THE NEW ARTHASHASTRA

A Security Strategy for India

Edited by
Gurmeet Kanwal

HarperCollins *Publishers* India

First published in India in 2016 by
HarperCollins *Publishers* India

HarperCollins Publishers India, Cyber City, Building 10-A, Gurugram, Haryana-122002, India
www.harpercollins.co.in

P-ISBN: 978-93-5177-751-9
E-ISBN: 978-93-5177-752-6

2 4 6 8 10 9 7 5 3 1

Typeset in 10.5/13.5 Minion Pro Regular at
SURYA, New Delhi

Printed and bound at
MicroPrints India, New Delhi

This product is made of FSC®-certified and other controlled material.

HarperCollins Publishers, Macken House, 39/40 Mayor Street
Upper, Dublin 1, D01 C9W8, Ireland

Dedicated to India's soldiers, sailors, air warriors and personnel of the paramilitary and police forces. All of them serve with a smile and never hesitate to make huge sacrifices for the nation.
May the nation never fail them.

Contents

Editor's Note

Unlike many other countries, India does not publish a formally articulated National Security Strategy or National Security Doctrine or a White Paper on National Defence. The advantages of publishing such a document are well known. First, a comprehensively formulated national security strategy reflects the national will to protect and promote national interests pertaining to security, and dissuades adversaries from attempting to play mischief. Second, it provides guidance to all stakeholders on policies related to national security. Finally, it offers reassurance to citizens that the government has initiated appropriate protective measures to safeguard national security.

My interest in India's national security strategy goes back to my tenure as a colonel in the Military Operations Directorate at the army headquarters, New Delhi (1996–98). As Director MO-5, I was dealing with threats, strategies and force structure. The realization had begun to dawn on policymakers that the challenges of national security went well beyond territorial defence. With Pakistan's proxy war expanding beyond Jammu and Kashmir and the growing China–Pakistan collusion in the fields of nuclear warheads, ballistic missiles and military hardware, the absence of a comprehensive national security strategy was sorely felt. We did try to initiate the process of drafting such a document but, in the absence of a central organization like the present National Security Council, inter-ministerial coordination was a daunting task.

Then, in my application for a two-year fellowship at the Institute for Defence Studies and Analyses (IDSA), on study leave from the army, I proposed to work on 'India's National Security Strategy' as my research project. The committee approved my fellowship but not the subject that I had proposed for research. I was directed to write an article in *Strategic Analysis*, the IDSA's bi-monthly journal, on my concept of a national security strategy for India—which I did—and work on another subject.

My interest in the subject remained constant over the years. Over a decade later, I asked a former national security advisor (NSA) at a conference in New Delhi why India did not have a formally articulated national security strategy and what he had done about it as NSA. He said he had tried his best to publish such a document in the public domain and that seven drafts had been prepared. However, he said, before the last round of comments from all the ministries concerned had been received, a new government was elected.

I was invited to deliver a talk at the National Defence College, New Delhi, on 'India's National Security Strategy and the Transformation Necessary to Achieve It' over two consecutive years. After the talk, the commandant, several members of the faculty and many student officers suggested that I write a book on the subject as they thought it was extremely important. I spoke on the subject at the College of Defence Management in Secunderabad also and the response was similar.

Given the complexities of the subject, it was clear to me that a book would take many years if I were to write it myself. Also, as I lack specialized knowledge of issues like maritime, cyber and space security, among others, I would be groping in the dark. A better alternative would be to invite the finest domain experts in the country to write on their areas of specialization and put it all together in one volume.

With this in mind, I approached Krishan Chopra, Publisher and Chief Editor at HarperCollins. He had previously edited my book *Indian Army: Vision 2020*. He quite liked the concept note that I sent him and approved the book. Edited volumes or anthologies are not easy to put together or to market and I am grateful to him for appreciating the desirability of bringing out a book on the subject and reposing faith in the authors.

All the authors are well-known practitioners and analysts and have a masterly grasp over their subjects. The book begins with a chapter on the conceptual underpinnings of national security strategy and covers India's defence policy, threats and challenges, national interests and national security objectives, defence cooperation and strategies to counter external and internal threats. It also includes the role of intelligence in national security, nuclear deterrence and maritime security strategy.

Besides these, there are chapters on cyber and space security, energy security, economic warfare, defence expenditure, research and development and the indigenization of defence production. It also has chapters on the defence policy of other major powers and India's grand strategy. In the concluding chapter, an endeavour has been made to draw up a national security strategy in respect of the major threats and challenges, including managing the rise of China, Pakistan's proxy war, peace and stability in the region and internal security.

While the book covers a fair amount of ground, it is by no means comprehensive. Several important aspects that are considered part of the national security paradigm today, like human security, food and water security and social security, could not be incorporated for want of space. Perhaps there is scope for a companion volume to be brought out separately.

Within the time that was available to them and the resources for research that were at their disposal, the authors have done a commendable job. The credit for the end result goes entirely to the authors and I am grateful to them for their efforts. If there are any shortcomings in the conceptualization of the chapters, or if a major facet of national security has escaped attention, the responsibility for the inadequacies is mine and mine alone.

This first attempt at publishing India's 'National Security Strategy' in the public domain is a labour of love and a collective gift to the nation from all the authors. We hope it will spur the government to finally publish a comprehensive document on the subject. As and when that happens, it will give all of us immense joy and quiet satisfaction.

Finally, it has been a pleasure working with all the authors as well as Team HarperCollins, especially the editor, Siddhesh Inamdar, and my grateful thanks to all of them.

GURMEET KANWAL
New Delhi
September 2016

Preface
The Conceptual Underpinnings of National Security Strategy

Professor Gautam Sen

Formerly Savarkar Professor of Defence Studies and head of the department of Defence Studies, University of Pune

Founder Director of the National Centre of International Security and Defence Analysis, University of Pune

National Security Strategy: An Overview

National security strategy is an integral part of a nation state's quest to safeguard its national interest. As a concept, it covers a vast domain and cannot be confined to any single discipline, nor restricted to any single methodology with which to find solutions, define policies, or create public policy orientations. There is no consensus on accepting a general theory applicable to all matters of security. The conceptualization of national security is beyond the realm of any single discipline because it covers the very foundation of a nation state on the one hand and the welfare, survival and continuation of human life on the other. Therefore, the approach to conceptualizing security has to be inter- and multi-disciplinary.

If one could compress the entire evolution of the world into a twenty-four-hour timespan, then modern civilization appears on Earth only in the last few seconds. Within this period, man has become the greatest threat to himself. Therefore, the focus of national security will eventually shift radically from the safety and sovereignty of the nation state to the much more complex concept of human security, which cuts across international borders and covers the hitherto 'non-traditional' security issues affecting the very existence of human beings and requiring the securitization of the economy, ecology, environment, energy and the rights of the unborn. However, for now, the world is still working on a model whose unit of analysis is the nation state.

Conceptualizing security in the context of this book will be Indo-centric. The year 2030 will be a landmark in world affairs. India's gross domestic product (GDP) is projected to increase to $8 trillion by then and its urban population is estimated to be 720 million. India has a rich culture and civilization and has been further empowered by its demographic dividend vis-à-vis an ageing Europe and North America. This will have great implications not just for India—its national security and its national interests—but also global politics.

But first, let us begin by understanding the evolution of the concept of national interest.

National Interest

A Brief History

In *The Idea of National Interest* (1934), American historian Charles Beard traced the history of the concept back to the sixteenth and seventeenth centuries, when modern nation states began to crystallize. Unsurprisingly, the rise of the nation state and the use of the term occurred at the same time. Beard found that after the development of the nation state and the appearance of nationalist sentiments, older terms—the 'will of the prince' and 'raison d'état'—lost their ability to mobilize public will. They were, therefore, replaced by references to 'national interests' and 'vital interests'. Other terms used for their mobilizing capacity included 'national honour', 'public interest' and 'general will.[1]

The early history of 'national interest', according to political scientist Joseph Frankel in his book *National Interest*, cannot be traced much farther back than the sixteenth century. Earlier societies that were in contact with one another often developed notions of self-interest based on language, a common political identity, survival, power and wealth, but conceived these notions 'within specific bargaining terms or conflict situations rather than in general terms'.[2]

Frankel writes that the concept could not be articulated in ancient Greece because of the blurring of distinctions between political and cultural communities and the absence of clear-cut political boundaries. Conceptions of common interests were restricted to the boundaries of individual city states in a manner analogous to that of the Renaissance Italians. During the Persian Wars these conceptions gave way to Panhellenic ideas and the more inclusive sentiment of a Hellenic cultural community. The Roman Empire accentuated the shift from a national to a catholic (universal) consciousness.

Frankel observes that in the Middle Ages, the nature of relations between individual political units and the Roman Empire and the 'confusion between politics and metaphysics offered no scope for the evolution of the idea of the "national interest"'.[3] In other words, 'empire' superseded 'nation' as a form of political organization.

Conceptualizing National Interest

In modern political life, 'national interest' has become a common term among politicians and political scientists. In nearly every discussion about changing foreign policy, national interest is treated as comprising a set of accepted tenets that support scholars or politicians when they present opinions. But there is no accepted common standard or definition of the concept of national interest, so the understanding of the role or meaning of national interest differs from one user of the term to another. This makes it nearly impossible to reach a consensus when debating foreign policy.

Such a superficial discussion is meaningless for policymaking. A debate without a common definition of national interest can never achieve a meaningful outcome. This type of debate does not help policymakers at all in judging which recommended policy serves national interests better. Therefore, it is necessary to establish common standards to define national interest. Without such common standards, it will be impossible to make the study of foreign policy scientific; it will also be difficult to have meaningful discussions on foreign policy.

Confused Concepts of National Interest

In the Chinese language, the concept of 'national interest' has two meanings. One is national interest in the context of international politics, meaning the interests of a nation state in the global arena. This concept must be contrasted with group interests, international interests or global interests. The other is state interest, or the interests of the state as the highest level in domestic politics, meaning governmental interest or a government that represents the people's interest. The interests of the state are more important than local interests, collective interests or individual interests.

In 1954, Mao Zedong, the then chairman of the Communist Party of China, at an extended meeting of the party politburo, said, 'Our policy towards farmers is not like the Soviet's, but it is one that takes care of both the interests of farmers and the interests of the state.' The national interest that Mao was talking about is in the category of domestic politics. In 1989, when Deng Xiaoping met with the Thai prime minister, he said, 'China wants to maintain its own national interest, sovereignty and territorial integrity. China also believes that a socialist country cannot violate other countries' interests, sovereignty or territory.' The national interest that he was talking about here meant national interest in the context of international politics. Premier Zhou Enlai said in 1949: 'When no war or violation takes place, national interests need to be protected domestically and internationally. In the international arena, diplomacy has become front-line work.'

Because of the dual meaning of 'national interest' in the Chinese language, some scholars have confused national interest with the interest of the state. They have, therefore, misunderstood the meaning of the concept of national interest in the context of international politics. Vladimir Lenin, the former leader of the Soviet Union, said that the state is an instrument of the ruling class in domestic politics. Because the ruling class controls the state, its interest and that of the state coincide. A state's interest is often contrary to that of groups other than the ruling class; therefore, national interest in terms of domestic politics does have a class nature.

However, a state in international politics represents a political entity that consists of four major elements: population, territory, government and international recognition. This state is sometimes called a country. After the modern nation state was formed, a country has also been called a nation. This is why the UN is called the United Nations. The term 'nation' is a political concept for all the people of a country. Its focus is national but certainly not class-based. The national interest in international politics includes the interests of the whole nation state. And both the ruler and the ruled share those interests.

Definition of National Interest

What exactly then is national interest? Napoleon Bonaparte had said that he was acting in the interest of France when he initiated his campaign against Russia in 1812, and later when he launched his desperate battle at Waterloo in 1815 in which he was defeated by the British and the Prussians. Adolf Hitler justified his expansionist policies, including the annexation of Austria in 1938, in the name of Germany's national interest. 'Friendly socialist' governments were installed in Poland and other East European countries by Joseph Stalin in the name of the Soviet Union's national interest in the first half of the twentieth century. President George H.W. Bush was acting in America's national interest when he led the war against Iraq on the question of its annexation of Kuwait. Benazir Bhutto thought that it was in Pakistan's national interest to destabilize the Indian state of Jammu and Kashmir.

Thus, several actions in global politics, howsoever problematic, are taken in the name of national interest. We must, therefore, try to find a commonly acceptable definition of it. The idea of national interest is singularly vague. It assumes a variety of meanings in different contexts. However, political scientists Norman Padelford and George Lincoln observe: 'Concepts of national interests are centred on the core values of society, which include the welfare of the nation, the security of its political beliefs, national way of life, territorial integrity and its self-preservation.'[4] According to another political scientist, Robert Osgood, national interest is the 'state of affairs valued solely for its benefit to the nations'.[5] And a third, Hans Morgenthau, maintains that the main requirements of a nation state are to protect its physical, political and cultural identity against threat from other states. Frankel writes about the aspirational and operational aspects of national interest. The aspirational aspects include the state's vision of good life and an ideal set of goals to be realized. Put into operation, national interest refers to the sum total of its interests and policies actually pursued.

Therefore, governments try to narrow down the definition of 'national interest' to defence, national security economy, inter-state and foreign commerce, foreign relations and the state of general national affairs.

The Global Order

The Contemporary Paradigm

The loss of bipolarity due to the demise of the former Soviet Union, the proliferation and weaponization of nuclear technology, and the complexities of globalization whose darker side is the evolution of international terrorism have made the study of security far more complex than even in the Cold War period. The armed forces, as an organization, will become even more significant for nation states from the point of view of containing internal security problems apart from maintaining the integrity of the nation state from external aggression and projecting power beyond territorial limits.

It is, hence, necessary to place ourselves on the track of thinking about theoretical concepts in conjunction with methods and methodologies in the complex mosaic of the use of force, international relations, diplomacy and the internal problems of nation states. The answers to this dilemma lie in how each nation state rationalizes its national interest. Also, national interest does not and cannot change with every change of government, be it a nation state which is developed, developing or underdeveloped.

Emerging New Global Order?

There are two questions that need to be addressed. First, has a specific pattern of global order emerged in the post–Cold War period? If so, what are its principle constituents? The second question is: should this order be defined in terms of globalization?

There is obviously a new pattern in international politics in the post–Cold War era as compared to the one that existed prior to it. The second question leads us to understand this contemporary order through the lens of globalization. There is a major debate raging on this to understand the exact meaning and processes of globalization. However, what is beyond doubt is that some kind of transformation is already under way.

A serious study to determine the overall character of the post–Cold War order is still in its infancy. We do not know how it will culminate. It is still not an enclosed period with a determinate ending like in the case of the period between the two world wars. While individual aspects of the present order can be identified (ethnicity, identity, peacekeeping, humanitarian intervention, globalization, integration, financial instability, terrorism and the war against it, weapons of mass destruction, regime change, and so on), there has been no general evaluation of its essential nature.

In the earlier period, the interest in the international order was largely 'negative' and lay in ensuring that no threats emerged from it. Today, there is a high level of integration and interdependence and hence the interest is 'positive', which makes the international order act as a great provider of a large amount of social good. The international order today can deliver information, access to global social movements, economic resources, human rights, interventions, action through non-governmental organizations at national and international levels, and the sharing of cultural artifacts.

It will be important to state that the new order which is unfolding is being pulled in a number of different directions. At one end of the spectrum, it continues to be largely state-centric, concerned with the structure of the balance of power, the polarity of the international system and the current form of collective security. At the other end is a widening agenda of order, which encompasses the relationship between economic and political dimensions, new thinking about human security, examining the consequences of globalization, human rights, and environmental security.

Fault Lines in the New Global Order

Conceptually one can identify two main theories which explain the post–Cold War world. The first is liberalism. Proponents of liberal persuasion include Francis Fukuyama, who wrote a seminal article titled 'End of History' in 1989. He contended that history since the end of the French Revolution has been driven by the core dynamic conflict between the forces supporting collectivism and those endorsing 'bourgeois' individualism. With the Russian Revolution in 1917 the balance began to tilt toward 'collectivism', and by the late 1970s it turned towards 'individualism' as the various attempts at economic planning in the Third World started to show signs of fatigue.

Thus the Cold War ended in terms favourable to the West, such that liberal economic values would prevail globally. Hence there was no alternative to 'bourgeois democracy' to take over globally, which in essence stated that while authoritarianism bred war, democracies brought peace. Higher the number of democracies, greater was the possibility of a peaceful world.

While the liberals painted a picture of a more peaceful world, the realists painted a bleaker one. They saw much more chaos and conflict occurring because the international system continued to remain competitive and anarchic. Past history showed the failures of building new world orders, as did the assessment of the world after 1989, with all the barbaric wars, failed states and collapsing regions. The inference was that there was nothing to be too optimistic about.

The three main political thinkers of the realist school to challenge the liberals were John Mearsheimer, professor of political science at the University of Chicago; writer Robert D. Kaplan; and Samuel Huntington of Harvard University. Mearsheimer analysed the structure of the international system during the Cold War in line with Kenneth Waltz's thesis which claimed that bipolarity produced stability after World War II, and therefore surmised that the collapse of this bipolarity could generate new problems, most dangerously by furthering nuclear proliferation.

He also postulated that the division of Europe and Germany after 1946 had created a new continental order and hence the unification of both would usher uncertainty. He argued that with the collapse of communism in the East, old ethnic hatred would resurface to thrust the continent back into chaos and bloodshed.

Kaplan in his study of the Cold War worked on the assumption that economics and human collapse in parts of Africa were also relevant to our understanding of the future character of world politics. He felt that in his real world, old structures and traditional certainties were fast disappearing, producing chaos and misery.

Huntington placed realism at the forefront of the post–Cold War debate. He warned about the world after 1989. He refuted the liberal argument by stating that the world now faced a clash of secular economic ideologies, which meant no end to conflict as such. He postulated that conflict would assume a new form, defined as the 'clash of civilizations', as an evolution of conflict in the modern world.

He argued that this conflict would be between the West and those other countries and regions of the world that did not adhere to such values as respect for the individual, human rights, democracy and secularism. Identity and culture would create antagonism and form the new fault line in the post–Cold War world, pitting those nations in Western Europe and the US which embodied one form of 'civilization' against those in the Middle East and Asia, and China and post-communist Russia, where the value system was profoundly different. He even warned that unless the West recognized this reality, it would be unable to deal with it wisely.

Conclusion

To sum up, Waltz's prediction about nuclear proliferation after the Cold War and the collapse of communism in the East, resulting in ethnic hatred; and Huntington's postulation that conflict would assume a new form due to the clash of civilizations have come true. Today, nation states—small or large, powerful or otherwise, democratic or non-democratic—have to formulate their individual national security strategies by factoring in their own national interest in the new world order emerging in the post–Cold War period.

Every nation state around the world will be affected by these happenings and India will be no exception. Hence, the theoretical moorings of India's national security strategy and its linkage to its national interest will underpin its policies and be crucial in how well it works.

1

Introduction
Defence Policy and Management of National Security

General V.P. Malik

Former Chief of Army Staff and Chairman, Chiefs of Staff Committee

'Of all the gifts that a king can give, it is not the gift of gold, nor the gift of land, nor the gift of cows which is important, but the gift of security.' —*Panchatantra*

'Protecting our nation's security—our people, our territory, our way of life—is my administration's foremost mission and constitutional duty.' —Bill Clinton, President of the United States, in his first National Security Review, 1996

'In a world of startling change, the first duty of the government remains the security of our country.' —David Cameron, Prime Minister of the United Kingdom, in 'National Security Strategy, 2010'

Introduction

India's national security spectrum is more complex today than it has been at any point in the past. Conventional military threats as well as non-conventional (or non-military) threats—arising out of economic backwardness, poor governance, international or intra-national terrorism, drug trafficking, gun running, ethnic conflicts, religious fundamentalism, caste or communal disturbances, economic subversion or failures, large-scale migrations, and even environmental pollution—impinge upon the security of the nation. They slow down the development of the nation. Such threats can emanate from unfriendly countries, non-state elements, or from within the country.

Defence, however, remains a dominant feature of national security: defence of territorial integrity from external attacks, proxy wars, insurgencies, terrorism, or any other type of internal security threats. Defence forces are also called upon for disaster relief and a wide range of crisis missions, from urgent evacuation of Indian citizens from foreign lands to the pulling out of babies from borewells.

Dynamic strategic and technological developments keep adding new dimensions to challenges, cause greater uncertainties, and reduce reaction time. The example of the turmoil in Yemen, from where 4,500 Indian workers and their families had to be evacuated in April 2015 while heavy fighting was going on, shows how new security-related problems can emanate unexpectedly, from unexpected quarters, and affect our national security.

In the contemporary context, the concept of national security goes well beyond narrow conceptions of external and internal security. It has multiple and interrelated dimensions, which demand integrated responses.

To deal with this entire gamut of national security issues, it has become necessary to review security threats and strategies and security management systems every few years. The security management system needs synergy and optimal utilization of all national resources, including the armed forces, to make the system efficient, resilient and speedily responsive.

Post-Independence Experience in Managing Security

Traditionally, the armed forces and civilian police forces of India have been responsible for territorial integrity and security, and for assisting civil authorities in other security and disaster-related tasks. Before Independence, they worked directly under the British. Our political leaders, who got us Independence, had neither the experience nor the inclination to meddle in military matters. The higher defence organization was a totally British affair. Even when the interim government came to power, and our leaders became members of the Viceroy's Executive Council, they had little idea of how the military was being managed.

After Independence, India adopted the higher defence organization establishment blueprint as recommended by Lord Hastings Ismay,[1] the then Chief of Staff with Lord Louis Mountbatten, British India's last viceroy and the independent nation's first governor-general. Ismay had suggested a Defence Department, with a series of committees such as (a) Defence Committee of the Cabinet, (b) Defence Minister's Committee (c) Chiefs of Staff Committee, and some of their sub-committees to ensure integrated functioning. Secretarial support for all these committees was provided by the Cabinet Secretariat, which included a Military Wing to coordinate the working of the Defence Committee of the Cabinet. The idea was to facilitate prompt decision-making on defence and other security issues, enable good coordination, and also to provide a direct interface between the highest political and executive (including military) authorities of the government.

The relevance and effectiveness of this organization in subsequent years needs to be viewed from two perspectives: (a) the developments and practices within the organization, and (b) the politico-military performance and achievements in wars and conflicts that followed.

Over the next five decades, although there was no major tinkering with the higher defence organization and its committee system, the role of the Defence Department (later re-designated as the Ministry of Defence, or MoD) underwent radical changes. It started at the level of Prime Minister Jawaharlal Nehru, whose disdain and distrust of the military and neglect of defence planning impacted this ministry and the armed forces. Nehru kept the armed forces outside the politico-military decision-making loop except when military operations became necessary. The idea of civilian supremacy over the military was implemented by designating the three service headquarters as 'attached offices'. With this nomenclature, the three service headquarters were reduced to being adjuncts of the MoD, controlled by civil servants under the defence secretary. India managed to develop a unique system: bureaucratic control instead of political control over the military.

Some other significant developments that took place were:

1. In 1952, the MoD published a document titled 'Organization, Functions, Powers and Procedures of Defence Headquarters, 1952'. This document stated that the status of the armed forces headquarters 'corresponds to that of an attached office of the secretariat of the civil side'. The service chiefs raised objections but were overruled.
2. In 1962, the Defence Committee of the Cabinet was re-designated as the Emergency Committee of the Cabinet (ECC), later changed to

Cabinet Committee on Political Affairs (CCPA), and much later, the Cabinet Committee on Security (CCS). The services chiefs used to attend meetings of the defence committee, but since the CCPA and CCS dealt with other matters besides defence, the military chiefs were asked to attend only 'as and when required'. The result was that while some prime ministers called them often, others very nearly forgot them. An example: in 1979, when the CCPA discussed the morale of military officers, only the defence secretary was present. The service chiefs were not invited. Even when defence plans were discussed, the service chiefs were excluded from the cabinet meetings.

3. A system of Raksha Mantri's (defence minister's) Morning Meeting was introduced in 1962. This dealt a deathblow to the Defence Minister's Committee, which worked with a formal agenda. Raksha Mantri's Morning Meetings did not have any fixed agenda.

Instead of working jointly with service headquarters and then issuing policies and directions, the MoD became a higher entity—an exclusively higher civilian headquarters controlling the three armed forces. The developed system not only gave civilian bureaucracy stifling control over the armed forces but also isolated them from all institutions outside the MoD. The committee system was undermined and the military got more and more isolated from the policymaking, planning and strategic decision-making processes. This isolation led to suspicion and friction between the civilian officials in the MoD and the service headquarters. To a considerable extent, this continues to date and has affected the ability of the military to interact, advise and perform.

The doyen of India's strategic thinking, the late K. Subrahmanyam, described this defence and security structure as one 'where politicians enjoy power without any responsibility, bureaucrats wield power without any accountability, and the military assumes responsibility without any direction'.

Politico-Military Performance

Despite reactive defence policies, ad hoc defence planning, poor and inadequate equipment, intelligence failures and strategic surprises, the armed forces—with few exceptions—continued to perform with professionalism and dedication. They achieved success in most conflict situations. But the chasm and mismatch between the operational and strategic levels became evident in almost all post-Independence conflicts.

In 1948, Prime Minister Nehru decided to approach the United Nations on the Jammu and Kashmir (J&K) issue just when the Indian Army had reached the gates of Muzaffarabad, the capital of Pakistan-Occupied Kashmir (POK) today. In 1954, India granted 'suzerainty' to China over Tibet without any quid pro quo and thus created a long-term security problem for the country, which continues to date. In 1962, the government at the highest level failed to resolve border issues with China and indulged in provocative forward deployments on the border without adequate military preparedness. After the 1965 war, the strategically important Hajipir Pass, which had been captured by the Indian Army in POK, was returned to Pakistan. This area is a major source of cross-border infiltration and terrorism today. After the 1971 war, India returned 92,000 Pakistani prisoners of war (PoW) without making Pakistan agree to a permanent solution on J&K.

Despite China carrying out its first nuclear weapon test (Project 596) in October 1964, India dithered for twenty-four years between the testing of a nuclear device (in 1974) and its nuclear weapon test (in 1998). Pakistan has targeted India with a proxy war in the form of terrorism since the 1960s—earlier through East Pakistan and now through all possible land, sea and air routes. India sent a peacekeeping force to Sri Lanka in 1987 and withdrew it under Sri Lankan and domestic pressure in 1989. We lost 1,155 soldiers but failed to meet any long-term strategic objective.

The hijacked Indian Airlines flight IC 814 on 24 December 1999 landed in Amritsar for refuelling but could not be stopped from taking off again due to poor crisis management and lack of coordination.

Despite major incidents like the Kargil war, the terrorist attack on Parliament in December 2001, on Mumbai in November 2008 and five major bombings/attacks on our diplomatic missions in Afghanistan, India has not been able to find a satisfactory political or military solution to this problem.

In hindsight, all these events demonstrate a poor grand strategic vision and lack of direction in planning and enabling desirable military and non-military capabilities. They also demonstrate a lack of coordination amongst leaders responsible for grand strategy, defence capability planning, military strategy, operational planning and execution. The lack of political guidance on these important security-related issues continues to be a major handicap even today.

Adoption of National Security Concept

Ever since well-known American writer and political commentator Walter Lippmann noted in 1943 that 'a nation has security when it does not have to sacrifice its legitimate interests to avoid war and is able, if challenged, to maintain them by war',[2] the concept of security of nations started changing globally. National security came to be understood as the ability of a nation to protect and preserve its independence, integrity and sovereignty against any external and internal threats and the promotion of its political, economic and social growth with equity.

It became an all-encompassing security concept that included multiple interrelated traditional (military) and non-traditional (non-military) dimensions of the nation such as food, energy and water security, and taking care of climate change, natural disasters and so on. This holistic approach ensured not only territorial integrity and sovereignty but also the greater ability of the nation to use all instruments of national power to be able to achieve the 'wholesome' security of the nation.

India's National Security Council

India made a short-lived attempt to set up a National Security Council as an apex agency to look after the country's political, economic and strategic security concerns in 1990. The present national security structure was established by the Atal Bihari Vajpayee government in November 1998. The National Security Council (NSC), headed by the prime minister, has ministers of defence, external affairs, home, finance, and the deputy chairman of the Planning Commission (now called NITI Aayog or National Institute for Transforming India Aayog) as its members. Other political leaders/officials may be invited to attend as and when required.

Its three-tier organization under the national security advisor (NSA) comprises the Strategic Policy Group, the National Security Advisory Board, and a Secretariat. The Strategic Policy Group is the first level of the three-tier organization. It forms the nucleus of the decision-making apparatus. The NSA is the principal coordinator for formulation and implementation of long-term national security policies, under the overall guidance of the prime minister and the NSC. He is the long-term strategic security planner. As per our nuclear doctrine, the NSA also heads the executive council of the Nuclear Command Authority and monitors the preparedness of the country's strategic forces to respond in accordance with the approved nuclear doctrine.

After the establishment of the NSC, India's defence policy and higher defence management system became an important adjunct of its holistic national security system. Unfortunately, the NSC, which should be looking into long-term strategic problems, does not meet as often as it should.

Post–Kargil War Reforms

The impact of the limited Kargil war, wherein Pakistani regular troops in the garb of jihadi militants intruded into Indian territory across the Line of Control (LoC) but were subsequently forced to withdraw, was immense. The war in its wake brought many geopolitical and geo-strategic changes in the subcontinent. The Pakistani military embarrassment resulted in a military coup and a change of polity. In India, the government realized that the national security apparatus, particularly the higher defence management organization, had become an embarrassment.

The Kargil Review Committee Report brought out many grave deficiencies in India's security management system. It also drew attention to the fact that our national leadership had failed to keep up with the complexities of national security management. Its recommendations led to the setting up of a Group of Ministers (GoM) to review the national security system in its entirety and formulate specific proposals for implementation. Both these committees took note of the deteriorating security environment and emphasized the need for changes in the national security system and for better defence and strategic management. The GoM noted, 'India's security scenario has witnessed nothing short of a sea change as a result of the end of the Cold War, the proxy war in Kashmir, militancy fuelled from abroad in many parts of the country, the revolution in military affairs and an increasing nuclearization of the neighbourhood.'[3]

The GoM broadly considered four major areas of national security, i.e., intelligence apparatus, internal security, border management and management of defence. It made important recommendations keeping in view the latest security developments in and outside the country which impacted India's national security environment and apparatus. These included the establishment of a separate Department of Border Management in the Ministry of Home Affairs (MHA), the principle of 'one border, one force' to be followed by border guarding forces, coordination of border intelligence, the Border Areas Development Programme, measures to check cross-border infiltration, gun running and drug smuggling, combating subversive propaganda and disinformation, and so on.

On the higher defence organization, the GoM observed that 'there is a marked difference in the perception and crisis of confidence among civil and military officials within the Ministry of Defence and service headquarters regarding their respective roles and functions. There was also lack of synchronization among and between the three departments in the Ministry of Defence, including the relevant elements of defence finance. The concept of "attached offices" as applicable to service headquarters; problems of inter-se relativities; multiple, duplicated, and complex procedures governing the exercise of administrative and financial powers; and the concept of "advice" to the minister have all contributed to these problems.'[4]

The GoM observed that the Chiefs of Staff Committee had serious weaknesses in its processes of providing single point military advice to the government, and of resolving substantive inter-service doctrinal, planning, policy and operational issues. This institution needed to be restructured to enable it to discharge its responsibilities efficiently, including the facilitation of synergized action.

Some other important comments were:

1. There were no clearly defined national security objectives. The defence planning process was handicapped due to the absence of a national security review or doctrine. It suffered from the lack of a holistic approach. Inter-service planning was budget-competitive and uneconomical.

2. The system governing defence acquisitions suffered from lack of integrated planning; weaknesses in linkages between plans and budgets; cumbersome administrative, technical and financial evaluation procedures; and the absence of a dedicated, professionally equipped common procurement structure within the Ministry of Defence.
3. There was no synergy between academic research and the government's security policy requirements. Both functioned without any linkages.

The GoM recommended the appointment of a Chief of Defence Staff in the MoD to (a) provide single point military advice, (b) hold administrative control over and manage strategic forces, (c) ensure intra- and inter-service prioritization of ten- and fifteen-year 'perspective plans', and also the five-year defence plans, and (d) to bring about improvement in the synergy among various units of the armed forces. The Chief of Defence Staff would work towards improving the uniformity of training in the three services and to reduce any 'overlap' and 'replication' in them.

It was also recommended that the service headquarters, which were considered as attached offices earlier, should be made part of the 'Integrated Defence Headquarters'. This new name was promulgated soon thereafter but no changes were made in the business rules, responsibilities assigned therein, or in the working procedures. The post of the Chief of Defence Staff was not created. The military structures continued to be based on the concept of single service management. No clear-cut system of single point advice after joint military deliberations was made possible.

The government created an 'Integrated Defence Staff', but by keeping it headless, it failed to provide an integrated and joint paradigm, much less give advice to the defence minister, prime minister or the CCS. As of date, each service headquarter continues to do its own planning and management of matters related to its own service. There is limited joint planning in military operations, logistics and on new technologies. On the same principle, each service chief represents only his own service and offers advice to the government related to his service.[5]

Current feedback shows that there has been no change in the responsibilities, accountability and procedures, or in the attitude of the officers posted in the different departments of the MoD. Inter-services cooperation across the entire spectrum of military functions remains weak. In the absence of direct military advice and framing of long-term policies, the bureaucratic wall between the political executive and the professional service chiefs continues to convert the concept of 'civilian political control' into 'civilian bureaucratic control'.

In June 2011 the government set up yet another task force under Naresh Chandra, a former defence and cabinet secretary, to carry out another review of the entire gamut of national security and defence preparedness and management. This task force had fourteen members, including three senior retired military officers, one from each service. The task force submitted its report in August 2012. The report has not been made public so far. It is believed to have covered external and internal security threats and challenges comprehensively and made some sensible recommendations.

Its recommendations included (a) creation of a separate permanent Chairman, Chiefs of Staff Committee, to exercise administrative control over the nuclear arsenal, head a separate joint special forces command, prioritize modernization of the armed forces and prepare annual defence operational status reports, (b) establishment of a bureau of politico-military affairs, (c) a national defence university, (d) an advanced projects agency under the scientific advisor to the defence minister, (e) cross-posting of civil and military officers in the ministries of defence and external affairs, and (f) promotion of self-reliance in defence weapons and equipment.

Till the writing of this book, these recommendations were still being 'studied in the government'. It is learnt that overwhelming opposition to its implementation comes from the MoD itself. The ministry does not even want a permanent Chairman, Chiefs of Staff Committee, to be invited for CCS and NSC deliberations.[6]

National Security Challenges and the Viability of India's Security Apparatus

All these aspects demand close coordination (and some integration) of ministerial structures within the Union government, and active public affairs policies. It implies that government departments working in relatively autonomous silos can no longer enable effective national security.

While evolving a holistic approach towards national security management, it would also be relevant to keep in mind that our country comprises a huge cultural and geographical diversity. Our nearly one and a quarter billion people represent multi-religious, multi-lingual and multi-cultural societies whose traditions, customs and socio-religious sensitivities are deep-rooted. In our vast, unfettered democracy, an unhindered interplay of socio-cultural traditions and religious practices, as seen in the 'ghar wapsi' campaign, internecine tribal violence in the north-east, and caste-based socio-political demands in north India, can generate discord and disagreements and lead to serious communal disturbances.

On the military front, it should be noted that globally the threat spectrum has undergone a major change. While conventional war as an instrument of foreign policy has become increasingly unviable due to very high costs, casualties and international pressures, sub-conventional conflicts and armed violence have become more prevalent. There is a greater likelihood of limited conflicts and wars in the future than that of all-out or general wars. It may also be noted that in the current strategic environment, wars, when they do occur, may no longer be taken to the logical conclusion of military victories, as was the case in the past. They would be conducted with the objective of achieving political successes rather than a military victory. In the Kargil war too, the political aim and term of reference prevented the military from escalating the conflict or crossing the LoC. With such a paradigm shift, the military has a much tougher job today. It has to be prepared for an elongated spectrum of conflicts ranging from law and order situations arising out of civil police control, insurgencies, terrorism, and different levels of wars—from conventional to those involving weapons of mass destruction (WMD).

In this strategic environment, the separation between tactical, operational and strategic levels of warfare has blurred. While there was always some degree of overlap between these levels, due to the increasingly pervasive influence of information technology (IT), this overlap has increased. A small military action along the LoC, or a terrorist's act in the hinterland, both tend to become issues for consideration and decision-making at the highest level. It is a situation wherein a junior military officer is expected to understand political considerations, and the political leader to know the tactical and operational considerations.

The intelligence cycle of collection, collation, synthesis and dissemination of information has to be speeded up.

The indication of major political and military objectives and the estimation of the likely duration of the war or the time available to the armed forces to execute their missions and achieve politico-military goals will be crucial for the planning and conducting of operations. This will require complete understanding between the political and military leadership. We can also expect fairly rigid political terms of reference, as were given during the Kargil war. In such a conflict scenario, politico-diplomatic factors will also play an important role. Careful and calibrated orchestration of military operations, diplomacy and the domestic political environment is essential for its successful outcome. Continuous control of the 'escalatory ladder' requires much closer political oversight and politico-civil-military interaction.

In the new strategic and technological environment, we have to develop more integrated capabilities so as to obtain the most optimum results. These capabilities require inter-service and not single service organizations. Elsewhere too it has become necessary to achieve greater synergy through integration and joint action. Integration does not mean 'unification' or subsuming the characteristics and importance of any of the armed forces. There are two aspects: greater and faster politico-military interactions and coordination, and the integration of the three armed forces verticals at the top. This integration should cover defence planning and force structuring, strategic and operational planning, budgetary economy and common personnel and logistics policies. This integration implies a joint doctrine, joint commands and staffs, and joint training for greater synergy for the effective utilization of military power. Jointness in military operations validates the well-known principle of war, the 'economy of effort'. It precludes wastage of resources by using an appropriate mix of force capabilities.

Ever since Pakistan launched a proxy war in Punjab and J&K, external and internal security management have been inextricably intertwined. As a result, despite different roles, characteristics and ethos, these forces have to work together in most crisis situations to achieve the desired results. The army, navy and air force, which are primarily engaged in wars over land, sea and air space, would have to fight jointly and depend heavily on other elements of the government. Thus there is an increasing requirement of interoperability within the armed forces and with civilian police forces. The backbone of such interoperability is a set of common interoperable standards and operating procedures. For maintaining internal security efficiently, we need greater interoperability in areas like surveillance, communications, intelligence and logistics.

In India, a serious problem that we face between the Centre and the states is over clear-cut jurisdiction and management of law and order, insurgencies and terrorism. These conflict situations are excessively intertwined today. Besides, left-wing extremist groups and terrorist groups like the Indian Mujahideen operate across many state boundaries, some even across national boundaries. Constitutionally, it is the prerogative of the states to manage law and order within their territories and the Centre has no basis for interfering in this arena. But there is also a provision in the Constitution which states that it is the duty of the Union to protect every state against external aggression and internal disturbances. Unfortunately, there is no political consensus between the states and the central government over homeland security infrastructure. The delineation of responsibilities and an effective mechanism for cooperation amongst intelligence and police forces of the states and the Centre is yet to be evolved.

In recent years, the cyber and space domains have added yet another complexity. The entire command and control mechanism of the civil and military authorities is dependent on space satellite facilities. Cyber attacks on critical civilian infrastructure would have far more significance than any damage to military installations. As national security can no longer be compartmentalized into purely civilian and military domains, any military cyber war infrastructure will have to work in close coordination with the National Information Board. The cyber protection strategy will need to provide a template on which a holistic government—that is, both civil and military—approach becomes possible.

On the nuclear deterrence front, India has always reiterated its commitment to a credible minimum deterrent posture with a 'no first use' condition. In a conflict with other nuclear-armed states, India would have to adapt its existing strategic and tactical doctrines to meet a possible situation where its leaders may have to consider the deterrence capability of nuclear weapons. To make its deterrence more credible and effective, the Strategic Forces Command would require the capability to shift nuclear assets from peacetime deployment to fully employable forces in the shortest possible time. This may include an 'alert deployment' requiring political concurrence. As the size and complexity of India's nuclear arsenal increases, different kinds of complications are likely to emerge.

The GoM report in 2001 had recommended the institution of a Chief of Defence Staff. This appointment has now become indispensable in order to develop, prioritize and optimally employ inter-services capabilities such as cyber, space, special and strategic forces and work alongside task forces responsible for non-military security missions. This urgently needed defence reform should be accompanied by the creation of joint service staffs down to the level of corps headquarters.

The empowered Chief of Defence Staff or a permanent chairman of the Chiefs of Staff Committee, with authority to override service chiefs, would bring a degree of coherence into the area of defence and operational planning, research and development in civil and military organizations, and in overall civil–military relations.[7] The next step will be to hasten the establishment of tri-service aerospace, cyber and special forces commands—already under consideration—to deal effectively with emerging challenges. This will have to be followed by tri-service integrated theatre commands to synergize the capabilities of individual services.

A strategy is of little value without the tools to implement it. The armed forces and central police forces, which carry the major burden of implementation, have to be better equipped and made more versatile to protect our security in this age of uncertainty. We cannot afford to be dependent on foreign countries for nearly 70 per cent of military hardware (world's largest importer!). No country can stake claim to the status of a major power unless it can design and produce a major proportion of the hardware required by its armed forces. Our military industrial complex requires an urgent review. The laudable objective of 'Make in India' in the field of defence can succeed only if the Defence Research and Development Organization (DRDO), defence public sector undertakings (PSUs) and the relevant private sector organizations are encouraged with a level playing field.

National security strategy also requires the creation (or revision) of institutional structures which create multi-disciplinary capacities for the implementation of strategy. This requires the deputation of civilian and military experts in its primary national security establishments and cross-deputation in ministries like defence, external affairs and home. The nation may even have to establish a national security cadre of personnel drawn from different areas of expertise.[8]

Articulation of National Security Strategy and Defence Policy

Unlike most developed countries, India does not have a documented national security strategy or defence policy, not even a white paper or a monograph.[9] A national security strategy and policy document would entail the identification of national interests, the determination of national objectives, the discernment of potential threats, and finally the development of a strategy to deal with these threats, covering the full range of political, economic, diplomatic and security interests.

Arvind Gupta, the deputy NSA and head of the National Security Council Secretariat in 2016, has given two reasons for this absence. First, there is no political consensus in the country on national security issues, including the most important external and internal security threats and challenges and on how to go about meeting these. Second, the government has not been able to address the crucial issue of coordination required to formulate and address these issues.

Further, he states, 'The National Security Council has been a useful invention but it is anaemic in terms of resources. More importantly, it lacks powers to enforce anything. The departmental interests are very strong and it becomes difficult to synchronize them. There is no common understanding among various segments of the government on what constitutes national security.' Gupta believes, 'In the absence of a coherent strategy, the government's responses will remain ad hoc and partial, which may prove costly. An official national security strategy document, for the next ten years, is required urgently. This will help clarify confusion over national security matters and consolidate the government's responses. More importantly, it will generate informed debate which will help build consensus.'[10]

Shyam Saran, former foreign secretary, prime minister's special envoy and chairperson of the National Security Advisory Board in 2016, also emphasizes the need for an articulated national security strategy. According to him, 'In order to ensure policy coherence, every country needs to articulate a national security strategy which enjoys broad political consensus and provides a stable and predictable template against which various component parts of the state can take decisions on a whole range of issues that they must deal with on a day-to-day basis. Without this overall strategy, national security decisions often take on ad hoc, fragmented, reactive and sometimes contradictory forms, and the state appears to lurch from one crisis to another.'[11]

As stated earlier, in the contemporary context, national security involves multiple dimensions which are closely interlinked through strong feedback loops. As an aspiring regional and global power, it is essential for the Indian government to publish its national security strategy every five to six years. This will involve drawing together and using all instruments of national power and ensuring that the sum of the national effort is much bigger than its component parts. Such a publication will help in strengthening a national consciousness, promote the economy and socio-economic development, and enable various stakeholders to understand their role in the overall national context. Establishments assigned to implement this strategy would then become capable of spotting emerging security risks in their respective fields and, with cooperation from others, would then deal with those risks before they became crises.

It is important to underline that a national security strategy document should be realistic and balanced. While recognizing challenges, it should also underline the opportunities that are available in an ever-changing world.

What about the defence policy? On 10 May 1995, Prime Minister P.V. Narasimha Rao had stated in the Lok Sabha, 'We do not have a document called India's defence policy. But we have got several guidelines which are followed, strictly followed and observed ... This policy is not merely rigid in the sense that it has been written down, but these are the guidelines, these are the objectives, these are the matters which are always kept in view while conducting our defence policy.'

Now that we have adopted the national security model, a well-defined national security strategy and its clear articulation are a prerequisite for the evolution of defence policy, defence planning and military doctrines to meet national goals. Based on that, the defence minister is to be responsible for evolving a defence policy and laying down the role and tasks of the three services as well as the DRDO, defence production agencies and other components forming the military establishment. As observed by K. Subrahmanyam, India has lacked an ability to formulate future-oriented defence policies, managing only because of short-term measures, blunders by its adversaries, and force superiority in its favour.

It must, however, be noted that the MoD does evolve a top secret document called the 'Raksha Mantri's Operational Directive' to the service chiefs after obtaining inputs from intelligence agencies and other ministries involved in internal and external security. Many experts are of the opinion that this cannot be equated with a comprehensive defence policy document. In the absence of such a policy document which articulates India's interests, purposes and goals, the government's policy directions are neither clear nor consistent in addressing long-term defence requirements.

National Security Decision-making Process

The existing national security decision-making process is fundamentally flawed. A few examples will illustrate its shortcomings.

In 1987, Prime Minister Rajiv Gandhi agreed to dispatch the Indian Peace Keeping Force during discussions with President J.R. Jayewardene in Colombo. That was a decision taken on the spot without consulting his cabinet or service chiefs. This impromptu decision resulted in the induction of the force at extremely short notice and without proper mandate, tasking, intelligence or equipment. In less than two months, instead of peacekeeping, this force was involved in heavy fighting with the Liberation Tigers of Tamil Eelam.[12]

In 1997, India signed the Chemical Weapons Convention and declared at the Organization for the Prohibition of Chemical Weapons that it possessed a stockpile of chemical weapons. India's three service chiefs learnt about this declaration from the newspapers. These weapons were not held by the armed forces but by the DRDO.

The fundamental flaw in the defence decision-making process starts from the business rules and transactions followed in the MoD. The MoD conducts its business as laid down in the 2nd Schedule of the 'Allocation of Business Rules and Transaction of Business Rules', wherein service headquarters are considered as attached offices. According to these rules, the responsibility for the defence of India, and every part thereof, including preparation for defence and for the armed forces of the Union, namely the army, the navy and the air force, has been vested in the defence secretary. The professional heads of the three services, charged with the command of the armed forces, are not recognized by these rules. There is no legislation in which their responsibilities and authority, other than disciplinary and limited financial powers, are mentioned. The service chiefs and their headquarters are consulted on security-related crises but are not part of the decision-making loop. The chiefs are invited by the CCS from time to time to discuss ongoing security crises but seldom discuss geopolitics, strategy or long-term national security planning. The NSC, which is expected to decide long-term contingencies and process long-term defence planning, meets rarely. There is little interaction between political and military leaders on the dynamics of geo-strategy and security-related environment and strategies. The lack of adequate military inputs into decision-making continues to remain the most significant lacuna.

Well-known strategist Kanti Bajpai once observed, 'Civilians have not sufficiently involved the military in issues where military advice and involvement is proper and vital on issues relating to national security. The military's role in threat assessment and military acquisitions has been unduly restricted. Its thinking on nuclear weapons has never been sufficiently sought or discussed.'[13]

Functional Problems in Peace and War

In peacetime, most of the decision-making in defence matters is institutional. It involves the service headquarters, Chiefs of Staff Committee, Raksha Mantri's Morning (and other) Meetings, and the CCS and other committees mentioned earlier. Proposals initiated by a service headquarter or in the MoD are briefly discussed in the committees mentioned earlier and then submitted on file. Each case is steered through multiple layers of bureaucracy that exist in the MoD, its finance wing and then in the Ministry of Finance before it reaches the CCS for final approval. The pace and the progress depend upon the experience and mindset of officers—civilian and military—who have to give comments. If someone appreciates the proposal, the file will continue to meander through the corridors, but if a person does not like or know what to do with the proposal, he or she can scuttle it or consign it to a deep hole in the cupboard, or send it back with some frivolous query.

The difficulties of integrated policy initiatives in the Chiefs of Staff Committee, the multiple layers of bureaucratic examination and control in the MoD and the service chiefs not being able to attend the CCS meetings when important strategic and defence policy and preparedness issues are discussed tend to make the decision-making process unbearably slow and frustrating. The disadvantages of such a process and its adverse impact on defence capabilities, planning and preparedness can be easily imagined. Five-year defence plans are prepared but seldom approved by the CCS. They seldom get implemented on time or as per given priority because the financial and negotiating control for major procurements rests entirely with non-users.

However, there are major changes in this process in a crisis situation or during a war. Let me give the example of the Kargil war, which was fought during my tenure as the Chief of Army Staff and chairman, Chiefs of Staff Committee.

In the initial stages of the war, the intelligence inputs were that the infiltrators were jihadi militants. There was no information about the direct involvement of the Pakistan Army in the infiltration. As a result, the Chiefs of Staff Committee and the CCS could not agree on the fuller employment of the air force lest it cause escalation of the conflict situation. The situation changed after a few days when we were able to assess correctly that the infiltration was done by the Pakistan Army and not jihadi militants. The Chiefs of Staff Committee then adopted an integrated military strategy and briefed the CCS accordingly. Everyone was closely enmeshed in the politico-military decision-making process thereafter.

The CCS met on a daily basis. Besides the prime minister and other members, the meetings were attended by the NSA, the cabinet secretary, the three service chiefs, the secretaries of the defence, home, finance and external affairs ministries, heads of the Intelligence Bureau and the Research and Analysis Wing, and the secretary, National Security Council Secretariat. Sometimes, for specific purposes, special invitees were called in.

It was a refreshing change in the decision-making process, both at the political level as well as at the armed forces level: open and direct. The political leadership received views of the service chiefs first-hand. After discussions, the executive authorities concerned, including the three chiefs, would obtain clear-cut directions from the prime minister. The NSA was always accessible and facilitated this process. These developments led to an integrated approach to conflict management with the political, economic, diplomatic, media and military aspects meshed cogently.[14] We were able to secure many important but long-stuck weapons- and equipment-related decisions from the CCS.

In an age of uncertainty, we need to be able to act quickly and effectively to address new and evolving threats to national security. That means having access to the best possible advice, and, crucially, the right people around the table when decisions have to be made. It means considering national security issues in the round, recognizing that when it comes to national security, foreign and domestic policy are not separate issues but two halves of one picture.

From personal experience, I consider the fundamentals of national security decision-making to be as follows:

- **Consideration of multiple factors**: Besides military factors, there are a host of other factors, like international relations, socio-politics, economy, finance, technology, communications, and so on. For optimal decision-making, these factors require vertical and lateral consultations/inputs from different ministries and departments. This includes intelligence inputs at the strategic and operational levels.
- **Time and opportunity**: The decision has to be related to the time and opportunity. One cannot keep waiting for 100 per cent inputs to arrive before taking a decision.
- **The Observe, Orient, Decide, Action and Information loops**: One must anticipate the reaction on political, economic, social and military fronts, both inside and outside the country.
- **Implementation is the key**: This is always more important and critical than planning.

At present, national security decision-making is marked by knee-jerk reactions to emerging situations. A committee nominated by the CCS should recommend and then implement crosscutting decision-making procedures.

A Suggested Outline for a National Security Strategy

For a nation to be able to successfully manage the threats, challenges and vulnerabilities that it is faced with, it must formulate a clearly thought-through national security strategy. As mentioned earlier, the Indian government does not publish a document called 'National Security Strategy'. In fact, the Indian defence policy is opaque and known only to a handful of government officials, if at all. As a regional power and an aspiring global power, it is essential for the Indian government to publish its national security strategy. Such a publication will enable various stakeholders to understand their role in the overall national context.

In the United Kingdom, the first task that the newly established National Security Council in 2010 completed was to write and approve the 'National Security Strategy'. This document has four parts: (a) the strategic context, (b) Britain's distinctive role, (c) risks to security and prioritization of risks, and (d) national responses. This document has been closely linked to a separate 'Strategic Defence and Security Review', which describes how the country will equip its armed forces and the police and intelligence agencies to tackle current and future threats effectively. The US has only one document, called 'National Security Strategy'. The latest edition covers in detail all aspects pertaining to (a) security (b) prosperity (c) values and (d) the international order.

The national security strategy document of India will need to cover the following important elements amongst others:

- **Definition of national security and its objectives:** This should define and state in broad terms both military and non-military objectives, for instance, protection and defence of territorial integrity and sovereignty; protection of the core values given in the Indian Constitution; major socio-economic developments and India's envisaged role in global and regional affairs.
- **An appreciation of the geopolitical environment:** An assessment of the geopolitical environment and how it affects India. This can

include the global transition into multi-polarity (no single world power or the bipolarity of the Cold War era); the comprehensive rise of China and its likely political, economic and military impact; growing dysfunctionality of the Pakistani state; the impact of the withdrawal of US and International Security Assistance Force (ISAF) troops from Afghanistan; the spread of Shia and Sunni-supported terrorism; developments in the Indian Ocean region and maritime security; militarization of space, challenges and threats to India's security due to cyber attacks, terrorism, asymmetric warfare and WMD proliferation; scarcity of energy and mineral resources, and implications of climate change on India's security.

- **Challenges from the neighbourhood:** Developments in the region, particularly the extended neighbourhood and the Indian Ocean, which may cause a backlash in or instability for India. How can India contribute towards stability through bilateral and regional cooperation?
- **Coping with challenges:** Having defined the challenges, the strategy document should broadly delineate how India intends to cope with these challenges and seek a role for itself to be able to contribute its efforts regionally or globally. For a realistic national security strategy, there must also be an appreciation of the ends and the means to be adopted to achieve them.
- **Military reforms and modernization:** The need for military reform is acute today. Necessary changes should be made in the defence structures for harmonious civil-military relations and improvement in weapons development, production and acquisition. Professionalization in the MoD should be enhanced through specialization of the civilian staff and substantive integration of uniformed personnel. Information warfare and cyber security issues should be given special attention.
- **Internal security:** This part will include issues such as left-wing extremism, ethnic conflicts in the north-east, J&K, communalism, corruption, religious fundamentalism and extremism, and regional and socio-economic inequalities. A counter-insurgency strategy aimed at dealing with insurgents and addressing the grievances of the alienated groups is needed. Required reforms in police,

intelligence, laws, and rules of engagement as well as improvements in coordination of resources should be covered.

- **Border Management**: The linkage between internal security and externally sponsored terrorism, fake Indian currency, money laundering, drugs, etc., may be specified. It should also cover aspects such as immigration policies and illegal cross-border movement.
- **Resources and capabilities**: Building of diverse capabilities will require focus on a strong economy, inclusive growth, human resource development and progress in technology in addition to development of hard and soft power through diplomatic and military means, governance reforms and through the creation of synergy between these channels. These should include (a) the approach towards achieving a strong economy and inclusive growth, (b) building capacities in research, development and technology to enable socio-economic development and self-reliance in the strategic sectors, and (c) creation of skilled human resources to take advantage of the demographic dividend India is presently enjoying.
- **Information policy:** An elected government needs to align public perceptions with the state's policy objectives through continuous engagement with its people. The channels of communication must be two-way, thus ensuring feedback. An institutional structure is required to disseminate and to receive information in a timely manner. Moreover, such information must carry credibility. The use of social media can become an important part of this endeavour.

Conclusion

National security decision-making in the current strategic environment is too vital a subject to be dealt with using watertight compartments. It requires frequent multi-disciplinary vertical and lateral consultations and much faster decision-making. Therefore, it is imperative that we change our mindsets and attitudes and look beyond narrow boundaries defined by turf and parochialism. We need many changes in the national security structures, processes and procedures which can make it more efficient, resilient and speedily responsive. It is only then that we can be secure internally and externally, fully prepared to take on the role that we see for ourselves as a regional power.

2

International Experience: The Defence Policies of Major Powers

Major General Dhruv Katoch

Former General Officer Commanding of an infantry division in Arunachal Pradesh and former Director, Centre for Land Warfare Studies, New Delhi

> 'Let us never forget that our way of life, our vision and all we hope to achieve is secured not by the rightness of our cause but by the strength of our defence.' —Margaret Thatcher,[1] former Prime Minister of the UK

The defence policy of a nation flows out of its perceived national interest. Across the world, most countries have local issues to contend with while determining their national interest and the consequent development of their defence policies. This chapter seeks to examine the formulation of policies by some key nations in the above context.

The United States

The core national interests of the United States are:[2]

- The security of the United States, its citizens, its allies and partners.
- A strong, innovative and growing US economy in an open international economic system that promotes opportunity and prosperity.
- Respect for universal values at home and around the world.
- An international order advanced by US leadership that promotes peace, security and opportunity through stronger cooperation to meet global challenges.

These four enduring national interests of the US are inextricably linked to each other and would be pursued simultaneously through diplomacy, economic development, cooperation and engagement, military capability and through the power of ideas. There is inherent synergy in the pursuit of these goals as positive action in any one area helps advance the others too. Thus, a strong economy provides the wherewithal for furthering security interests. Similarly, a secure environment enables the growth of a strong economy. Both contribute to advancing US interests in maintaining its leadership role in world affairs, which in turn helps to promote the values which the US holds dear.

It is also apparent that besides its primary commitment to protecting the American people, the US also views itself as a protector and promoter of international security. Its commitments to allies, and the lead role it intends to play in supporting what it views as a 'just and sustainable international order', would require unmatched global military capabilities. These objectives would, therefore, be reflected in the policies and steps being taken in that direction.

The US is singularly blessed in that, unlike many countries across the globe, it faces no military threat from its neighbours. After World War II, the prime security challenge for the US was the containment of the Soviet Union. The period 1947–91 witnessed the Cold War—a state of political and military tension between the US and its North Atlantic Treaty Organization (NATO) allies on one side and the Eastern Bloc, represented by the Soviet Union and its allies of the Warsaw Pact of 1955 on the other. With the dissolution of the Soviet Union in December 1991, the US emerged as the sole superpower, to face a different set of challenges, characterized by a changing world order.

While the threat of a nuclear conflagration was considerably reduced after the end of the Cold War, the US still viewed the spread of nuclear weapons as posing the gravest danger to its people as well as the global community. Its policy thus remains focused on addressing concerns arising out of weapons of mass destruction (WMD), particularly nuclear weapons. The attacks of 11 September 2001 brought home to the US the fact that it had to also contend with violent extremism. The impact of globalization and the general advancement in military capabilities across the world has given rise to a third set of vulnerabilities. These include threats emanating from the space and cyberspace domains, the security of energy supplies, the dangers of climate change and pandemic diseases and the failure of states endangering regional and global security. The US thus seeks to 'adapt, reshape and rebalance' its military to prepare for the strategic challenges and opportunities the country is likely to face in the future. The 'Quadrennial Defense Review 2014', building on the '2012 Defense Strategic Guidance', has accordingly prioritized three strategic pillars: defending the homeland; building security globally by projecting US influence and deterring aggression; and remaining prepared to win decisively against any adversary should deterrence fail.[3]

The US economy remains the foundation of US power. Its economic strength is closely tied to a stable international order, underwritten by the US military's role and that of its allies and partners in ensuring freedom of access and the free flow of commerce globally. The US defence policy thus aims to sustain its global leadership role and protect and advance its other core interests by leveraging the strength of its economy and its military capability and through a network of alliances and partnerships across the globe. Its defence strategy is thus based on three pillars, each mutually reinforcing and interdependent. These are:[4]

- To protect the homeland, to deter and defeat attacks on the US and to support civil authorities in mitigating the effects of potential attacks and natural disasters.
- To build security globally, in order to preserve regional stability, deter adversaries, support allies and partners, and cooperate with others to address common security challenges.
- To project power and win decisively, to defeat aggression, disrupt and destroy terrorist networks, and provide humanitarian assistance and disaster relief.

For the US, its nuclear deterrent is the ultimate protection against a nuclear attack. Through extended deterrence, it also serves to reassure its distant allies of their security against regional aggression. The global reach of US security and its ability to combat terrorism across the world reassures its allies, and, most importantly, reduces the likelihood of such threats finding their way back to US shores. The US defence doctrine, therefore, seeks to ensure the capability of its armed forces to simultaneously defend the homeland, deter aggression and assure allies through forward presence and engagement, and carry out sustained, distributed counter-terrorist operations. Should deterrence fail at any given time, it seeks force capability to defeat a regional adversary in a large-scale multi-phased campaign, and deny the objectives of, or impose unacceptable costs on, a second aggressor in another region.

The US views future conflict as ranging from hybrid contingencies against proxy groups using asymmetric approaches to a high-end conflict against a state power armed with WMDs or technologically advanced anti-access and area denial (A2/AD) capabilities. With this in view, the US defence policy aims to be ready for the full spectrum of possible operations. In this the US aims to retain its technological edge, through priority investments in science, technology, research and development, both within the defence sector and beyond, to include both the space and cyberspace domains. To counter violent extremism across the world, it seeks to use a combination of economic, diplomatic, intelligence, law enforcement, development and military tools. There is greater emphasis placed on building partnership capacity, especially in fragile states, while retaining robust capability for direct action, including intelligence, persistent surveillance, precision strikes, and special operation forces.[5]

The force structures required for achieving the aims set out would be:[6]

- Maintaining an air force with global power projection capabilities.
- Sustaining a world-class army capable of conducting the full range of operations on land, including prompt and sustained land combat as part of large, multi-phase joint and multinational operations. This will involve maintaining a force of 440,000 to 450,000 soldiers, an Army National Guard of 335,000 soldiers, and a reserve of 195,000 soldiers.
- Maintaining a naval capacity to build security globally and respond to crises.
- Maintaining the role of the Marine Corps as a vital crisis response force.

This implies capabilities including:

- Effective nuclear capacity to achieve deterrence, including updated delivery, warning, command and control, and weapons systems.
- Cyberspace capability to enhance ability to conduct cyberspace operations worldwide.

- A multi-layered approach to deter attacks on space systems while retaining response capabilities should deterrence fail.
- Air and naval capability to increase the ability of the joint forces to counter A2/AD challenges.
- An adequate missile defence system and precision strike capability across the globe.
- Intelligence, surveillance and reconnaissance (ISR) capability to support global situational awareness, counter-terrorism and other operations.

As the US has clearly stated end-term goals with respect to the capabilities required of its military, and as the financial means of securing those ends are declining, the US is resorting to innovation and rebalancing in many areas. It is now shifting to restore its readiness for the full spectrum of potential conflicts. It is looking at a forward posture across the globe which is permanent, prepositioned and has surge capability to deter adversaries and to reassure allies. It is also looking at enhancing the capability, capacity and readiness of its forces. The US aims to have the best trained, best equipped and best led fighting force on the planet. While doing so, it remains cognizant of the fact that this takes time, it takes money and that this edge is perishable.

The United Kingdom

Britain is a country whose political, economic and cultural outreach far exceeds its size. Ten per cent of its population permanently lives overseas. Its national interest is visualized in the promotion of six strategic aims. These are:[7]

- A free and democratic society properly protected from its enemies.
- A strong, sustainable and growing economy.
- A healthy, active, secure, socially cohesive, socially mobile, socially responsible and well-educated population.
- A fair deal for those who are poor or vulnerable.
- A vibrant culture.
- A beautiful and sustainable built (sic) and natural environment.

Based on its national interest, Britain's 'National Security Strategy' sets out to ensure a secure and resilient UK by protecting its people, economy, infrastructure, territory and ways of life from all major risks that can directly affect them, and to shape a stable world by acting to reduce the likelihood of risks affecting the UK or its interests overseas. It seeks to achieve this through application of instruments of power and influence to shape the global environment and tackle potential risks at source.[8]

During the Cold War years, the threat of Soviet armies spread across half of Europe posed an existential threat to Britain. Post the Cold War, however, the UK faces neither major state threats nor any existential threat to its security, freedom or prosperity. Potential threats can, however, emanate from a myriad of sources to include terrorism, cyber attack, unconventional attacks using chemical, nuclear or biological weapons, as well as large-scale accidents or natural hazards, each having the potential to do grave damage to the country. Presently, the UK views international terrorism as a prime threat to the country.

Potential threats that the country can face have been characterized as hostile intelligence-gathering activities, the disruption of critical services, and the exercise of malign influence over citizens or governments. The conventional domain is expected to be characterized by greater difficulty in securing access to and freedom of manoeuvre in conflict environments, and unclear battle lines in a battlefield that may contain local people and the media as well as adversaries. Lines of communication could be vulnerable to disruption and all actions could be subject to scrutiny in the media and courts and by society at large. While international terrorism is presently viewed as the prime threat to the UK, future scenarios could change. The ability to identify risks and opportunities at the earliest possible stage and to maintain highly capable and flexible armed forces so as to retain the capability to exercise military power when necessary therefore assumes significance.[9]

The UK believes that the protection of its national interests requires continued full and active engagement in world affairs. Its economy must compete with the strongest and the best and the entire government effort overseas must be geared to promote trade, which is the lifeblood of the economy. It must also stand up for the values the country believes in—the rule of law, democracy, free speech, tolerance and human rights—to ensure that they are upheld and respected in the world. Hence the need for power projection capabilities to act well beyond its shores and to have a strategic presence wherever it may be required, both individually and with its alliance partners, principally the US and NATO. With this in view, there are three principal elements in the UK's strategic policy framework. These are:[10]

- The ability to respond to the highest priority risks by maintaining key counter-terrorist capabilities, developing a transformative programme for cyber security, focusing on efforts to counter natural hazards and integrating diplomatic, intelligence, defence and other capabilities to prevent international military crises, while retaining the ability to respond should they nevertheless materialize.
- To respond to the low-probability but high-impact risk of a large-scale military attack by another state, through deterrence including nuclear deterrence, partnership with allies and the ability to regenerate capabilities given sufficient strategic notice.
- To identify and manage risks before they materialize in the UK, as well as to maintain a broad spectrum of defence and other capabilities to deter, contain and engage developing threats on ground.

Maintaining a wide set of alliances and partnerships remains a key facet of Britain's overall security architecture, and its relations with the US are essential to deliver the security it needs. In addition, through the NATO and other alliances, it seeks to share security needs and gain collective security benefits.

The armed forces are the core of Britain's security, providing the means to threaten or use force when other levers of power are unable to protect its vital national interests. The country's defence policy hence aims to retain a full spectrum of military capabilities that would provide the greatest utility to the UK as well as its allies, and to maintain collectively the ability to reconstitute or regenerate capabilities that may be required in the future. The latter would require investment in key technologies.

While the UK is downsizing its forces, it aims to retain their geographical reach and their ability to operate across the spectrum of conflict: from high-intensity intervention to enduring stabilization activity. The focus would be on tackling risks before they escalate, and on exerting influence, as part of a better-coordinated overall national security response, with the option of force being used when the national interest is at stake. The UK will maintain the ability to act alone where it does not expect others to help, but will also work with allies and partners to share the burden of securing international stability. The UK also seeks to invest in programmes that will provide flexibility and advanced capabilities, and reduce legacy capabilities, whose use is less likely in a world of precision weaponry, and where the battle space increasingly involves unmanned and cyber operations. As part of Britain's defence policy, the military has been given the following tasks:[11]

- Defending the UK and its overseas territories.
- Providing strategic intelligence.
- Providing nuclear deterrence.
- Supporting civil emergency organizations in times of crisis.
- Defending the UK's interests by projecting power strategically and through expeditionary interventions.
- Providing a defence contribution to the UK's influence.
- Providing security for stabilization.

The UK has identified the force structure for the military to be in place by 2020. In the maritime environment, Future Force 2020 will be able to provide: continuous nuclear 'at sea' deterrence; maritime defence of the UK and its South Atlantic Overseas Territories; an enduring presence within priority regions of the world to contribute to conventional deterrence and containment; powerful intervention capabilities from surface and submarine fleets; the ability to land forces from the sea by helicopter and over the beach with protective vehicles and supplies from specialist ships; and the ability to command UK and allied naval forces at task force level.[12] A key capability is the UK Trident programme, which encompasses the development, procurement and operation of the current generation of British nuclear weapons, and the means to deliver them. Trident itself is an operational system of four Vanguard-class submarines armed with Trident II D-5 ballistic missiles, able to deliver thermonuclear warheads from multiple independently targetable re-entry vehicles. It is the most expensive and the most powerful capability of the British military forces.

Carrier strike capability will be based on a single carrier, with a second kept at extended readiness. The UK will complete the construction of two large aircraft carriers and retire the ones in use, as it believes that only aircraft carriers can provide the ability to deploy air power across the world without needing friendly air bases on land. The surface fleet will consist of nineteen frigates and destroyers, providing military flexibility across a variety of operations, from full-scale naval warfare to providing maritime security. The Royal Marines, 3 Commando Brigade will provide the key element of the High Readiness Response Force.[13]

For the land environment, Future Force 2020 will be able to provide light specialist forces for short-duration interventions and sufficient multi-role forces to provide flexibility for larger or more complex intervention operations, or to undertake enduring stabilization operations. Capabilities will include five multi-role brigades and sixteen air assault brigades, besides others. In the air environment, Future Force 2020 will be able to provide air defence of the UK and its South Atlantic Overseas Territories and a credible and capable combat air presence to contribute to conventional deterrence and containment. It will also provide an expeditionary combat air contribution to enduring land operations, strategic and tactical airlift and other air power capabilities, including intelligence, surveillance, target acquisition and reconnaissance (ISTAR), helicopters and Royal Air Force (RAF) Regiment ground units.[14]

UK defence policy is now in a transitional phase, requiring a major, challenging programme of change within set financial perimeters. The UK is moving towards leaner, better-coordinated structures and processes in order to ensure efficient and effective delivery of strategic defence and security priorities.

Germany

Germany is the largest country in Europe and has more common borders with neighbours than any other European nation. Due to its geostrategic location, it has a higher potential for conflict with neighbours than for any other European country. With the destruction of Germany in World War II, and its division thereafter, West Germany sought a foreign policy that allowed it to cope with the past and achieve stability and acceptance in the international system. It sought to integrate itself into Western institutions and define itself as part of a Western alliance, a process known as Westbindung or Einbindung. Simultaneously, it sought better relations with East Germany and the Soviet Union to reduce tensions and to deal with the reality of German division.[15]

There was an inherent dualism in German foreign policy. It publicly condemned war and focused its post-war re-education efforts towards demilitarization and de-Nazification of society. At the same time, it had to be prepared for defence against the Soviet Bloc. The prime German interest at this stage was in achieving unification of the two wings of the country, and this was sought by integrating with the West through institutional and multilateral mechanisms. While integration was viewed by the Western powers as a means to keep Germany under check, the Germans themselves saw it as an opportunity to establish the legitimacy of the new state and become an actor in the post-war system.

While Western nations were not keen that West Germany should rearm, security commitments forced it to change their minds. They had to either accept an expensive and untenable military burden or treat Germany as a political equal for the defence of Europe. The German policy of Einbindung created the framework for stability in western Europe and also led to the unification of Germany after the collapse of the Soviet Union.

After the fall of the Berlin Wall in 1989, Germany used its alliances with the European Union (EU) and NATO to further its national interests. Here the national interest sought was 'peace', given the two disastrous wars fought by Germany in the first half of the twentieth century. Germany's size and economic prowess made it a major player in Europe, but it lacked the strength to prevail in the world on its own. Its economic growth was largely a product of its exports to European markets, and its cherished social model was sustainable largely because Germany was embedded in the deep structures of the EU.[16]

It was West Germany's first post-war chancellor, Konrad Adenauer, who had welcomed the prospect of bringing Germany's first successful democracy into an eventual 'United States of Europe', and that policy continues. But this distant goal has been kept in a dialectic relationship with national interest. Even a decade after German unification, the state clung to the raison d'état of the old Federal Republic rather than formulating its new national interest. Germany thus continued to conduct its foreign policy on an economic agenda rather than a political one, and its defence policy was subsumed in the larger construct of a pan-European security architecture.

This defined the national interest and accustomed the initially disoriented Germans to the democracy set forth in the Basic Law[17] and to the completely new conditions of the international system. By the threshold year of 2000, German foreign policy might best be summed up as moving irreversibly towards handing Europe the sovereignty of a state founded on the Basic Law.[18]

With a change in the international scene post 11 September 2001 and America's response in the form of the war on terror, there is growing scepticism in Germany about the decade-old assertion that the EU could be expanded and strongly integrated, and that this integration was in Germany's interest. As part of its security commitments, Germany has been drawn into political crises in Afghanistan and in the Middle East, which made it dawn on the German people that it might not be so wrong to rediscover German national interest after all, especially when other states in the EU still ranked the interests of their own states first and consequently pursued policies to serve that interest.[19] While Germany's national interest seems tied to its economic development, through its policy of Einbindung, the spirit in which to pursue and articulate self-interest exists in Article 56 of the Basic Law.[20] Germany, however, awaits actors who can articulate it in credible, precise and yet also internationally acceptable terms.

In tune with its policies, Germany has refrained from developing a high military profile to support its foreign policy, preferring to contribute to international stability through non-military means. Its security policy remains hinged on development of the Euro-Atlantic community and strengthening of the Europeans' capability to act, within the frameworks of the EU and of NATO. This has led to a downsizing of its force structure post the end of the Cold War. In 1985, at the peak of the Cold War, the overall defence expenditure of the Federal Republic of Germany (or West Germany) amounted to 3.2 per cent of the gross domestic product (GDP). The improved security climate after the end of the Cold War resulted in reduced budgetary support for defence to 1.5 per cent of GDP. This further reduced in real terms from 47.3 billion deutsche mark (DM) in

2000 to 39.7 billion DM in 2006—a drop of about 16 per cent.[21] Since 2006, the defence budget is in the range of 1.2 per cent of GDP.

The manpower of the force was also drastically reduced. In 1985, at the peak of the Cold War, the Bundeswehr had an active strength of 478,000 military personnel (including reserve training posts), of which almost 48 per cent were conscripts. The Federal Forces' mobilization strength amounted to 1,250,000 soldiers, and the strength of civilian personnel forming the administrative back-up of the military organization was nearly 170,000. By 1998, the Bundeswehr's active strength had fallen to less than 335,000 military personnel, the proportion of conscripts had shrunk to about 42 per cent, the estimated mobilization strength had been halved and the civilian component had shrunk to 125,000 personnel. By 2010, the active strength of military personnel had further reduced to 250,000 and that of civilian employees to 75,000.

By 2017, the Bundeswehr is envisioned to consist of no more than 185,000 active duty military and 55,000 civilian employees. This posits up to 10,000 soldiers being deployable simultaneously in two areas of operation. In the new personnel structure, the army, air force and navy will consist of approximately 62,000 soldiers, 32,000 airmen and 16,000 sailors, and the Joint Support Service and the medical service will consist of roughly 46,000 and 19,000, respectively.[22] (The remaining members are distributed among equipment, infrastructure, human resources and other services.)

With reduced manpower come cuts in prospective procurement and decommissioning of active systems. Although the German navy is to remain more or less the same (albeit at a lower level of personnel), these reductions will strongly affect Germany's army and air force. The tank holdings of 350 Leopard 2 tanks will be reduced to 225 and the armoured personnel carrier Puma/Marder from 410 to 350. There is also a substantial reduction in artillery and helicopters. For the air force, there is a prospective reduction of the Eurofighter Typhoon from 177 to 140 aircraft and in the combat aircraft Tornado from 185 to 85 aircraft.[23]

The rationale for force reduction is provided by the Defence Policy Guidelines (DPG) and Eckpunkte (principles), both published in May 2011. They explain Germany's vested interest in a stable, liberal international order and analyse current and likely future threats to that order. The 'new orientation' seeks to develop a sleeker force that is highly deployable and effective in crisis management and crisis resolution missions. As per the DPG, 'The ability to fight ... is thus a benchmark for operational readiness.' The new orientation's force structure is 'breadth rather than depth' (Breite vor Tiefe), meaning a preference for 'a little bit of everything' over further military specialization.[24] This strategy incurs deficits in sustainability and effectiveness in operations but is said to give Germany a key political role in cooperating with European partners of small and medium size. By offering broad basic capabilities, Germany allows other partners to develop highly specialized forces that can then be pooled and shared in common operations—presumably, at times, under German leadership—and with financial benefits for all.

There has been an apparent shift, however, as seen in pronouncements made in the 2014 Munich Security Conference. German President Joachim Gauck, along with Foreign Affairs Minister Frank-Walter Steinmeier and Defence Minister Ursula von der Leyen, clearly outlined visions of German policy that differed considerably from historical precedent. The statements made in the conference were telling: 'Germany's culture of restraint must not become a culture of standing aloof', 'Indifference is not an option' and 'Germany must be ready to do more to guarantee the security that others have provided for it for decades' were some of the statements made and coming from Germany, bordering on the revolutionary.

German political leadership is, however, aware that the government's manoeuvrability in redefining defence policy depends on obtaining strong public support. This means that change can only start from home and has to be introduced carefully. They would have to overcome the weakness of the German defence identity, overturn the enduring pacifism in German society and bridge the gaps between politics and the military persisting from the Cold War, with many people still considering the military a peculiar instrument, and certainly not a 'good' or 'normal' part of the government's toolbox.[25]

However, Germany's political leadership remains instinctively reluctant to use hard power, believing that force rarely produces the desired result and always incurs political costs at home. As a nation deeply ashamed of the horrors of Nazi militarism and having been re-educated as free-riding consumers of security, Germany still struggles with the appropriate approach to military means as an instrument of foreign policy.

Russia

Post World War II, the Soviet Union emerged as a superpower in competition with the US to form a bipolar world. Competing ideologies led to the Cold War between the two, which finally ended in 1991 with the dissolution of the Soviet Union. Russia, as the successor of the Soviet Union, is today grappling with the contradictions between imperial nostalgia on the one hand and the dramatic decline in its power after the Soviet collapse on the other. While Russia remains a well-established sovereign state, it is still seeking a balanced strategy of relationships with the newly independent states that have emerged within the borders of the former Soviet Union.

Russian national interests have been enunciated in the 'National Security Concept of the Russian Federation', approved by Presidential Decree No. 24 of 10 January 2000,[26] and in the 'National Security Strategy of the Russian Federation up to 2020', approved by Decree of the President of the Russian Federation No. 537 on 12 May 2009.[27] There is an element of vagueness in the way the national interest has been enunciated in these two documents, perhaps reflecting differing perspectives within the Russian elite and also indicating a somewhat opaque political process. In broad terms, Russia's national interests could be said to encompass the following:[28]

- Upholding Russian sovereignty, preventing military aggression against Russia and its allies and preventing major terrorist attacks within the country.
- Maintaining nuclear deterrent capability as a guarantor of Russia's sovereignty and great power status; preventing the use of nuclear weapons or other WMDs against Russia and preventing proliferation of nuclear weapons and delivery systems in the post-Soviet space.
- Ensuring conditions for the peaceful and democratic development of the state.
- Assuring continued revenue flows from Russia's energy exports

and ensuring that other states are not able to exercise leverage over Russia's energy exports.

- Sustaining Russian influence in the post-Soviet space and denying competing powers or alliances the ability to dominate the post-Soviet space, thereby strengthening its position as a great power and as one of the influential centres in a multipolar world.

After the break-up of the Soviet Union, Russian policy remained ambivalent in its attitudes and policies towards the Commonwealth of Independent States (CIS). Up to the mid-1990s, Russia's main concern was to restore at least minimal security in the region by ending the civil war in Tajikistan, peacemaking attempts in Abkhazia and Transnistria and mediation of the Azerbaijan-Armenia conflict around Nagorno-Karabakh. Russia also aspired to secure its own role as the major transit operator in energy supply from Central Asia and the Caspian basin to Europe.

Politically, Russian leaders preferred formal confirmations of loyalty from their neighbours to ensure truly effective cooperation. Until 2005, friendly relations with Ukraine were based on Kiev's access to cheap Russian oil and natural gas and on Moscow's readiness to allow gas supplies to be delivered from Turkmenistan to Ukraine. Economically, however, Russia gained little from accommodating the interest of CIS countries, as concessions were rarely mutual. At the beginning of the new century, Vladimir Putin adopted a more critical approach towards 'Western expansionism', as he described NATO and EU enlargement. Russian economic cooperation with the CIS countries came to be measured in terms of their political loyalty, with greater attention being paid to the military-political component of cooperation.[29]

During this period, Russia also launched multilateral cooperation between post-Soviet countries and other regional powers that took a cautious stance towards the West. In 2001, the Shanghai Cooperation Organization was created as an instrument to increase Russia's influence in Central Asia and balance Russian-Chinese interests in the region. It has since preferred to restrict cooperation with either those countries which followed in the footsteps of the EU and the US, or those trying to undermine Russia's dominance as an oil and gas transit power like Azerbaijan and Turkmenistan.

Post 2008, when the armed conflict between Georgia and Russia showed the ambiguity of Russia's positioning in the CIS, the leaders of the Kremlin apparently realized that the true strengthening of Russian influence in the post-Soviet space was possible only through economic incentives for political integration and led to efforts to form the Eurasian Economic Union. There is thus an effort to consolidate those parts of the former Soviet Union that are still not incorporated in other blocks.[30] Effective collaboration and cooperation with CIS members, however, remains a vital component in providing for the military security of the Russian Federation: to enable the state to react to a crisis situation in its initial stages and to achieve its foreign policy goals.

Despite the end of the Cold War, the majority of the challenges confronting Russia internationally stem from US aims to remain the world leader and to occasionally unilaterally tailor the political map of the world. Russia, occupying one-seventh of the world's territory and straddling two continents, feels slighted by such attempts, having always been a key player in European and global politics. Attempts by the US and its allies to undermine regimes favourable to Russia are matters of concern, as are US 'Velvet Revolution Technologies' policies, disguised as support for greater democracy, in which huge monies are being pumped in to activists to mobilize corresponding audiences. US attempts to achieve invulnerability in the military sphere, through its Ballistic Missile Defence Programme, also upset the concept of mutually assured destruction and put Russia at risk. In addition, Russia finds itself the target of a carefully planned information warfare campaign.[31] Russian concerns could thus be seen as:[32]

- A weakening of Russia's political, economic and military influence in the world.
- Strengthening of antagonistic military-political blocs and alliances, especially NATO's expansion eastwards.
- The possible emergence of foreign military bases and the presence of major military forces close to Russia's borders.
- Threats from the use of WMDs against Russia and its allies.
- Territorial claims on Russia, the weakening of the process of integration within the CIS and conflicts breaking out and escalating

near to the borders of the Russian Federation and the external borders of CIS member states.

- Growing technological asymmetry, which could provoke a new round of the arms race and radically alter the forms and methods of warfare.
- Threats arising from international terrorism.

Russian defence policy seeks to progress towards nuclear arms control, elimination of WMDs, furthering international cooperation in the fight against transnational crime and terrorism, and building measures to ensure international supervision of the export of goods and technologies, especially over the provision of military and dual-purpose services. While the Russian Federation prefers political, diplomatic, economic and other non-military means to prevent war and armed conflicts, it would maintain sufficient military power to ensure its own security, to include nuclear deterrence as well as conventional capability to provide effective protection against aerial attack, perform missions to repulse aggression in a local war and to carry out strategic deployments for missions in a large-scale war.[33]

Russia's military doctrine was published in February 2010. There appears to be ambiguity in Russian thinking between a desire to create a force with global reach akin to the Soviet era, or smaller armed forces for homeland security and anti-terrorist missions. The military doctrine reflects, to a large extent, the views expressed in the National Security Concept of 2000. A significant change, however, is on nuclear retaliation in case of a nuclear attack. The concept paper of 2000 posited nuclear retaliation in the event Russia is attacked by nuclear weapons. The new doctrine goes further and advocates nuclear retaliation in case of non-nuclear WMD attacks on Russia or its allies, as well as in cases where aggression against the Russian federation with the use of conventional weapons endangers the very existence of the state. This reflects Russian security concerns over actions by NATO in extending its influence eastwards. The reference to protection against aerial attack reflects a growing appreciation of US technological capability, as reflected in the war in Kosovo.[34]

An analysis of the August 2008 Russia–Georgia conflict showed up weaknesses in C4I2SR (command, control, communications, computers, intelligence, information, surveillance and reconnaissance) capabilities and in joint planning, forcing a realization in the Russian establishment that the state lacked the means to fight a modern war.[35] This, and ongoing efforts by the US to create global missile defences, encircle Russia with military bases and expand NATO, forced a new configuration of the country's armed forces and a rearmament effort.[36] The military was downsized to under a million from the 1.2 million personnel held in 2008, and the four-tier command system of military districts, armies, divisions and regiments was reduced to a basic two-tier system of strategic commands and fully manned brigades that could be deployed for combat operations within a few hours (termed 'permanent readiness brigades'). On 5 March 2010, President Dmitry Medvedev stated that the reorganization had been completed and set a ten-year target for modernization of the forces. The reorganization basically affected the army, which saw 203 partially staffed divisions being converted to eighty-five brigades and elimination of 20,000 tanks from a holding of 22,000.

Russian fears of a US or NATO-led attack, similar to NATO actions against Serbia in 1999, led to the creation of the Aerospace Defence Operational-Strategic Command. Formerly known as the Moscow Air Defence District Special Purpose Command, the new command has unified aerospace defences by bringing existing systems of air and missile defence, missile attack warning, and space surveillance under its ambit, with a view to detect the initiation of an attack and to warn the state leadership in order to facilitate further decisions to detect, destroy, suppress, or close down the assets used in an attack.

Russia's military doctrine calls for the technological independence of its military weapons manufacturing capability, especially its strategic systems. The military aims to increase the share of modern weaponry to 70 per cent by 2020 by upgrading 11 per cent of military equipment each year. The procurement programme lays emphasis on nuclear weapons and delivery systems for the Strategic Rocket Forces; fifth-generation fighter aircraft for the air force; ships and submarines for the navy; and air defence systems, digital communications means, and intelligence capabilities. However, there are serious problems associated with the desired aim of manufacturing all weapons indigenously. Adequate funding is not available for research and development, and many of the erstwhile production facilities are in the newly independent republics. Though Russia has endeavoured to establish business relations with the republics, it has shifted to foreign weapon purchases that emphasize technology transfers.[37]

As part of defence reforms, Russia is consolidating its 1,500-odd defence research institutes, design bureaus and industries, all of which are either partly or wholly owned by the state and which employ about 3 million workers, through the establishment of the Rostekhnologii (Russian Technologies) State Corporation. The aim is to boost the high-technological transformation of defence and non-defence industries, foster sales of high-technology goods in domestic and foreign markets, and attract investment.[38]

Russia remains a major global arms exporter, accounting for about 25 per cent of total arms sales worldwide. As an extension of its homeland security, it seeks to project capabilities in the territories of Soviet successor states through leases for bases and other military facilities. There is no plan to reduce such commitments. However, global power projection capabilities appear to have lower priority right now. Increased military spending may impact Russia's economy, taking away much-needed funds from their social and development sectors. However, an invigorated defence sector could also contribute to an improved economy if corruption and inefficiencies are controlled.

Overall, defence reforms as of now appear to be reasonably successful, and Russian military capability as of now stands enhanced. It has the requisite capability in the nuclear field, but its global power projection capabilities remain limited. Nevertheless, the combat readiness of the armed forces in local and regional conflicts, in counter-terrorism, in combating insurrections in the North Caucasus, and in exercising military influence within the CIS stand enhanced.[39]

China

China sees itself in historical terms as a unique power with an unbroken history and culture that goes back 5,000 years. It is conscious of its history and of its rising power status in a world that is moving towards multipolarity. China claims this rise to be peaceful, and one which does not intend to challenge the existing international system through military expansion or to seek to create another international system outside the existing system through confrontation.

For long, China has spoken of its national interest though generic formulations. These were defined for the first time at the July 2009 US–China Strategic and Economic Dialogue, when the then Chinese state councillor, Dai Bingguo, listed national security, sovereignty and territorial integrity and economic and social sustained development as China's core interests.[40] Subsequently, the white paper issued by China in September 2011 on 'China's Peaceful Development' also stated that 'China's political system established by the constitution and overall social stability' were components of its core interests.[41] In 2006, it identified Tibet and Xinjiang as core interests. Prior to this, Taiwan was the only specific issue identified as a core interest.[42]

Chinese conceptions of and prioritization of its core interests have been impacted by changes in political dispensations and perceptions of national concerns. For Mao Zedong, the political and security interests of the state were paramount and were closely allied to the ideology of the state. His identification of Chinese policies with the larger cause of 'world socialism' led to an overemphasis on self-reliance and the ill-fated economic policies of the Mao era.[43] His successor Deng Xiaoping shifted emphasis to economic development, which he considered the 'core' national interest—and peace was vital to achieve it.[44] Thereafter, Jiang Zemin expanded the idea of economic security to include technological security and ecological security. His successor, Hu Jintao, while continuing with the polices of his predecessor, promoted the concept of 'peaceful development' (heping fazhan). This construct continues to date.

While the core national interests of China appear to be relatively stable as of now, the policies to achieve these remain fluid. Chinese national interest could expand in line with its growing economic interests, and could in future encompass securing energy and strategic resources for continued economic development. This could lead to a deviation in the stated goal of peaceful development.

A major internal security challenge for China is controlling internal instability, brought about by high unemployment (8 to 10 per cent in urban areas), a large floating population and social inequity. The number of 'mass incidents', the term the Chinese government uses to describe public protests, is in excess of 100,000 a year. Another internal security challenge is the separatist movement in both Xinjiang and the Tibet Autonomous Region. The East Turkistan Islamic Movement in Xinjiang also presents China with its most significant terrorist threat. This and other Uyghur separatist groups have reportedly trained in Afghanistan to fight with the Taliban and al Qaeda, and resort to violence, bomb attacks, assassinations, and street fighting.[45]

Externally, China's major security challenge comes from the US. While China does not envisage a military conflict with the US, its leadership is concerned about US military deployments and capabilities in the region that have the potential to threaten the country.[46] The protection of sea lines of communication (SLOCs) is also a major concern for China, as a disruption of its energy supplies can adversely impact China's economic development. Within the region, China seeks to address Russian and Japanese military capability. China has a territorial and boundary dispute with India, and has contesting claims with Malaysia, Philippines, Vietnam, Brunei and Indonesia over the Spratly Islands. It also has a dispute with Vietnam over the Paracel Islands and with Japan over the Senkaku Islands.

However, it is the Taiwan issue that holds the greatest import for China as a military clash across the Taiwan Straits could end up in a China–US military confrontation. Internally, the mishandling of the Taiwan issue could trigger off social instability and a power struggle in China.[47] While Taiwan's politics since 2005 have been developing in favour of China, and the Taiwanese leadership has been trying to reduce tensions, strong opposition to and mistrust of Beijing still exists. China is inclined to show its military might to prevent any attempt by Taiwan to move towards independence. Taiwan thus remains a long-term security challenge requiring Beijing's constant focus and attention.

China's concerns over its territorial disputes is closely related to its domestic politics, such as Chinese nationalism, and results in increased assertiveness over such claims. The Senkaku Islands, claimed by both Japan and China, are a potential source of conflict between the two countries. While the Japanese constitution forbids the country to maintain an offensive arsenal, its technological prowess, high per capita income and clear military capabilities give the country a strong military edge as a defensive force. Japan, hence, is perceived as a threat for China with its extended maritime reach and as a key US ally.

Though China's dispute with India is of a lower priority, it is concerned about Indian military capability, as India has had easier access to advanced military technology from around the globe. India's cooperation with the US is apparent in space technology, which is of growing potential military import. China is also concerned about India's nuclear and missile capability, which can now target major Chinese cities.[48] The bilateral disputes that China has with Vietnam, Philippines, Malaysia, Brunei and Indonesia have the potential to strain and stall relations with the Association of South East Asian Nations (ASEAN) as a whole. Also, Vietnam's history of conflict with China and its place in the collective Vietnamese memory serve to complicate China's relations with Vietnam.

The US's involvement in the South China Sea is also a matter of concern. The US declaration that it has a 'national interest' in the continued freedom of navigation in the region at the July 2010 ASEAN Regional Forum meeting at Hanoi is viewed as an effort to scuttle the bilateral negotiations that China favours on the issue.[49] It also provides the US and Japan a reason to expand their military footprint in China's immediate neighbourhood, with a consequent threat to the safety of its SLOCs, which could be interdicted.

The defence policy of China has been enunciated in a paper titled 'The Diversified Employment of China's Armed Forces' of 16 April 2013, issued by the Information Office of the State Council.[50] The fundamental principles enunciated in the paper are:

- Safeguarding national sovereignty, security and territorial integrity, and supporting the country's peaceful development. The policy purports to be defensive, advocating attack only if attacked. However, what constitutes an attack has not been specified.
- Aiming to win local wars under the conditions of informationization and expanding and intensifying military preparedness. In this China has undoubtedly been influenced by the conflicts in Iraq and Afghanistan, where the use of advanced technology had a dramatic impact on operations conducted. China aims to promote

military preparedness in all strategic directions, intensify the joint employment of different services and arms, and enhance war-fighting capabilities based on information systems.

- Formulating the concept of comprehensive security and effectively conducting military operations other than war. Here, China's armed forces have a role in maintaining internal order and negating threats to peace and stability within the country. They also have a role in disaster relief and providing security support for Chinese interests overseas.
- Deepening security cooperation and fulfilling international obligations. This refers to promoting and establishing collective security mechanisms and military confidence-building mechanisms with other countries' armed forces, to include confidence-building measures (CBMs) in border areas. Cooperation is sought in the maritime domain, UN peacekeeping missions, international counter-terrorism cooperation, international merchant shipping protection, disaster relief operations and the like.
- Acting in accordance with laws, policies and disciplines. This basically suggests that China's armed forces will act in accordance with the law of the land and on the basis of the UN charter and other universally recognized norms of international relations to ensure the legitimacy of their operations involving foreign countries or militaries.

China's armed forces are composed of the People's Liberation Army (PLA), the People's Armed Police Force (PAPF) and the militia. The PLA is composed of the PLA Army (PLAA), PLA Air Force (PLAAF), the PLA Navy (PLAN) and the PLA Second Artillery Force (PLASAF).

The PLAA is composed of mobile operational units, border and coastal defence units, and guard and garrison units, and is primarily responsible for military operations on land. In line with the strategic requirements of mobile operations and multi-dimensional offence and defence, the PLAA has been reoriented from theatre defence to trans-theatre mobility. It is accelerating the development of army aviation troops, light mechanized units and special operations forces, and enhancing building of digitalized units, gradually making its units small, modular and multi-functional in organization so as to enhance their capabilities for air–ground integrated operations, long-distance manoeuvres, rapid assaults and special operations. It has a strength of 850,000, spread over seven military area commands (MACs). The border and coastal defence forces of the PLAA are stationed in border and coastal areas, and on islands. They focus on combat-readiness duties for safeguarding the security and stability of the borders and coastal areas. China has signed border cooperation agreements with seven neighbouring countries, and established mechanisms with twelve countries for border defence talks and meetings.

The PLAN is responsible for safeguarding its maritime security and maintaining its sovereignty over its territorial seas along with its maritime rights and interests. It is composed of the submarine, surface vessel, naval aviation, marine corps and coastal defence arms. The PLAN too is modernizing its forces for comprehensive offshore operations, to include blue water capability. It has a total strength of 235,000 officers and men, in three fleets. In September 2012, China's first aircraft carrier, Liaoning, was commissioned into the PLAN.

The PLAAF is responsible for its territorial air security and maintaining a stable air defence posture nationwide. It is primarily composed of aviation, ground air defence, radar, airborne and electronic countermeasures (ECM) arms. It is strengthening the development of a combat force structure that focuses on reconnaissance and early warning, air strike, air and missile defence, and strategic projection. It has 398,000 officers and men, and an air command in each of the seven MACs.

The PLASAF is a core force for China's strategic deterrence. It is mainly composed of nuclear and conventional missile forces and operational support units, primarily responsible for deterring other countries from using nuclear weapons against China, and carrying out nuclear counter-attacks and precision strikes with conventional missiles.

The PAPF's main tasks include performing guard duties, dealing with emergencies, combating terrorism and participating in and supporting national economic development. In wartime, it is tasked with assisting the PLA in defensive operations. The militia is an armed organization composed of the people not released from their regular work. As an assistant and back-up force of the PLA, the militia is tasked with participating in the socialist modernization drive, performing combat readiness support and defensive operations, helping maintain social order and participating in emergency rescue and disaster relief operations.

While China is set to strengthen its military commemorate with its economic power, a comprehensive modernization of armed forces remains financially and technologically challenging to China, forcing it to set priorities among different services. Given that a number of its present and long-term security challenges centre on maritime security, Beijing is likely to give PLAN the priority in the coming years.

3

Threats, Challenges and Vulnerabilities

Lieutenant General B.S. Pawar

Former Director General, Army Aviation, and Commandant, School of Artillery, Devlali

Introduction

The twenty-first century has seen the global order in a state of flux and turmoil. The rise of China and the realignment of forces between the US and China in the Asia-Pacific, the Arab Spring and the rise of the Islamic State of Iraq and Syria (ISIS), the Iranian nuclear issue and the continuing turmoil in the Afghanistan–Pakistan (Af–Pak) region make the Indian security environment both complex and dynamic.

Neither today's conflicts nor tomorrow's wars will have clearly definable two-dimensional battlefields, thus giving way to a battle space. Full-scale conventional war is less likely in the future. Wars will be short and intense and the geostrategic reality, which dictates that conflicts will take place in a nuclear environment, points to wars of limited duration in which all elements of combat power will be optimally used to achieve decisive results. Conflicts will be fought in all spaces—land, air, sea, undersea, space, cyberspace, the electro–magnetic spectrum and, most importantly, in the minds of the leadership and population of the country. Future wars will transcend geographical boundaries and will be technology-intensive, ambiguous and complex. The impact of technology will be far more evident. These wars will be fought on all fronts—physical, economic and psychological—and characterized by uncertainty and reduced time for decision-making.

Instability in the Horn of Africa, and the growth of piracy, maritime crime and terrorism will continue to pose security challenges to sea lines of communication (SLOC) in the Indian Ocean Region (IOR). The presence of extra-regional powers like China, the US, France and the UK in the Indian Ocean will be a source of tension as these powers, especially China, tend to expand their influence over the oceanic waters by claiming sovereignty over vast tracts of exclusive economic zones (EEZ). Exploitation of minerals and oceanic riches is also likely to remain a source of conflict in the years ahead as land-based sources are exhausted and new discoveries are made deep in the waters beyond. The fielding of large fleets in the IOR will militarize these waters on a large scale for the first time in history. This militarization could be in the form of cooperative state structures combating non-state actors, as existing in the Horn of Africa, or competitive, conflict-prone ones, as in the South China Sea.

Sub-conventional conflict perpetrated by non-state actors will increase both in scale and technology. The spectrum of conflict could range from that between states to that with non-state actors and state proxies, resulting in blurred boundaries between regular and irregular warfare. These groups could, in the future, acquire better capability and greater lethality to pose a serious threat, especially in the case of acquisition of weapons of mass destruction (WMD). Non-state actors and asymmetric threats will take the centre stage in future security situations. Armed forces will be required to undertake low-intensity border wars as well as combat insurgencies fuelled by foreign powers. Such conflicts are likely to go on indefinitely as conflict resolution requires many contradictory influences. There are more chances of hybrid conflicts involving conventional as well as sub-conventional threats.

Challenges like energy scarcity, water scarcity, health threats and mass migrations will manifest themselves as discernible threats. Depleting reserves of crucial natural resources like water and energy, especially oil, will mean greater rivalry for markets and resources, thereby increasing regional instability. Cross-border migrations resulting in demographic inversions are likely to increase, especially in impoverished regions, creating large-scale demographic upheavals leading to grave security threats. Global warming and disaster management will be issues to contend with. Disasters are likely to be exacerbated both in frequency and intensity, resulting in increased deployment of armed forces for the same, affecting their operational capability. Global warming's greatest impact will be on the availability of water, escalating tensions in the region.

Changes in the structure of the global economy, communications and new technology ushered in by the Revolution in Military Affairs

(RMA)—a military-theoretical hypothesis about the future of warfare—will continue to have greater effects in the coming decades. The economy will play a very crucial role in the national security dynamics of a nation. Offensive use of information warfare, especially in cyberspace, and options of non-contact war will give the adversary the ability to cause disruption and destruction and degrade war-waging potential even before the battle is actually joined. New threats to national security emerging from terrorism, ethnic diversity, proliferation of small arms, narcotics trafficking and religious extremism will be challenges to contend with in the region.

Threats and Challenges: External and Internal

As India enters the global arena as a power of the future, its external and internal environment are in a state of flux. For India, the external security environment is undergoing a paradigm shift. The accrual of potentially destabilizing Chinese military and economic power; the proliferation of the cyber, space, missile and nuclear domains in India's neighbourhood; the US drawdown from Afghanistan; maritime rivalries in the Indian Ocean; and the global economic meltdown and its security implications are few such realities. The uncertain future of Pakistan as a consequence of its political, economic, ethnic and sectarian conflicts, the increasing radicalization of its society, and its amassing of nuclear weapons and missiles at the 'fastest rate in the world' are of serious concern to India. Simultaneously, the widening contours of international terrorism, threats posed by left-wing extremism, the insurgency in the north-east, social conflicts on communal and caste lines catalysed by vote bank politics and a volatile polity compound and vitiate the Indian internal security landscape.

India faces diverse external threats and challenges. It has to manage its over 15,000-km-long borders with seven countries, sections of which are contested or not formally demarcated on the ground or constitute only an agreed line of control. Additional problems emanate from open or porous borders. India has a long coastline of over 7,500 km along with an extended maritime zone, island territories, SLOCs for its trade and energy flows and offshore oil installations. India would wish to proceed on its peaceful path of development; however, it would be naïve not to take into account the threats and challenges it faces in this regard both in the conventional and sub-conventional domains. These could be from regional powers, proxies, non-state actors or global threats with their own manifestations in the South Asian context.

India has the disadvantage of being situated in close proximity to what is being described as the epicentre of global terrorism. The tribal region near the Afghanistan–Pakistan border has been constantly drawing the attention of America's global war on terror since 2001. India's increasing relevance to the US strategic canvas, its troubled relationship with Pakistan since Independence, the deteriorating and unpredictable relationship with China, the unstable political climate in Nepal along with its Maoist insurgency, the mistrustful relationships with Bangladesh, a Sri Lanka ravaged by civil war and an authoritarian Myanmar are challenges India has to contend with.

China: The Long-term Challenge

China–India relations have been marked by distrust and fear on both sides since the 1962 war, which resulted in China usurping the Aksai Chin area in Jammu and Kashmir (J&K), giving it easy road access from the Tibetan plateau to the remote Xinxiang region in the west. More than fifty years after that war, tensions between India and China are rising again. Their entire 4,057-km-long border—one of the longest in the world—remains in dispute without a clearly defined line of control in the Himalayas separating the rival armies.

This situation has persisted despite regular talks since 1981 to settle their territorial disputes. The latest talks, the eighteenth round, between the special representatives of the two countries held in March 2015 have yielded little. These talks, in fact, constitute the longest and most futile negotiating process between any two nations in modern world history.

Additionally, China's rise in the past three decades has given it tremendous weight in international political and security circles. China has patiently been working towards building military–economic and political alliances around India's periphery (the String of Pearls strategy) and remains India's number one security threat. It has provided consistent military assistance to Pakistan for use against India, funded armed rebels in the north-east and has continued to up the ante in diplomatic circles through stapled visas, visa denials and so on. In addition, the Chinese have, in the past decade, rapidly built up superior civilian and military infrastructure along the Indo-Tibetan border, thereby vastly improving their military capability in Tibet, which is India-specific. India's defence infrastructure vis-à-vis China's leaves much to be desired despite the push given by the Narendra Modi government.

In the recent past, China has been sending clear signals to the world and specifically to India of a new, assertive border policy. This is evident by way of its shrill political rhetoric, frequent transgressions across the Line of Actual Control (LAC) and unprecedented cyber attacks on Indian networks. The simmering Sino-Indian tensions threatened to become an open conflict in 2013 when Chinese troops crossed the disputed border in the Ladakh region (Depsang Valley), establishing a camp 19 km inside Indian territory. This episode showed that stoking tensions with Japan, Vietnam and the Philippines over islands in the South and East China Seas did not prevent an increasingly assertive China from opening yet another front.

However, what took the Indian establishment by surprise was the incursion of People's Liberation Army (PLA) troops in eastern Ladakh (Chumar and Demchok) during the high-profile visit of Chinese president Xi Jinping to India in November 2014. Such actions no doubt are a demonstration and endorsement of China's assertiveness. The fact remains that with its stated peaceful rise giving way to an increasingly sharp-elbowed approach to its neighbours, China has broadened its core interests and territorial claims while showing a growing readiness to take risks to achieve its goals. It is obvious that the growing economic and trade ties between the two countries have not translated into improved relations.

From the above it is evident that China poses a long-term threat/challenge, and hence limited/full-scale war cannot be ruled out. Settlement of the border dispute by use of force may evolve as an option if the difference between Indian and Chinese capabilities continues to grow. China has substantially increased its defence spending, which is now three times that of India, at $136.3 billion. Belying the present stability of the relationship there is the reality of a 'trust deficit'. Notwithstanding the ongoing dialogues on trade and security, the absence of any serious negotiation on the settlement of the border and the fallouts of China's policy on South Asia and the IOR are likely to increase the trust deficit.

Pakistan: A Receding Threat

Nuclear deterrence and mutually assured destruction usually freeze conflicts and pave the way for détente, as they did between the US and the Soviet Union. But little has changed in the Pakistani outlook, even after the induction of nuclear weapons in the subcontinent. There is little recognition that, with nuclear weapons, Pakistan no longer has any reason to feel insecure about being overrun by a larger Indian conventional force. Instead, to counter India's so-called 'cold start doctrine' (which India denies), it has introduced another dangerous dimension into the India–Pakistan military equation by developing tactical nuclear weapons.

In fact, it is this insecurity that dictates its Afghanistan policy to keep India out, based on its fetish for the concept of strategic depth and fears of encirclement by India and Afghanistan. The notion of an existential threat to Pakistan is now only psycho-political and ideological. Pakistan has already lost four wars with India and half its territory in the process—the erstwhile East Pakistan, which became Bangladesh in 1971.

As for J&K, jihadi militancy since 1989 has failed to wrest Kashmir for Pakistan from India, as have war and military confrontation. Pakistan, however, continues with its confrontationist policy vis-à-vis India with no change in its policy on Kashmir. Therefore, the perennial challenge before the Indian defence establishment is to manage both the covert and overt threat from Pakistan. The low-intensity conflict in J&K, abetted and sponsored by the Pakistani military, is likely to continue. Pakistan remains one of India's principal worries on both the external and internal security fronts. Besides, on the basis of its long-standing strategic partnership with China, it can stretch the capabilities of India's armed forces in the eastern sector.

Present trends bode ill for Pakistan, and unless it changes tack, it will continue to be a source of instability and terror in the region. The large nuclear arsenal and its security is a major cause of concern. It is likely to remain on short fuse with the possibility of conflict always looming large.

Pakistan–China Collusion

The core of China's strategy in the South Asian region revolves around its strategic alliance with Pakistan by providing it unprecedented levels of nuclear and conventional military support. Pakistan has almost become a vassal state of China as it has even allowed the positioning of Chinese troops in Pakistan-Occupied Kashmir (POK). This aspect was further reiterated during the visit of Xi Jinping to Pakistan in April 2015, with Pakistan terming it as a fate-changing event. While addressing a joint session of Pakistan's parliament, Xi termed China's friendship with Pakistan as transforming into a strategic partnership for mutual benefit and reaffirmed its support and solidarity for the sovereignty, independence and territorial integrity of Pakistan.

The mutual strategic need has spurred Pakistan and China to achieve military interoperability unmatched even by the US–NATO (North Atlantic Treaty Organization) alliance at the height of détente in the 1970s. As a consequence of interoperability, the Pakistan military could well use China's military capabilities in addition to its own to increase its options both in north Kashmir and the Line of Control (LoC). In addition to the 2,395-km-long economic corridor being established, connecting Xinjiang to Gwadar port through Gilgit–Baltistan in POK, China has also agreed to strengthen bilateral cooperation in space, providing remote-sensing and telecommunication technologies. As per defence analysts, by the end of the decade, this corridor will provide Beijing new transportation links to faster deploy its forces to areas disputed by Pakistan and India.

This is a worrisome development for India. In view of the above, it will not be wrong to construe that in any future conflict, both countries colluding with each other to carry out mutually supportive military operations against India is a reality. For India, this implies fighting simultaneous wars on two widely separated fronts, virtually amounting to a two-front war.

Afghanistan

The Talibanization of Afghanistan, aided and abetted by Pakistan, constitutes a major threat. The deteriorating security environment in the Af–Pak region is the greatest challenge to regional stability and India.

The area is the main centre of Islamic extremist fundamentalism, drug trafficking and illicit trade in arms. The turmoil in Afghanistan is likely to intensify with the drawdown of US-led forces, and the next arena of conflict between Pakistan and India could well be Afghanistan, with no perceptible change in the aggressive and intrusive policy of Pakistan towards India vis-à-vis Afghanistan. The Pakistan Army has a perennial fear of strategic encirclement by India and Afghanistan, and it believes that a pliant, pro-Pakistan Taliban regime in Afghanistan is necessary to ward off this danger. According to strategic thinkers in Pakistan, any regime with close ties to India should not be allowed to continue in Afghanistan as it may pose danger to the very existence of Pakistan. Pakistan's military establishment believes Afghanistan provides vital 'strategic depth' to Pakistan, where it could relocate armament and crucial bases out of India's military reach.

Questions have been raised not just about President Ashraf Ghani's foreign policy pivot but also the potential loss of influence built by the Indian government over the past few years under the Hamid Karzai administration. It is true that Ghani's political manoeuvring has indeed put China and Pakistan ahead of India in the country's sphere of influence for the time being, and this will clearly cause a great deal of unease in Delhi, which is the fifth biggest aid donor to Afghanistan today. India has provided around $2 billion in aid to Afghanistan since 2002 for highways, roads and infrastructure development, health care and education. In October 2011, India and Afghanistan signed a historic strategic partnership agreement—the first that Afghanistan signed with any country—whose relevance is today in doubt.

Nonetheless, it is the entrance of China as a mediator between Kabul and the Taliban that seems to have taken India by surprise. Chinese policy on Afghanistan since the beginning of 2014 has been proactive. In November that year, Chinese diplomats reportedly visited Peshawar to push ahead with the mediation process, followed by the Taliban delegation visiting Beijing. The outcome expected from China's mediation is to bring the Taliban to the negotiating table and somehow try to integrate them into the country's political process. The fact that President Ghani's first port of call after taking power was China, followed by Islamabad and Washington, with India figuring in the itinerary much later in April 2015, is a clear pointer towards the India–Afghanistan ties hitting a strategic low. These developments do not bode well for India and need to be watched closely.

The Immediate Neighbourhood

Unfortunately, with the exception of Bhutan, India's other neighbours don't provide any succour to military planners and political leaders, and some are as challenging as China and Pakistan. While Nepal is in the grip of political turmoil since the ouster of King Gyanendra in 2008, India has to play its cards carefully lest it be seen as having a big-brother agenda. India and Nepal share an open boundary with free exchange of people and currency across borders. Although few contentious points do remain in Indo-Nepal relations, they should not be allowed to obstruct India's efforts in ensuring political stability in this strategically important neighbour, where the Chinese have already made numerous strategic inroads with the support of the Maoist leadership. The proactive stance of the government in the wake of the devastating Nepal earthquake was a step in the right direction.

Bangladesh, on the other hand, is showing signs of delivering on the stated policy of the government of Prime Minister Sheikh Hasina of not letting her country's soil to be used for anti-India activities. This was aptly demonstrated when her government recently handed over many high-profile terrorist leaders hiding in Bangladesh. India has also reciprocated with a huge $1 billion in economic assistance in the form of a line of credit. The clearance of the settlement of the land boundary bill with Bangladesh by the Indian parliament has hopefully set the tone for further cementing relations. India should actively continue to engage with Bangladesh, seeking cooperation in destroying the terrorist infrastructure of the Harkat-ul-Jihad-al-Islami (HuJI), as this remains a challenge for Indian security agencies.

Although India at first neglected its relationship with Myanmar's military rulers, there have been improvements in the past few years in bilateral relations. China has been investing in Kyaukpyu and Sittwe as commercial ports on the west coast close to India's north-eastern states. Both of these ports can be used as naval bases, and this is a major security concern. India urgently needs to co-opt Myanmar to curb the north-eastern rebel groups that find shelter in dense forests along the international border with Myanmar. Moreover, India needs to increase its economic and military cooperation with Myanmar in the coming years.

India also faces competition from China in keeping Sri Lanka attuned to our interests. The civil war in north-east Sri Lanka has imposed huge emotional and economic costs on the Tamils there. Thus, encouraging cordial linguistic relations in Sri Lanka by persuading the Lankan government to ensure equitable distribution of resources and fair treatment of ethnic minorities is a priority for Indian foreign policy mandarins.

Sub-conventional Threats

Internal security is currently viewed as the most vulnerable aspect of India's national security. Its import is borne out by the country's long historical experience of fighting insurgencies and state-sponsored terrorism in J&K and the north-east.

While development and sustained growth are expected to improve the internal situation, these threats are likely to continue in the future. The proxy war and insurgency, fuelled, aided and supported by Pakistan and China in J&K and the north-east respectively, are a major internal security threat. This threat is also manifesting itself in the Naxalite-affected areas. Irregular or asymmetric wars involving non-state actors may occur concurrently across the entire spectrum of conflict. The prevalence of such groups in armed conflicts has added layers of complexity to conflict management and resolution. It is noteworthy that the Kargil Committee Report (2000) and the Report of the Group of Ministers on National Security (2001) had both underlined the criticality of internal security issues and recommended a sharp increase in national capacities to confront the same.

Left-wing extremism and Naxalite violence is rapidly emerging as a major threat with distinctive features. This is the threat identified by former Prime Minister Manmohan Singh as the greatest internal security threat facing the nation. Though an internal threat, it could be exploited by both Pakistan and China.

Meanwhile, Pakistan, which harbours a compulsive hostility towards India and lacks capabilities to achieve its politico-strategic objectives through military or political means, continues to engage in covert actions as an instrument of state policy to bleed India. There are indications that the American withdrawal from Afghanistan is likely to further embolden Pakistan to continue to wage the asymmetric conflict with India with renewed vigour. The new Pakistani game plan could pose multiple threats, ranging from persistent terror attacks to low-intensity conflicts waged through sub-national, ethnic or religious groups recruited from within India; the surfacing of the Indian Mujahedeen is one such example. These attacks combined with internal disturbances will aim to erode the economic, socio-cultural and political foundation of our society and can prove dangerous for India's security. The current doctrinal concepts for combating Pakistan-sponsored terror and subversive activities may prove largely ineffective unless we are able to anticipate and pre-empt future Pakistani plans with some exactitude and evolve appropriate models for dealing with the challenges that post-modern covert warfare may pose.

China has also been actively supporting and fuelling the insurgencies in the north-east in terms of weapons, logistics and finance, especially in Nagaland, Assam and Manipur. In a recent development, nine militant groups from the north-east, including the National Socialist Council of Nagaland-Khaplang (NSCN-K) and the United Liberation Front of Assam (ULFA) faction led by Paresh Baruah, have come together with Chinese blessings to form a United Front in a meeting held in Myanmar. The Chinese intelligence is reported to have played an active role in encouraging these disparate groups to form a common platform against India. The aim seems to be to keep the environment boiling in the north-east in view of Chinese claims on Arunachal Pradesh. As brought out earlier in the chapter, India needs to work together with Myanmar to counter these moves.

Nuclear, Biological and Chemical Threat

The region encompassing south and east Asia is home to the largest concentration of nuclear-capable states. The nuclear overhang is more volatile in the India–Pakistan context, compared to the relatively stable India–China context. Proliferation of nuclear technology—rogue elements getting their hands on WMDs—is a serious threat and challenge. Nuclear weapons have encouraged greater reliance on proxy, low-intensity and asymmetric warfare. The role of biological weapons in a no-contact war cannot be overemphasized.

The threat of chemical and biological terrorism emanating from non-state actors, including Islamic jihadi organizations, remains a major concern in the Indian subcontinent, especially India, which has been vulnerable to jihadi violence from across borders. Even though no terrorist group, including the al Qaeda and Lashkar-e-Taiba, has achieved success in employing these destructive and disruptive weapon systems or materials so far, in reality they have been seeking to acquire these WMDs and know-how. The Indian government needs to recognize this threat and accord high priority to tackle the same.

Aerospace Threats

Outer space and cyberspace systems have been critical in enabling modern warfare, specifically for strike precision, navigation, communication and information gathering. Undoubtedly, outer space–cyber space is the new combined military high ground of the twenty-first century, as both break the historical constraint of domination through physical control of territory, leading to militarization in both domains. In the context of outer space, every country around the world understands the seminal importance of safe, secure and sustainable access to and use of outer space. This also includes the freedom from space-based threats, the physical and operational integrity of manmade objects in space and their ground stations, as well as security on Earth from threats originating in space.

Asia today is host to four major space powers, namely, Russia, China, India and Japan, and among these Russia and China have demonstrated anti-satellite capabilities. India is also well on its way to becoming a global space power and is looking at a similar capability. China has been the most proactive in forging multilateral space cooperation programmes around its sub-region. The Asia-Pacific Space Cooperation Organization (APSCO), headquartered in Beijing, is an inter-governmental organization with full international legal status. It has fourteen members including Pakistan and Bangladesh, with the main thrust being towards space science, technology applications and research and development, aimed at the peaceful use of outer space. In addition, China's Beidou

Regional Navigation Satellite System, consisting of a constellation of thirty dual-use satellites, is expected to be deployed by 2020. China proposes to reserve 60 per cent of Beidou for commercial purposes and the balance 40 per cent for military applications. What is of concern is that China has also given access to Pakistan for the use of Beidou—a number of ground stations are being built in Pakistan.

India can no longer remain a mute spectator in the aerospace arena either in the immediate sub-region or in the larger Asia–Pacific region. The importance of space diplomacy as a tool of regional security cannot be overemphasized. The creation of long-term linkages through civil space cooperation programmes, allowing participating countries to become invested in combating/achieving common challenges/objectives, impacts overall national security, of which space security is an inherent component. Space could be the new frontier of conflict in the future.

Maritime Security

The IOR has been the vortex of intense maritime activity over centuries and has today emerged as the world's centre of gravity in the maritime domain. This region is home to nearly 2.6 billion people who live on the rim or the shores of the Indian Ocean (nearly 30 per cent of the world's population). It is also rich in oil and mineral products and has emerged as the world's global economic highway. This makes the environment in our region extremely dense due to increased maritime activity and numerous SLOCs.

India, due to its geographical location, faces a multitude of maritime threats and challenges. These relate mainly to the security of its island territories, oil platforms and rigs, SLOCs, sea piracy and terrorist attacks like the one in Mumbai. However, the main challenge remains mostly from China, both commercial and military. The docking of a Chinese submarine and a warship at Colombo in 2014 has left no doubts about Chinese intensions—this move is certainly seen as 'inimical' to India's interests in the region.

China's proposal for establishing a Maritime Silk Route is a move viewed suspiciously by India. According to some analysts, the aim is to give a peaceful and economic angle to the 'String of Pearls' port facilities set up in India's neighbourhood. This certainly is a cause of concern for

India, and many in the Indian security community do not see this as a legitimate reflection of Chinese commercial interests in the region or its strategic interest in protecting its SLOCs.

The other threats and challenges in the maritime domain are non-traditional and as wide and varied as they come. These include grappling with sea piracy, maritime terrorism, drug running, arms and human trafficking and poaching/fishing in deep-sea areas. Out of these, piracy and terrorism have assumed major dimensions and need to be addressed. The Indian Navy, along with the other world navies, has deployed its ships in the Gulf of Aden and off the coast of Somalia, the epicentre of piracy, in various task forces to combat this threat. India's vast coastlines remain vulnerable to maritime terrorism, which is a major challenge to be addressed because non-state actors have anonymity of identity and intent.

For India to retain its dominant position in the region and safeguard its commercial and strategic interests, it is time that India turned its strategic vision towards the IOR. India's maritime interests could be compromised in the future if the SLOCs in this region are blocked or hindered in any way, especially given past historical instances of power rivalries in the region. With the major global powers already having a naval presence in the region and China increasing its footprint in a well-thought-out strategic context, India cannot afford to remain a passive bystander, as its supremacy in the region is slowly and invisibly dented. Early pre-emptive steps to include the region in its security grid would be in India's interest and in the interest of the IOR.

Information and Cyber Security

Information warfare will gain more relevance and will be the next arena for intensive conflict, with no physical boundaries or attribution of blame. It will also constitute the silent war that will carry on during peacetime. With an increasingly wired society, it will pose a major 24x7 threat to national security. Cyber war as a form of no-contact war can target the populace and influence minds. This form of warfare is likely to be a major national security threat in the future, both during peace and war, as it is a shift from the physical to the perceptual domain. There are obvious military risks to computer and communication systems. There is also the vulnerability of critical civilian infrastructure to cyber sabotage, like the banking system, power infrastructure, nuclear plants and telecom networks. These attacks could be from nation states or non-state actors, but the lines would be blurred, as one would be clueless as to who perpetrated them or where and when they may strike again. Both the dominating powers in the cyber warfare arena, i.e., the US and China, regularly utilize cadres of cyber attackers and defenders from within their populace. These cadres typically operate on the fringe of legality and are similar to the pirates of the high seas in olden times. The Chinese appear to have gained an edge in this form of warfare.

Cyber security breaches are increasing the world over and India cannot ignore its impact. There is a dire need to protect Indian cyberspace from sophisticated cyber attacks. Keeping this threat in mind, the Government of India enunciated its first National Cyber Security Policy in July 2013 with the aim to build a secure and resilient cyberspace for its citizens, business and the government. However, the challenge of a cyber policy lies in its operationalization and implementation, with military establishments developing indigenous capability for cyber defence. Calling cyberspace a new domain of warfare, the US Department of Defense set up the US Cyber Command in 2011 for defending its interests in cyberspace, calling it the latest global combat zone. India also needs to put in place its Cyber Command organization at the earliest.

Natural Resources

One of the critical factors affecting the security of a nation is adequate access to natural resources. The sharpening geopolitical competition over natural resources has already turned some strategic resources into engines of power struggle. Water, mineral ores and fossil fuels like coal, oil and gas are resources of the greatest strategic import. They not only hold the key to development but also, in the case of water, to human survival. Food production is closely intertwined with water and energy, whereas water and energy are closely connected with each other.

While it has been rightly said that the twenty-first century will be Asia's century, this is also likely to be accompanied by an insatiable appetite for natural resources. This has set off a sharpening resource competition between Asian economies and far beyond in other continents like Africa, aggravating disputes over resource-rich areas. This is best exemplified by the resurgence of territorial and maritime disputes in the East and South China Seas. Both China and India being the power engines of growth in Asia are likely to confront each other in this war of resources.

Conflict over Water

Population pressures and changes in climatic patterns are having adverse effects on the availability of water while demand continuously expands. Fresh water, although a renewable resource, is a finite commodity whose quantity has virtually remained the same since the dawn of civilization. Around the world, pressure to control and access water-rich areas is increasing, resulting in geopolitical tensions. This is likely to be a major security concern in the future, both domestically and internationally. India shares rivers and watersheds with Pakistan, Nepal, Bhutan, Bangladesh and China (Indus, Brahmaputra, Ganga and Barak). While India has a formal treaty for sharing of river waters with Pakistan, no such treaty exists with China. The Chinese plan to divert the Tibetan rivers is in fact a major security challenge.

The struggle for water is set to define many inter-country relationships in the coming years. At a time when territorial and separatist struggles are being increasingly driven by resource issues, water indeed is becoming the new oil. But unlike oil, dependence on which can be reduced by tapping other sources of energy, there is no substitute for water. The danger that riparian disputes could escalate to overt conflicts looms large on the horizon in the future.

Energy Security

Oil is a critical energy resource. Depletion of this resource in the future will spark tensions and could be a major trigger for conflict. The highest consumption of oil is by both China and India, being the fastest growing economies and developing countries in the world. Tensions due to this critical resource are already mounting in the South and East China Sea. While China has managed to secure new hydrocarbon supplies through pipelines from Kazakhstan and Russia, this option is not available to India. India remains dependent on oil imports from an increasingly unstable Persian Gulf. There is an urgent need to look at alternative energy sources like nuclear and solar to meet India's growth requirements within the security paradigm.

Global Warming

The effects of global warming are already resulting in large-scale migrations of human populations, causing an ethnic and religious imbalance. Cross-border migrations will result in demographic upheavals leading to grave internal security threats. Food and energy security will pose grave challenges and be a volatile trigger for conflict. Health catastrophes and epidemics like the ebola virus and avian flu will throw up greater challenges for nation states to confront. Disasters are likely to be exacerbated in frequency and intensity, increasing the employment of armed forces to address these threats. Three major disasters in the region in the recent past (Uttarakhand and J&K floods and the Nepal earthquake) are pointers in that direction.

Indian Diaspora

The large Indian diaspora, spread all over the world, and its security and safety is a major challenge. This was starkly evident during Arab crises in which a sizeable Indian diaspora had to be moved out of countries like Syria, Libya, Egypt and Iraq due to ISIS violence. The latest in this arena has been the evacuation of 5,600 displaced personnel from war-torn Yemen (Operation Rahat) in April 2015 and massive humanitarian relief and rescue operations after the devastating earthquake in Nepal (Operation Maitri) the same month. In fact, in both these operations India proved that not only was it capable of providing safety and security to its own diaspora but was also able to help nationals of other countries as well. Out of the 5,600 people evacuated from Yemen, 940 nationals were from forty-one other countries, including Britain, France and the US. Protection of the Indian diaspora and ensuring its security and safety will remain a major security challenge in the future.

Economic Warfare

Economic warfare is the direct or indirect manipulation of an economy by a state or non-state actors, or any other entity through legal or illegal means. It has been waged between states for centuries and continues to be waged today, causing economic instability in the targeted country. The axiom that that there can be no economic development without adequate security and that there can be no security without economic development holds very true today. In our region, Afghanistan, and to a lesser extent Pakistan, are clear examples of this interdependence of security and economic development.

Serious economic threats are most likely to emerge from the exploitation of small vulnerabilities in the system at times when confidence in the economy and our ability to protect it are low. Given exponential increases in the electronic management of the financial system, governments face vulnerabilities and potential mass effects that neither governments nor the private sector could have ever imagined. Accordingly, suitable policies, regulations and practices related to protecting the financial sector and mitigating future threats need to be evolved. India is far behind in this area.

The terror strikes of 9/11 and 26/11 were both aimed at the commercial hubs of New York and Mumbai, with the sole aim of striking at the very core of the respective country's economic system. While the effect on life and property may not be catastrophic to a nation, the economic costs can be enormous in such organized and externally supported terrorist attacks. Transnational organized crime, terrorism, insurgency, drug trafficking and counterfeit currency have been clearly recognized as handy tools for perpetrating economic warfare against a nation. While India has been a victim of these tools for some time now, to its credit it has shown enough resilience to thwart their effects on its economic growth, development and stability.

However, in the cyber realm, state and non-state actors can wreak havoc on a country's economy, striking when the economy is most susceptible. Cyber espionage is not only a threat to Indian businesses and commerce but can also be used to generate useful information for manipulating public opinion and influencing legislation. However, despite the multiple government agencies engaging in securing India's national security, there is no single entity that oversees the efforts to protect the country's economy from outside attacks. There is a need for partnership between the government and the private sector, as the government has the authority and the private sector the means to secure our economy and find the best way to tackle this threat.

Religious Extremism

One of the major internal security threats that India today faces internally is religious extremism. Fair and transparent law enforcement and quick, efficient judicial apparatus are required to stem the tide of religious extremism in the country, related to both the minority as well as majority communities.

Other challenges to internal security are astoundingly high levels of corruption, political factionalism and caste wars, all of which require seasoned and firm political vision.

Conclusion

Fundamentally, the Indian security environment is skewed, with multi-dimensional threats posed by two nuclear powers acting in collusion in our neighbourhood. The concept of India's strategic autonomy will be called into question if India does not develop demonstrable military capability and upgrade its doctrinal thinking in tune with the changing nature of wars and the prevailing environment. Strong dissuasive capability backed by political resolve is required for India to protect its interest and shift from a pure territorial bias to a more interest-based capability. Even more important is reorientation of the political mindset that looks upon soft power and status quo as the best options, leaving India open to coercion and dealing with unabated proxy war.

The twenty-first century has been spoken of as the Asian century. Aspirations of this large Asian populace, their desire for development, and demographic pressures, amongst others, constitute a heady and explosive mix with a potential for conflict. India, due to its location, size and democratic strength, must be the catalyst to ensure regional peace and security. This can only come about if backed by technological, economic and military prowess.

4

National Security Objectives

Lieutenant General Aditya Singh

Former General Officer Commanding-in-Chief, Southern Command, and member, National Security Advisory Board

The Need

National security is a multifaceted and all-encompassing concept related to building comprehensive national power. In it, internal and external security share a symbiotic relationship. A country's external security is organically linked to its internal strength. External challenges can be met by effective diplomacy and adequate defence capability. For internal stability, strong political institutions, economic growth, social harmony, an efficient law and order machinery, expeditious judicial relief and good governance are prerequisites. It is an integrated whole which requires a coordinated and comprehensive approach for realization. Security begets stability and each feeds on the other to provide an environment for development.

Central to this are India's citizens. Simply put, the safety, well-being and right to life of every Indian in conditions of internal and external peace should be India's supreme concern. India's tradition of promoting peace and amity in the Indian Ocean Region (IOR) and in South-East Asia through soft power dates back two millennia. The long-term interests of India can only be served by regional peace and stability. With over one-sixth of the world's population, India can serve as an example in the quest for global peace and stability while being self-reliant in safeguarding its national interests. Its religious, linguistic and cultural diversity, woven into a harmony over centuries through a process of assimilation, gives it the potential for working to bridge differences between nations, cultures and faiths.

India's Constitution provides the basis for building a democratic, pluralistic and secular society in a federal structure. With large numbers of poor—deprived of adequate access to education, health care and other basic facilities—the state remains responsible for their welfare through policies of inclusive growth. Thus, the objective should be to provide an environment wherein every Indian is given a stake in the country's prosperity, social peace and stability.

As discussed earlier, India faces diverse external challenges. It has to manage its 15,000-km-long border with seven countries, sections of which are contested or not formally demarcated on the ground, or constitute only an agreed line of control. Additional problems emanate from open or porous borders. It has a long coastline of over 7,500 km, along with an extended maritime zone, island territories, sea lines of communication (SLOC) for its trade and energy flows, and offshore oil installations. The IOR, therefore, figures prominently in India's security calculus.

India's security is best served by a peaceful, stable and friendly neighbourhood. Territorial, religious and ethnic issues, extremism, terrorism and transfers of nuclear and missile technologies, however, are factors that cause instability in South Asia. Equations within the region have also been disturbed by external influences. The security dynamic has been further affected by limited intra-regional economic cooperation. Added to this are the internal challenges which, apart from those mentioned above, include economic disparity, left-wing extremism, population pressure, illiteracy, organized crime, governance, connectivity and so on. All these impact security.

In the near term, global issues of energy, food and environment security will create new challenges. There are also emerging aspects of knowledge and information management, freedom and equity in the use of space and cyberspace, trans-border crimes, pandemics, and the misuse of social media and the Internet, as well as the issue of global commons. All these are dynamic and morphing at an increasing pace. Scenarios thus have to be anticipated and solutions put in place. The luxury of time does not exist.

To build this comprehensive power and ensure stability, there is a need to outline the broad principles and objectives of national security for India. Definition of goals and the overlaps will provide a framework for policy formulation as also strategy flow. As clarified above, these goals need to be kept under constant review.

Broad Objectives

The Constitution provides the basic structure for governance and progress. The broad contours to fulfil the aspiration of every Indian, as also to ensure internal and external security, are:

1. Maintaining the unity and territorial integrity of India.
2. Working towards a peaceful, prosperous and friendly extended neighbourhood.
3. Creating credible capacities for conventional as well as non-conventional defence and dealing with asymmetric threats such as cross-border terrorism.
4. Sustaining high rates of inclusive economic growth.
5. Ensuring political stability, internal social harmony, law, order and justice; and
6. Building wide consensus in polity on the basic parameters of foreign and domestic policies based on informed awareness and understanding of issues.

The achievement of these goals requires a mix of external, defence, economic and internal objectives, which could then serve as guidelines. While the problems of India are not unique, they still require an 'Indian' solution within its federal structure. The information and technology revolution provides scope for innovative outreach and execution.

Ideally, objectives must be time-bound. However, this may not be possible, as the situation will continue to change. This aspect could be incorporated in the strategy and plan for implementation. For ease of understanding, these goals have been grouped under 'parent' heads. All these goals need to be formalized under the aegis of the National Security Council (NSC), backed by political consensus, and disseminated.

External Affairs and Defence

India must seek to maintain independence in its foreign policy choices, while working in partnership with all friendly countries on issues of common interest. As a leading power destined to play an increasingly important regional and global role, India has to retain the freedom and capacity to deal with all actual and potential power centres in the world on the basis of equality and mutual confidence. For this it must:

1. On a regular basis issue a white paper defining its objectives in the neighbourhood, region and beyond. This must be based on stipulated principles.
2. Identify the need for manpower and resources to fulfil these aims.
3. Optimize and synergize available assets and set up structures for implementation.
4. Provide for systems of outreach and connect.

Further, India must accord the highest importance to developing mutually beneficial ties with its neighbours on the basis of equality, respect for sovereignty and non-interference in their internal affairs. It must clearly establish that it is willing to work with the neighbours on any common agendas that will strengthen regional bonds and help create a climate of peace and security in the region. There is vast potential for mutually beneficial programmes and economic linkages, which must be pursued in a transparent manner.

India must defend its legitimate interests against any encroachment by others and protect its territorial integrity with all means at its disposal. India must seek to resolve all outstanding issues relating to its land and maritime borders through negotiations. While being committed to this, it must strengthen its defensive capabilities on its borders so as to deter any attempt to alter them by force or subversion.

India must project itself to the world as an example of a well-functioning multi-religious, secular society. The success of its model is vital for peace and stability in this region, involving the welfare of over one-fifth of humankind. India must strive with like-minded countries to prevent the forces of religious extremism from enlarging their strategic depth in the region and counter their destabilizing impact on India's external as well as internal security.

India must enhance economic cooperation in South Asia, essential for increasing prosperity in the whole region, bilaterally as well as multilaterally, by supporting the South Asian Association for Regional Cooperation (SAARC) and organizations like BIMSTEC (Bay of Bengal Initiative for Multi-Sectoral Technical and Economic Cooperation). India's expanding economy and its high growth rates create opportunities for it and its neighbours to move up the economic growth ladder together.

India must promote, with the Gulf countries, an enhanced economic partnership and free trade agreements similar to those concluded with individual Asian countries and the Association of South East Asian Nations (ASEAN). This would be in keeping with India's ties with the region by way of energy supplies, manpower export, remittance flows and the potential of investment of the region's financial surpluses in the growing Indian economy, especially in infrastructure.

India must establish close relations with IOR countries in view of the common interest in securing SLOCs. A large part of the global hydrocarbon and trade traffic passes through these waters that contain two of the world's most important choke points—the straits of Hormuz (between the Gulf of Oman and the Persian Gulf) and Malacca (between the Malay Peninsula and the Indonesian island of Sumatra). India recognizes its strategic position and role as a responsible member of the international community in ensuring that the Indian Ocean remains a safe zone for trade and commerce. The Indian Navy must plan for this in partnership with other nations.

India must recognize the notable role of the Indian diaspora in extending India's soft power and building bridges between the countries of their residence and India in diverse areas in a manner compatible with their obligations to their country of adoption and their country of origin.

India must build defence capabilities based on current and future threat assessments through periodic strategic reviews, with a coordinated intelligence system integral to this exercise. The defence objectives include:

1. Building capacity to confront two adversaries simultaneously in all domains and while ensuring security of the rear areas.
2. The armed forces must have the capability to deter any adversary from initiating a conflict. To achieve this, they must possess the requisite conventional strength, including force projection capabilities for intervention operations.
3. They must be capable of undertaking intense operations at short notice across all domains. This would include engaging sub-conventional, irregular forces and non-state actors.
4. Having the capacity to counter and initiate operations in the information warfare (IW) and non-contact domains.

5. Having the ability to engage forces propagating fundamentalism, separatism and secession.
6. Having the capacity to undertake sustained operations under nuclear, biological and chemical (NBC) conditions.
7. Building expertise in conducting peacekeeping and peace enforcement operations.
8. Possessing resources and training to undertake disaster management and providing humanitarian assistance, including that for the Indian diaspora.
9. Building adaptability in a fast-changing world to absorb and benefit from technology. This would include aids for quick decision-making.

Ensuring integration within the armed forces and joint structures is critical. Current and emerging threats require joint organizations. The creation of a Chief of Defence Staff with a combined headquarters and functional commands for military aspects in space and cyberspace is overdue. There also has to be closer coordination between various organs of government dealing with external challenges, i.e., the foreign service, intelligence agencies, armed forces, as also other agencies like the ministries of home, finance, information and so on. The armed forces must transform and restructure to synergize capacities. The concept of theatre commands needs to be implemented. A joint doctrine for employment of the armed forces needs to be enunciated and implemented, if required by a parliamentary decree.

Accelerating the creation of an indigenous defence production base with access to state-of-the-art technology is also crucial. An independent defence and foreign policy is seriously constrained by high dependence on defence equipment imports. Revamping of defence-related research and development (R&D) as well as the high technology base in the country has to be undertaken with the participation of the private sector. Relations with traditional defence partners must be maintained even as new relationships are forged as necessary in order to boost local production, including co-production. An integrated headquarters can work to ensure prioritization of acquisition. Defence can be a catalyst for the Make in India initiative.

The emerging threats of IW, both in the defensive and offensive domains, have to be addressed, and the ability to tackle the increasing reach of social media has to be built. This would include incorporating technology and dealing with the role of the media. IW's all-encompassing reach makes it an ideal domain for non-contact war. India lags far behind.

India must uphold the professionalism of its armed forces, which operate under the control of the civilian leadership within the constitutional framework. The armed forces are an intrinsic part of the strategic planning process in which they should be appropriately integrated. They must maintain a high level of preparedness for all threats and challenges, including the above-mentioned threats from space and cyberspace. Military effectiveness must be enhanced through increased capability for joint operations.

Mutual confidence building must be stepped up through international military cooperation. Synergy between the military and diplomacy must receive renewed attention to further bonds within the region.

India must build its strategic deterrent capabilities without getting involved in any arms race. These capabilities must be exercised in accordance with the laid-out nuclear doctrine. This must be regularly reviewed based on technological changes and adaptations. At the same time, India believes that its own security and that of the world as a whole is best served by the total elimination of nuclear weapons. To that end it must cooperate with any time-bound, universal, verifiable and non-discriminatory steps in that direction.

Combating terrorism by all possible means, including strengthening border and coastal defences in order to stop infiltration, is a key focus area. Politically mobilizing neighbouring countries to extend their cooperation in eradicating the networks on their soil is important, as is galvanizing the international community to progressively control and eventually eliminate the menace through collective efforts as enjoined by relevant UN resolutions. India must reserve, in all instances, the right to take appropriate action in the face of cross-border terrorism directed at it.

Economic Development

Economic well-being promotes security, as people who are better off tend to have a greater stake in furthering peace and stability. Thus, promoting rapid, sustained and broad-based economic development is the cornerstone of any edifice of security. Job creation to meet the aspirations of the increasing number of youth is central to this. This requires special emphasis on developing human resources and skills.

India must address growing inter- and intra-regional disparities by expanding educational and employment opportunities and encouraging entrepreneurship and self-employment, especially for the rural and tribal areas, economically disadvantaged sections of society and in remote locations.

Encouraging manufacturing competitiveness by the effective development of indigenous capabilities, along with international cooperation in trade and transfer of technology, is also very important. The Make in India programme—along with simpler rules for starting ventures, pragmatic labour laws, tax and other incentives, support infrastructure and availability of land—forms part of this. This will include identifying key sectors for industrialization and then putting in place plans to increase the share of manufacturing to at least 30 per cent of the economy.

India must enhance capacities to bid globally and competitively for natural resources. Identifying and working to build stocks of strategic commodities such as rare earths is vital, as is ensuring adequate reserves in the field of energy.

Developing critical infrastructure and industry with security systems takes priority. Security and protection must be incorporated into the design itself. Financial, transportation, health, civic services and e-governance networks must incorporate robust security.

Food security is crucial for strategic autonomy. India can achieve this by focusing on research in agriculture for increased food production for the growing population by increasing yields, allowing thereby also for the expansion of forest cover to protect the country's rich biodiversity. This will also include research for exploiting the resources of the sea.

Improving energy efficiency, cutting down the carbon intensity of the economy and developing unconventional and renewable energy resources to reduce environmental damage and to realize the key strategic goal of ensuring energy security is key. The issue of climate change has to be addressed on the basis of international equity, while preserving India's long-term development prospects and shared global responsibility.

Education, Technology and Connectivity

Scientific and economic development is based on the quality of education. Perhaps the greatest neglect after Independence has been the lack of emphasis on basic education. A literate populace understands, demands and works towards security. While this realization has dawned, its implementation is still far from complete. True security can only come about with education. Thus, the transformation of India into a knowledge society must form part of the national security objectives. The National Knowledge Commission in its report[1] had put forward recommendations that need to be implemented. Further, India must improve the standards of education from the primary level to the university.

Technology, in its various forms, must be used to secure India, whether in terms of food, resources, health, infrastructure or services. The reach of the Internet and cloud computing has opened up new vistas to reach out across India. The National Knowledge Network (NKN)[2] is being set up and a study needs to be undertaken as to how it can meet security objectives.

Developing a coordinated structure for cyber security and IW is pivotal. This is an all-encompassing domain and potential for misuse or damage without attribution is vast. Internet connectivity is central to the path India has chosen to follow for its development, hence its security and protection is paramount. While military aspects will be looked after by the armed forces, similar measures need to be put in place for the public and private domain. The aim must be to set up an empowered overarching body like the Atomic Energy Commission that can coordinate and put in place mechanisms in this regard. The present edifice under the National Security Council is inadequate. With the growth of the Internet and allied services, vulnerabilities are expanding and must be addressed on priority. This includes potential for damage though social media.

India must accord greater importance and resources to cutting-edge research in science and technology. This will encompass inter-disciplinary research for technological innovation and its application to meet India's needs. It shall also form part of the comprehensive cyber security regime mentioned above and provide capacity to monitor and disable disruptive communication networks and ensure connectivity at all times. Emerging benefits such as those in the field of information technology (IT) and the global system for mobile communication (GSM) are to be exploited in keeping with public and security interest.

Special emphasis must be placed on emerging fields such as bio-technology, nano technology, green technology, and alternative sources of energy. India needs simple, cost-effective solutions. Innovation and research need to be encouraged and rewarded.

India must put in place systems to hold and protect knowledge. Presently, all data and information is being held in servers under the control of the US. Social apps such as Facebook, Viber, Twitter, WhatsApp, and platforms such as Google and e-marketing sites hold vast amounts of information data that constitute security vulnerabilities. India needs to set up domestic systems with back-up facilities. With its vast IT potential and numbers, this should be possible. Planning and implementation of this needs focused attention, especially with respect to security. The same is the case for operating systems (OS) for sensitive networks, such as those for strategic weapon systems. All this can only be ensured under a strong structure as proposed above.

Given the limitations of the administrative, law enforcement and judicial agencies, it is important to determine how technology can ensure delivery. There is vast scope in policing and governance. The modernization and training of law enforcement agencies in IT also has to be ensured. Planning for the delivery of quality services through the NKN is an area of opportunity.

India must encourage and support language training and translation. While this should primarily include the languages of our neighbours, even study and instant translation of Indian languages will aid in security and national cohesion.

Political Stability and Social Peace

Fostering national cohesion based on the unifying power of justice and the rule of law is crucial so that people are motivated to remain together in a state of creative freedom. Good governance is central to this. Restoring integrity in public life by reversing the rise of corruption is important because corruption detracts from good governance. Corruption can be combated with greater transparency, right to information and accountability. Here, too, the Internet can play a vital role.

It is also important to reduce the scope for arbitrary exercise of power by the political leadership over the bureaucracy in general and police and security agencies in particular. This will restore the stability of institutions and provide for a security net for meaningful action. The present environment deters decision-making and promotes the status quo.

The government must promote social cohesion, counter radical ideologies, treat all citizens as equals and ameliorate the conditions that give rise to feelings of neglect. The resolution of issues and redressal of grievances must be through dialogue and peaceful constitutional means. Violence must be dealt with resolutely.

Police reforms have to be undertaken on a priority basis. These are long overdue and have been resisted. Policing remains a huge weakness in the system and cause for insecurity. The manpower, equipment, and technological and infrastructural needs of the police must be met to enable them to function professionally and effectively. The police must increase their collaboration with local communities to build up public confidence and enhance their ability to uphold the law in a non-discriminatory manner.

Dealing with terrorism, extremism and organized crime as grave threats to national security is vital, and India must take all necessary measures, including diplomatic, economic, administrative, legal and executive, to combat them. This will necessitate intelligence sharing, well-coordinated mechanisms, financial checks, and closing of all available routes for illicit arms, ammunition and explosives. Simultaneously, it must be ensured that at the ground level, more so in rural areas, governance, relief and justice are provided in a fair and transparent manner and public confidence built up.

Revamping the justice system will provide for timely decisions. It has, in a manner, collapsed under the weight of its own processes and contributed to a lack of faith in the order and consequent scepticism. Maintenance of law and order requires a revamp.

India must expedite the development of infrastructure, especially in remote and border regions, to inter alia develop the ability to handle disruption of essential supplies and services due to natural or manmade causes. Connectivity, outreach and growth in border regions will also contribute to the physical security of borders.

Public health must be given urgent attention, especially with respect to the disadvantaged classes and remote regions. The threat of epidemics, pandemics as also the fallout of natural disasters must be planned for. The state has a major role in this through effective contingency planning, management, capability building amongst the community and appropriate partnerships with the private sector.

Media and social networks play a vital role in open societies. Logic dictates that it must be constructive. However, this is seldom the case, and potential for damage and creation of disharmony is vast. The state needs to devise policies and regulators that permit freedom but at the same time prevent misuse.

Preserving India's diversity and permitting people of all identities to pursue their way of life in consonance with the fundamental provisions of the Constitution is equally necessary.

Internal Security and Emerging Challenges

Though primarily a state subject, internal security issues transcend boundaries and require a coordinated approach. Left-wing extremism poses a major challenge and warrants separate identification and planning. In addition to the aspects of governance mentioned above, there has to be a special effort made for outreach and development. The writ of the state must run.

Special efforts are to be made to foresee and plan for non-traditional threats and emerging challenges such as those from NBC agents, immune viruses, paucity of water, climate change and so on. Institutions and organizations must be tasked to undertake scenario building and planning exercises.

Global Outreach and Consensus

The world is now increasingly interdependent. Resources will continue to be at a premium and India will have to work in partnership for a sustainable planet. Ensuring access to the global commons in an equitable manner must be the guiding principles when laying down objectives.

Detailed knowledge and study in the domains of oceans, polar regions, atmosphere, space and cyberspace is needed to ensure India's interests are protected and negotiations are on the principles of fairness, equity, sharing and for the common good. This human resource capital needs to be ensured.

Consensus Building

Laying emphasis as a democratic polity on people's informed awareness, understanding and support for the country's security doctrine and strategies is crucial. India must encourage education and discussion in the domain of national security. All major powers have institutions for defence studies. India needs to step forward to promote awareness and understanding.

India must also seek inputs from opinion makers, academics, think tanks, non-governmental organizations (NGOs) and retired public servants.

Formalization

There is a lamentable lack of a strategic culture in India. It appears to be a historical legacy and there are no formal doctrines or guidelines for national security. It is, therefore, not surprising that there is very little understanding as to what constitutes the security needs of the nation. Arvind Gupta, the current deputy national security advisor, wrote in 2011: 'India needs a National Security Strategy urgently. The world is changing very fast. New security challenges have arisen. In the absence of a coherent strategy, the government's responses will remain ad hoc and partial. This may prove costly.'[3]

There is very little discourse in the media or amongst academics. Only a handful of universities offer courses in defence and strategic studies. The much-touted Indian National Defence University, which was sanctioned in 2010, is unlikely to come up before 2019.

Compare that with India's major neighbours. Both Pakistan and China have established institutions and accord considerable importance to defence and security matters. China regularly issues white papers on defence and strategic issues. Government structures accord greater importance to matters of security. India, by contrast, is far behind and vulnerable. Interest in security issues is episodic, event-related and not a part of the developmental process. There is limited understanding on what constitutes national security, with the result that there is no comprehensive planning.

As a first step, the government, after reviewing the current milieu, needs to formalize and issue a white paper on what constitutes national security and what needs to be done. Security provides peace and stability, the bedrock for economic growth. Given that this is the aim of any government, political consensus should be easy to obtain. Speaking at a workshop on national security on 5 March 2014, Shyam Saran, the then chairman of the National Security Advisory Board, had mentioned that a draft of the National Security Doctrine had been prepared and would be placed in the public domain for discussion. This has not transpired. In its absence there is no clarity on what constitutes India's approach to security. A comprehensive paper is long overdue.

As mentioned earlier, this should ideally be a statement of national objectives not directed at any other nation. It has to be in the public domain and discussed amongst the academic and strategic communities. It would form the basis for planning strategies for implementation. Models are available and it need not be a very long document. It should, however, define what the objectives are, as also the cross linkages. It needs to be based on the Constitution and India's federal structure. Each ministry, state, institution and organization would then be able to plan for implementation.

There is apprehension that once formalized, the government will be accountable to meet these objectives and that such a document may become a liability. It is for this reason that the public paper should be a statement of broad aims, with the details for implementation left to the stakeholders. It can also be argued that in the absence of such stipulations, no one can really understand what national security involves. Issuing of these objectives as a doctrine is thus necessary. The added advantage of a public document is that it will be available to other nations and clearly indicate India's position.

Strategy and plans for execution based on defined objectives will be both public and in-house, based on the need to know. Thus, while a national cyber security policy or doctrine will be for all, plans pertaining to offensives in this domain will be covert. As clarified above, these objectives are based on the current circumstances. These will be constantly reviewed based on changed circumstances and relevance.

Conclusion

There is a clear and urgent need for definition and statement of national security objectives. These would explain needs and components of national security and lay down goals with the overall objective of growth and betterment. The instruments of state functioning within the parameters of the law will take into account the elements of these objectives in the conduct of the country's foreign, defence, political, economic and social policies. Such enunciation will also take into account concerns of other nations and clearly specify and define India's approach to security and how it seeks partnerships for regional peace and stability.

This comprehensive approach to national security will enable India to protect the life, liberty and welfare of its citizens from external and internal challenges and threats from both state and non-state actors, and ensure an environment for steady, all-inclusive growth.

5

Beyond Non-Alignment: New Imperatives for Defence Diplomacy

Dr C. Raja Mohan

Director, Carnegie India, and contributing editor on foreign affairs for the Indian Express

Introduction

The idea of non-alignment, the dominant motif of India's international relations since Independence, limited the nature and extent of India's defence partnerships with other countries in the second half of the twentieth century. Non-alignment was itself the flip side of India's inward economic orientation, a conscious choice made by the new rulers of Delhi. As the Cold War enveloped the world soon after India's Independence, the new nation was determined to stay away from military blocs led by the United States and the Soviet Union. This core principle, that participation in military blocs would limit India's freedom of foreign policy choice, was in many ways the essence of Prime Minister Jawaharlal Nehru's emphasis on non-alignment. After his death, non-alignment increasingly became a mantra that was interpreted as prohibiting any significant military–political engagement with countries big and small. These three principles—economic self-reliance, non-alignment, and military isolationism—came to define India's worldview and its international identity, and were widely considered immutable. But, by the turn of the 1990s, when the end of the Cold War coincided with the collapse of the old Indian economic system, all three principles came under stress.

After decades of import substitution and state control of the economy's commanding heights, Delhi turned, if only reluctantly and cautiously, to liberalization at home and reconnecting with global markets. As a result, India's growth rates have picked up and its relative weight in the international system has increased since the 1990s. By

2015, India's gross domestic product (GDP) of $2 trillion ranked it seventh in the list of the world's leading economies. This new weight was not just about an expansion in the size of India's economy but its very nature. From a closed economy, India became a deeply interdependent one in the twenty-first century. Imports and exports add up to a sum that is nearly 50 per cent of its GDP. This extraordinary international exposure includes an ever-expanding dependence on imported energy resources, including hydrocarbons and coal. This structural change in the economy has presented new imperatives for India's foreign policy and national security strategy. As the Indian military prepares to deal with these challenges, expanded cooperation with other countries has become a major imperative.

The changed economic orientation has also had a lasting impact on India's international relations. The collapse of the Soviet Union demanded that India overhaul its foreign policy root and branch. While the public emphasis on non-alignment and strategic autonomy endured, there was no escaping the need for significant adaptation across all areas of Indian diplomacy and foreign policy. This included a renewed engagement with the US, Europe, Japan and China, with whom India's relations steadily declined during the Cold War. India's quest for markets, capital and technology demanded a greater outreach to the West. The decades after the 1990s saw India reconnect with its extended neighbourhood and seek an improvement of ties with its immediate neighbours.

As India restructured its foreign policy, renewed defence engagement became an important part of India's diplomatic toolbox. While this engagement was tentative and cautious, defence cooperation and military exchanges have steadily grown since the 1990s and cover a wide range of bilateral relations and multilateral forums. Broader strategic trends, especially the changing balance of power in Asia and the Indo-Pacific, have lent a greater salience to India's defence diplomacy in the twenty-first century. The rise of China, its growing military prowess and its expanding strategic influence in India's neighbourhood have been major factors propelling India's military diplomacy. From the general perception of equality with China in the past, Delhi now finds that the strategic gap with Beijing has widened considerably. In 2015, China's GDP at $10 trillion was five times the size of India's. Its defence spending too is nearly four times bigger. While China's economic growth rate has begun to slow down and India has shown renewed signs of acceleration, this gap is likely to persist for quite some time. As Delhi comes to terms with this gap, the question of deeper defence cooperation with the US and its allies has come to the top of India's diplomatic and security agenda. At the same time, a growing number of medium powers and smaller countries in Asia and the Indian Ocean are looking to Delhi to shore up their defence capabilities amidst the flux in the regional environment. While the change in India's defence diplomacy has been slow and incremental, there is no denying its increasing significance in India's national security strategy.

Non-Alignment and Military Isolation

When India became independent in 1947, the Cold War divisions were beginning to congeal in Europe and expand into Asia. As India sought to insulate itself from the impact of the Cold War, Delhi was deliberate in its choice of 'military isolationism' at the global level. Independent India's isolationist impulse was, in part, a reaction to the expansive external use of Indian armed forces during the nineteenth century and the first half of the twentieth. The armed forces under colonial rule initially focused on domestic constabulary functions and the defence of ever-shifting frontiers, but beginning in the late-eighteenth century, the Raj also put them to expeditionary use. Through the nineteenth century, Indian troops saw action in theatres ranging from Egypt to Japan, and from southern Africa to the Mediterranean.[1]

British use of Indian armed forces surged in the first decades of the twentieth century. During World War I, nearly 1.2 million Indians were recruited for service in the army. When it ended, about 950,000 Indian troops were serving overseas. According to the official count, between 62,000 and 65,000 Indian soldiers were killed in that war. In World War II, the Indian Army saw action on fronts ranging from Italy and north Africa to east Africa, the Middle East and the Far East. In South-East Asia alone, 700,000 Indian troops joined the effort to oust Japanese armies from Burma, Malaya and Indochina. By the time the war ended, the Indian Army numbered a massive 2.5 million men, the largest all-volunteer force the world had ever seen.[2]

As the Indian nationalist movement gathered strength after World

War I, it rejected the use of Indian military manpower for imperial purposes and without the consent of the Indian people.[3] While there was considerable support in the national movement to the British during World War I, it largely evaporated by the time World War II broke out. The Indian National Congress acknowledged the threat of fascism but was unwilling to support the British war mobilization without a clear timetable on independence. Others like Subhas Chandra Bose saw the war as an opportunity to oust the British with support from Germany and Japan. Bose raised the Indian National Army and established a provisional government of India with the support of imperial Japan. The Indian communists were the only ones to support the British, but only after Germany attacked Soviet Russia in 1941. It was no surprise, then, that the divided national movement could not leverage the Indian Army's extraordinary contribution to the Allied victory in the negotiations with the British on the terms of independence, the distribution of the spoils of the war and the construction of the post-war international order.

At the end of World War II, many Asian nationalist leaders complained to Jawaharlal Nehru, who was heading the interim government in Delhi, about the use of the Indian Army to protect British and European interests rather than the national liberation forces in the colonial world. Given his strong solidarity with the anti-colonial struggles everywhere in Asia, Nehru was not going to accept the use of the Indian Army to repress liberation movements. Once the Indian Army came under the full control of the new nation, he explicitly rejected its use for expeditionary operations. As Cold War military blocs confronted India, he declared that India will not align with either the East or the West and will pursue an independent foreign policy. Besides defining the national orientation as non-alignment, India moved towards the construction of a broader forum of solidarity among other newly liberated nations. The effort that began at the Asian Relations Conference in Delhi (1947) and the Conference of Afro-Asian Nations at Bandung in Indonesia (1955) led to the eventual formation of the Non-Aligned Movement (NAM), which met at the summit level for the first time in 1961. If rejecting bloc politics was central to India's national idea of a Non-Aligned Movement, the movement's membership was limited to those countries that did not have foreign military bases on its soil.

In the years after Independence, India slowly wound down its external military links with Great Britain, forged over a period of nearly two hundred years of colonial rule. While London and Washington would have preferred to see a measure of coordination among the armies of the commonwealth against the emerging global communist threat, India's new approach of non-alignment ran counter to it. Nehru chose to remain a part of the Commonwealth, but only after making it clear that India will have nothing to do with the Western military alliances.[4] To be sure, Great Britain was a major source of arms supplies to independent India, but little more than that in the first years after Independence. Other European arms suppliers like France were eager to enter the Indian market. But it was the Soviet Union that eventually became the main defence partner for India in the Cold War period.

If non-aligned India disentangled itself from the military relationship with Britain, it was not going to allow itself to be tied down by the new partnership with Soviet Union. As it sought weapons from the Soviet Union at the turn of the 1960s, India was careful to circumscribe its military engagement with Moscow. Despite being bound to the Soviet Union through the friendship treaty of 1971, India carefully avoided undertaking joint exercises or other service-to-service contacts with Moscow.[5] During the Nehru years, India did seek to develop military cooperation with other developing countries like Egypt and Indonesia, but the effort petered out sooner rather than later.[6] Nehru's successors were increasingly reluctant to offer military cooperation and support to friendly countries, like Singapore, that sought them in the mid-1960s.

One major exception to India's military isolationism in the Cold War period was Delhi's active participation in the international peacekeeping operations authorized by the United Nations Security Council (UNSC). This would seem to be a continuation of the Raj legacy of expeditionary operations in a different form after decolonization. The huge 'military surplus' of the subcontinent created during the British rule has endured despite all the political changes of the past six decades: Partition, permanent Indo-Pak conflict, the occupation of Tibet by China and the resultant Sino-Indian military tensions on the Indo-Tibetan border. Despite these challenges, the now-separate armies of India, Pakistan and Bangladesh are among the major contributors to UN peacekeeping forces.[7]

But this extraordinary role is widely overlooked in international debates on peacekeeping, particularly in India's case. While China's more recent contributions to international peacekeeping are widely noted and assessed, there is less appreciation of India's sustained and significant participation in UN military operations. After the domestic political controversy in the early 1950s over participation in the UN intervention forces backed by the West in Korea, India carefully avoided joining great powers in their military activity during the Cold War period. Delhi squared its new commitment to international peacekeeping with the policy of non-alignment by conspicuously limiting its participation to only those operations that had the mandate of the UNSC. India became one of the biggest contributors to international peacekeeping from the 1950s onwards.[8]

A second and equally important exception to India's military isolationism during the Cold War was New Delhi's continuing role after Independence as a security provider to the smaller states of the subcontinent. In the colonial era, the British Raj was the preeminent power in the Indian Ocean and was the guarantor of security for a number of states abutting the subcontinent. This primacy of the Raj has been described as the 'India Centre' in the system of British imperial defence. Yet, the Raj was not merely an extension of London's policies in the Indian Ocean littoral. It devised and implemented policies that arose out of the geographic and political imperatives of securing India.[9] Partition had ruptured the strategic unity of the subcontinent and enormously weakened the so-called 'India Centre' in Asian security affairs. The Cold War and the re-emergence of a centralized China in control of Tibet and Xinjiang likewise chipped away at the presumed primacy of New Delhi in the region. Yet, India sought to preserve all it could of its once-impressive glacis in the subcontinent.

Independent India revived the British Raj's protectorate arrangements with Nepal, Bhutan and Sikkim in 1949-50. Sikkim was eventually integrated into India, and New Delhi saw itself as responsible for both the external and internal security of the Himalayan kingdoms.[10] While military diplomacy was an important component of India's engagement with Nepal and Bhutan, Delhi also used coercive diplomacy as well as military force in its immediate neighbourhood. India's military interventions in East Pakistan and Sri Lanka and other instances of its use of force, however, are not part of the discussion here. Like the Raj, independent India claimed an exclusive sphere of influence in South Asia. An Indian version of the Monroe Doctrine for the subcontinent, aimed at preventing other major powers from intervening in the region, became an integral element of India's policy, although not always successful. It also argued that its own conflicts with neighbours should be managed in a bilateral rather than a multilateral context and viewed with great suspicion the interests of major powers in its neighbourhood. To the extent it could, New Delhi also sought to prevent its neighbours from granting military bases and facilities to great powers.[11]

Re-engagement after the Cold War

After the Cold War, as India reconfigured its economic and foreign policies, it was inevitable that it would take a fresh look at its military isolation of the previous decades. The logic of economic globalization, and the need to reconfigure its relations with the major powers after the collapse of the Soviet Union, were imperatives that India had to tackle with a measure of urgency. Soon after the demise of the Soviet Union, India launched a military engagement with the US. The basis for the interaction between the Indian and US armed forces was provided by the so-called 'Kickleighter' proposals of the early 1990s.[12] Named after the then US commander of the Pacific Armies, they provided a framework for service-to-service interaction between the armed forces. After that, the floodgates of India's defence diplomacy opened up. Although it was subject to many hiccups, political and bureaucratic, the vector of India's military engagement with the rest of the world has been on a rapid upward trajectory. India has bilateral defence cooperation agreements with more than forty countries: from Brazil in Latin America to Australia in the Pacific and from Mozambique in Africa to Mongolia in inner Asia.[13] These agreements, which vary greatly in their scope and intensity, can be grouped into three categories: major powers, immediate neighbours and other actors of interest to India in the Indian Ocean littoral and beyond.

Starting with the major powers, India's defence cooperation with the US is probably the most expansive in terms of the areas covered. It has also, not surprisingly, been the most politically controversial at home and of special interest to the world. For a country that had little defence interaction with India since Independence, except for a brief period from the late 1950s to the early 1960s that was marked by Sino-Indian tensions, Washington has emerged as a major defence partner of India. The US now conducts more military exercises with India than with any other partner. After a period of stop-and-go interaction between the armed services, they have taken off since the George W. Bush administration came to power in 2001.

India, which never bought a single weapons platform from the US in the Cold War period, has acquired, since 2005, a number of systems, including the landing platform/dock (LPD) ship *Trenton*, C-130 and C-17 military transport aircraft, and P-8 maritime surveillance aircraft. Starting from a zero base at the turn of the 2000s, India's defence purchases from the US have rapidly grown, making Delhi Washington's biggest arms buyer.[14] Even more significant has been the 2005 framework agreement that defines a number of political missions, including peacekeeping, humanitarian relief and maritime security, for operational cooperation. The agreement was a clear departure from the tradition of India's defence engagement in one important sense. None of independent India's defence cooperation agreements with other powers in the past identify explicit political missions. The agreement also calls for greater defence industrial collaboration.[15]

While India and the US have made much progress on defence cooperation in the 2000s, its trajectory has not always been along predicted lines and has moved ahead only in fits and starts. India's forward movement on defence engagement with the US has opened the door for a similar, but on a much lower scale, interaction with Great Britain, France and Russia. The new relationship with Washington has been absolutely instrumental in deepening defence ties with US allies in Asia like Japan and South Korea, and Australia.[16] India has also begun a tentative military exchange with China that includes high-level exchanges, port calls and joint exercises. Larger political mistrust, however, continues to limit the Sino-Indian military exchanges.[17]

India's security diplomacy with its neighbours falls into a separate category of its own. If inherited political legacies make Delhi a hesitant partner for defence cooperation with great powers, India's smaller neighbours have had problems of their own in drawing close to India in the military arena. In the case of Pakistan, there are additional problems with their own great significance. Since the end of the Cold War and amidst their emerging nuclear capabilities, India and Pakistan have been encouraged by great powers to embark on greater military and nuclear confidence-building measures (CBM). The international community has been deeply concerned about the prospect of a conventional military conflict escalating to the nuclear level, and the inadequate arrangements for crisis management in South Asia. From the late 1980s to the end of the 2000s, the two countries negotiated a range of nuclear and military CBMs.[18]

But Delhi and Islamabad have found it hard to institutionalize any contact between the two military establishments outside of a hotline that operates between the two headquarters.[19] One problem is the resistance of the Pakistan Army to service-to-service interaction with its Indian counterpart. Given its exalted position in the nation's political system, the Pakistan Army does not see the Indian Army as an equivalent. Not surprisingly, it has been reluctant to embark on even the simplest military CBMs, like exchange of military bands or visiting each other's staff colleges. The military CBMs between the two sides are negotiated by the foreign secretaries of the two countries.

India's military engagement with the armed forces of Bangladesh too had been virtually non-existent until the late 2000s. With the cooling of the relationship since the mid-1970s, Delhi did not make much of an effort at military diplomacy in Dhaka. That has changed in the last few years; India has recognized the importance of engaging the army as an institution and has actively sought to intensify its ties since 2008. The broad framework agreement for cooperation signed by prime ministers Manmohan Singh and Sheikh Hasina in 2011 has provisions for substantive military and security cooperation.

In an interesting development in 2011, India signed a strategic partnership agreement with Afghanistan that includes the option of substantive Indian military support to Kabul.[20] The agreement came amidst the impending US withdrawal from Afghanistan and unresolved tensions between Kabul and Islamabad. While the agreement might have considerable geopolitical possibilities, the military cooperation between Delhi and Kabul is constrained by geography and the hostility of Pakistan.

India's military ties with smaller states too have begun to acquire some traction. After the failed intervention in the Sri Lankan civil war in the late 1980s, Delhi has returned to engage the armed forces of the country. While Colombo has responded positively, Delhi is constrained by the opposition of the Tamil Nadu government. Colombo's inability to resolve the Tamil ethnic question after its victory in the civil war had made it difficult for Delhi to be seen as extending military cooperation.

In Nepal, while India maintains a close relationship with the national army, there is widespread political opposition to the 1950 India–Nepal treaty that provides for a close military partnership. This treaty is seen in Kathmandu as unequal and hegemonic. Delhi has been willing to revise the treaty but is yet to find a stable interlocutor who can change the terms of the pact. Meanwhile, India revised its 1949 treaty with Bhutan in 2007 to make it more in tune with contemporary realities while retaining the essence of the security partnership between a large state and a tiny partner. In 2011, India also signed a new partnership agreement with the Maldives that focuses on deepening maritime security cooperation. Despite the many difficulties, Delhi is on the road to modernizing its security ties with most of its neighbours, except Pakistan.[21]

Unlike the major powers and immediate neighbours, where political issues limit the possibilities for military diplomacy, the context has been far more welcoming for Delhi's defence diplomacy with major regional actors and critically located small states in the Indian Ocean littoral that India considers its extended neighbourhood. The enthusiasm for defence cooperation with India has been widespread in Africa, the Indian Ocean littoral, East Asia and the Pacific.[22] In fact, the early focus of India's defence diplomacy after the Cold War was South-East Asia. The objective was to reverse the mistrust that had accumulated during the 1980s, when India was seen as a proxy of the Soviet Union and hence a threat to the region. In the last two decades, India has gone way beyond that initial objective to establish substantive defence cooperation and military exchanges with all the major South-East Asian countries, including Thailand, Malaysia, Singapore, Indonesia and Vietnam. The Indian Navy has been at the forefront of lending a military dimension to India's Look East policy unveiled in the 1990s.[23] Over the years, India's military diplomacy has expanded to cover Mongolia in inner Asia, north-east Asia and the south Pacific. Some have characterized this engagement as an effort to counter-balance China. Delhi is a long way from becoming a challenger to Beijing in South-East Asia and the Pacific.[24] India's current focus is on establishing itself as a player of some relevance over the longer term in East Asia and the Pacific. Delhi is acutely conscious of its severe limitations in projecting power into the Pacific littoral.

The Indian Ocean, however, is another matter. It has attracted much attention from India's defence diplomacy in recent years.[25] Given its geographic centrality to the Indian Ocean, Delhi is determined to consolidate its strategic advantages in the littoral. The entry of China into the Indian Ocean has added yet another incentive for India to step up the pace and intensity of its defence diplomacy. In recent years, India has concentrated on deepening security cooperation with Mauritius, Seychelles, Mozambique and Madagascar in the western littoral; Oman, Qatar and the United Arab Emirates in the Arabian Sea; and Myanmar in the Bay of Bengal. India's security diplomacy is not confined to the nations on the littoral. India has sought to develop military cooperation with central Asia, and there has been much speculation about an Indian military base in Ayni, Tajikistan, but the reports have never been confirmed.[26] India has also sought to develop military cooperation with medium powers outside its extended neighbourhood.

After the Cold War, India's military diplomacy has not been limited to bilateral engagement. India began to shed some of its earlier political hostility to multilateral security initiatives. Much of its traditional suspicion of multilateral security arrangements arose from its opposition to US alliances like the SEATO (South East Asia Treaty Organization) and CENTO (Central Treaty Organization) that were set up in the 1950s. India was also deeply sceptical of collective security proposals that emanated from the Soviet Union. India did not welcome Leonid Brezhnev's 1969 proposal for Asian collective security and was not willing to see its own bilateral treaty of 1971 as part of such a system.[27] India also remained ambivalent to Mikhail Gorbachev's proposal for Asian collective security in 1988.[28]

India's traditional preference for defence bilateralism was slowly complemented by a number of new multilateral initiatives. In its outreach to South-East Asian countries in the 1990s, Delhi unveiled the 'Milan' multilateral exercises in 1995. It has now been institutionalized as a biennial event that draws in a large number of countries in the Indo-Pacific littoral.[29] In 2008, India took another initiative by convening the Indian Ocean Naval Symposium (IONS) that brought together all the navy chiefs from the Indian Ocean.[30] In 1996, India joined the security forum of the ASEAN, the ARF (ASEAN Regional Forum). In 2005, ASEAN leaders invited India to join the East Asia Summit process that was to focus on broader political and security issues facing Asia. In 2010, India attended the first expanded gathering of the ASEAN Defence Ministers Meeting, which was dubbed ADMM Plus.[31]

In assessing India's new security multilateralism, it is difficult to miss one paradox. While India has been eager to join the new Asian multilateral institutions, its participation in these forums has been quiet and low-key. Many leaders of the ASEAN have often complained about India's lacklustre performance in the East Asian multilateral institutions. Yet, India has also shown leadership in creating new institutional mechanisms like 'Milan' and the IONS. Delhi seems far more comfortable in multilateral military institutions set up under its leadership rather than those where the agenda and direction are set by others.

India has also begun to let its military forces occasionally participate in multilateral coalition operations. In the tsunami relief operations at the end of 2004, the Indian Navy joined forces from the US, Japan and Australia. This was probably the first time that India was participating in a military coalition. But the enduring opposition to any multilateral military activity came to the fore in September 2007, when India conducted joint naval exercises with the US, Japan, Australia and Singapore. Amidst the Chinese objection to these exercises and the protests by communist parties at home, the political leadership of the defence ministry sought to step back from multilateral defence diplomacy. India has also begun to develop minilateral cooperation with some of its neighbours. For example, India signed a trilateral agreement with Maldives and Sri Lanka on deepening shared maritime domain awareness in the Indian Ocean. India hopes to expand this framework to include Mauritius and Seychelles.[32]

Constraints: Organizational and Political

The scale and scope of India's defence diplomacy has steadily expanded since the end of the Cold War. Nevertheless a number of factors—including organizational and political—continue to constrain their reach and effectiveness. At the organizational level, the shortage of staff in the headquarters of the Ministry of External Affairs (MEA) and the Ministry of Defence (MoD) remains a major impediment. While India's defence engagement with other countries has grown manifold in the last two decades, the number of officers servicing it in the two headquarters remains virtually the same. Second, the MEA and the MoD do not appear to be on the same page when it comes to defining the objectives of India's military diplomacy. While the leadership of the foreign office has come to value the possibilities of military diplomacy, the MoD remains deeply conservative and has been reluctant to plunge deep into military diplomacy. Linked to this is a third problem that is rooted in the peculiar structure of India's civil-military relations. Few democracies have the kind of overwhelming dominance of the civilian bureaucracy over the services that has been institutionalized in India.[33] Not surprisingly, the civilian bureaucracy is none too enthusiastic about giving the military services greater room for international engagement.

If India needs a new tool kit for a military diplomacy that is in tune with its rise on the world stage, Delhi is some distance away from developing effective policy instruments and institutions. While there is a growing demand for security assistance from India, Delhi is yet to put in place adequate domestic capacities for military training and arms production. India has large training establishments that can be ramped up to service the new global demand, but India's ability to supply arms has been severely constrained by the absence of a domestic defence industrial base. India has been a major importer of weapons system on the world market and is yet to develop domestic capacities to export them to other countries and leverage it as part of the nation's defence diplomacy.

Beyond the organizational challenges, Delhi will need to resolve a number of political and strategic ambiguities to strengthen its military diplomacy. There are at least three contentious issues in India's national security debate that constrain its defence engagement with other nations. The first is the tension between India's notions of 'strategic autonomy' and 'military partnership' with great powers, especially the US. Since limiting military entanglement with other powers was central to the conception of India's non-alignment, India's expanding defence diplomacy with the US has repeatedly run into roadblocks from the left and the right of the political spectrum. The idea of 'interoperability' with the US armed forces remains a taboo for the political establishment.[34] Many in Delhi associate this with the danger of becoming a military subaltern to the US. Part of the problem also stems from the entrenched suspicion of American intentions regarding India. While the political mistrust in the US has significantly come down, there is enough residue that limits India's military diplomacy. It is interesting to note that the many political objections raised in relation to the US are rarely put forward in dealing with other powers.

The second tension is between the traditional imperative of territorial defence and the new logic of securing India's growing interests far from its shores. The Indian political and bureaucratic leadership continues to recoil at the ideas of 'power projection' or developing 'expeditionary capabilities' for the Indian armed forces. Yet, they frequently call upon the security forces to cope with emergencies in distant lands. The Indian Navy had to evacuate thousands from Lebanon in 2006 and Libya in 2011. While the logic of a widening security perimeter for a globalizing India begins to impinge on Delhi, the Indian security debate tends to be reticent about acquiring and deploying the instruments of power projection.[35]

The third tension is between the logic of India's own forward military presence amidst expanding global interests and the traditional opposition to foreign military bases. To be able to operate in distant waters, the Indian Navy will need what might be called 'turn-around' facilities around the Indo-Pacific littoral. To acquire such facilities, India will have to develop a range of special political relationships and military partnerships. It was precisely these arrangements of the superpowers that the Indian security discourse had rejected outright during the Cold War. The Indian strategic community now objects to China's efforts to develop maritime access in the Indian Ocean. While India's ideology of non-alignment prevents it from accepting a junior partnership with a larger power, the logic of Delhi's expanding interests demands developing military presence in and security cooperation with smaller countries.

In fact, many smaller nations that face threats from other powers are beseeching India to contribute more to their security. The logic of this universe is indeed very different from the one that India is coming from, and its national security debate will be under pressure to adapt.

The Modi Effect: Beyond Non-Alignment

If these tensions seemed irresolvable at the end of the decade-long rule of the United Progressive Alliance (UPA) in Delhi, Prime Minister Narendra Modi has signalled a more assertive foreign policy and greater interest in defence engagement since he assumed power in 2014. At home, Modi has sought to plug one of the biggest gaps in India's defence policy—the inability to produce weapons. His 'Make in India' initiative has led to the liberalization of norms for foreign direct investment in the defence sector, de-licensing of a number of items for production in the private sector, and encouragement of large Indian companies to participate in the production of weapons at home. All these steps have improved the prospects for the development of a strong domestic defence industrial base.

Externally, Modi has discarded some of India's defensiveness in the engagement with the US in the security sector. If defence cooperation between the two countries had slowed down under the UPA, Modi has seemed eager to consolidate the partnership. He had no hesitation in renewing the ten-year defence framework that was expiring in 2015. His government also ended Delhi's dithering on the Defence Technology Transfer Initiative (DTTI) with the US. A more positive approach under the new government was reflected in the decision to work together with the US on the development of the next aircraft carrier in India.[36]

Modi also restored Japanese participation in the Malabar naval exercises in the Indian Ocean.[37] The UPA government, bending under pressure from the Left and concerned by the Chinese reaction to the multilateral naval exercises involving the US, Japan, Australia and Singapore in 2007, had pulled back to limit the military engagement with the US to the bilateral plane. Modi's new self-assurance in playing the new geopolitics of Asia was also reflected in his decision to elevate the India–US–Japan dialogue from the official level to the political level. The foreign ministers of the three countries met for the first time in

October 2015 on the margins of the United Nations General Assembly in New York.[38]

The new enthusiasm for defence partnership with the US was accompanied by a greater willingness to strengthen security ties with the US allies in Asia: Japan and Australia. Besides shedding inhibitions on engaging the US and its allies, the Modi government has stepped up efforts to raise its independent military profile in the region. It has been more willing than the UPA to speak up on issues relating to China's maritime territorial disputes with its neighbours, intensify military cooperation with Vietnam and initiate defence exchanges with the Philippines. If its 'Act East Policy' signalled a new determination to stand up and be counted in East Asia, the Modi government also outlined an ambitious policy to build on its natural advantages in the Indian Ocean.[39] These new initiatives mark a definitive shift away from the traditional defensive mindset in Delhi on global security issues. They also showcase a shift from the past emphasis on 'strategic autonomy' to the notion that India can be 'a leading power' in the international system.[40]

While Modi's instincts in favour of a more expansive defence diplomacy are striking, he faces much ambivalence in the political class including his own party, massive inertia in the bureaucracy, and the lack of sufficient national capabilities in implementing his strategic aspirations. Yet, looking ahead, it is possible to imagine that Delhi's military diplomacy will acquire greater traction in the coming years. There will be greater regional and international demand for India's military services, support and cooperation. Besides the pull factor, there is also the push factor in India's defence diplomacy. As its interests expand—and India will have to secure them far from its shores—Delhi is likely to reach out and build defence partnerships with countries big and small. Despite the entrenched resistance to security sector reform, the new imperatives of national security are likely to prevail, in the coming years, over the inherited ideology of non-alignment.

6

The Future of Intelligence

Vikram Sood

Former Secretary, Research and Analysis Wing,
Government of India

> 'War is hell. Spying is much, much worse. Wars you can win. But in espionage there are no winners because it never ends.'[1] —Matthew Aid, *Intel Wars*

> 'Nothing should be as favourably regarded as intelligence; nothing should be as generously rewarded as intelligence; nothing should be as confidential as the work of intelligence.'[2] —Sun Tzu, *The Art of War*

Author's Disclaimer: This chapter has been written about intelligence needs in a generic sense and is not meant to be a critique or a defence of any existing intelligence organization in India. The stress is on preparing for future threats that may be considerably different in their nature and effects from what India faces today as it is feared that we are not truly prepared to handle the emerging situation.

The Conventional Intelligence Milieu

Any meaningful, coherent intelligence and security system in a country has to be designed for the preservation and furtherance of the national strategic and security objectives. This system should focus on present needs and prepare for the future. In India's context, intelligence activity would have to keep pace with globalization and India's growing relevance in the global order; the continuance of existing threats from hostile and ambitious neighbours; international terror, which may morph in unpredictable ways; and the continuing evolution of technology, which again has a multiplier effect on the threats of the future. These developments have also altered the scope and meaning of security, which now has a much wider connotation.

Global powers with global interests, like the US, have massively overhauled and upgraded their intelligence systems, with a disproportionately large reliance on technical means of collection and on the privatization of the means of both collection and analysis. Countries like ours, although threatened in the neighbourhood with one hostile neighbour and another with global ambitions, have been forced to move slowly, essentially for want of resources and priorities. Global interests and threats, being such as they are today, are impossible for one agency to handle.

Intelligence operations are driven by threat perceptions, strategic interests and capabilities. Threat perceptions in the early days after Independence were military threats and subversive activity from Pakistan, a vague suspicion about the West arising from the socialist-nationalist ethos of the government, and a more or less undefined threat from communism while seeking friendship with the Soviet Union. China was considered a threat by sections of the Indian leadership including Sardar Valabhbhai Patel, but Prime Minister Jawaharlal Nehru tried to keep the Chinese at bay through what he hoped would be conciliatory diplomacy. China was added as a real threat only after 1962.

The main charter in the early days for Indian intelligence was the communist threat, as it was under the British. The 1962 war with China led to the creation of the Aviation Research Centre for air reconnaissance and electronic intelligence, and the Special Service Bureau, a guerrilla unit to counter any future Chinese attacks in the Himalayan region, whose role was later altered to that of a border patrol force. A special operations group was also established. It was felt, after the 1965 war with Pakistan and the Mizo uprising in 1966, that the Intelligence Bureau (IB) had far too many internal responsibilities, and that it was necessary to create an external intelligence agency. In September 1968, the Research and Analysis Wing (R&AW) was established, which became the key external intelligence arm of the Indian state through an executive order of the government (and not through any legislative enactment).

The Kargil war of 1999 led to the creation of the Defence Intelligence Agency and the National Technical Facilities Organization (renamed National Technical Research Organization) for the collection of technical intelligence. They were modelled on the National Security Agency (NSA) of the US and the Government Communications Headquarters (GCHQ) of the UK. Several other intelligence coordination and assessment units were created following the reports of the Kargil Review Committee and the G.C. Saxena Task Force on Intelligence. The terror attacks of 2008 in Mumbai led to the creation of the National Investigation Agency. A National Counter Terror Centre planned after the attacks has been stillborn, as has been the National Intelligence Grid.

Governments invest billions of dollars in acquiring or manufacturing the most sophisticated weaponry possible in the hope that this arsenal would be a deterrent against the enemy and the weapons would never be used. However, this arsenal needs periodic upgrading. A smart and effective intelligence mechanism developed at a much lower cost can certainly prevent a war and the losses therein—even though it may not by itself win a war. But such a mechanism, to have a chance to be effective, must keep pace with emerging threats, and would therefore need similar upgrading.

Conventional, unconventional and sub-conventional threats occupy the minds of military planners. There is one aspect that has begun to change the nature of these threats. This is the exponential development of easily available high-speed massive capacity information technology, accompanied by the miniaturization of weapons technology and surveillance capacities. Much of the former is available to the average man on the street at low or no cost to be used, misused or abused. It may be that in the years ahead, the expensive weapons of war may be rendered unusable by technology, or even substituted by it.

The Twenty-first Century Technology Blitz

The current century's security and intelligence scene is going to look increasingly different from that of the previous decades as time goes by. Not many of us have fully grasped the significance and speed, or even the range of this change.

The Internet began as a military creation by the Defence Advanced Research Projects Agency (DARPA) of the US Department of Defense. The Internet's original purpose was to be the alternative means of communication in case of a nuclear attack. Today this has immense geopolitical and intelligence ramifications. It is universally available. Undoubtedly, this provides immense advantages to science, medicine and education, air traffic control, other means of communication, banking, and in every walk of life: incomes have grown, manufacturing has benefitted and the world has become smaller in space and time. There are a billion or more Facebook users who have happily shared their personal details, which are useful to the lawbreaker and potentially to the law enforcer as well as the intelligence agent. Users have downloaded billions of apps, which are now used for anything from personal banking to paying taxes and bills, saving and sending photos and music, and reading newspapers and magazines. The Internet is accessible from smartphones that are becoming cheaper by the day, and from iPads, laptops, high-definition televisions (HDTVs) and Apple TVs.

Global strategist and consultant Marc Goodman graphically and lucidly describes the direction the dark side of technology is taking in his remarkable book *Future Crimes.*[3] Of course, this includes terror and associated activities by lawbreakers as well as state-sponsored attacks on other targets. He points out that the Internet and the speed, stealth and scope of communications will continue to alter the abilities of the enemies of the state. The changing nature of threats and the technological revolution have altered not only the targets of intelligence operations but also the processes of collection of intelligence. Human sources will remain the link between the real and the virtual world but will also remain the core of classical intelligence. Inevitably, the surveillance of these new methods of communication will be technology-intensive, intrusive and expensive. This can only mean that the debate between the needs of security and principles of privacy will never be satisfactorily resolved.

The twenty-first century will be known as the period that adapted to the computer age in all its aspects. From banking transactions, financial deals, the electric power grid, train systems, air traffic control, military hardware, hospitals and medical treatment to traffic signals—any kind of communication is now linked to computers. All our systems, institutionally and at a personal level, are so dependent on the Internet that is controlled from outside our territory that we do not realize this acute dependency. Technology is overtaking our lives at an exponential rate, and intelligence agencies have to be prepared for the worst.

In 2000 there were 360 million people online. By 2005 the figure had gone up to 1 billion, and it doubled in the next six years. Google estimates that by 2020 the entire world will be online. If the enemy were to be able to cripple these systems, there would be unimaginable chaos, with the country caught in a digital gridlock, unless there is a credible back-up.[4]

Smarter weapons that 'think', designed as precise missions to maximize damage and minimize own casualties, are the trend now. Five years ago, the US military was working on miniaturized technology to make unmanned aerial vehicles (UAV) the size of birds and much more lethal, making the current Predator-armed UAV obsolete.[5] Latest indications are that US military scientists have in fact invented CICADA, a close-in covert autonomous disposable aircraft, a drone that could fit in the palm of a hand and eventually cost as little as $250. Imagine the impact on terrorism and military operations this could have globally.[6]

The US Navy has been researching towards building a drone army of unmanned autonomous robots for naval, aerial and ground combat. The DARPA continues to research 'smart dust', which is a surveillance system the size of a pinhead. Once developed and deployed, swarms of millions of these could be dropped in an enemy zone to provide detailed surveillance intelligence and also support offensive military operations. Nano weapons would render present unwieldy weapons obsolete and 'smart weapons' would replace the present dumb missiles. Robotic armies and battalions would make military interventions more tempting.[7]

This is the shape of threats that will emerge later in the century. All this will impact intelligence collection and operations in the future.

The Age of Computer-savvy Crooks and the Cyber World

As was to be expected, the Italian Mafia, the Chinese Triads and the Colombian drug cartels have also made the technology jump. They have taken advantage of the speed of transfers of funds, the anonymity of the activity and the fact that cyberspace is thinly policed. This has helped them reap huge profits. Their main activity remains narcotics smuggling, human trafficking and counterfeit currency. All these are connected with the spoils and reach of terrorism, one feeding off the other. Added to this are organized groups in cyberspace that also indulge in phishing, fake pharmaceutical ads, denial-of-service attacks, extortion, child pornography and other crimes.[8]

Hackers are another rampant and fast-growing category of criminal activity. They are today highly organized and professional. They work in syndicates as they steal computer identities, commit credit card and other banking and financial frauds. In October 2013, criminal hackers broke through the Adobe systems and stole 38 million account login IDs and passwords, along with millions of credit card numbers. They also stole more than 40 gigabytes of computer source codes of Adobe's flagship products. Consequently, criminals could sell Adobe products and could do this also by altering the codes and inserting any number of back doors and malware without the unsuspecting customer ever getting to know this. Even Symantec, the makers of Norton Antivirus, had its source code broken. Nevertheless, the software security business is destined to grow and could reach nearly $100 billion in size by 2017 or so.[9]

According to research by Verizon Business Services in 2013, in the case of 62 per cent of these illegal intrusions, it took two months to detect. Another survey by Trustware Holdings also threw up similar findings. This means that it takes up to seven months for systems to detect that they have been breached by a criminal, corporate competitor or a foreign country, and most of these are detected by customers, law enforcement officials or contractors, and not by the company's elaborate firewalls. The Verizon study also revealed that in about 75 per cent of the cases, the defences of an average computer system were breached within minutes of the attempt. Only in 15 per cent of the cases it took a few hours. As Goodman says, 'In today's world, hackers are living unfettered and free inside your very own data systems for months and months, watching, waiting, lurking and pillaging everything from your passwords to work projects to old selfies.'

Goodman also says, most tellingly:

> The next Industrial Revolution, the Information Revolution, is well under way, with massive yet unrealized implications for our personal and global security ... there is the proverbial technological train that is leaving the station, one that is rapidly and exponentially picking up speed. There are signs of it everywhere, if one knows where to look.

Goodman describes these thus:

> Just over the horizon are newly emerging technologies, including robotics, artificial intelligence, genetics, synthetic biology, nanotechnology, 3-D manufacturing, brain science, and virtual

> reality, that will make today's cyber-crime seem like child's play. These innovations will play essential roles in our daily lives in just a few years, yet no in-depth, broad-based study has been completed to help us understand the unintended attendant risks they pose...[10]

In typical intelligence terminology, this would be called blowback effects—the unintended consequences of innocent technological research and application.

There is another category distinct from international cyber-crime syndicates: the hacktivists, who are politically motivated cyber attackers and are some of the most influential and powerful groups in cyberspace. Some of these groups are Anonymous, LulzSec, AntiSec, WikiLeaks and the Syrian Electronic Army. Anonymous has been powerful enough to attract the attention of the GCHQ in the UK and for it to launch denial-of-service attacks against this group in order to try to disrupt its activities. Generally, hacktivists can be globally relevant as they were in the case of the Arab Spring, especially in Egypt. *Time* magazine recognized this when it included Anonymous in its list of hundred most influential people in 2012.[11]

States often use the covert option to further and protect their interests. The authorization by US president George W. Bush in 2006 to launch Operation Olympic Games for the insertion of the Stuxnet worm to attack Iran's nuclear facility in Natanz was one such known use. For a country that watches 5 billion emails in a day, and given its global interests, resources and technological abilities, this surely was not the only operation of this kind. This is apart from listening into phone calls and covering all the various new apps that are used. Imagine the downstream activity that would involve more technology and expertise to convert this data into information, and then knowledge and finally intelligence.

The Israeli Air Force attack in 2007 on the Syrian nuclear facility in the Deir ez-Zor region also required that the Syrian air defences be hacked in advance by the Israelis. This is going to be the pattern for the future and India needs to be prepared for this and other similar attacks. The Chinese have stolen technology secrets from the US, including the designs of the submarine-launched miniaturized nuclear missile W-88. The US has alleged that the Chinese have clandestinely acquired sensitive

American technologies for nuclear weaponization, improvement of the performance of their space rockets and missiles, submarine detection techniques, improvement of the People's Liberation Army's (PLA) telecommunications capability and supercomputers.[12]

The Age of Digital Jihad

It is well known that terrorists began using the Internet and modern communications much sooner than the counter-terrorists did. Besides, they operate on a different budget scale and different security norms. Chat rooms help recruit new members. Clandestine financial transactions, clandestine communications and dissemination of propaganda, as witnessed graphically in the recent case of the Islamic State of Iraq and Syria (ISIS), show that the battle is not just with guns and ammunition. As far back as 2002, the al Qaeda–linked Jamaah Islamiyah had raised funds for the Bali bombings by hacking into Western bank accounts. Philippine police unearthed a telephone hacking scam in 2011 where hackers worked on AT&T customers and cost the company $2 million in written-off frauds. This hacker cell was working with Jamaah Islamiyah, which funnelled millions back to a Saudi-based terrorist organization. This in turn funded the Lashkar-e-Taiba (LeT).

In West Asia, the ISIS has shown tremendous adaptability to the networking of its propaganda effort. It has its presence on all types of social media networks, and they rapidly open new accounts once the old ones get closed down. They design their programmes and videos according to target audiences. For the East, they are bloody and fear-inducing; for the West, they are coherent, cool and clean. They manipulate video games for children, relying on subtle and appropriate imagery.[13]

The extensive use of the Internet by terrorists has prompted counter-terrorist experts to refer to the Internet as a 'terrorist university'—as it enabled terrorists to learn new techniques, acquire new lethal skills and launch cyber attacks. Online documents like *The Mujahedeen Poisons Handbook*, containing homemade recipes for poisons and poisonous gases, and the 600-page *Encyclopaedia of Jihad* are primers for jihadi knowledge. The LeT had used modern technology and communications to great effect during the Mumbai 2008 massacre.

Nightmare for Intelligence Services

These fall under several categories, starting from the lone unknown terrorist or jihadi plotting in front of a computer to Julian Assange, Bradley (Chelsea) Manning and Edward Snowden, who became world figures when they chose to challenge the institutions for which they worked on the grounds of conscience. The ease and speed with which data was transferred only means that similar transfers can take place again or are still taking place. All this requires extensive and even aggressive surveillance, which is not always possible in a democracy.

The question to be asked is, given how the threats will be operationalized in the future, do the present organizational structures have the ingredients to deliver, and what is required to be done to attain that capability? This has to be done in India by Indians and it cannot be a copy of another system.

Forecasting Growing and Evolving Threats

Thus, some of the questions we should be asking are: What are the security threats that India would face in 2025 or 2030? What kind of an intelligence organization would thus be needed either to protect our interests by preventing others from upstaging us or, if required, to reverse the trend among our rivals? Does the present organization have the ingredients to deliver? If not, what needs to be done so that we are not found wanting in 2025? In doing so, we have to evolve our own systems and not just copy others.

Reforms in India have had two characteristics. They have concentrated on providing better career opportunities within the existing concerns, and on the creation of new agencies. There has been no reform that seeks to build the strengths of the organizations. In-house reviews that deal merely with career enhancements are inadequate. Reforms have to be more fundamental and far deeper, have to be done in the fullness of time and not when a crisis has begun to loom. In India, reforms have been episodic, usually following a debacle and not based on periodic threat assessments. This is something that has to be done by the strategic and intelligence community including the armed forces, or, if the threat is economic or technological (cyber, for instance), along with other appropriate experts.

National threats have changed but traditional threats from traditional adversaries will continue, whether they are conventional, sub-conventional or involving weapons of mass destruction (WMD). The meaning of security is now larger to include resource security, market and investment security, and cyber security. Intelligence and security agencies will have to continue to watch and counter this much larger threat.

There are other transnational threats that no single agency or single country can handle. Besides, there is no knowing how the new threats will evolve. The rapidly changing technological applications bring their own threats. Catastrophic terrorism, cyber terrorism, remote-controlled missile attacks and virtual wars are the other new threats. International trade and commercial transactions have become faster and more intricate; banking transactions move at the speed of lightning. Information-technology-driven globalization also covers the criminal world. Interaction between narcotics smugglers, arms merchants, human traffickers and terrorists is that much easier, faster and safer. Added to this are radical religious terrorists who are affecting India and the rest of the world most dramatically, supported not only by Pakistan but also by a number of new players in the Arab world who see themselves threatened either by Israel or Iran.

As such, we need to be looking at reforms from the following perspectives:

Starting Early

It must be borne in mind that we have to begin preparations now for the next two decades or more considering that it takes about ten to fifteen years for an intelligence officer to gather experience in various aspects of intelligence in order to mature. A young recruit who joins at the age of twenty to twenty-two will be at his or her peak between the ages of thirty-five and fifty. Thereafter he functions mostly as a senior supervisor.

Improve, Not Merely Control

Thoughtful supervision and mindless control are two different issues. In India, reform has mostly meant more organizations, more posts and more control. True reform would consider past experiences, present conditions and evolving threats to make a judgement on the kind of intelligence agency required, say, fifteen to twenty years from now. True reform is also best achieved and is reasonable when carried out from within. This would obviously mean a thorough evaluation of the abilities of the agencies that exist and what needs to be done so that the intelligence agency of the day twenty years from now is in a position to deliver at that time. No such exercise has been seriously carried out in India. Intelligence reforms in India have remained sporadic and crisis-linked. Also, reforms in India have essentially been about exercising greater control without seeking to improve the performance.

Any intelligence organization that is manned by careerists who are either too old to be moulded or are too risk-averse is on a sharp downhill trajectory. Any government of the day must guard against this because faulty or inaccurate intelligence is far more dangerous than no intelligence.

Accountability and Empowerment

In a democratic system, it is desirable to have a measure of clarity in the working of intelligence agencies, both to define purpose and to ensure that tasks assigned are performed within the charter. Therefore, while on the one hand accountability of intelligence may be considered essential, it is meaningless without a legalized existence, a legalized charter, empowerment and then accountability. Legislation, therefore, has to be an aid to intelligence and not an impediment; it should encourage performance, risk taking and not stifle initiative and make the organization risk-averse. There must be a clear demarcation of responsibilities allowing for the necessary overlap. Each intelligence organization must have a clearly defined legalized charter.

Previous attempts at a bill were expectedly thrown out because it was designed to run the intelligence apparatus as a human rights organization. The private member's bill, 'The Intelligence Services (Powers and Regulation) Bill, 2011', did not make any progress in the Lok Sabha as it was far too stifling in its endeavour to provide accountability without flexibility and empowerment. All the various extensive controls suggested would have killed any intelligence organization. As a principle, external controls by those with little or no knowledge of intelligence functioning have to be minimized as they only lead to bottlenecks. At the same time, internal controls have to be made stricter.[14]

Recruitment Patterns Need to Change

This would mean looking at the recruitment pattern, evaluating the talent required in the future, and creating an organizational structure that would draw in talent or outsource some aspects and recruit from the open market. Personnel to be recruited would include linguists by the hundred, in Chinese, Arabic of different dialects, Persian, Hebrew, Pushto, Darri, Urdu, Balochi, Sindhi, Nepali, Tibetan, Bangla, Bhasa Indonesia, Malay, Japanese, Russian, French and German. These requirements are bound to grow as the country's interests grow. Intelligence organizations need to recruit skilled workers massively, including mathematicians to break cipher codes, cyber security experts, hackers, software experts, hostage negotiators, scientists, robotic experts, military experts, issue experts and economists and financial whiz kids who understand international financial systems. Intelligence operatives at all levels have to be net-savvy as the future will be determined less on the battlefields and more in cubicles and on screens. Mid-career course corrections and training are very necessary to update the skills of existing personnel. Rigidity in functioning and unimaginative supervision have no place in an intelligence organization, as rigid parameters will curb the flexibility that is key to its efficient running.

The skills required are so varied and the price to be paid for such skills so high that all agencies will need to think of ways and means of attracting and retaining this talent. This perhaps will be the biggest challenge for the government while preparing an intelligence organization for the future. Intelligence organizations not only need to have language skills, interrogation skills, ability to deal with hostages, area and issue expertise, and operational skills of a special kind individually, but also must understand that there can be no hope for victory without international cooperation. The traditional route of recruiting officers through the organized civil service should be abandoned and talent needs to be found in the open market.[15]

Commenting on the recruitment pattern, this author had said in a report in 2006:

> The age of the generalist and the bird of passage is surely over. An officer on deputation comes without area expertise, language

> skills and does not necessarily have the attitude, time or incentive to acquire these skills during his tenure, long or short. The chief motive of such an officer on deputation is to hope for a comfortable foreign assignment without adding much to the experience basket of the organization. Officers on deputation these days come with additional baggage—most are politicized or unwanted in the states. It is, therefore, a fallacy to assume that the salvation of intelligence organizations lies in greater induction from existing services.[16]

All intelligence organizations may be better served by dedicated long-term personnel with just a few areas of expertise, or regional experts co-opted for specific projects. The R&AW, for instance, is now more than forty years old and does not need periodic induction of deputations whose arrival and departure do no add to the strength, skills and experience of the organization. On the other hand, there is inherent danger that officers who come and go carry back with them secrets of the functioning and other details about the organization. The government must take a call on whether or not it is a good practice to expose such details to those who will leave after a few years.

Selection of the Heads of Organizations

Selection of the head of an intelligence organization is a very important issue. Intelligence agencies are complicated secret organizations where functioning is compartmentalized on the basis of the need-to-know principle and very few ever get to see the entire working of the organization throughout their careers. It is, therefore, most desirable to always have, as the person heading the organization, someone belonging to the system. Besides this is good for the morale in organizations where there is no public recognition and no chance of lateral mid-career movement. The government would also have to seriously consider fast-tracking talent based on suitability rather than relying simply on the seniority principle. This naturally means that the government would have to consider sizeable signing-off packages for those whose career has no future.

It has been the experience of many that threats sometimes emerge suddenly or change equally suddenly. This requires repositioning of material and human resources. It has also been the experience of many that by the time sanctions/approvals are obtained from the Ministry of External Affairs (MEA) and the financial advisor, considerable time elapses, with the result that the threat is inadequately covered, or worse, not covered at all. Heads of intelligence organizations should have powers to relocate resources on their own according to the perceived need. Each organization should have this surge capacity.

Strengthening the Counter-terrorism Grid

Disclosures in the media about the number of terrorist cases where the courts have acquitted or released suspects in terrorist cases for want of evidence only suggest weaknesses in our counter-terrorism grid. Repeated cases of this nature only strengthen perceptions about policing that are not healthy for law and order and lower the image of the police and intelligence agencies. Obviously there is a need for strengthening and training our personnel on the ground, modernizing their training and equipment and increasing their numbers.

Indian intelligence not only has to pre-empt a terror strike and neutralize terror groups and cells, but also has to eliminate such threats when they become live. This means sharper intelligence, greater coordination between intelligence organizations, greater support from the government, continued psychological warfare (psywar), the ability to take covert punitive action at a time of choosing and finally backed by the ability of the armed forces to escalate sharply, if required.

Political and Strategic Clarity

Intelligence success depends on the clarity of purpose set out by the political leadership, the dynamism of the organizational leadership, in-house talent and morale, and the milieu in which it works. The collection of intelligence is not an end in itself; therefore, its product is very often only as good as its consumers' use of intelligence.

As threats change with time, organizations must be able to surge and redeploy or augment capacity quickly when a threat not anticipated earlier emerges or increases. Experience has been otherwise. The system gets enmeshed in endless bureaucracy of justifications and finances required to be given to external financial managers, with the result that sanctions and approvals are never received in time, affecting intelligence collection work down the line. There is, therefore, a need to 'debureaucratize' intelligence systems, not tie them up with promotions in the central staffing pattern schemes, because they do not compete with the rest of the general system and seek promotions within their own systems. Intelligence organizations have to be leaner, sharper and quicker off their feet than in the past if they are to succeed in performing their tasks.

Lessons from Other Nations

The 9/11 attacks altered security perceptions, needs and priorities in the US. The security apparatus grew almost overnight; a stringent Patriot Act that curbed individual rights was approved by Congress; and a new agency, Homeland Security, was up and about. The numbers handling intelligence reached 210,000 by 2012 in seventeen intelligence agencies in the US. Kabul alone had 700 case officers, with presumably a comparable number in Islamabad. Both the Defense Intelligence Agency (DIA) and the Federal Bureau of Investigation (FBI) grew phenomenally. The FBI now has its own fleet of 132 surveillance aircraft and helicopters owned by different front companies in the US. Private American corporations increasingly collect and analyse data on behalf of the US government. Even special operations have been outsourced in some cases.[17]

America has been in an enormous, mostly unacknowledged, surveillance overdrive to sweep in all possible intelligence that might lead to the exposure of terror links and plans. Disclosures by Edward Snowden reveal that the NSA was watching hundreds of international companies and organizations, including in countries closely allied to the US, in an effort to find security weaknesses in cell phone technology that it can exploit for surveillance.

In a hugely networked existence, intelligence analysts can no longer be thinking in terms of sections or specific unrelated subjects. Traditional demarcations are disappearing and analyses will have to be across the board. Therefore, traditional hierarchical patterns will also need to be recast. Since so much material is available openly, there is such a monumental overload of data, information and disinformation that it is difficult to distinguish which of this makes for knowledge and security. As a result, the pressures on intelligence producers and analysts are going to be much more. Analysts will need to have the ability and training to make sense of the vast fund of information and match it with the secret information that may be available. In fact, the ability to make sense of open data would be a desirable professional qualification. It can no longer be a take-it-or-leave-it approach. Increasingly, intelligence outputs will have to cater to what the consumer/client wants.

Elsewhere in the Western world, especially in the US, a new arrangement has come into being. An intelligence-industrial complex like the military-industrial complex that had typified US capitalism is now functioning. In fact, this is much more intricate and larger if one converts this into a military-intelligence-industry-private-military-contractors complex. The US intelligence community outsources about $50 billion in business annually, which consumes about 70 per cent of its budget. Different intelligence agencies and the Pentagon have partnership arrangements with giants like IBM, CACI and Boóz Allen Hamilton.

The Central Intelligence Agency (CIA) and Amazon Web Services signed a $600 million agreement in the summer of 2014 which would allow sharing of information between Amazon and the seventeen intelligence agencies of the US, and an Amazon-built cloud will operate behind the intelligence community's firewall.[18] This kind of cooperation is now common and shows that other agencies have realized the need to get truly net-savvy.

This may not be the model for India to follow but there is no way that there can be any effective functioning of intelligence agencies in the future without some involvement and reliance on the private sector, especially in the realm of the Internet, communications and technology. In India we need to think of this now if we are to be in a position to handle emerging threats.[19] Recruitment to the agencies and private–government tie-ups will have to be specialized and not left to routine civil service recruitment systems.

Psywar: The Art of Winning and Influencing Nations

Intelligence agencies will need to use soft power as an intelligence weapon and also as an influence weapon. US and Western intelligence and the Russians have used the media, non-governmental organizations (NGOs) and influential individuals extensively as part of a psywar to influence perceptions and weaken the opposition or claim successes. These are those who can help change mindsets and perceptions abroad and at home.

Again, not enough attention is paid in India to this resource mostly because it is difficult to audit this financially and anyone expecting immediate returns on investment is bound to be disappointed. On the other hand, terrorists have used the Internet and electronic, print and social media much more effectively. Here, again, the private sector will have to be searched for talent and ingenuity.

America fought its psywar in the Cold War era to keep communism at bay and to save Europe from Soviet plans with the help of personalities like Noel Coward, Arthur Miller and Norman Mailer, and the Rockefellers and Henry Fords. There were many more. Michael Josselson of the CIA led this multi-million-dollar campaign, operating on the principle of plausible deniability, for more than a decade. This cultural propaganda campaign later covered thirty-five countries under the umbrella of the Congress of Cultural Freedom. The congress funded magazines, held art exhibitions, organized philharmonic orchestras, ran a radio station from Germany which quickly acquired twenty-nine other stations, and also ran the *Encounter* magazine for a number of years.[20]

The Cold War was thus won also through the sustained efforts of the cultural cold warriors. A peacetime campaign is far more difficult to manage as personalities clash, perceptions change and there is impatience because the results are not immediately tangible.

Effective psywar is the ability to put forward and defend an idea, or to offer a better way of life that is appealing to the recipient and not merely the giver. The ultimate test of a successful psywar or propaganda tool is when it appears never to have been carried out at all, and when it is able to make the audience ask for things that can be given to it. The favoured tactic could be the 'necessary lie' that is based on some basic truth for it to be acceptable. It was this absence of any truth in the allegations that Saddam Hussein had acquired WMDs and was in cahoots with the al Qaeda that led to a catastrophic campaign.

Conducting a long-term psywar campaign during peacetime against an implacable foe whose long-term objectives are at variance with current overt declarations requires unusual tenacity and hard work. In India, we are facing this kind of a situation today. This requires a constant effort of the kind the West made against the communists during the Cold War and has still sustained against Russia.

Since perception building is a long-term project that relies solely on the transient bureaucrat, equipped with opinion but without expertise, the system is left stultified, dogmatic and even totalitarian. It has become necessary to involve private entrepreneurs with the skills and imagination for making plausible programmes. At the same time, this cannot be left entirely to various private TV and news channels acting like unguided missies. We need to have the equivalents of Reuters, Agence France-Presse (AFP), Cable News Network (CNN) and the British Broadcasting Corporation (BBC); the last two, though independent, have governmental financial backing and there are broad guidelines for their world services.[21] It is also important for the credibility of such ventures that they are not required to support government policy in all its aspects.

The Indian challenge is to make our presence felt abroad without this being seen as another boring government enterprise. A country that aspires to greater glory must have a credible voice that is heard. Image building is important and can be a collective national enterprise. Image building and perception management do not have to be a sinister venture.

Hard Power for Special Operations Capabilities

While it is essential for any country to have a top-end intelligence system for the collection of intelligence, in modern times it is necessary to aggressively push a country's interests or to send a message to a recalcitrant opponent that he is not willing to receive otherwise. Thus, any intelligence organization that is working abroad needs not only intelligence collection abilities, which is stating the obvious, but also the ability to carry out special operations of the kind that the CIA, Mossad of Israel, Secret Intelligence Service (SIS) of the UK, and the KGB of the Soviet Union have conducted in the past. There has to be capability, patience and tenacity to hunt down those who have damaged Indian interests. Recourse to the UN or seeking the assistance of other powers cannot always be the solutions. There has to be a political climate and ethos that allows this to be done, while being aware that there could be failures. Political leaders should ideally set the goal, not the means.

In the world of intelligence there are no arrangements based on friendship; there are only relationships based on interests. But soft power is only effective if there is hard power to back it.

Conclusion

Threats to India will continue to morph and new ones will be added in the years to come. The country's security requirements will change too, given its increasingly active role in international affairs. India will need a first-rate, state-of-the-art intelligence service that will cater to the new requirements. Its leadership should be such that it is willing to take calculated gambles. All the major arms of intelligence—the IB, R&AW, DIA, National Technical Research Organization (NTRO), Directorate of Revenue Intelligence (DRI) and other economic intelligence services—will need to be continually strengthened, revamped and reoriented from time to time, keeping in mind the security threats in the foreseeable future. Creating intelligence systems when the threat has already evolved is doing that too late. As already mentioned in the beginning, doing this when the crisis is upon us means intelligence is doomed to fail.

The important requirement is going to be an intelligence system that is empowered to address the fast-changing and growing security threats and that is flexible and alert enough to change priorities to make the most optimum use of limited resources.

Intelligence cannot and does not function in a vacuum; nor is it an end in itself. It is a consumer-driven service requirement and works in a given political, security and bureaucratic surrounding. Its utility and efficiency was best described by Sun Tzu:

> Unless someone has the wisdom of a sage, he cannot use spies; unless he is benevolent and righteous, he cannot employ spies; unless he is subtle and perspicacious, he cannot perceive the substance in intelligence reports. It is subtle, subtle, subtle.

7

Nuclear Deterrence and India: Doctrine, Strategy, Force Structure and Operationalization

Dr Manpreet Sethi

*Senior Fellow and Project Leader, Nuclear Security,
Centre for Air Power Studies, New Delhi*

India refrained from accepting nuclear deterrence as a framework for its own security despite the nuclear test by China in 1964, or even after its own peaceful nuclear explosion in 1974. The apparent focus of Indian nuclear diplomacy remained on getting the world to acknowledge the dangers of nuclear weapons and pressing the nuclear weapon possessors to move towards universal nuclear disarmament. By promoting international security, India hoped to achieve national security.

By 1998, however, India was compelled to make a choice. Disarmament was nowhere on the horizon; the Non-Proliferation Treaty (NPT) had been extended indefinitely at the 1995 Review and Extension Conference; the Comprehensive Test Ban Treaty (CTBT) had been put out for signature and was likely to freeze India's non-nuclear status without addressing the nuclear threat from China or its nexus with Pakistan; Pakistan had declared itself nuclear capable in 1987 and its adventurism with terrorism had grown. India's security concerns and the non-proliferation pressures combined to push the country to test its nuclear weapons and adopt nuclear deterrence as a security strategy.

Having made the choice, however reluctantly, India has since been engaged in giving nuclear deterrence a credible form through an effective strategy premised on a sound, logical and suitable doctrine. This chapter fleshes out the Indian approach to nuclear deterrence as evident in its doctrine, strategy, force structure and operational dimensions. It explains the logic of India's choices and the merit in sticking with some of them, offers suggestions on enhancing the credibility of deterrence, and sets priorities for operationalization.

Indian Approach to Nuclear Weapons

Till such time as nuclear weapons persist in national nuclear arsenals across the world, India too is compelled to hold on to them for the sake of its security. However, India has maintained a very narrow view of employing nuclear weapons only for deterrence. It seeks to deter by threatening retaliation of a kind that would negate the benefits that the adversary hopes to gain by using them in the first place. India eschews the idea that nuclear weapons could be effective for fighting a war or for prevailing over the adversary given their destructive potential, which makes their use unthinkable for a rational political end. Prime Minister Atal Bihari Vajpayee had stated in Parliament in 1998 that India did not 'intend to use these weapons for aggression or for mounting threats against any country; these are weapons of self-defence to ensure that India is not subjected to nuclear threats or coercion.'[1]

Interestingly, this idea of deterrence, at one level, does not impose very demanding needs on nuclear hardware. The numbers game is of relatively less importance for India as compared to nations that view nuclear weapons as viable war-fighting tools. Nor is it necessary to have an elaborate command and control system that perfects the logistics of first strike. But, at the same time, the credibility requirements that can assure retaliation of a kind that is seen to be unacceptable by the adversary are extremely complex. This is what poses a unique challenge in operationalizing India's nuclear strategy. In order to do so prudently, it is imperative that national security decision makers, political and military, have a good understanding of what credible nuclear deterrence demands. More may not be better if less can suffice. But less may not suffice if the nature and capability of the adversary is not correctly understood. A right balance, therefore, is required to juggle many factors and calculations. It is in this context that the nuclear doctrine plays a critical role.

India's Nuclear Doctrine: The Making and Logic of Its Essential Attributes

A nuclear doctrine is a set of guiding principles that encapsulates the philosophy or explains the raison d'être of one's acquisition of nuclear weapons. It answers the fundamental questions of when, how and where the weapon should be used in the cause of national defence. The doctrine, therefore, serves as a conceptual framework and conveys a sense of the country's worldview, what it seeks to do, and how. Beliefs reflected in a nuclear doctrine emanate from the strategic culture of a nation and essentially reflect its personality, or the idea of the nation. Seen thus, the doctrine is relatively abiding and timeless. It changes when the nation decides to amend its core values or belief systems.

At another level, the doctrine also explains the manner in which nuclear weapons would be employed to meet the purpose that they have been acquired for. Thus, the doctrine provides direction on issues pertaining to force structure and force posture. By doing so, it becomes a guide for nuclear strategy. It enables the determination of the size and nature of the nuclear arsenal, including delivery systems; it helps decide the type of command and control systems employed, as well as the type of retaliation, and hence the identification of targets; and finally the deployment status of the arsenal.

It is remarkable that India formulated a nuclear doctrine just fifteen months after the conduct of its nuclear tests in May 1998. This task was performed by the first National Security Advisory Board (NSAB) constituted under the chairmanship of the late K. Subrahmanyam. On 17 August 1999, the group presented a draft nuclear doctrine to the national security advisor, Brajesh Mishra. The government decided to make this draft public, thereby opening it for debate and discussion within the country and outside. Indeed, the national and international strategic communities were taken by surprise not just by the speed with which the task was completed but also by the rather uncharacteristic transparency shown by the government on a subject traditionally kept behind thick veils of secrecy. The objective was to clear the air by unambiguously stating a political role for the nuclear weapon and explaining the manner in which India planned to 'put it to use'. As is evident, right from the beginning, the country was trying to stabilize the situation the best it could despite being compelled to accept certain basic requirements of nuclear deterrence.

The document produced by the NSAB has essentially remained a draft since the governments since 1999 have not accorded it the status of a formal doctrine. However, on 4 January 2003, the Cabinet Committee on Security (CCS) issued an operationalization note that accepted most of the principles of the nuclear doctrine and laconically outlined operational arrangements governing India's nuclear capability. This has since come to be known as the 'official' nuclear doctrine. The following sub-sections examine the attributes of this publicly declared Indian nuclear doctrine.

Credible Minimum Deterrence (CMD)

The first dictum as mentioned in the CCS Review of the Operationalization of India's Nuclear Doctrine is 'building and maintaining a credible minimum deterrence'. As mentioned earlier, while building and maintaining a stockpile of nuclear weapons is indeed critical for deterrence, the rejection of the concept of nuclear war fighting frees India from the need to match the nuclear arsenal of its adversaries weapon for weapon. American political scientist Kenneth Waltz had stated several decades ago: 'Forces designed for war fighting have to be compared with each other. Forces designed for war deterring need not be compared. The question is not whether one country has less than another, but whether it can do unacceptable damage to another.'[2]

With the principal role of India's nuclear force being to protect the nation from nuclear blackmail and coercion, instead of any desire to annex or mount aggression or indulge in terrorism from behind the shield of nuclear weapons, the country is satisfied with CMD. Stockpile accumulation of the kind that the US and Russia are engaged in, running into hundreds of thousands of strategic and tactical nuclear warheads, is dismissed as useless. Official pronouncements, however, have refused to be drawn into quantifying the minimum. Rather, the actual size and composition of the nuclear arsenal is left to the assessment of threats and India's own technological capability. Jaswant Singh, India's then foreign minister, had said in 1998: 'The minimum is not a fixed physical quantification. It is a policy approach dictated by and determined in the context of our security environment. There is no fixity. Therefore, as our security environment changes and alters and as new demands begin to be placed on it, our requirements too are bound to be evaluated.'[3]

While the determination of CMD would change with the transformation of threat perceptions and technological developments (such as the deployment of an effective ballistic missile defence by an adversary), it definitely need not seek superiority or even parity with an adversary's nuclear forces in the number, yields or types of weapons. All that is required is an 'assured counterstrike capability' that can inflict 'unacceptable damage' on the enemy despite suffering a first strike. CMD, therefore, imposes two prerequisites for credible deterrence.

First, how to estimate the 'unacceptability threshold of the adversary'. Strategists have warned of the dangers of mirror imaging, where one assumes that what is not acceptable to self would also not be acceptable to the other. In order to make a correct assessment of what an adversary might actually find unacceptable, a deep study of its strategic culture (based on the historical experiences of the wars it has fought), socio-psychological make-up, economic growth (the more developed the country, the lesser the loss it would be willing to take as a result of a nuclear exchange), and nature of the political system (the more closed a system, the greater the loss it could take), among other factors, is necessary.

Fortunately, it is not very difficult to impose punishment with nuclear weapons. By their very nature, they cause huge damage to life and property unrestricted in time and space. Moreover, given the high density of population in this region, punishing a first user with unacceptable damage neither calls for the kinds of numbers that the superpowers built, nor the kinds of yields that they experimented with. A sufficient number of kiloton weapons dispersed intelligently over the target and made to explode at an intelligent height to maximize damage suffice for credible deterrence.

In this respect, the aspersions cast on the thermonuclear capability of India are quite irrelevant. It may be recalled that in 2009, a set of Defence Research and Development Organization (DRDO) scientists had questioned the veracity of the results announced by the Department of Atomic Energy (DAE) on the thermonuclear yield of the test. The DAE had defended its stand. Irrespective of which side one believes, the point is that nuclear weapons, even if not of megaton yield, are still powerful deterrents. The weapons dropped on Hiroshima and Nagasaki in August 1945 were only 15-20 kiloton in yield. And yet they scarred the human mind enough to not merit a repeat performance.

Of course, there is an argument that H-bombs make more economic sense when carried on expensive, inaccurate intercontinental ballistic missiles (ICBMs). They provide more bang for the buck. But, given the number of people who would be threatened by India in case of a counter strike on cities, can the loss of life and property caused by a kiloton weapon be less of a deterrent? Would it matter to the adversary, or to India, whether the destruction was caused by a fission or a fusion weapon as long as it caused damage unacceptable to the adversary in relation to the objective being sought? In the current international climate, it is virtually impossible for India to consider more tests to establish its thermonuclear capability to the sufficient satisfaction of the sceptics. But, fortunately, desirable though it might be considered by some, it is not essential for deterrence.

The second requirement of deterrence of the kind that India seeks relates to the criticality of ensuring that sufficient warheads and delivery vehicles survive a first strike and are available for retaliation. This calls for survivability measures such as hardened silos, mobile launchers, deployment beyond the reach of hostile delivery systems, dispersion of the arsenal on a triad, and a pre-determined chain of succession, including alternative ones, for the weapon release authority. Reliability of the delivery vectors is critical for deterrence credibility. This includes dependability of communication (that the correct message is delivered at the right time for launch) and reliability of launch (that the missile actually lifts off); of the booster (that it ignites in time); of separation (of the booster from the missile after burn out); of penetration (despite enemy air defence systems); and of detonation at the designated target.

While each of these requires technological sophistication, fortunately, deterrence is dependent more on mind and perception management, to convey the idea of nuclear damage, than inflicting the damage itself. The requirement of numbers, therefore, is tempered by the nature of the deterrence being envisaged by India.

No First Use (NFU)

The second clause of the 'official' nuclear doctrine refers to 'a posture of no first use'. It clearly states that nuclear weapons 'will only be used in retaliation against a nuclear attack on Indian territory or on Indian forces anywhere'. This stance, yet again, derives from the unique Indian approach that considers nuclear weapons useless for fighting a war. Therefore, India has opted to free itself of the decision of having to use the weapon first. It seeks to deter the use of the weapon by threatening retaliation of a kind that would wreak intolerable damage. This view has been criticized by military strategists at home for adopting a pacifist position and ceding the initiative to the adversary. Meanwhile, strategic analysts have dismissed it for being declaratory and hypocritical. Unfortunately, the military logic of NFU and the strategic sense underpinning it have never been adequately understood or explained.

According to a well-known American military strategist, Barry Posen, 'A military organization prefers to fight its own war and prevent its adversary from doing so ... An organization fighting the war it planned is likely to do better than one that is not.'[4] This is because offence allows the military to stay with its pre-deliberated course of action while denying the adversary the advantage of being able to play his moves. With conventional weapons, it is possible for the armed forces to stick to their standard operating procedures (SOPs), choose the time and place of action, thereby increasing the chance of their victory, or reducing the damage of war on themselves.

This equation, however, gets skewed with the entry of nuclear weapons. In a situation where both sides have secure counter-strike capabilities, even if not the ability to cause mutual assured destruction, a nuclear first strike, however splendid it might be, cannot rule out nuclear retaliation. Hence, the calculation of the first user cannot be limited to the damage caused by its first strike, but must also take into account the damage that it will suffer from the adversary's response. Therefore, an offensive nuclear strategy can neither assure victory nor promise no nuclear damage to self. And, given the nature of the weapon whose effect transcends space and time, no rational government can brook such nuclear damage as acceptable.

This logic prompted India to accept NFU as a doctrinal principle. Some have argued that India was trying to earn brownie points or blunt international opprobrium when it accepted NFU. This is not true. These might have come along as incidental collateral benefits of the NFU doctrine, but it was the military logic that held sway over a majority of the NSAB members.[5] They discussed the issue at length and found many advantages of NFU. But, before discussing these, it would be worthwhile to examine two scenarios in which it is believed India might be tempted to use nuclear weapons first.

One such situation is visualized in the context of a conflict with China. In a hypothetical scenario, if India was facing the prospect of conventional defeat, it is assumed that it might be tempted to use nuclear weapons. But the question that needs to be answered is: how would India gain by using the nuclear weapon? In fact, once it has done so, its fate would shift from being defeated-now-but-living-to-fight-another-day to one of severe damage/annihilation since China would certainly respond with nuclear weapons too.

Jonathan Schell, American author and campaigner against nuclear weapons, explained this dilemma well when he questioned, 'For how can it make sense to "save" one's country by blowing it to pieces? And what logic is there in staving off a limited defeat by bringing on unlimited, eternal defeat? Nuclear deterrence is like a gun with two barrels, of which one points ahead and the other points back at the gun's holder.'[6] Robert McNamara, former US secretary of defence, made a similar argument based on his experience of more than forty years of making and overseeing nuclear war plans. He wrote, 'During that time [when in office], I have never seen a piece of paper that outlined a plan for the United States or the North Atlantic Treaty Organization to initiate the use of nuclear weapons with any benefit for the United States or NATO ... To launch weapons against a nuclear-equipped opponent would be suicidal.'[7]

Indeed, there is no way to effectively contain a nuclear strike and there can be no guarantee against unlimited escalation once the first nuclear use/strike occurs. Therefore, India would not have defended itself even after using the nuclear weapons first. It might have the satisfaction of having wrought nuclear damage on the adversary, but it would also carry the guilt of having brought a nuclear strike upon itself.

A second scenario revolves around the question of whether India should stick to NFU if it learns that the adversary is preparing for a nuclear strike. Should nuclear pre-emption then not be the right step? The answer to this lies in understanding that even preparation is no guarantee of nuclear strike. Rather, it may well be part of a strategy of 'coercive diplomacy.' It is not a coincidence that nearly all of the more than fifty incidents of the threat of use of nuclear weapons so far have actually intended coercion.[8] Despite the apparent show of readiness, there could still be a chance that the adversary does not actually fire the weapon. A country, even with a first use doctrine, may or may not use its nuclear weapons despite projected preparedness. But after having been struck, and where the first strike has not been disarming or decapitating (which is well-nigh impossible with the kinds of arsenals that nuclear states today have), retaliation would be a certainty.

Therefore, under neither of these circumstances does it seem to make sense to use nuclear weapons first. In fact, the act of using nuclear weapons first is not as easy as it is believed to be, since the first user has to take into account not just what would happen in the first phase of war, but also how it would proceed, and end scenarios which are not easy to coherently contemplate in the presence of robust retaliatory capability. Hence, even countries with a first use strategy find it very difficult to actually credibly execute it. Rather, the idea appears politically limiting. This is a thought worth considering since conventional wisdom contends that first use is more liberating compared to a counter-strike strategy. But serious thought to the actual execution of first use reveals the complexities involved in doing so. After all, the purpose of first use should be to convey deterrence through communicating four essential messages:

1. I will not hesitate to use the weapon first.
2. By doing so, I would be able to substantively improve my situation.
3. My first strike will interfere with and degrade your second strike capability.
4. I will be able to come out of the crisis looking better after the use of the nuclear weapon than without its use.

The credibility of this communication, however, is seriously jeopardized if the adversary has a survivable nuclear force. Retaliation, in that case, complicates the calculations of the first user regarding how it could 'look better' after suffering nuclear damage to itself. As graphically explained by a strategist, 'Engaging in a nuclear war with a nation with whom one is in a condition of mutual vulnerability would be like running a red light across a high-speed, heavily travelled, multilane highway under conditions of near-zero visibility. One might make it safely across, but one could not form a reasonable expectation that one would.'[9]

Therefore, the essential question that the first striker has to consider is whether in a state of mutual vulnerability, he could emerge in a better position against one who can retaliate. On the other hand, the messages that an NFU state must convey credibly are:

1. I will not be the first to use nuclear weapons.
2. But any first strike or first use (irrespective of yield, target or extent of damage) would trigger assured retaliation to cause damage of a kind that would be found unacceptable.
3. My counter strike will ensure that your material situation is worse off after your having used the weapon first.
4. I might suffer losses, but you will not escape either and you would have brought it upon yourself. The choice, therefore, is yours to make.

As is clear from the above, NFU bravely concedes the onus of escalation to the adversary. But in doing so, it actually liberates itself in many ways. For one, it is beneficial from the point of view of nuclear arsenal requirements. First strike postures based on the projection of nuclear war fighting require large arsenals of first strike weapons (such as accurate missiles with multiple independently re-targetable vehicles); nuclear superiority to carry out counter-force attacks against an adversary's retaliatory forces; and elaborate and delegated command and control structures to handle launch on warning or launch under attack postures, or to launch simultaneous nuclear attacks from and over dispersed forces. NFU, on the other hand, requires nuclear forces that have ensured survivability through a mix of measures that include hardening of nuclear storage sites, deception, mobility, dispersal over different delivery vectors, and a level of defence. The core of this strategy lies in projecting the invulnerability of a sufficient part of the arsenal to even a worst-case first strike, and a near automaticity of retaliation to cause damage that the adversary is unlikely to find acceptable vis-à-vis the gains made.

Secondly, the NFU is liberating from the point of view of military command and control. It allows the military to adopt a more relaxed position rather than straining at the nuclear leash in a hair-trigger alert posture that can easily fall prey to misperceptions. Moreover, it does not have to perfect the logistics of a meaningful first strike, which would involve coordinating a nuclear attack on a diversified arsenal with speed and surprise to hit the adversary's forces before they can be launched or dispersed. It involves addressing complicated questions such as whether to launch aircraft first or missiles, how many to launch in the first wave, and so on. A credible first strike requires forward deployment of nuclear forces, which increases the likelihood of accidental or unauthorized use. LOW (Launch on Warning) / LUA (Launch under Attack) postures require pre-delegation of authority to launch nuclear weapons and this can never be a risk-free option. Responsible command and control is not easy to enforce at each level, given that, in times of crisis, lack of information, misinformation and misjudgements could become causes of confrontation without either side having the intention to precipitate one. McNamara once said, 'It is correct to say that no well-informed, coolly rational political or military leader is likely to initiate the use of nuclear weapons. But political and military leaders, in moments of severe crisis, are likely to be neither well-informed nor coolly rational.'[10] NFU eases this dilemma.

Ironically, this becomes liberating for the adversary too, which, paradoxically, is beneficial to the self. NFU alleviates the adversary's insecurity by relieving pressure on launching a pre-emptive strike. If the adversary were constantly under fear that a nuclear strike was imminent, his own temptation to use his nuclear force would be higher. But NFU helps to mitigate the 'use or lose' pressure and thereby lessens the potential for crisis since it sends a message that does not place the adversary on edge at all time.

Finally, NFU frees the political leadership from the psychological pressure of taking the difficult decision of using a WMD. This is sure to weigh on him/her personally for the damage caused and for the international opprobrium for having breached a nuclear taboo. And, to top it all, to do so in the knowledge that one's own vulnerability to retaliation can yet not be escaped. Therefore, rather than retaining the first use/strike option, it would be better to deter by threatening assured retaliation. Deterrence is, in fact, the only real defence against nuclear weapons.

In view of all of the above, NFU appears far more sensible and credible. While a country would find it very difficult to use the weapon first, the decision to retaliate would be far easier, seemingly legitimate and more guilt-free to make. In fact, by projecting assured retaliation, a nation displays greater confidence, and hence greater deterrence credibility. And by establishing the nuclear weapon as an instrument of punishment through retaliation, the country lessens the possibility of deterrence breakdown, and thus minimizes, if not prevents, the very use of nuclear weapons. NFU actually encourages the possibility of 'no use' instead of 'sure use'. This is clearly demonstrated in the following table.[11]

Nuclear Posture, Country 1	Nuclear Posture, Country 2	Nuclear Threshold	Chance of Nuclear War
First Use	First Use	Low	Very High
No First Use	No First Use	High	Very Low/Nil
First Use	No First Use	Relatively High	Relatively Low

Evidently, then, through NFU coupled with assured retaliation, a country can rein in the initiative in favour of no use of nuclear weapons. Unless the adversary is completely irrational, has suicidal tendencies or is utterly unmindful of national survival and international public opinion, the possibility of a nuclear war should not arise.

Operationalization of Nuclear Strategy

While the Indian nuclear doctrine is propounded on sound logic, aspects of its operationalization into a credible deterrent strategy still require some pieces to be built, further improved or effectively communicated. Such a strategy must be built on the three pillars of capability, resolve and communication. The following paragraphs identify the developments as well as the milestones yet to be achieved.

Capability Build-up

While CMD requires India to build an arsenal sufficient to inflict damage that is thought to be deemed unacceptable by the adversary, NFU imposes the requirement of building this number and capability in a manner that ensures retaliation after absorbing a first strike. For effective deterrence, therefore, a certain amount of nuclear hardware—nuclear warheads and delivery vectors—is critical. The five nuclear tests in 1998 have equipped India with the capability to build a range of nuclear weapons—from sub-kiloton to thermonuclear. India's nuclear doctrine, however, has eschewed the need for the first kind, commonly referred to as tactical or battlefield nuclear weapons, since India does not believe that nuclear wars are fightable for any rational gains. India conveys deterrence through the threat, nay promise, of punishment through assured retaliation. Therefore, the doctrine makes it clear that the adversary's use of any type of nuclear weapon would be met with a punishing response.

To credibly support this response, delivery vectors of adequate ranges and reliability are required. Efforts have been visible in the development and gradual deployment of a number of land-based ballistic missiles to fulfil this role. Short-range Prithvi and intermediate-range Agni variants are already operational. Graduating to the next level, long-range, cannisterized Agni V missiles are likely to become operational by 2020. This would enhance India's deterrence, especially vis-à-vis China. However, work on other technological capabilities is necessary to further the cause of credible deterrence.

The most urgent pending task is the operationalization of the sea-based leg of India's nuclear triad. While mobility is an important advantage of land-based missiles, and most Indian missiles are rail and road mobile, the highest level of survivability lies in placing nuclear-tipped missiles with sufficient ranges on nuclear-powered submarines (SSBNs). This is the most survivable of the three delivery vectors, and hence the projection of credible deterrence is best achieved through SSBNs carrying submarine-launched ballistic missiles (SLBMs) of adequate ranges. INS *Arihant*, India's first SSBN, currently undergoing rigorous sea trials, marks but the start of what will be a long journey towards building an operational SSBN force. While more boats are planned, India is still lagging in the range of the SLBMs. What have been tested so far—and that too from underwater pontoons, not submarines—are the K-15 with a range of 700-750 km and, in March 2014, the K-4 with a range of 2,000 km.[12] These ranges are insufficient for credible deterrence against China. The missiles have to go up to at least 5,000 km and more to reach targets whose loss would be deemed unacceptable by Beijing while India's own platforms stay out of harm's way. A submarine-launched version of Agni V should be the next technological milestone in service of credible deterrence.

Secondly, focus has to be retained on improving the penetrability of Indian missiles. Given China's BMD, though currently of limited capability, Indian missiles will have to be equipped with countermeasures to evade interception in order to convey the capacity to cause unacceptable damage. Development of multiple re-entry vehicles (MRVs), which hit the same target with many bombs, and manoeuvrable re-entry vehicles (MaRV) that can drastically change trajectory to evade interception in the terminal stage, are capabilities that will help in buttressing deterrence. Meanwhile, MIRVed (multiple independently targetable re-entry vehicles) technology that allows independently targetable warheads on the same missile need not be an immediate priority. MIRVed missiles have essentially been seen as first-strike weapons and do not find a place in India's NFU strategy. However, given the trend towards this development in the region, India would be prudent to keep options open while it focuses on other more urgent tasks towards enhancing the credibility of deterrence. Alternatively, it may also be wise to engage in nuclear arms control to cap the deployment of MIRVed missiles.

Another technology of concern is the BMD. India has repeatedly conducted successful interceptions in the endo- and exo-atmosphere on the basis of which the DRDO maintains that a missile shield is ready to be deployed over Delhi and Mumbai. As the government now contemplates sites for BMD deployment, it must consider how this capability can best serve the nuclear strategy, given the complex missile threat environment that it has to function in. China currently has the biggest arsenal after the US and Russia. The DF-21s, which are the medium-range ballistic missiles of relevance to India, have reportedly increased from about twenty in 2005 to nearly four times that figure today. More than a thousand conventional or nuclear-capable short-range ballistic missiles are reportedly deployed. China has also paid particular attention to improvements in the penetrability of missiles to breach US BMD, and its missiles are known to have not only simple countermeasures but also the capability to launch MIRVed and MaRVed missiles to evade interception.

Pakistan too has been regularly conducting tests of either its very-short-range missile Nasr (60 km), the short-range Abdali (350 km), the cruise missiles Babur or Ra'ad, and the long-range Shaheen 1 and 2.

In the face of such threats, how can India best employ its BMD? The answer lies in using the capability intelligently not for the defence of individual cities but to use it for strengthening India's nuclear deterrence. This essentially means deployment of BMD for the protection of nuclear command and control centres, or missile/nuclear warhead storage sites and so on as a first step. This will communicate the certainty of retaliation to the adversary and add weight to India's NFU commitment by conveying confidence in the survivability of its own nuclear capability. This would, in turn, help in reducing pressure on the adversary to use its nuclear weapons quickly lest it loses them to an Indian attack. Above all, BMD on retaliatory assets would credibly convey that any use of the nuclear weapon against India will not go unanswered and result in unacceptable damage. In the process, India would end up protecting the entire country rather than just Delhi and Mumbai.

Political Resolve

The actual use of the nuclear weapon is a political decision. Therefore, for deterrence to be credible, evidence of political will, including through an organizational set-up reflecting institutional decision-making is crucial. There is a dire need for conducting periodic scenario-building exercises and regular threat assessments to equip the political leadership with the requisite understanding of how to play the sophisticated game of nuclear deterrence.

From the messages that emerge from Pakistan, it seems that it believes that its nuclear weapons have obviated the possibility of a conventional Indo-Pak war because India would never have the motivation or the will to initiate such a war owing to the fear of escalation. In making such an assumption, Pakistan does not doubt India's capability but its resolve to use it. To address this supposition, two issues beg consideration from India. One, communication of political will to punish when acts of terrorism or transgressions occur, and, secondly, communication of a kind of retaliation that appears credible.

Communication and Signalling

Indeed, the most important pillar of the credibility of deterrence is communication. Building a nuclear capability is meaningless if the adversary does not know about it, misreads it, or if it doubts the resolve to put it to use. It is critical, therefore, to convey a coherent and consistent message so that the adversary does not premise his own nuclear strategy on mistaken assumptions.

Fortunately, the communication of resolve can be displayed across a range of issues. In fact, the resolve does not have to be conveyed through the conduct of a conventional or nuclear war. That would be foolish. But its evidence on issues as varied as stringent law and order enforcement at home, firmness in policymaking and pursuit of inter-state relations, and zero tolerance for terrorism can effectively convey determination. More specific to the nuclear domain could be actions such as providing information on the regular meetings of the Political Council of the Nuclear Command Authority to consider India's threat environment, or on the conduct of military war games envisaging the use of nuclear weapons by the adversary and their successful neutralization.

The second aspect of communication relates to the credibility of the kind of punishment that the adversary is being threatened with. The NSAB draft doctrine had qualified retaliation as 'assured punitive'. But the 2003 CCS note changed this to 'massive retaliation'. Coming in the aftermath of the long mobilization of Operation Parakram that achieved little by way of India's objective of getting Pakistan to give up terrorism, and following the delineation of vague, ambiguous but very low redlines by Pakistan,[13] it was felt that the use of the term 'massive' would better deter Pakistan from contemplating easy or early use of nuclear weapons since India's response would be suicidal for it.

However, the change of language has come in for criticism from within the country and from across the border for failing to enhance the credibility of deterrence. It has been argued that during the Cold War, even after building the kind of stockpile the US did, it gave up massive retaliation as an incredible strategy. In the Indo-Pak context, it has been questioned whether India would undertake massive retaliation in response to Pakistan's use of low-yield nuclear weapons in the battlefield. The general assumption is that a small sub-kiloton weapon used over counter-force targets would not elicit a nuclear response from India, which would come under pressure to refrain from escalation.

This argument, however, shows a lack of understanding of nuclear terminologies. The CCS note of 2003 clearly states: 'Nuclear retaliation to a first strike will be massive and designed to inflict unacceptable damage.' A first strike, as different from first use, amounts to a large-scale use of nuclear weapons with the intention of taking out retaliatory assets. In response to this kind of an attack, how can India's retaliation be anything less than massive? So there is no dichotomy here.

A related issue of concern is the type of response from India to the use of tactical nuclear weapons (TNWs). At the time that the doctrine was enunciated, this capability had yet to enter the India–Pakistan nuclear equation and hence there is no explicit mention of this. Nevertheless, the message that any use of a 'nuclear' weapon would evoke retaliation is loud and clear. In the case of TNW use, the Indian leadership could well decide the type and extent of retaliation, but there is no doubt that it would be assured and punitive. Therefore, the onus of using nuclear weapons first, and the choice of kind of use (small or large), has been left to the adversary. India promises retaliation. But, in order to enhance deterrence, India would do well to focus on improving the expression of resolve for a counter strike to cause disproportionate loss to the adversary. It must convey that it may not climb the escalation ladder one step at a time. Just as Pakistan claims that there is a one-rung escalation ladder that would move from India's conventional response to a nuclear riposte, India should communicate that it too has a one-rung ladder that would take nuclear use (in battlefield or otherwise) to a nuclear retaliation resulting in substantial damage.

For this message to carry weight, it is important that there is greater transparency of the military dimension of nuclear command and control, including redundancies that assure automaticity of nuclear response. This could be done by strengthening the public profile of the Strategic Forces Command (SFC). The knowledge of the existence of this tri-service organization and a calibrated transparency would send a signal of intent and purpose to the adversary. As said by an analyst, 'It makes no sense to surprise an opponent with unanticipated retaliation when a clear signal could have deterred unwanted activity in the first place.'[14]

Therefore, indications of measures being taken to ensure the survivability of the chain of command at the primary, secondary and even tertiary levels would be prudent.

Lastly, it must be mentioned that the Indian nuclear doctrine begins and ends with the aspiration for a nuclear weapons–free world (NWFW). This is not mere rhetoric but the indication of a deep-rooted belief that nuclear weapons are dispensable as long as it happens as part of a universal, verifiable process. India moved towards nuclear weapons reluctantly, and despite their possession continues to maintain that its security interests, besides the larger cause of morality and humanitarianism, would be better served through their elimination. In an NWFW, India can be regionally more secure—free from the Pakistani use of terrorism from behind the shield of the nuclear weapon, from the threat of nuclear coercion or blackmail from China, and from the China–Pakistan nuclear collusion. However, until such a world can be realized, India's unique brand of nuclear deterrence premised on a small arsenal that is not on hair-trigger alert but geared towards assured punitive response adequately provides for the country's defence.

Recommendations for India's Nuclear Strategy

1. CMD and NFU are built on sound logic and must be retained and upheld. In fact, sticking with these in the face of the development of sophisticated technologies and the emergence of vested interests of military and departmental turf wars will be the real challenge for India in the years ahead. The understanding, therefore, that CMD and NFU provide credible deterrence in a most cost-effective and stable manner will be critical.
2. Further capability build-up is necessary on the following fronts:
   a. Quick operationalization of Agni IV and V.
   b. Full operationalization of the sea-based leg of the triad with the construction and induction of more SSBNs.
   c. Range enhancement of SLBMs.
   d. Optimal utilization of BMD for the protection of nuclear retaliatory assets rather than over cities. The guarantee of retaliation through the evidence of survivability of the arsenal is the key to deterrence as much as the knowledge of each other's vulnerability to nuclear damage.

e. Development and induction of MaRVed missiles to defeat the adversary's BMD is more a priority than the development and deployment of MIRVed missiles. The latter may, in fact, be counter-productive for deterrence stability.

3. Display of resolve through calibrated transparency and better signalling—occasional statements by relevant officials, knowledge of existence of SFC and its fast-evolving capabilities to fulfil its mandate, knowledge of conduct of war games that take the nuclear scenarios into account, and more.
4. Remain open to opportunities for confidence-building and arms control measures with nuclear-armed adversaries. BMD, MIRVed missiles and doctrinal transparency may be considered amongst the first candidates for such measures.
5. Continue to support/suggest initiatives in the pursuit of an NWFW.

8

Managing External Threats

Kanwal Sibal

Former Foreign Secretary and India's Ambassador to Russia and France

Two-Front Threat

The external threats to India's security must be properly identified before a clear national strategy to deal with them can be forged. We have two nation states on our borders that claim our territory, and both are nuclear and cooperate together strategically to contain us. This makes our security environment almost unique. Pakistan is unrelenting in its hostility towards India despite radical changes in the international environment. It has deployed the arm of terrorism against us for decades with impunity. We have to contend with growing Chinese power in our other neighbouring countries, which court China to balance India's overwhelming weight in the subcontinent. China is becoming successful in gaining access to the Indian Ocean through Pakistan and Myanmar, adding to India's concerns about being strategically encircled. The spread of extremist Islamic forces in West Asia, coupled with the increased radicalization of Pakistan and the resurgence of the Taliban in Afghanistan, puts pressures on India's multi-religious society, with implications for our internal security. India's energy, manpower and financial interests in the Gulf need to be protected against various forms of instabilities and sectarian rivalries in the region.

A state must, before all else, protect its borders and its territorial integrity against external threats. India faces a distinct challenge in this regard. Most major countries have settled borders, but almost our entire northern border with Tibet is unsettled, while with Pakistan we have a Line of Control (LoC) in Jammu and Kashmir (J&K) and not an accepted border. Worse for us, China and Pakistan, the two countries which occupy Indian territory and claim more of it, are strengthening their strategic collaboration to our detriment.

To face this double threat, our defence capabilities have to be scaled up appropriately. We have to be prepared in principle for a two-front conflict, which imposes a singular burden on us. China has become the world's second largest economy and is developing its all-round military capacities with its growing financial resources. Its annual outlays on defence are increasing; it is developing advanced platforms and technologies. Conscious of its growing economic and military power, it is becoming more assertive in its territorial claims in the western Pacific, occupying and undertaking reclamation works on reefs in the South China Sea. It is adopting this rather aggressive posture in the face of US power in the region.

In the case of India too, China has become more provocative in its claims on Arunachal Pradesh, despite the several bilateral confidence-building and border management agreements and the establishment of the special representatives (SR) mechanism to resolve border differences. It has begun to refer to Arunachal Pradesh as 'South Tibet'. It has thus effectively hollowed out the purpose of the SR mechanism by amplifying its territorial claims. It has developed its military infrastructure in Tibet dramatically, far more than would be necessary to control Tibet, considering that for decades the Dalai Lama has proved his commitment to non-violence and, unlike in the case of the Uighurs in East Turkestan, the Tibetans are not committing violence against Chinese authorities. In other ways too, it is unilaterally consolidating its territorial claims, as, for instance, by shortening the length of the India–Tibet border, issuing stapled visas to those from Arunachal Pradesh, affixing revised maps of China's borders on newly issued Chinese passports that show large parts of India as Chinese territory and distributing them to the People's Liberation Army (PLA).

It is true that despite the unsettled border, strident Chinese territorial claims and military deployments on both sides, no violent incident has occurred on the border for several decades. Both sides have placed emphasis on maintaining peace and tranquillity, confidence-building measures (CBMs), procedures to follow when patrols come face to face, more elaborate border management agreements, additional meetings between area commanders and the like. All these steps reduce the threat of violence but do not altogether remove it. India has to constantly work on improving its military position on the ground by raising more units, acquiring better equipment and building improved infrastructure to match the capacities China has developed.

The irony is that no peace dividend is available to the Indian side from all these CBMs and improved border management accords. The 1993, 1996, 2005 and 2013 agreements have not reduced bilateral mistrust and the defence burden on India. The decision to raise two mountain divisions, a strike corps and an independent mountain brigade is the fruit not of enhanced confidence in China but uncertainty about its medium- to long-term intentions. We have stationed our front-line aircraft in the east and opened up advanced landing grounds in the north, all indications of increased military preparedness. Our strategic programmes, especially the development of Agni missiles and enhanced undersea capabilities, are directed at countering the Chinese threat. China, however, has already developed impressive military capabilities for countering US power, which can simultaneously address the challenge of steadily increasing Indian military strength at the strategic level. But at the local level on the Tibetan border, the disparity in strength is being narrowed.

Resolution of the Territorial Dispute

When borders between two major countries remain contested; one side makes expansive claims; frequent intrusions take place into pockets of disputed areas; and military preparations to gain local advantage continue, the latent danger of an actual flare-up remains real. By defining the Line of Actual Control (LAC) on the ground, this danger can be reduced considerably, though without a finally settled border, India's compulsion to strengthen its defensive capabilities on the border will remain. The Depsang incident of May 2013 and Chinese intrusion into Chumar in Ladakh during the official visit of Chinese president Xi Jinping to India in September 2014 are reminders of the perils of the present situation, which cannot be eliminated entirely by entering into yet more agreements on border management.

The SR mechanism has not produced any significant result since it was set up in 2003. The Chinese side essentially repudiated its mandate by subsequently enlarging its claims in the east and affirming them aggressively, objecting to visits by the prime minister and other leaders to

Arunachal Pradesh and opposing even small development projects there, financed by international financial institutions. If its commitment to the SR mechanism was genuine, the Chinese side should have worked to lower territorial tensions during the period of negotiations and not stoke them by becoming more emphatic in its claims and staging incidents in Ladakh. If its forceful claims are intended to intimidate or bully India, that would be a commentary on China's approach to its relations with India. Eighteen rounds of SR talks have been held to date without China budging from its position that India must cede vitally strategic areas in the east that are actually not under China's control, and which would involve transfer of populated areas, contrary to the guiding principles and parameters agreed to in 2005 on resolving the border issue.

In assessing the Chinese threat to us, we must take into account the import of statements by its president about China's determination not to make any concession on territorial issues, and its aggressive conduct in the South China Sea and East China Sea on territorial and maritime boundary issues. China is cognizant of US power and its defence commitments to countries threatened by China's claims and actions, but this is not deterring it from adopting these defiant postures. This has lessons for us. If China is pursuing a more muscled strategy in the western Pacific compared to its less confrontational approach towards India for the present, it may be for several reasons.

They may want to avoid opening up two fronts at the same time or push India into either joining the US rebalance towards Asia more decisively, or into strengthening military ties with Japan and Australia as well. They might also be wary of the consequences of mounting tensions with India on the Tibetan question. Under cover of engagement with us, they have made important strategic inroads into our neighbourhood, where they may not want to be challenged more frontally by us. India has, in fact, been put in a situation where it cannot object to improved relations between its neighbours and China when it itself is seen pursuing a similar objective. The more China succeeds strategically in the western Pacific, the more potent the strategic threat from China to us will become. Our defence planning has to take cognizance of this. An India–China rapprochement can change the geopolitics of Asia and beyond, but this does not seem to be part of China's long-term vision of its international role. We have to live with this reality.

China's rising power affects all its neighbours, but for India it has implications of its own. The US as the world's foremost economic and military power has sufficient capacity to deal with China's rise, even if it loses some ground. Its naval deployments close to China's coasts are formidable; it has military alliances and bases in the region. The US is exercising extended power in the western Pacific, far away from its own shores, as part of its global dominance. Japan is a formidable economic power and possesses strong and capable armed forces, but, as a non-nuclear power, it is dependent for its security on the US. The South-East Asian countries are too small individually to stand up to China. Some are allied to the US, while others protect their security interests through the structures of the Association of South East Asian Nations (ASEAN) and involvement of outside powers, including India, to balance China's influence.

India is uniquely placed as, unlike the US, it is a direct neighbour of China. It is the only other large country in Asia that can genuinely balance China in the Asian political and security structures. Empirically, India's rise, even if delayed, will counter Chinese hegemony in Asia. However, the economic and military gap between the two has grown over the years, giving China greater resources and confidence to handle India in the years ahead. India is not a member of any military alliance and has to face Chinese power on its own. Its historical attachment to non-alignment and the continuation of the spirit of independence in the making of foreign policy, rooted in its democratic politics, account for this reality.

With the strengthening of the Russia–China relationship, supply of advanced Russian weaponry to China, growing economic linkages between the two countries, and the change of power equations between them increasingly in favour of China, India's position becomes even more vulnerable in the case of rising India–China tensions. India may not be able to count on Russian support as Russia–China ties have become considerably stronger than India–Russia ties. That India and Russia have a close political understanding and a history of mutual confidence will not be enough to draw Russia on our side in any confrontation with China. US/NATO (North Atlantic Treaty Organization) pressure on Russia, the policy of sanctions and the demonization of the ruling Russian political class headed by President Vladimir Putin are being balanced by the Kremlin through the exercise of its eastwards option. The strategic stakes for Russia in its China relationship because of the revival of Cold War policies against it by the West have clear implications for us.

So far, India's strategy has been to keep the border situation under control through CBMs, continuing negotiations on resolving the border issue, not allowing differences over the border to block the rest of the relationship, and leveraging China's economic rise to India's advantage wherever possible by trading more with China, allowing Chinese companies openings in our power and telecommunication sectors despite security concerns, and attracting Chinese investment in improving India's poor infrastructure, especially in railways and in industrial parks. Simultaneously, the approach has been to downplay incidents on the border, avoid responding to China's provocative statements on Arunachal Pradesh and respect Chinese sensitivities over Tibet. This strategy has given China the upper hand in all aspects of the relationship, with no incentive to change its position on the territorial issue, even though China's claims on us stem from its occupation of Tibet against the wishes of the Tibetan people who contest the occupation.

Managing the China–Pakistan Collusion

Beyond its own capacities to pressure India militarily, China has vitally damaged Indian security by transferring nuclear and missile technologies to Pakistan, India's congenital adversary. Pakistan too claims Indian territory in J&K, just as China occupies a sizeable chunk of it in Ladakh. Whereas China pursues a strategy of avoiding military incidents on the border that could cause casualties, Pakistan has actively sought to disturb the status quo by direct military aggression, infiltration of terrorists, ceasefire violations, inciting violence in J&K through its proxies, and encouraging separatists in J&K to keep the situation continually on the boil politically.

Pakistan is using the instrument of terror against India as state policy. It declares openly its 'political, moral and diplomatic' support to 'freedom fighters' in J&K, seeks external intervention on its behalf against India, constantly targets India at international forums and at the Organization of Islamic Cooperation (OIC), besides using the Islamic card to interfere in our political relations with other Islamic countries. In doing all this, Pakistan's conduct differs from China's. China keeps its doors open to India but exploits Pakistan's animosity towards India to serve its larger strategic ends: to impede the rise of India and the expansion of its regional power.

China's strategy is to encourage Pakistan in its confrontational policies with India by giving it vital political, military and moral support, even on the issue of terrorism. China's recent decision to block a United Nations Security Council inquiry into the financial arrangements to obtain bail for the mastermind of the 2008 Mumbai terrorist attacks, Zakiur Rehman Lakhvi, is evidence of this. Prime Minister Narendra Modi raised this issue with the Chinese president at the BRICS (Brazil, Russia, India, China, South Africa) summit at Ufa in Russia in 2015, with a parrying response by the latter. The Chinese spokesperson subsequently reaffirmed support for Pakistan. The Chinese special envoy to Afghanistan too dismissed the charges against the Pakistani Inter-Services Intelligence (ISI) for its truck with terrorism.

China bolsters Pakistan's position on J&K by insidiously questioning India's sovereignty over the state in various ways, including by denying a proper visa to our army commander there even when he was to travel to China for official defence-level talks. While it opposes any assistance from international financial institutions to projects in Arunachal Pradesh because it is 'disputed' territory, it is engaged in major strategic and other projects in Pakistan-Occupied Kashmir (POK), even though Pakistan harps that Kashmir is 'disputed' territory whose sovereignty should be decided through a plebiscite in accordance with relevant UN resolutions. The announcement by China and Pakistan of the highly strategic China–Pakistan economic corridor that would link East Turkestan with Gwadar is not possible without traversing territory that is legally Indian and recognized as legally unsettled even in the 1963 China–Pakistan border agreement. India needs to step up its political opposition to this project that will potentially strengthen the China–Pakistan nexus enormously, cut off India from Afghanistan and Central Asia even more, make China a third party in the resolution of the Kashmir issue, and further erode our claim to POK while leaving open the legal position of the part of the state under our jurisdiction.

It suits China to have India bogged down in a simmering conflict with Pakistan. Our military's preoccupation with Pakistan makes us exceedingly cautious towards China to avoid two-front pressures. Pakistan's hostility towards India also keeps the South Asian Association for Regional Cooperation (SAARC) weak and prevents India from consolidating SAARC under Indian leadership, besides preventing it from playing any significant role in Central Asia, which is a situation that also suits China's interests. Even if we become stronger militarily, we will not have a solution to easier connectivity to Central Asia or greater cohesion of SAARC. This will ultimately depend on the scale and rapidity of India's economic rise and Pakistan's political evolution towards a more normal country.

Pakistan has leveraged its nuclear capability to use its terrorist arm against India, dramatized by the brazen Mumbai attacks in 2008. Exposed by their enormity and the incontestable link with Pakistan, its agencies have been cautious since then not to engineer any massive acts of terrorism against India for fear of reprisals, but it has found every procedural ground not to try those involved in the Mumbai attacks despite Indian and international exhortations. It has not dismantled the India-related terrorist infrastructure in the country and, indeed, continues to nurture it as an asset to be used in future contingencies. India has not found an effective answer to Pakistan's strategy of terror. It hesitates to retaliate militarily because of the risks of escalation, especially as Pakistan has acquired nuclear weaponry. Pakistan has calculated that limited activity on the LoC and on the terrorism front will not provoke an Indian military strike inside Pakistani territory. Should a major terrorist attack compel India to think of a limited but potent strike across the border, Pakistan is threatening to retaliate with the use of tactical nuclear weapons. The so-called 'Cold Start' doctrine of the Indian Army has been hyped up by Pakistan to justify the development of tactical nuclear weapons, lowering in the process the threshold of its use of nuclear weapons against India.

Despite its loud non-proliferation rhetoric, imposition of sanctions against countries suspected of developing nuclear capabilities and even recourse to military strikes, the West has adopted a complacent attitude towards Pakistan's nuclear activities, its stated readiness to use nuclear weapons against India, the rapid expansion of its nuclear arsenal, its obstructionism in Geneva on the Fissile Material Cut-off Treaty negotiations and so on. Pakistan's aggressive conduct in stoking tensions with India is actually used by Western non-proliferation lobbies to create scare scenarios of a nuclear stand-off in the Indian subcontinent and lobby for imposing nuclear restraints on India by calling for strategic stability in the region. While India is not hampered in steadily developing its credible minimum nuclear deterrent by external pressures, its security situation is not helped because of the lack of any pressure on Pakistan's adventurist nuclear policies.

Despite rising international concerns about the increasing radicalization of Pakistani society; the proliferation of jihadi groups, many nurtured by the Pakistan state itself, and the spread of terrorism within the country because of the general deterioration of internal conditions; sectarian conflicts; and the compulsion to cooperate with the US to exercise some control over terrorism from Pakistani soil targeting Afghanistan, Pakistan is escaping real pressure from the West on its nuclear policies. While the West, led by the US, has put enormous pressure on Iran on the nuclear question, even threatening military action and, indeed, suffocating Iran financially through stringent sanctions, Pakistan is being treated benignly.

Some Western think-tank elements have begun advocating a nuclear deal with Pakistan on the lines of the agreement with India, indicating a strong nuclear bias in favour of Pakistan for political reasons. China has, of course, given Pakistan a nuclear deal of its own to parallel the one given by the US to India, without the restrictions the US has imposed on India as part of the nuclear deal. It is buttressing Pakistan's nuclear capability in violation of its Nuclear Suppliers Group (NSG) obligations, without any visible opposition from the US. The high level of international tolerance of Pakistan's nuclear policies suggests that considerations of checkmating India strategically and creating a nuclear balance in the subcontinent are not absent from the calculations of even some of our 'strategic partners'.

Pakistan apart, the external threats to our security are compounded by Chinese inroads into other countries in our neighbourhood—Nepal, Bangladesh, Sri Lanka and the Maldives. These countries play the Chinese card against us in varying degrees. They continue to be wooed by the

Chinese politically, economically and even militarily at the cost of our interests. A more muscular approach by us would invite accusations of hegemony and could push them even further into the arms of China. We have an open border with Nepal; the development of road and rail links across Tibet to the Nepal border by China will thus raise new security challenges for us. The Chinese presence encourages the traditional anti-Indian forces in Nepal to continue breeding a sense of alienation towards India. China has already made strong inroads into Myanmar, though of late the Myanmarese are trying to limit this penetration.

By pushing proposals like the Bangladesh–China–India–Myanmar (BCIM) corridor, China aims at bringing the areas bordering Yunnan into China's economic orbit, which in turn will increase China's political influence in the area. We are already concerned about the flow of arms from China to insurgents in our north-east and the revival of violence by Naga groups, in which we see a Chinese hand. The BCIM corridor would imply allowing our north-east, which is underdeveloped and inadequately integrated with the rest of India, to fall into China's economic orbit. With the security dangers of this so evident, India should not be encouraging this Chinese strategy, as we are doing, until such time as China's territorial claims in this area are withdrawn or amicably settled. Meanwhile, India should accelerate the build-up of east-west connectivity, linking itself increasingly to Myanmar and Thailand and further on to South-East Asia up to Vietnam.

China's maritime strategy requires a strong Chinese presence in the Indian Ocean littoral, whether in the Bay of Bengal or the Arabian Sea. The latest white paper on China's military strategy stresses the great importance China lays on guarding maritime rights and interests, and protecting strategic sea lines of communication (SLOC) and overseas interests. It asserts that the PLA Navy will add the duty of 'open seas protection' to 'offshore waters defence'. In this strategy, ports in Myanmar, Bangladesh, Sri Lanka, the Maldives and Pakistan become important. India dominates parts of the Indian Ocean geographically as well as militarily because of its strong navy. The Andaman and Nicobar islands give us the inherent capacity to control the Strait of Malacca. For the present, China's naval presence in the Indian Ocean is limited, though with the development of its nuclear submarine fleet, our security will be challenged in the future. Already Chinese submarines have docked in Sri Lanka and Pakistan.

China seeks to disarm our security concerns about its Indian Ocean strategy by proposing our participation in what it calls the maritime silk route (the so-called One Belt) extending from the Pacific to the Indian Oceans. This is a counter to the American–Japanese concept of Asia-Pacific security. By offering its cooperative version in the garb of trade connectivity, China is seeking political legitimization of its increasing presence in the Indian Ocean and drawing attention away from its muscle-flexing in the western Pacific. India has to find an answer to China's success in roping in some of our neighbours to support its grand strategic design of extending its influence throughout the region backed by its huge economic and financial strength.

China's Quest to Dominate Asia's Strategic Landscape

China's strategy is to erode the preponderant US role in large parts of Asia. As a counter, India needs to strengthen its overall ties with Japan and continue to collaborate with the US in the Indian Ocean. We should be willing to strengthen trilateral India–Japan–US maritime cooperation in the Asia-Pacific region. In the east, India's possession of the Andaman and Nicobar islands stretches our frontiers to the choke-point of the Strait of Malacca. The Bay of Bengal has Bangladesh, Myanmar and Thailand as littoral countries. This stretch of the sea is our link to South-East Asia and beyond, and is of vital importance for buttressing our Look East policy. The security of the SLOCs in an area where the only regional blue water navy is that of India gives us an important strategic role.

India, despite its size and power, is, ironically, a country most targeted by terrorism from its own neighbourhood. Although terrorism is now considered a global threat to be fought collectively by the international community, India continues to be threatened by Pakistan-based terrorism without Pakistan being summoned by the international community, through the UN, to eradicate it. The US and its allies want Pakistan to control terrorist activity directed at them in Afghanistan, and deal as well with domestic terrorism that could destabilize the country from within and bring other problems in its wake. Terrorism directed at India remains a secondary Western concern. US pressure has, however, not been strong enough to compel Pakistan to break its links with the Haqqani group. (The US does not treat the Taliban as a terrorist group.)

The rise of religious extremism within Pakistan and the surrounding Islamic world, extending now to north Africa, is creating conditions for more jihadi violence. Pakistan's failure to take any substantive step to try those responsible for the Mumbai terrorist attack of 2008 and the unwillingness of its leadership to accept that terrorism remains a crucial outstanding issue in India–Pakistan relations indicate that the nexus between the jihadi groups and political and military power centres in Pakistan will not be easily broken. India by itself lacks the capacity to coerce Pakistan to abjure terrorism as an instrument of state policy, especially as Pakistan now has nuclear cover for its delinquency. Pakistan sees the extremist religious forces that resort to terrorism as allies against India and, potentially, in the takeover of Afghanistan after the Western forces depart.

Within SAARC, apart from the Hamid Karzai government castigating Pakistan for its sponsorship of terror, the other countries distance themselves politically from the problem. Each of them, barring Bhutan, has an interest in maintaining good ties with Pakistan for a mixture of motives that include leveraging Pakistan's hostility towards India to their own advantage and wariness of being dominated by India. SAARC conventions on combating terrorism have little meaning given Pakistan's complicity with terrorist groups. Pakistan in fact uses Nepal and Bangladesh as bases for infiltrating terrorists into India, or, in the case of Bangladesh, using local extremists for targeting India, though with Sheikh Hasina's government in Bangladesh this activity has been greatly curtailed.

Sections of Indian public opinion hold India's lack of adequate strategic thinking responsible for not being able to secure its own neighbourhood. The argument is that India as the biggest country in the region has the primary responsibility for managing the regional environment. India is accused of not being sufficiently generous towards its neighbours and of reluctance to make unilateral concessions to them, especially on the economic side, when, as a huge economy, it can easily absorb the limited sacrifice expected of it. In the process, it is believed, it can attach the neighbouring economies to itself in a mutually beneficial manner, which, in turn, would make it difficult for other governments to pursue adversarial policies beyond a certain point. Poor border management and the failure to create proper border posts and customs infrastructure are viewed as other examples of insensitivity to the need to facilitate relations with neighbours.

India cannot control the strategic situation in the subcontinent by isolating itself from external powers. From the viewpoint of India's South Asian neighbours, realpolitik would demand that they try to balance India's weight by bringing external powers into the subcontinent, giving themselves greater margin of manoeuvre vis-à-vis India. They would thus be able to obtain more concessions from India, besides making themselves more eligible for economic and military assistance from powers wanting to check its rise or impose costs on India for not following policies congenial to their interests. Pakistan has, of course, in its obsessive pursuit of 'parity' with India and a pathological refusal to accept any status of inferiority vis-à-vis it, has been most instrumental in facilitating the entry of outside powers in the subcontinent. In Nepal, China is becoming more assertive in demanding that it be treated at par with India, one example of which was to ask for its 'Friendship Treaty' with Nepal to match the one with India. With the Maoists now a powerful political force in Nepal, and given their ideological compulsions in favour of China, the political terrain has become more favourable for the latter for the expansion of its influence there. This can only make India's task of handling Nepal more difficult.

China's position in Bangladesh is entrenched. Even the friendly government of Sheikh Hasina would want to maintain close ties with China for the many benefits it can derive from it, including giving India an incentive to woo Bangladesh more. China has earned the gratitude of the Sri Lankan government by supplying it arms that helped in defeating the LTTE militarily. Sri Lanka, along with Myanmar, Bangladesh and the Maldives, is a target for the naval ambitions of China in the Indian Ocean area to protect its vital lines of communication through these waters. The so-called 'String of Pearls' strategy—labelled 'One Road' now—involving the construction of new port facilities in these countries, may be projected as commercial at present but it certainly has military goals in the longer term. To promote these objectives, China is bound to step up further its engagement with these countries, especially with increasing material means at its disposal, posing further challenges to India's equities in its neighbourhood.

China can claim the right to take dispositions in the Indian Ocean area to protect its trade and energy flows. The countries with which China is cooperating are independent sovereign countries and have economic and investment plans of their own to which China, with its vast financial resources, can contribute. Ultimately, for India's neighbours, it is a question of political judgment how far they should be cognizant of India's concerns and avoid becoming platforms for tensions between India and others.

Bangladesh has shown an unprecedented willingness to deny safe havens to anti-India insurgents and discuss transit issues. If it opens up doors for Indian investments in the country, as was agreed during Prime Minister Narendra Modi's visit there in June 2015, the complexion of the economic as well as political relationship can change substantially. Bangladesh can play a critical part in linking the eastern region of South Asia to Myanmar, Thailand and beyond. A solution has to be found, however, to the problem of illegal Bangladeshi migration into India. With the settlement of the boundary issue and the vexed question of enclaves by the Modi government, the prospects for improved all-round ties with Bangladesh have opened up.

India's relations with the Maldives need to be nurtured, especially in view of the attention it is receiving from China at the highest level. Bhutan has been the only real success story in terms of India's relations with its neighbours. Bhutan has border differences with China. It has kept its distance from Pakistan and the great powers as well, giving them little scope for interfering in its relations with India. This underscores the point that good relations between India and its neighbours depend not only on wise policies on our side but also, equally, on the pursuit of wise policies by our partners.

Beyond the threat of terrorism and Islamic radicalism emanating from Pakistan, India cannot ignore the mounting danger of a wider religious radicalization of West Asia eventually spilling over into India. The politically misconceived regime change policies of the US/NATO in West Asia have unleashed Islamic extremism in the whole region, with a potential impact on Afghanistan. The Western military intervention in Iraq has spawned today the Islamic State in parts of Iraq and Syria. That Syrian territory has been captured by these elements flows from the backing the West has given to extremist forces in Syria in a bid to topple the regime of Bashar al-Assad. Libya has descended into lawlessness, with extremist forces fighting each other for control and fuelling the spread of the al Qaeda in sub-Saharan Africa. The Gulf states have fuelled these extremist forces—not to mention the contribution of Turkey's pernicious role in Syria—both in collaboration with the West and also independently to bolster Sunni extremism against the Shia crescent embodied by Iran and its allies in the region.

The collapse of the Iraqi army in Sunni-dominated western Iraq raises concerns about the capacity of the US-trained Afghan army to withstand a potential Taliban onslaught in Afghanistan. If Afghanistan were to get seriously destabilized by these extremist religious forces, the strategic space for these obscurantist elements will expand enormously, with seriously adverse fallouts in the region that has either other Islamic countries or large populations of Muslims living in non-Muslim countries. A triumphant radical Islamic ideology can be destabilizing for the religiously composite societies of South Asia. Pressure on India from these forces would grow. Extremist forces in Pakistan itself would become more unmanageable, with security consequences for India. The problem for us is that the spectre of these threats cannot be dealt with militarily. The only practical solution will be to strengthen the defences on our borders and handle our internal situation with greater vigilance.

Devising a Coherent Strategy

If our security horizon extends from the Strait of Malacca to the Strait of Hormuz, then we have to devise strategies to counter threats to our interests in this wide space. The developments in the Gulf area, which lies within India's security parameter, have a major impact on India. Six million Indians are employed in the Gulf, sending back almost $35 billion in remittances. This region is the largest supplier of oil and gas to India, meeting 70 per cent of our energy needs. This area is the heart of Islam, and influences and ideologies emanating from there have an impact on our immediate external environment and indeed, to an extent, our internal situation. It will serve us well to remember that if India had not been divided in 1947, its western frontier would have extended to the Persian Gulf.

A critical component of our strategy would be the continued strengthening of our naval power. Our visible naval strength in the Indian Ocean will not only act as a deterrent against any Chinese browbeating in the Himalayas, but a powerful Indian Navy can also change, in our favour, the security environment in the Gulf. Our large dependence on the Gulf in terms of manpower, energy and financial resources is not backed by any security architecture in which we participate. The Pakistan dimension is a huge handicap for us in this regard. The US has a strong military presence in the Gulf, but US policies in the region are also the source of the instabilities ravaging this larger region, and this includes the partisan US role in the emerging Shia–Sunni conflict pitting Saudi Arabia against Iran. We have no control over this dynamic, which can potentially cause enormous problems for our interests in the region. If with the shale gas revolution, US strategic interest in the region relatively declines, the current levels of security provided by the US for ensuring the flow of oil into the international market could go down. A robust Indian Navy gives us increased options to forge the required political arrangements and deal with a potential crisis.

Where does the US, the world's foremost political, economic and military power, figure in our strategy to meet the external threats to us? The strategic competition between the US and China is growing, notwithstanding the close economic and financial ties between the two. US–China tensions are growing in the western Pacific. The US rebalance towards Asia is seen by the Chinese as a strategy to contain China. Our growing strategic ties with the US are viewed by China with concern. China believes that the US intends to incorporate India into its 'pivot' towards Asia, and would want to thwart this process. This would explain China's readiness to engage with India in efforts to improve ties, especially economic, without yielding, however, on the border issue and its relations with Pakistan. China may be reasoning that India has de facto accepted China's strategy to give priority to maintaining tranquillity on the border rather than making the resolution of the border issue an overarching political prerequisite for building stronger ties, and that both sides can keep stating the need to settle the border quickly, primarily for public consumption. As regards relations with Pakistan, the Chinese may reason that if India can live with close US–Pakistan ties and even US arms aid to Pakistan, it has no choice but to live with a strong China–Pakistan axis.

India has the choice of forging closer military ties with the US, going beyond what is envisaged at present, namely, joint military exercises on land, sea and air; procurement of US platforms and arms; and some tentative steps to involve US companies in defence manufacturing in India, as part of a strategy to strengthen its hands vis-à-vis China. The US seems keen to build a stronger military relationship with India. It has shown interest in sharing some advanced naval technologies with India, including probing the possibility of involvement in India's indigenous aircraft carrier plans. At some stage, it would want India to sign the three foundational agreements necessary for advanced technology transfers: the Communication and Information Security Memorandum of Agreement (CISMOA), the Logistics Support Agreement (LSA) and the Basic Exchange and Cooperation Agreement (BECA). India may remain cautious on this score so as not to get too tied into US military strategies in the region and lose its autonomy in decision-making.

During Prime Minister Modi's visit to the US in September 2014 and President Barack Obama's visit to India in January 2015, a strategic understanding on the Asia-Pacific region and Indian Ocean issues has, however, emerged. This shift in India's strategic thinking is reflected in the Joint Strategic Vision for the Asia-Pacific and the Indian Ocean issued during the January visit. In it, India took a more public position against China's maritime threats, as the document referred to 'the importance of safeguarding maritime security and ensuring freedom of navigation and overflight throughout the region, especially in the South China Sea'. It spoke of developing a roadmap that 'leverages our respective efforts to increase ties among Asian powers', enabling India and the US to 'better respond to diplomatic, economic and security challenges in the region'. It also envisaged, over the years, the strengthening of regional dialogues, and investing in trilateral consultations with third countries in the region and the like.

In his joint press conference with President Obama in September 2014, Prime Minister Modi stated that the US was intrinsic to our Look

East and Link West policies, which suggests a growing role for the US in the making of our foreign policy. During President Obama's January visit, the joint statement noted that India's Act East policy and the US's rebalance to Asia provided opportunities for India, the US and other Asia-Pacific countries to work closely to strengthen regional ties. This implicitly endorsed the US rebalance towards Asia and connected our Act East policy to it. So far, India has been hesitant to be seen drawing too close strategically to the US because of Chinese sensitivities, but this is changing. By strengthening relations with the US (which is strategically an Asian power), Japan and Vietnam and, at the same time, seeking Chinese investments and maintaining a high-level dialogue with it, India has begun to play the same game that China does with India, which is to seek to build overall ties as much as possible on the economic front, deny any negative anti-India element in its policies in our neighbourhood, but pursue, simultaneously, strategic policies intended to contain India's power in the subcontinent and delay its regional extension to Asia.

A point to consider as we strengthen our strategic ties with the US is the content of US–China ties, especially economic and financial, that far exceeds that of India–US ties. Even US allies in Asia like Japan are not too certain of whether, in the face of a real threat of a conflict over the Senkaku Islands, the US will be willing to enter into a military conflict with China. This explains why Japan is widening its strategic options—despite a military alliance with the US—to countries like India to counter China in Asia. India has to, therefore, be careful about how far it wants to go with the US with a view to improving its bargaining power with China. The US is drawing India into its Asia-Pacific strategy to counter China, whereas China threatens India primarily on our land borders and in our neighbourhood. India's security challenges, therefore, remain unaddressed in the Asia-Pacific context. Curbing China's assertiveness in the western Pacific collectively by member countries, of course, aids India's security indirectly by placing constraints on China's expansionism in its own periphery.

The other point to consider is the US–Pakistan equation. The US recently announced $1 billion of military aid to Pakistan. Its position on the Taliban is against our strategic interests in Afghanistan. It needs Pakistani cooperation to secure its withdrawal from Afghanistan as smoothly as possible, with a readiness to make some concessions to the Taliban under the guise of reconciliation. Its position on Pakistani sponsorship of terrorism against us remains essentially rhetorical, though it is helping to build up our counter-terrorism capabilities, which is of value. It is not taking any visible step to curb Pakistan's expanding nuclear programme and the China–Pakistan nuclear collaboration. Its soft approach on sanctioning Pakistan contrasts with the draconian sanctions imposed on Iran and tough sanctions on Russia on the Ukraine issue. In short, in practical terms, both US and China are bolstering Pakistan militarily, collaborating actively or passively in the build-up of Pakistan's nuclear capacities, and either letting Pakistan escape accountability for its terrorist affiliations or protecting it from international action. In sum, India's experience of US policy in the last several decades is that it will not take a clear-cut position on India–Pakistan issues, will try to maintain some balance in its relations with the two countries, and will not seriously sanction Pakistan for its terrorist links.

Any national strategy to meet external threats has to have strategic autonomy as its core. For a large country like India, with the potential of becoming a big power in the future, strategic autonomy is the only choice. By virtue of its demographic, geographic, economic and military size, India must lead. India cannot subordinate itself to the policies and interests of another country, however powerful. Indian political and public opinion, the functioning of its democracy, the traditions that have been established over decades by the practice of non-alignment, all these factors will not allow India to become an appendage of another power. Even when it was much weaker than it is today and had to bear pressures during the Cold War, it chose to remain outside the block system. It does not, however, have the kind of comprehensive national power today that will enable it to actually lead from the front. It is, therefore, in a 'transit mode' today, as it were—not strong enough to lead but sufficiently strong not to be led. Strategic autonomy for India means that as far as possible it would like to rely on its own judgement on international issues, balance its relations with all major countries, forge partnerships with individual powers and take foreign policy positions based on pragmatism and self-interest and not any alliance or group compulsion. This serves India's strategic interests and its security the best.

Strategic autonomy allows India to improve relations with the US and China while maintaining close ties with Russia at the same time. We can forge stronger ties with Japan and still seek a more stable relationship with China. We can draw closer to Israel—Modi will be the first Indian prime minister to visit the country—and maintain very productive ties with the Arab world. It means that India can have strategic partnerships with several countries, as is the case at present—with the US, France, Germany, the UK, the EU, Russia, China, Japan, Brazil, Saudi Arabia, Australia, Canada, Kazakhstan, Afghanistan, Vietnam, Iran and the like. It means that India can be a member of BRICS and the RIC (Russia, India, China) dialogue, as well as IBSA (India, Brazil, South Africa), in which either Western countries are not members, or the agenda is to forge partnerships amongst non-Western countries with a view to bringing about changes in the functioning of the international system and reform the international political, economic and financial institutions, at present dominated by the Western powers, to reflect the shifts of political and economic power that have taken place in the world after 1945.

Finally, no country can have a credible national strategy to ensure its security at the required levels unless its military strength derives from an autonomous indigenous base. Our external security apparatus suffers from a major weakness because we are almost 70 per cent dependent on the import of arms. It does little honour to India and how we manage our defence that India should be the world's largest importer of arms. Even as regards arms imports, our dilatory and corruption-tainted procurement procedures have led to inordinate delays in acquisitions and gaps in our military preparedness. The Modi government is stressing the need for the indigenous manufacture of arms, for which the foreign direct investment (FDI) ceiling for investment in the defence sector has been raised from 26 to 100 per cent. Despite Western arms embargoes on China since 1989, it has succeeded in developing its arms manufacturing industry in an impressive way. We need to emulate its example in all available practical ways.

To conclude, a national strategy for dealing with external threats could contain several elements. Foremost in this would be to develop an indigenous defence manufacturing base. The Modi government is focusing on this need. To achieve this objective rapidly, the government is encouraging the private sector to enter into foreign collaborations to build platforms and bring in technologies. As part of this priority, our defence procurement procedures have to be rationalized to cater to defence needs and not be obsessed with curtailing corrupt practices.

Devising a strategy to deal with China is exceptionally difficult in view of its phenomenal rise, the gap that has developed between us in economic and military strength, and the strategic initiatives China is taking to expand its influence in the Indian subcontinent, Asia as a whole, and in the Indian Ocean—all in the context of unrelenting territorial claims on us. We have to accelerate the improvement of our military infrastructure on the Tibetan border and raise additional forces for border defence. Our strategic programmes need accelerated development, as this would increase our political space vis-à-vis not only China but also all other powers. It is vital for our security in the Indian Ocean area to expand our naval power, including strengthening the Andaman and Nicobar Islands militarily. We need to carve out political space for ourselves on the Tibetan question. The Chinese make outrageous claims on 'South Tibet', which requires adding some nuance to our position on Tibet. We should express our wish for a solution to China's internal problem in Tibet because it affects India–China ties. We should call upon China to seek a negotiated settlement with the Tibetans so that India–China relations can be normalized. Even as we seek more economic ties with China, we should not lose sight of China's cyber capabilities when opening up certain sectors to Chinese companies. Even otherwise, we need to strengthen our capacities to defend ourselves against cyber attacks. The China–Pakistan Economic Corridor should be strongly opposed as it traverses territory that is legally Indian. The BCIM corridor is against our strategic interest and should not be promoted. We should encourage Japan to invest in our north-east and contribute to building east-west connectivity.

We have to find an answer to the terrorist problem we face from Pakistan. A limited military response in POK in retaliation to another major terrorist attack emanating from Pakistan would be essential to raise the costs for Pakistan for its unacceptable conduct and deter it from using this instrument against us. We would need to develop tactical nuclear weapons to neutralize the capability that Pakistan has developed.

The Modi government is wise in strengthening relations with neighbours. They should be drawn into the Indian economic orbit as much as possible. We should proceed with sub-regional cooperation within SAARC as Pakistan will continue to hold back the organization from realizing its potential. China's entry into SAARC should be opposed. We must persevere in our involvement in Afghanistan's development so that the goodwill there towards India is preserved.

More attention needs to be paid to Myanmar to deal with actual and potential threats from anti-Indian insurgencies in the north-east, apart from balancing China's influence there. Our Look East policy needs to be pursued vigorously to raise our profile in South-East Asia. We should strengthen our strategic ties with Japan as much as possible, including trilateral naval exercises with Japan and the US in the Indian Ocean.

The expansion of strategic ties with the US should continue, even if aspects of US policies in our region are not in our interest. We should not, however, compromise our strategic autonomy. Russia should remain a vital political and military partner so that the strategic balance in our foreign policy is preserved. The West's policies towards Russia are not in our strategic interest.

We should maintain a balance in our ties with Iran and the Arab world and avoid getting involved in regional and sectarian rivalries in the region as this can affect our security. Iran remains important for our energy security and transit requirements to Afghanistan and Central Asia, while our equities in the Arab world, especially the Gulf countries, remain of prime importance. Our defence ties with Israel have greatly expanded and need to be nurtured for defence requirements and anti-terrorism capabilities. Despite geographical handicaps, we should pay attention to Central Asian countries so that this region does not escape our strategic net.

The answer to Islamic radicalism and its potential impact on us lies in improvements in our internal security apparatus, as the dynamic of these forces is outside our control.

9

Crafting a Strategy for India's Maritime Security

Admiral Arun Prakash

Former Chief of Naval Staff and Chairman, Chiefs of Staff Committee

India's Maritime Awakening

Given that 70 per cent of the globe is covered by the seas, the effective employment of maritime power has always garnered for a nation a position of political and economic influence as well as military ascendency. American maritime strategist Rear Admiral Alfred Thayer Mahan commences his authoritative commentary on the influence of sea power on history by seeking to draw historical lessons from transnational conflicts.[1] Starting from the victory of Greek naval power over the Persians at Salamis in 480 BCE, he goes on to cite Hannibal's defeat by Roman General Scipio Africanus in 202 BCE and Napoleon's rout by Wellington in 1815 to offer conclusive evidence that it was always the dominant sea power that prevailed over the mightiest opposing armies.

As a general rule, Indians have been remiss not only in their failure to record history but also in the inability to learn from their past. The 'continental mindset' of Indian kings and princes as well as their successors, our post-Independence decision makers, is attributable to this failing. In this context, Indians owe a debt of gratitude to the diplomat-historian, Sardar K.M. Panikkar (1895–1963), who undertook painstaking research to rediscover India's glorious maritime past and published a seminal essay titled 'India and the Indian Ocean' in 1945. Panikkar found ample evidence of the salience of sea power in India's history. While India did not embark on imperial adventures, it did project its 'soft power' through the medium of the sea to establish extensive dominance over South-East Asia during the first millennium CE. Known in Sanskrit as 'Suvarnabhumi' (Golden Land), this region constituted a veritable Indian 'cultural empire', established by merchants, religious teachers, artisans and craftsmen who had been carried to these distant shores over centuries by intrepid Indian seafarers following a hoary maritime tradition.[2]

Two historical realities provide further corroboration of the crucial role played by maritime power in India's destiny. A succession of foreign raiders, from Central Asia, Iran and Afghanistan, encouraged by the weakness of Indian rulers, have historically intruded through the north-western mountain passes into the rich plains of north India. Many of these invaders stayed on to rule, were gradually assimilated into the permeable fabric of India's rich culture and became Indians.

This was not so with those who came by sea to our shores; the conquest and colonization of India by small European powers, commencing with Vasco da Gama's arrival in 1498, was rooted in mercenary and exploitative motives as well as religious fervour. In the words of historian Paul Kennedy, 'God, the gun and the sailing ship became the three pillars of an expanding Western civilization.'[3] Lacking enterprising princes and merchants, India, once a great maritime power, lagged behind in shipbuilding technology as well as seafaring skills. Unable to fend off the European seaborne onslaught, it became a colony for the next two centuries.

Panikkar, in his essay cited above, while reminding his countrymen of their long and glorious maritime past, vigorously promoted the idea of a strong navy for independent India. Writing in 1902, Admiral Mahan had said, 'War has ceased to be the natural, or even normal, condition of nations, and military considerations are subordinate to the other great interests they serve: economics and commerce.'[4] He insisted that since the true path to national prosperity and greatness lay in peacetime trade, ensuring access to sources of economic well-being, i.e., foreign trade, commerce and natural resources, is of paramount importance.

In our own context, the dramatic growth of India's economy has been stimulated by the powerful phenomenon of globalization, leading to not just large foreign direct investment (FDI) in India but also heavy Indian investment abroad, including that in energy resources. Thus, along with an Indian diaspora of over 20 million, we also have growing economic interests worldwide. India's economy and its progress and prosperity depend on international trade, which is carried overwhelmingly by sea. Energy, the lifeblood of our industry, is also similarly dependent on the sea.

Fortuitously, the past fifteen to twenty years have witnessed a 'maritime awakening' amongst India's traditionally land-oriented decision-making elite. A series of developments, including the ongoing phenomenon of globalization; the drama of rampant piracy; the exposure, in November 2008, of India's soft coastal underbelly; and the spectre of a growing Chinese navy served to bring sharp focus on maritime security. A powerful catalyst was provided by the navy's active outreach to its counterparts internationally and its diplomatic fallout. For example, the 'Malabar' series of annual naval exercises have served as a subtle but powerful cementing force in bilateral relations even without a formal India–US alliance.

Need for a National Maritime Strategy

The fact is that India is a maritime nation, not just by historical tradition but also because its geophysical configuration and geopolitical circumstances make it as dependent on the seas as any island nation. Located astride vital shipping lanes, India occupies a dominant maritime position.

Jutting a thousand kilometres into the ocean named after it, the Indian peninsula is rimmed with 7,500 km of coastline, 200 major and minor ports, offshore islands, and a huge exclusive economic zone (EEZ) with fishery resources and energy potential. India's economy is heavily dependent on foreign trade and energy imports, over 95 per cent of which come via Indian Ocean sea lanes.

Given these circumstances, India should have long ago crafted an all-encompassing national strategy defining a holistic approach to the oceans that surround it. Parented by a national grand strategy, such a document would have identified India's maritime areas of interest and described the economic, political, military, scientific and technological objectives that it would seek therein. The strategy would, then, have addressed ways and means of achieving these objectives.

While none of this actually happened, the Indian Navy on its own initiative issued the military component of such a strategy in 2006. A year later, a declassified version titled 'Freedom to Use the Seas: India's

Maritime Military Strategy'[5] was made public. But so far there are no signs that a national-level maritime vision or strategy is being contemplated by those responsible for India's national security.

Given India's rapidly growing economic, military and geopolitical profile, the formulation of a national maritime strategy is overdue. Unless this is done, the Maritime Military Strategy would remain hollow for want of the substantive national underpinning necessary. Before embarking on an examination of such a project, it would be useful to reflect on the underlying causes for the existing intellectual void.

India's Strategic Culture

The contemplative Indian often tends to agonize over past historical events, wondering why, for example, in India's history, invasions over its north-western passes were never stopped or defeated. Why were rulers of Indian states unwilling to unite against invaders, and why was no thought given to the strategic defence of India as a whole or to maritime defence?

In contemporary times, India's failure to define and articulate a coherent strategic identity has been highlighted by foreign analysts like George Tanham, who have drawn attention to a 'historic lack of a strategic thought process in Indian society'.[6] Such commentary has raised hackles in India, causing many Indians to hark back to 'Chanakya-niti'[7] and Nehru's policy of non-alignment, insisting that a hidden streak of inherent strategic sense does run through Indian culture.[8] Notwithstanding such assertions, however, the fact is that India is a young nation state that has remained tentative and unsure about the use of power.

A Western political construct of the Cold War era may have some relevance here. Seeking a rationale for the startlingly different responses of the Soviet and American leaderships to similar situations, researchers devised a new tool for political analysis and forecasting, calling it 'strategic culture'. Today there is an agreement that it is a nation's distinctive strategic culture which shapes its policies relating to the role of military force in international affairs, as well as the conduct of politics, diplomacy and foreign affairs.[9]

Since strategic culture has come to be used as an index for assessment, it is interesting to note Tanham's remark that 'status and symbolism matter greatly in Indian society',[10] and hence the possibility that certain military capabilities such as nuclear weapons, ballistic missiles, and a blue water navy may have been acquired by India merely as symbols of 'great power' status without a clear-cut notion of their practical utility.

Tanham's caustic remark is a reflection of our ruling elite's failure to understand that the security policies of a state must be rooted in clearly identified vital interests and should be guided by a vision of its place in the world. An enunciation of national aims and objectives helps in policy formulation and in visualization of the nation's military capability. But in all the years since Independence, India has neither issued a defence white paper, nor undertaken a defence review, nor formally articulated national interests and objectives encompassing the various aspects of national security.

The most deleterious consequences of this have been felt by the armed forces, which have had to extemporize and undertake planning in a strategic void. Indians are no doubt justified in resenting the condescending remarks of foreign analysts, but the fact remains that the ruling elite has largely abdicated its national security responsibilities. While India's politico-bureaucratic complex loses no opportunity to emphasize the importance of 'civilian control' over the military, rarely have they spelt out the political aims underpinning the nation's post-Independence military operations or provided strategic guidance to the armed forces.

Under such circumstances, the emergence of the Maritime Military Strategy was a remarkable development, but perhaps not enough. In this context, it is instructive to note in passing the politico-military interface that shapes national security policies in the US. Nothing illustrates US political oversight of the armed forces better than the fact that the post–World War II form, structure and character of the US military have been shaped substantially by two acts of the US Congress: the National Security Act of 1947 and the Goldwater–Nichols Defence Re-organization Act of 1986.

As far as political guidance to the armed forces is concerned, the US Congress has mandated the Department of Defense to undertake a Quadrennial Defense Review, which spells out a national defence strategy by defining force structures and the budgetary support necessary for the military to execute its allotted missions.[11] Apart from this, direction to the military is provided by a National Security Strategy, a National Military Strategy, a US Armed Forces Doctrine and a Strategic Guidance document, issued periodically to the Department of Defense, under the hand of the commander-in-chief, the President of the USA.

The Roots of India's Maritime Strategy

Compelling Factors

By way of contrast, India's Maritime Military Strategy declares in its opening pages that it draws inspiration from something as lofty as the Constitution of India, written in 1947.[12] It also finds some guidance from other pedestrian documents such as the Ministry of Defence Annual Report and from an occasional edict known as the Defence Minister's Operational Directive.

The debate whether strategy should drive force architecture or the other way round has always simmered below the surface in the Indian Navy. However, as long as it was Soviet admirals who prescribed the hardware to be offered to India at 'friendship prices', there was little choice in the matter and the Indian Navy innovated doctrine and tactics on an ad hoc basis as it went along. The final decade of the last century, however, saw a number of factors coalescing to propel the navy leadership towards a long-overdue enunciation of India's relationship with the seas. Prime amongst these were: (a) the putative Revolution in Military Affairs (RMA), (b) disintegration of India's main arms supplier, the Soviet Union, followed by (c) the opening of India's economy and (d) its entry into the nuclear weapons club.

Moreover, by then, indigenous warship building in India had come of age and this, coupled with the diversification of military hardware sources, opened up many options as far as acquisition of technology and platforms was concerned. The navy felt that it was (unlike its sister services) finally in a position to create a maritime force to match the strategy that it would now craft. A clear articulation of the attributes of maritime power and the roles and missions of the navy as an instrument of state power was also considered necessary, not just for educating India's decision makers and national security elite but also for familiarizing the navy's own middle-ranking leadership with the arcane logic and use of maritime power.

Notwithstanding these good intentions, a catalytic spark was required to trigger the process of strategy–policy formation.

The Catalytic Spark

This was provided by Rear Admiral K. Raja Menon, a retired navy submariner and one of India's most cerebral military thinkers, who had written a book titled *Maritime Strategy and Continental Wars* in 1998. Menon's book argued that nations like India whose preoccupations are mainly continental have difficulty visualizing and crafting a maritime strategy. As a benchmark for a plan's acceptance as 'maritime strategy', he stipulated that it must 'affect the national political purpose'.[13]

However, he had to contend with nineteenth century geo-strategist Sir Julian Corbett's historical tenet that major issues between nations have rarely been decided by naval action alone. According to him, wars have largely been won by what the army can do against the enemy's territory and national life, or by what the fleet can do to help the army attain its aims. Menon recommended the use of modern technology to 'speed up the battle', offering the navies of continental powers options that would enable them to influence land wars.[14]

Certain sections of this book struck a chord with the senior navy leadership. They took Menon's advice to forget 'ship counts' and grasp the RMA in order to substitute rather than complement existing forces.[15] Many of his specific prescriptions for smaller navies, relating to communications satellites, special forces and aerial reconnaissance, were actually translated into policy initiatives by Naval HQ during 2004–06.

A maritime doctrine having already been issued in 2004, Menon's assistance was also enlisted by the navy in formulating the new Maritime Military Strategy. He can, thus, be termed a major catalyst for the intellectual renaissance of the Indian Navy. It bears mention in passing that the momentum of this renaissance also saw a few other beneficial fallouts as far as the strategic planning process of the navy was concerned.

For example, in 2004, the Ministry of Defence (MoD) approved the navy's long-standing demand for the creation of a maritime think tank. Originally conceived as a forum to revive 'maritime consciousnesses' in the country and enable freewheeling professional discussion within the navy, on the lines of the US Naval Institute, it has acquired a much more ambitious charter as the National Maritime Foundation.

In order to provide impetus to creative doctrinal thinking, the position of 'Flag Officer Doctrines and Concepts' was created in 2005, in Mumbai, in close proximity to the Western Fleet and some operational-evaluation groups. In Naval HQ, a small group of cerebral officers was constituted as the Directorate of Strategy, Concepts and Transformation and placed directly under the navy chief to encourage 'out of the box' thinking. In order to bring sharp focus on foreign cooperation and expedite assistance programmes, it was brought under a newly created Assistant Chief of Naval Staff. To engender a long-term perspective in the navy's quest for of self-reliance, a Principal Directorate of Indigenization was created in Naval HQ to consolidate endeavours in this critical area.

The Maritime Doctrine and Strategy

As discussed earlier, the inability of Indian statesmen to apply themselves sufficiently to strategic issues has not only precluded the definition of tangible national aims and objectives but also kept them from specifying political ends for any of the post-Independence military operations. This vacuum hindered the evolution of strategy and rendered military force planning an arbitrary process.

Given the set of factors described earlier, the navy took up the challenge of bridging the intellectual gap and drawing up a roadmap to synergize its maritime endeavours. This resulted in the Maritime Military Strategy. The strategy was followed by a document titled 'Maritime Capabilities Perspective Plan' (MCPP), which set out the capabilities required for the former's execution. While the MCPP has remained classified, sanitized versions of the other two documents have been released for public consumption. All of them are subject to periodic revision/updating.

This triad has served to provide the long-overdue intellectual underpinning for the planned growth of India's maritime power and also provided a clear roadmap for roles, missions, force architecture, technology induction and an operational philosophy for the navy. They attempt to conform to India's national security objectives and the worldview of its politicians—to the extent that these are known.

The Maritime Doctrine

The Maritime Doctrine clearly outlines the Indian Navy's four basic missions, which span the full spectrum of conflict, encompassing the military, diplomatic, constabulary and benign roles. Of these, the last three are clearly undertaken in peacetime, but the military role encompasses 'deterrence', which is a function that spans both peace and war.

The navy aims to achieve conventional deterrence by maintaining preponderance in conventional maritime capability, i.e., a sufficiency of warships, submarines and aircraft which will undertake the full gamut of operational missions, the idea being to never leave friends as well as potential adversaries in doubt about India's capabilities at sea.[16]

Deterrence, on the grand strategic plane, involves the deployment of nuclear weapons as political instruments of state policy, their actual use being contemplated only *in extremis* in the second-strike mode. Having crossed the nuclear Rubicon in 1998, India is now committed to maintaining a minimum credible deterrent under a self-imposed condition of no first use (NFU). The induction of the nuclear-propelled submarine INS *Arihant* into its strategic forces will mark the first step towards acquiring the third leg of the nuclear triad pledged in India's nuclear doctrine.

The Maritime Strategy

The Maritime Military Strategy describes how maritime forces can be deployed to interdict the enemy's foreign trade lifeline in an attempt to starve its industry, economy and people, and bring its military machine to a halt. The impact of this 'commodity denial' regime, also termed the 'indirect approach', requires finite time to take effect. Factors like the enemy's dependence on imports, his buffer stocks and ability to restock via land routes will decide the effectiveness of these indirect operations, and that is why a superior navy would like to prolong a war so that the adversary can be subjected to progressive strangulation.

In the other 'direct' mode of creating an impact on the land battle contemplated by this strategy, the enemy's homeland is targeted by naval platforms delivering weapons from the sea, undertaking amphibious operations or inserting special forces.[17] Adapting these concepts to the

Indian environment, the Maritime Military Strategy encompasses the resolute and judicious deployment of maritime forces in both direct and indirect operations. This aims to ensure that the impact of sea power is felt on the land battle, both in the short and long terms.

In order to obtain the maximum synergy and advantage from its superior numbers as well as capabilities, the navy considers it necessary to fight what the Soviets used to call an 'all arms battle' at sea.[18] By ensuring reliable and secure communications between warships, aircraft and submarines, it should be possible to concentrate their firepower in a geographical location and inflict heavy attrition on the enemy. Shore-based Indian Air Force strike aircraft would make an important contribution here. With network-centric operations linked by a navy-owned satellite, implementation of this concept should not pose a problem.

India's Maritime Military Strategy aims to provide an overarching rationale for the creation and deployment of naval capabilities during peace, crisis and conflict. In doing so, it also provides guidance in areas such as deterrence, war fighting, maritime contingency planning and scenario building. Its contours are shaped by three major factors: (a) the need to protect India's national interests, population, resources and diaspora (b) to underwrite India's 'strategic autonomy' by supporting foreign policy and (c) to assure safety of trade and energy transit by upholding freedom of the seas and compliance with international norms.

Need for Revision of Strategy

Strategies are inherently time-bound, and the navy had undertaken to review the Maritime Military Strategy ten years after the promulgation of the classified version. However, the quantum of change that has taken place in the intervening decade will call for a major re-appraisal of the environment and, perhaps, a corresponding re-formulation of the strategy. Since such an exercise is understood to be currently underway in Naval HQ, it would be pointless attempting to predict its nature and substance here. However, it may not be out of place to draw attention to a few factors that would have an influence on the review.

The Geopolitical Situation

At one end of the threat spectrum facing India is the twin nuclear menace posed by neighbours China and Pakistan, with the latter foolishly brandishing tactical nuclear weapons. At the other end is the hazard of Islamic fundamentalist terror outfits that form an integral part of Pakistan's low-cost proxy war against India. The unforeseen rise of the Islamic State in the Middle East could have grave implications for India if it spills over into an unstable Afghanistan and a strife-torn Pakistan.

China has made Pakistan the centrepiece of its anti-India grand strategy, and, by arming it to the teeth with conventional and nuclear weaponry, it has completely skewed the natural balance of power on the subcontinent, placing India in the jaws of a pincer. China is also flexing its muscle in the South China Sea and making economic as well as military inroads into the Indian Ocean Region (IOR). President Xi Jinping's strategic 'One Belt, One Road' initiative envisages the establishment of Chinese economic hegemony over the Indo-Pacific region.

China's geographic proximity and its huge economic and military disparity vis-à-vis India leaves the latter with no option but to find a modus vivendi and even seek cooperation, in economic and other fields, till a resolution can be found to bilateral border disputes. Given China's immense logistical and overall superiority on the Himalayan borders, there is a view that India needs to look seawards for a countervailing maritime strategy, using its peninsular configuration, island territories and growing maritime power to dominate Indian Ocean sea lanes and exploit China's putative 'Malacca dilemma'.[19]

There is also a view that this may be the appropriate juncture for India to invoke 'Chanakya-niti' and, without overtly threatening containment, seek partnerships and alliances with other nations with whom there is a convergence of security interests vis-à-vis China.

Coastal Security

The erection of fencing along the India–Pakistan international border, as well as the Line of Control in Jammu & Kashmir, is a major factor that has forced Pakistan to modify its proxy war strategy and start using the sea as an alternative infiltration route across India's west coast. In 1993, a few tonnes of arms and explosives, landed by the Pakistani intelligence agencies on the Ratnagiri coast, were transported by the Indian underworld to perpetrate the Mumbai carnage. Fifteen years later, a Pakistan-trained terrorist group sailed by boat from Karachi and landed in the heart of Mumbai to wreak havoc on the city for three days.

The 26/11 terror attack on Mumbai clearly highlighted the poor state of our intelligence, the gaps in ocean surveillance and the huge challenge of effectively policing and guarding a long and vulnerable coastline. In the years since this outrage, a number of measures have been implemented to rectify the lacunae in our coastal security.

In a somewhat convoluted arrangement, the navy has been designated as the 'authority responsible for overall maritime security', and existing commanders-in-chief of the Eastern and Western Naval Commands have been designated as 'Cs-in-C Coastal Defence'. At the same time, the Coast Guard has been designated as the 'authority for coastal security' in territorial waters, and the Director-General, Indian Coast Guard, has been designated as 'Commander Coastal Command'. The state governments have been tasked with raising marine police forces for the security of the coastal belt. Responsibility for overall coordination between state and central agencies in matters relating to coastal security rests with the Coast Guard.[20]

The coastal security paradigm is extremely complex and involves not only Centre–state relationships but also cuts across many agencies and organizations. Given the overlap of functions and responsibilities, there is a distinct possibility of confusion in live operational situations. By involving itself in coastal security issues, the navy also risks dilution of its 'blue water' focus. There is, thus, a need for the navy to undertake a critical re-appraisal of the existing allocation of responsibilities.

Advances in Technology

Access to technology and the ability to absorb and exploit it will continue to have a vital impact on the effectiveness of navies. If 'revolutions' are marked by non-linearity in the progression of events, military affairs have certainly been in the throes of a revolution since the 1980s. Galloping advances in weapon, sensor, platform and information technologies have taken navies on an exponential path of capability growth.

In the Indian Navy's context, the RMA has manifested itself in the recent induction of a large aircraft carrier with supersonic fighters, a nuclear attack submarine, advanced long-range missiles and torpedoes, phased-array radars, airborne early-warning helicopters, modern anti-submarine warfare (ASW) patrol aircraft and unmanned aerial vehicles. A dramatic development has been the launch, in 2014, of a dedicated naval communications satellite, the GSAT-7. This has provided data networking facility for all navy platforms deployed in the IOR.

This infusion of technology needs to be internalized by the navy through the process of 'transformation'. Essentially based on a willingness to constantly challenge old thinking and introduce new concepts, transformation encompasses not just the creation of capabilities by the use of technology but also changes in organizational relationships, war-fighting concepts and doctrines as well as strategies.

Only when the Maritime Military Strategy takes into account this rapid infusion of advanced technologies will the navy be able to fully leverage its new capabilities to tilt the maritime balance at sea.

Nuclear Deterrent

Operating a viable submarine-based deterrent is a complex undertaking and requires many components. It must have a number of ballistic missile submarines (SSBNs) armed with nuclear-tipped missiles of inter-continental range, as well as a small force of nuclear attack submarines (SSNs) for protection of the deterrent and for interdiction of shipping. Such a mix of SSBNs and SSNs, once at sea, will invest India with the 'strategic autonomy' that it seeks and the means to forestall attempts at maritime hegemony or domination of the IOR.

It appears that the Government of India has accorded approval for the creation of a small standing force of SSBNs and SSNs.[21] Apart from the formation of necessary command and control structures as well as submarine safety organizations and procedures, the navy would need to generate the necessary operating procedures and doctrines. While the deployment of the deterrent would entail a separate, highly classified strategy, it must also find mention in the new Maritime Military Strategy, insofar as it impacts the navy's conventional operations.

Having undertaken a cursory foray into the contours and proposed revision of the Maritime Military Strategy, it is time to examine the bigger maritime picture, because the two are inextricably linked.

A National Maritime Strategy

The concept of maritime power encompasses far more than what most people seem to imagine and certainly goes well beyond merely a 'fighting navy' that we have been discussing so far. Making a passing reference to the national maritime infrastructure as an asset whose growth would be desirable, the current Maritime Military Strategy also mentions the technological capacity building that would be required to underpin the naval build-up. But experience tells us that mere mention will not suffice. In fact, one could go so far as to say that the Maritime Military Strategy may fail to meet its aims and objectives unless undergirded by an overarching National Maritime Strategy that focuses, holistically, on maritime capacity building as a national endeavour.

It is clear that the government is not oblivious of the huge unexploited potential residing in the maritime sector, because three successive ministers of transport and shipping have issued three 'maritime perspective plans': 'Sagarmala' in 2003, 'National Maritime Development Plan' in 2005, and 'Maritime Agenda: 2020' in 2012.[22] A common thread running through these documents is their ambitious concept, unrealistic targets and absence of a roadmap or monitoring process.

Against this backdrop, the concluding part of this chapter highlights some of the major initiatives around which a proposed national strategy for India's maritime security needs to be built. To be titled the National Maritime Strategy, it would keep clear of issues relating to national defence as well as military response to threats, which will continue to remain under the purview of the Ministry of Defence.

A Whole-of-Government Approach

Admiral Mahan, while stipulating the conditions vital to the maritime power of a nation, also included 'character of the government and its institutions'.[23] In our case, this lacuna is apparent in the neglect shown by the Government of India towards the maritime sector since Independence.

Today there is no single government agency that has either the span of responsibility or the authority to act as the focal point for India's maritime policies and interests. As many as sixteen different ministries, departments or organizations (including the Indian Navy and the Coast

Guard) are involved in ocean-related matters and, most of the time, there is a lack of coordination between the different organs of the government.[24]

Moreover, generalist bureaucrats have been placed in positions that require specialist maritime knowledge and expertise. This has resulted in a lack of direction and even confusion in certain areas like coastal and port security, traffic management, pollution control, fisheries regulation and anti-piracy measures. While the trauma of the 2008 terror attack on Mumbai did trigger many security reforms, the reallocation of duties between the navy and the Coast Guard may have heightened ambiguity in the coastal security scenario.

The most important feature of a National Maritime Strategy would be the adoption of a 'whole-of-government' approach towards maritime security, which would bring together all government agencies and activities under a single structure. This would require the constitution of a ministerial-level working group on maritime security that will address and take decisions on all cross-cutting maritime security issues. Directly under the ministers, a secretariat in which all maritime stakeholders are represented would work to enact and implement ministerial decisions.

An Industrial Underpinning

In a quirk of circumstance, India has become a military and economic entity with great-power aspirations before it has become a significant industrial power or even a major trading nation. Thus India finds itself in an anomalous situation wherein it possesses nuclear weapons and the world's third or fourth largest armed forces but has to support their operational needs through massive imports.

Ironically, the government owns a vast research and development (R&D) and industrial complex dedicated to defence which would be the envy of many nations, but it has failed to deliver for many reasons. While a willing and capable private sector has been excluded from defence production, many public sector undertakings have been engaged merely in the assembly of imported kits while claiming 'transfer of technology' and 'indigenization'. This is in stark contrast to the outstanding performance of India's space and atomic energy departments, which have learnt to stand on their own feet and have remarkable achievements to their credit.

The navy's indigenization is, thus, only 'skin deep' and its operational readiness remains hostage on the one hand to the inefficient and complacent public sector, and, on the other, to unreliable foreign suppliers. Neither liberalized FDI nor the Make in India campaign is likely to have a substantive impact on defence production unless there is a radical change in approach. This would involve a sharply enhanced focus in the National Maritime Strategy on R&D by roping in our private sector and academia as well as the Indian diaspora in the US and elsewhere.

An important component of the National Maritime Strategy would be a plan for the dissolution of the current structure of the defence R&D as well as military-industrial complexes, followed by a drastic re-structuring in a private–public mode.

Shipbuilding

While the basic driver of shipbuilding is global seaborne trade, it is a strategic industry that an emerging power like India has been gravely remiss in not nurturing. Apart from constituting the foundation and support of a nation's maritime power, the shipbuilding industry generates huge secondary and tertiary benefits in terms of ancillary industries, skilled manpower and employment creation, which can transform India's economy.

Just over 10 per cent of Indian-flagged merchant vessels have been built in our shipyards, because of higher costs, longer delivery periods and indifferent quality. Countries like China, South Korea, Japan and even Vietnam and the Philippines have created shipbuilding industries that produce quality ships at competitive prices. While these nations have monopolized the world's shipbuilding market, India has short-sightedly failed to capitalize on its natural advantages to create a dynamic shipbuilding and ship repair industry.

Indian shipyards contribute a dismal 1 per cent of the global market share, and providing a boost to India's shipbuilding industry should form the third prong of the National Maritime Strategy. This will require the designation of shipbuilding as a strategic sector and initiation of grassroots measures for engendering ship design and building skills, like creation of industrial training institutes (ITIs) and faculties of naval architecture. The provision of active support in terms of levies, financial subsidies and tax exemptions would also be necessary.

Ports and Harbours

There is inadequate realization of the contribution of ports and harbours to the economy's health in peacetime as well as in war. The navy is a regular user of all major Indian ports, and resident in many of them. While peacetime naval operations are profoundly affected by the functioning of these ports, in wartime it will be the navy's responsibility to guard them and ensure their safe and efficient functioning.

Many of the major and minor ports are badly congested, poorly managed and lacking in facilities for dredging, mechanization and storage. They are inadequate to meet the cargo throughput requirements of our growing economy. Many of the navy's larger warships cannot find berths because of insufficient depths available even in our major harbours. Indian ports suffer in comparison with the efficient cargo handling and quick turnaround times available all over the Asia-Pacific, including China.

Most Indian ports are already operating at close to 100 per cent capacity, and expansion programmes will require massive investment to bring them to international standards. Moreover, unless hinterland connectivity in terms of efficient railroad and fast highway connections is available, investment in ports may be rendered unfruitful.

A master plan for rapid development and modernization of our ports and harbours should form the fourth prong of the National Maritime Strategy.

Shipping Industry

A nation's merchant fleet is a strategic national asset, both in peace as well as in war. Today, crude oil and natural gas carriers, container ships and Ro-Ro ferries are almost as important as warships in the security matrix. During war, a key objective of the belligerents will be to deprive the opponent's industry of vital raw materials and fuel, and to starve his civilian population by attacking merchant shipping. Ideally, therefore, the country should own and control as much of its shipping as possible so that it can ensure adequate reserves.

India's merchant fleet, the fifteenth largest in the world, has remained static at about 1,000 ships totalling 10 million tonnes. This fleet can carry less than 10 per cent of our foreign trade, and is not only woefully inadequate for India's needs but also lacks container, product and specialized carriers. Dependence on foreign shipping means not just a loss of earnings but also represents a strategic vulnerability.

Considering the fact that the Indian seaborne trade is set to double by 2020, the Indian shipping tonnage needs to be speedily augmented in order to arrest further decline in the strength of Indian flagged vessels. This should form the fifth prong of the National Maritime Strategy.

Foreign Cooperation

Maritime diplomacy figures prominently in the Maritime Military Strategy, but with one eye on enhancing interoperability and the other on 'shaping the maritime battle space'. In view of its important foreign relations connotations, maritime cooperation must find an important place in the National Maritime Strategy as a foreign policy initiative.

Concerns are frequently voiced in India about China's 'String of Pearls' and, the more recent, 'Maritime Silk Route' strategies. The challenge for India lies in crafting long-term alternatives based on economics, geopolitics and hard as well as soft power. The navy certainly has a role because smaller neighbours seek maritime security either through direct naval presence or through requests for material aid, training assistance and advice. The response to such requests is not always prompt due to differences of perceptions between the navy, the diplomats and the defence bureaucracy. After the navy's sterling performance during the 2004 tsunami, India's neighbours expect prompt assistance in times of natural calamities. Humanitarian assistance and disaster relief must, therefore, form a vital component of the National Maritime Strategy, with contribution from the armed forces as well as civil agencies.

India has been trying to give substance to its vision of the Indian Ocean as a unified geopolitical space by creating multilateral forums. An example is the Indian Ocean Rim Association (IORA) formed in 1997, with trade and economic cooperation as objectives; another is the Indian Ocean Naval Symposium (IONS), initiated by the Indian Navy in 2008 to bring together the IOR navies. So far these bodies have seen limited success, but they have great potential and may soon find greater regional resonance.

India is often accused of being over-possessive of the Indian Ocean, even to the extent of attempting to impose its version of the Monroe Doctrine in the region. This criticism is misplaced, and as a benign 'security provider' for the region India should give renewed impetus to a coherent and holistic approach to foreign maritime cooperation as the sixth component of its National Maritime Strategy.

Development of Island Territories

The critical strategic importance of India's island possessions in the Bay of Bengal as well as in the Arabian Sea has not been adequately appreciated by its decision makers. Distant from peninsular India, the location of these islands throws up security challenges, including the possibility of Kargil-like intrusions on some of the uninhabited ones. At the same time, they form a springboard from where India can reach out and project power, exert influence or strike bonds of friendship, especially in our South-East Asian neighbourhood.

Development of these islands is in the hands of a high-powered Island Development Authority, which seems to have become moribund. A combination of administrative lethargy coupled with excessive zeal by environmental lobbies has stalled developmental initiatives and kept these islands in a time warp akin to India's north-east. Island development is an issue of vital importance for national security and must find prominent mention in the National Maritime Strategy.

Maritime Domain Awareness

A key national security requirement is the effective understanding of all activities, events and trends within any relevant domain—air, land, sea, space and cyberspace—that could threaten India's safety, security, economy or environment. Maritime domain awareness (MDA) is the effective understanding of anything associated with the maritime domain that could impact the nation's security, safety, economy or environment. It enables the early identification of potential threats and enhances appropriate responses, including interdiction at an optimal distance with capable prevention forces.

Intense maritime activity in the Indian Ocean and the huge area that has to be kept under surveillance requires substantial reconnaissance and surveillance capabilities. The expected advent of the Chinese navy, especially its nuclear submarines, into the Indian Ocean will lend urgency to the MDA task. Post 26/11 there has been considerable progress towards the evolution of a multi-layered surveillance capability that includes communication and surveillance satellites, a coastal radar chain, surface and airborne patrolling and data fusion centres.

However, MDA is an ever-expanding challenge that requires technology as well as close cooperation with regional and other partners. Although it is a component of the Maritime Military Strategy, it must figure prominently in the National Maritime Strategy too.

Finally, a mention needs to be made of a strategic maritime asset that has unfortunately not received the attention and priority it deserves.

Seabed Exploration

India is the owner of a huge EEZ and was granted the status of a 'pioneer investor' in a large swathe of the Indian Ocean seabed by the International Seabed Authority as early as 1987. The ocean bottom promises to yield vast resources of mineral wealth, embedded in poly-metallic nodules, which lie on the ocean floor.

India's Department of Ocean Development and now the Ministry of Earth Sciences have shown perfunctory interest in seabed research. On the other hand, China has established a huge lead in the area of seabed exploration technology by producing the world's deepest diving vehicle, which can go down to 7,000 meters. If information about the presence of strategic rare-earth metals on the seabed is true, India needs to accord priority to seabed exploration programmes as part of the National Maritime Strategy so that it is not left far behind.

Conclusion

India is a peninsular nation with an ancient, if forgotten, maritime heritage and vital maritime interests which are growing by the day. Many important aspects of our national life and economy depend on our commercial connections to the wider world, a majority of which are provided by sea lines of communication. India's trade-dependent economic progress is undergirded by these essential components of maritime power, but a lack of strategic vision has resulted in failure to exploit the maritime sector in a holistic manner.

A strong and balanced navy is vital for the protection of these maritime interests and for India's march towards major power status. Such a force will soon be a reality, largely through the foresight and vision of India's naval leadership. In the absence of higher direction, the navy has also crafted for itself a maritime doctrine and strategy.

However, it is necessary for India's decision makers to understand that the navy by itself constitutes just one pillar of the country's maritime capability, and without the rest of the structure, including political guidance at the strategic level, the edifice of naval power will remain hollow. The Maritime Military Strategy must be linked to and become a component of an overarching national strategy for India's maritime security.

Another factor in Mahan's list of conditions affecting sea power is 'national character and aptitudes',[25] wherein he focuses attention on mercenary instinct and a propensity for trade and enterprise as traits that predisposed nations to becoming great sea powers. While the Indian proclivity for commercial enterprise is acknowledged worldwide, a national effort—such as the one initiated by China[26] in the last decade—at reviving its ancient maritime tradition has been wanting. Inspiring amongst the general populace—especially the youth—an enthusiasm for the sea and affinity for seafaring activities should form an important component of the new strategy.

A nation with India's maritime assets, challenges and opportunities urgently needs to conceive a National Maritime Strategy, which will create synergies and draw maximum advantage from the maritime sector. Till then, a competent and powerful navy notwithstanding, India's economic interests will remain under-developed and its maritime security vulnerable.

10

A Counter–Proxy War Strategy for Jammu and Kashmir

Lieutenant General Syed Ata Hasnain

Former General Officer Commanding of the Indian Army's Chinar Corps in Kashmir. He is a graduate of the Royal College of Defence Studies, London; Asia-Pacific Center for Security Studies, Hawaii; and Kings College, London. He is now associated with several think tanks in New Delhi.

In the hierarchy of India's national security issues, Jammu and Kashmir (J&K) takes the top spot. Unlike the perception that it is all about military and border/territorial security, J&K is also as much about India's emotional security, because it is one of the oldest national security issues still alive. It is also an issue that has dictated the trajectory of our relationship with Pakistan, which has been, and is likely to remain, a major adversary.

This chapter examines the dynamics of J&K as a source of insecurity, how it came to find itself set up for exploitation, and the launch of proxy war by Pakistan. It also looks at the status of the conflict after twenty-five years of bloodletting, and at how we need to deal with the issue to negate the frailties that have come to be associated with J&K in order to counter the sponsored proxy war launched against us.

The history of the J&K problem is well known and not necessary to recall, except for a few landmarks that are significant in the progressive deterioration of India–Pakistan relations over J&K. In legal terms, the Instrument of Accession signed on 26 October 1947 by Maharaja Hari Singh is the basis of India's right to the territories of the entire state. Our stance is reinforced by the joint resolution of the two houses of Parliament, passed on 22 February 1994, calling for the return of all the territories of J&K to India. Pakistan emphatically rejects the authenticity of the Instrument of Accession. It lays its claim on an infirm rationale of the state demographically having a Muslim majority, and thus adhering to the framework of the merger of princely states set up by the departing British at the end of their colonial presence in the subcontinent.

It chose to use force to settle the problem through the launch of the first conflict in 1947-48. By this it came to occupy certain territories before the ceasefire was brokered under an UN agreement, and a Cease Fire Line (CFL) was created. The CFL resulted in the occupation of parts of J&K by Pakistan, and the agreement was based upon the principle of vacation of that territory by its forces and the conduct of a plebiscite to ascertain the choice of the people. However, Pakistan has chosen to ignore that basic principle, continued to lay claims on the entire state and attempted to change the status through the use of force.

Roundly defeated militarily in 1971, it received magnanimous treatment at the historic Shimla summit in 1972, in which India chose not to force the settlement but to resolve the issue progressively and bilaterally by mutual consent. India has since then strongly maintained the non-tenability of the UN agreement and accepted the temporarily delineated Line of Control (LoC) as an interim measure. Both sides strongly man the LoC with their regular troops to prevent its sanctity being breached by the other side.

It is, however, important to recall that Pakistan's strategy has all along been to somehow keep the focus on the LoC, to sensitize the international community and remind it of the existence of the J&K problem. It has also regularly strategized to keep the flames of separatism alive in the state as a means to bolster its claims. Much against the spirit of bilateralism laid out in the Shimla Agreement, it has frequently raised the issue at international forums. It may also be relevant to mention that Pakistan has also complicated the issue by the illegal ceding, to China, of over 5,000 sq km of territory in the Gilgit–Baltistan area of J&K in 1963.

Pakistan's unsuccessful attempts to change the status quo by force, in 1947-48, 1965 and 1971, sent home the clear message that it did not possess the military capability to achieve its aim. In spite of that, Pakistan has constantly endeavoured to create conditions to secure an advantage by which India will be forced to either cede the entire state or agree to a UN-brokered plebiscite. The latter, no doubt a part of the original UN resolution, has been overtaken by the run of history and is no longer considered valid by India.

Pakistan's Approach, 1972–89: The Build-up to Proxy War

To arrive at any strategy to counter the proxy war efforts of Pakistan, it is necessary to first examine how it came to realize that proxy war was the most prudent method to contain and target India. Post the 1971 war, Pakistan displayed grudging acceptance in executing the provisions of the Shimla Agreement. However, the spirit of retribution for the loss of half its territory has never been out of Pakistan's mind. In fact, it intensified in the wake of the Pokhran nuclear test in 1974, which threatened a completely asymmetrical situation in the subcontinent. India's nuclear test was never aimed at Pakistan and was more a demonstration of India's will to more proactively pursue its security interest vis-à-vis China. It was, however, interpreted differently by Pakistan's security establishment, leading to Prime Minister Zulfiqar Ali Bhutto making his famous statement that Pakistan would eat grass and leaves but have the bomb. While Pakistan may have been led by a civilian government from 1972 to 1977, its disgraced army never really gave up power and continued to influence policy towards India, a policy essentially caustic, reflecting the seething anger within. Bhutto, as one of the architects of the policy towards erstwhile East Pakistan, never held back either.

Three important things occurred in this period which helped shape the future discourse of policy towards India and the launch of proxy war. First, the experiment with civilian government came to an end with the unceremonious dismissal of Zulfiqar Ali Bhutto (he was subsequently hanged in 1979), and the return of the Pakistan Army to power in 1977 under General Zia ul Haq. Zia's approach was clear. Retribution for 1971 would come not through direct military confrontation but by other subtle means that would exploit India's identified vulnerabilities—its heterogeneous make-up and religious and communal frailty. To do this, Pakistan needed identification and greater affinity with the Islamic world, as a back-up; it chose to align more vigorously with Saudi Arabia, from where it could draw financial and religious support by acting as its surrogate on Iran's eastern flank. The newfound financial clout of Saudi Arabia, enabled by the rising power of oil as a weapon, as well as the need of the Saudi monarchy to have additional protection within its country gave Pakistan the opportunity to align itself by providing military support to Saudi Arabia. A full Pakistani brigade was stationed at Riyadh for this purpose. The Iranian revolution of 1979 worried Saudi Arabia and reinforced its own need to support Pakistan. This is how Pakistan's strong relationship with Saudi Arabia was enabled, and it gave the former a back-up, a form of assured security.

Second, the Soviet invasion of Afghanistan, also in 1979, threw up greater opportunities for Pakistan and embellished its own strategic importance in the eyes of the West, especially the US. Pakistan's territory became the launch pad for the US-initiated irregular war to defeat the Soviet Union. In fact, this war was one of the triggers which contributed to the end of the Cold War. It was facilitated by Pakistan's Inter-Services Intelligence (ISI), which used surrogate mercenaries from all over the Islamic world. Impassioned as they were with religious (read Islamic) fervour, this was the beginning of the so-called jihadi wars, and the ISI learnt many lessons through the experience it gained in the ten-year irregular conflict. It was at this time (early 1980s) that the insurgency in Punjab commenced.

The ISI, in cooperation with the other security agencies of Pakistan, synced together to form the virtual 'Deep State', which sensed an opportunity. A proactive involvement in Punjab through financing, arms supply, narcotics and subterfuge ensured that the insurgency remained active for over ten years. In fact, that one of India's most developed states and segments of one of its most patriotic communities could be misled and sponsored to fight for a separate nation was an achievement of sorts for Pakistan and its Deep State. While separatism did not ever become a serious threat, there were times when the Punjab issue appeared to put India's experienced political leadership under severe test. For over ten years Pakistan could create cracks in India's nationhood, but the latter's stamina and inherent strength as a nation withstood this. It nevertheless gave Pakistan and its agencies enough experience to handle future situations, and to set these up in their favour.

The third aspect, partially already referred to in passing, was the religious fervour which General Zia ul Haq managed to inject into the spirit of Pakistan. This was one of the most important factors that enabled Pakistan to undertake its mission of seeking revenge for 1971 through the weakening of India by its policy of a 'thousand cuts'. Christine Fair, in her seminal work *Fighting to the End: The Pakistan Army's Way of War*, does not lay the responsibility for the Islamization of Pakistan on Zia but rather on the manner in which Pakistan developed as a nation right from its foundation. Her broad opinion is based upon the observation that Pakistan always considered itself a weak state and clung to faith as the unifier, which then received a boost when it lost its confidence after the defeat in 1971.

The late 1970s, with the impetus from the Iranian revolution and the period of the irregular war in Afghanistan, gave Pakistan the opportunity to ride on the back of faith. Zia analysed deeply and found that the Saudi-supported Wahabi faith could be what would allow Pakistan to take the lead and be counted among the flag bearers of Islam. It would further endear Pakistan to Saudi Arabia, besides impassioning the Pakistan Army. Using this ideology, Pakistan could attempt influencing the Sunni majority within Muslims in India and spreading radical ideas to endear Indian Muslims. This would create schisms in India's progressively strengthening secular system. The existing antipathy of the Pakistan Army towards India and the notion of Pakistan being a pure Islamic state were assiduously exploited by Zia to inculcate radical beliefs within the Pakistan Army, with faith becoming the driving force for the management of its strategic interests.

Zia's belief that India and Pakistan could not live in peace with the hangover of the latter's military defeat was to an extent strengthened in the face of India's aggressive military posturing in 1987 with Operation Brasstacks. In the run-up to this and through the 1980s, Zia adopted the policy of ambiguity regarding its nuclear weapons programme. He informally attached the label 'Islamic Bomb' to get Islamic nations to identify themselves more positively with Pakistan. This increased his confidence, and as nuclear technology was acquired clandestinely, the confidence continued to grow. The opaqueness connected with the programme as well as the ambiguity assisted in enhancing Pakistan's perceived military capability. An important aspect which developed as a spinoff of the clandestine nuclear programme was the development of Pakistan's diplomatic capability. Denial became its watchword in the pursuit of its strategic interests. All this was ignored by the US because of its need for Pakistan's support to fight the Soviets right through the 1980s.

The combination of nuclear ambiguity, concept of denial,

radicalization of the rank and file of the army, empowerment and experience of the ISI and the diplomatic corps, increasing affinity with the Arab world and the urge for early retribution against India ensured that Pakistan's confidence surged through the crucial period of the 1980s. In addition, the notion that Pakistan lost its eastern half more because of India's subterfuge and betrayal by the Bengalis and less because of military reasons continued to drive the Pakistan leadership's thinking. The developing psyche as a result of all of the above was the driving force behind Pakistan's understanding that it could target India effectively through threshold activity without the employment of military resources. As a back-up for anything going wrong or Pakistan crossing the threshold of India's tolerance, its military resources backed by the as yet untested nuclear programme were sufficient deterrence. It only awaited the opportunity to bring things to a head, and that came its way in 1989-90. Zia was dead by then, and an inexperienced Benazir Bhutto, wishing to prove her patriotic fervour and maintaining a relationship with the army, did the honours of initiating conflict.

The Situation in 1989-90: Ripe for Exploitation by Pakistan

From 1984 to 1989, India was in the midst of absorbing Rajiv Gandhi's leadership style, including the new drive towards technology. His coterie comprising the energetic General Krishnaswamy Sundarji and Minister of State for Defence Arun Singh dominated the strategic scene. It was the period in which India saw its first ever out-of-area security commitment in the form of the Indian Peace Keeping Force in Sri Lanka (launched in August 1987). The Bofors scandal in 1987 marked the downturn of Gandhi's stable government. In the same year, the J&K elections and the subsequent allegations of rigging initiated low-level street turbulence and conditions leading to a public order situation in the Valley. The year also saw Sundarji's ambitious Operation Brasstacks, which almost brought India and Pakistan to a state of conflict.

If 1987 was the year triggering rumblings in India's strategic environment, 1989-90 will be remembered for the rapidly altered international strategic environment, as well as a negative national scene. The Berlin Wall fell, symbolizing the end of the Cold War and the beginning of the process of evolving a new world order. The break-up of the Soviet Union was on the cards, and it finally happened in 1991. In the process, the energy released from the dying moments of the communist heyday started to manifest itself in the form of ethno-religious conflicts such as in the Balkans.

Within India, 1989 saw political turbulence of a high order. The Congress government fell and was replaced by a conglomerate of parties, with political stability remaining elusive. The Mandal agitation hit the streets in 1990, causing deep schisms in Indian society. Economically, these were bad years, and foreign exchange reserves were fast dwindling. The Indian Army was as yet committed in Sri Lanka to the tune of four frontline divisions. Punjab was burning with the militancy already supported by Pakistan. To top it all, Pakistan decided in 1989 to conduct Exercise Zarb-e-Momin, an army-level offensive exercise which was supposed to be Pakistan's answer to Operation Brasstacks. In New Delhi, it was assessed that the exercise could well convert into a lightning strike by Pakistan's offensive reserves.

Kashmir's militancy broke out in late 1989, although trans-LoC movement was rife right from 1987. Sensing the opportunity to score a point over the opposition, Benazir Bhutto was quick off the blocks. With shrill rhetoric she called for azadi, a major change from the avowed Pakistani intent of merging J&K with Pakistan. It was realpolitik, pandering to public sentiment, which was against India in the Kashmir Valley. It needed to be rallied and focused. In the days without 24x7 channels and satellite TV, no Internet and no social media, it had to be done on outmoded radio stations and the clarion call had to be given from mosques. That is how the mosques of Kashmir got involved in the militancy very early.

From a military perspective, what were India's resources to immediately respond to the trigger that Pakistan was providing by proxy? The entire Valley segment of the LoC was held by the 19 Infantry Division. The 28 Infantry Division, today's mainstay at Kupwara, was then deployed in Ladakh and oversaw Siachen operations. The 19 Infantry Division was anyway responsible for the sanctity of the LoC; it could not be employed in an anti-militancy role. To do that, the army rushed the 39 Infantry Division, a reserve division no doubt but with no understanding of anti-militancy operations. The Border Security Force (BSF) was there in fair numbers, but again with no training to handle militancy or, worse, street protests. The series of street massacres by India's security forces, now glorified by separatists, became bynames—Gwakadal, Bijbehara, Handwara and Sopore besides many others. It was Pakistan's sponsorship which urged the emerging separatist leaders to take to the streets. Organized militancy was some time away, but passions could be aroused quite easily as casualties mounted among civilians. Pakistan played the game most assiduously as sentiments spiralled out of control.

Pakistan's Proxy War and Lessons from the Low-intensity Conflict

A broad understanding of the progress of proxy war in J&K gives lessons in how it should be countered in the future. Pakistan chose to launch a proxy war for many of the reasons already spelt out above, the primary one being its full knowledge that Kashmir could not be wrested by conventional military means. As the situation presented itself and panned out from 1987 to 1992 or so (classified as classic conflict initiation) Pakistan used a combination of POK-trained militants (later classified as terrorists because of the methods used), plainclothes Special Service Group (SSG) leaders in safehouses in the Valley, grenade attacks, improvised explosive devices (IEDs) and ambushes against soft elements to engage the army.

The relatively low-density presence of the army in the hinterland and in urban centres such as Srinagar, Anantnag and Sopore forced the army to adopt defensive measures. In terms of offensive operations, large-scale cordon and search operations (CASO) characterized the response. While terrorists were killed in large numbers, the civil population was subjected to intense pressure; this included government servants and white-collar workers. It was part of the ISI's strategy to force the Indian Army to react strongly against the populace, creating antipathy among the more affluent segments. Since intelligence was poor and the J&K police were not yet trusted, the flow of information, let alone intelligence, was restricted, forcing the army and other security forces to impose measures such as multiple vehicle check points to detain suspects and restrict the freedom of movement. Unable to halt the free movement of civilians, particularly the youth, to and fro across the LoC, hard measures had to be adopted, leading to civilian casualties.

For a sponsor of proxy war, all of the above are results that are sought. Civilian casualties, restrictions on the movement of people, check points, interrogations and custodial deaths created a greater will to resist. As martyr graveyards and unmarked graves proliferated, the movement escalated. The induction of foreign fighters by Pakistan was an astute step after realizing that these were available in abundance, their cost was a pittance, and that the local Kashmiri terrorist was not sufficiently radicalized to wage jihad. Besides, they added to the numbers and provided leadership on the basis of their experience in Afghanistan. It is only the arrival of the first Rashtriya Rifles (RR) sectors and units that provided the recommended structure and means of a proper counter-infiltration (CI) grid to the army. The raising of two HQ CI forces in south Kashmir and Doda district and the induction and settling down of the 8 Mountain Division in north Kashmir strengthened the grid. Once the grid was in place, and serious coordination with J&K police was possible, the situation started to turn around.

Focused CI efforts were some years away. It was almost impossible to seal the LoC, and right through the 1990s up to mid-2004, the army's efforts produced results, but these were insufficient to control the 'mathematics of terror'. The latter is a term peculiar to J&K; it essentially reflects the end-year results in terms of the number of terrorists killed and those infiltrated across the LoC. Pakistan's proxy war would succeed as long as the numbers infiltrated exceeded those killed.

A most essential aspect of the proxy war was its classification as jihad. Without this label it could not be expected to draw the kind of support it did. There is no gain from hiding the fact that without the religious fervour, an irregular war which thrives on people's support cannot be fought. The ISI learnt this early in Afghanistan and the US assisted it by drawing hordes of unemployed young men from different Islamic countries, fired by the passion to save Islam and to promote it. Jihad became the by-word and the symbol of Islamic unity. In many ways, even more than the Bosnian conflict, it was J&K which provided the tonic for jihad. The proximity of Pakistan and the proxy support it extended, the presence of seasoned mujahideen from the Afghanistan war and the availability of a geographically isolated Muslim population that perceived itself wronged were all ingredients of the irregular war.

The triggering of radical Islamic passion led to the targeting of Kashmiri Hindus, both Pandits and Rajputs, the former being in larger numbers. Around 350,000 were virtually evicted. As long as Kashmir and Kashmiri Muslims were identified with tolerance and the Sufi concept of syncretic existence, the populace could not be expected to rise with the hatred which was necessary to bring about an internal war for azadi. Violence against the community was planned and executed such that it would create fear and exodus. The Indian government and the intelligence agencies did not understand the larger game plan. That Kashmiri Hindus virtually became internally displaced people outside Kashmir remains a major obstacle to the resumption of normalcy in J&K twenty-five years later. Pakistan, interestingly, now opposes their return on the grounds that it would upset the demographic balance, conveniently forgetting the demographic change of POK.

The Kargil Trigger

Many reasons have been ascribed to General Pervez Musharraf's decision to launch his Kargil misadventure in 1999. It is not important to discuss the relative importance or applicability of these; all we are concerned with is whether it had a link with the proxy war in J&K. The simple answer is 'yes'. The situation in J&K in 1999 wasn't exactly floundering, but the role of the foreign terrorist (not so much the Pakistani terrorist) was being questioned by the local people. The arc of terrorism had not effectively spread to the Hindu-dominated areas of Jammu and Udhampur. The ISI had plans to push in a large number of Pakistani infiltrators but required more energy from the Kashmiri fighters and the people to believe in the feasibility of ejecting India. Most importantly, there was a need to force the Indian Army to redeploy so as to recreate space in Kashmir, which was inching towards being controlled by the army. The 1998 tourist season wasn't too bad, and 1999 could be better, bringing a semblance of normalcy that India was seeking.

In effect, Musharraf's strategy may not have worked towards gaining Siachen, but it had results in Kashmir. The most important was the physical space which was created in north Kashmir with the rapid movement of the 8 Mountain Division to Kargil. The areas around Sopore and Lolab Valley got flooded with terrorists, and it was learnt that Handwara had the presence of a few ISI regulars who directed the operations. At this time the fedayeen attacks commenced, forcing the Indian Army to adopt defensive measures and more forceful methods for intelligence gathering, which had a cascading effect on the relationship with the local people.

When in 2008 the situation was seen to be flagging again, a fresh spurt was provided by the manipulated events leading to the Shri Amarnathji Shrine Board agitation. This was after the army's successful counter-infiltration run had reversed the 'mathematics of terror' between 2004 and 2007. Sensing the return of 1998, Pakistan looked for opportunities to give another push to the movement. The ongoing efforts of the Shri Amarnathji Shrine Board to improve the facilities for pilgrims were branded as anti-Valley, anti-Islam and anti-environment, thus providing a trigger for the launch of an agitation which took the streets of Kashmir by storm, and led to a major standoff between the Valley and the Jammu region. Stone-throwing mobs were instigated by separatists and the resistance took a completely different turn, arousing passions. The agitation remained on course for the better part of three years.

It is important to note here that the proxy war has run a dynamic course from 1989 onwards. There have been peaks and troughs, but the main 'way points' have been:

1. 1989: The launch in 1989 symbolizing mass resistance and street turbulence.
2. 1991-92: Enhanced induction of foreign terrorists freed from commitment in Afghanistan. This gave a boost to the movement when the perception started forming that the local Kashmiri may not be able to sustain a long-drawn proxy war.
3. 1999: With foreign (non-Pakistani) terrorists reducing in strength, the proxy war took a downturn in 1998. It was crucial to give it a fillip. The events relating to Kargil helped breathe life into the campaign.
4. 2004-07: The construction of the LoC fence brought focus on CI operations while anti-terrorist operations led to the elimination of a large number of terrorist leaders. The movement appeared to be flagging.
5. 2008-10: In particular, 2008 was significant for the return of street turbulence. The years 2009 and 2010 were characterized by the

continuance of turbulence brought on by the exploitation of triggers and astute propaganda.

6. Although 2011 was a peaceful year, partially due to the army's proactiveness and partially because of agitation fatigue, the energy from the agitation continued with many attempted triggers.

The conclusion that can be drawn is that the proxy war has never been static. Pakistan finds innovative ways to sustain it. There are uncontrollable triggers always available to be exploited, and the environment is conducive to such exploitation. Pakistan's twenty-five years of efforts have created a clientele which is available for its proxy support. The army takes its time but has answers to contain the proxy war. However, a transformative approach to nudge the situation towards conflict termination on our terms is eluding it. How exactly has the social environment of J&K changed over these twenty-five years, making the conditions easy to exploit, and how can the nation, the state and the army counter it and possibly put a permanent end to it? This forms the theme of subsequent analysis.

Political, Social and Economic Environment and Impact on Separatism

The subsequent analysis is for the purpose of defining the social environment of J&K and how, if at all, Pakistan can exploit it for continuing its proxy war. Three factors need examination: religion and ideology as a single entity, politics and demography. In the field of religion and ideology it has already been brought out that the idea of proxy war against India emanates from the understanding that India is a weak state because of a heterogeneity that has not fully achieved integration. Pakistan's belief is that Kashmir's Muslim population remains completely outside the realm of integration, to the extent that it is not even integrated with Indian Muslims. Kashmir's inclusive Sufi Islamic culture has already been majorly dented by the Wahabi ideology propagated by Saudi Arabia and Pakistan. An estimated 800 mosques, owing allegiance to the Ahle Hadis sect, have sprouted all over Kashmir. A large number have also come up in the Rajouri area. These mosques preach an ideology of an extreme kind, which helps to propagate the message of allegiance to the Islamic Ummah, thus giving a religious colour to the internal conflict.

India's agencies looking after J&K have failed to stem this tide in spite of being fully aware of the problem. A counter movement to restore Kashmir's rich Sufi tradition and tolerant outlook is the only way to prevent proliferation of this culture, which promotes separatism. The mosques of J&K must return to the Sufi tradition and be in the control of Sufi clergy, who are extremely rare to find in the state these days. It is not easy to interfere in the affairs of the mosque due to the prevailing sentiments, but attempting to work through the route of Sufi culture would be a more pragmatic way to counter the Wahabi ideology rather than a direct confrontation over mosques.

The demographic break-up of J&K and, even more interestingly, the divisions within the Kashmir Valley, offer some fascinating ideas. Arun Kumar, an RSS ideologue, in his extensive study came up with the interesting deduction that separatism runs in the sentiments of only five districts of Kashmir. The Shia Muslim population, forming approximately 12 per cent of the population, has no separatist tendency at all. This sentiment is prevalent primarily in the Sunni Kashmiri population of the Valley floor. Pakistan's efforts are, therefore, concentrated primarily on the Sunni segment, and ardent efforts are being made to spread the sentiment to the Pahari and Gujjar areas. In the late 1990s and in the early years of the new millennium, efforts were made to spread the arc of radical terror well outside the Valley towards Jammu division. It led to the invoking of the Armed Forces Special Powers Act (AFSPA 1990) in the Jammu division in 2001.

The politics of J&K has an indirect hand in promoting separatism. The persistent clash between the Jammu and Kashmir divisions for the political, economic and social space hampers integration in the Valley. The people of Jammu region have never supported Article 370 and stiffly resist any notion of removal of AFSPA. For Pakistan, Article 370 and AFSPA are cards that can be used to manipulate sentiments.

The other politico-religious card available for Pakistan's ready exploitation is the presence of a large number of Hindu shrines in the Kashmir region, the most prominent being the Shri Amarnathji Shrine and the Kheer Bhawani temple in Ganderbal. Many more shrines revered by the Kashmiri Pandit community dot Kashmir's landscape. Historically, the Kashmiri Sufi tradition respected the diversity of shrines and a large number of Sufi shrines also exist in the same landscape. But at the instigation of separatists, a demand has found a place in the politico-religious discourse to restrict the numbers of pilgrims visiting Hindu shrines on the pretext of preventing ecological damage to Kashmir's environment. The counter to this is better and more proactive perception management to highlight that the people of Kashmir benefit from the high number of footfalls in the mountains. The larger issue of Kashmir's inclusive culture also needs to be brought to the fore.

Although elections were introduced early in the period of strife (1996), the issues concerning governance have provided even more triggers. It comes to Pakistan's aid that the state's elected governments and substantial packages of assistance have not helped the people. Corruption is not of Pakistan's creation but hampers integration. There is a need for the induction of a select cadre of incorruptible administrators and better financial controls and accountability. There is no obstacle to this except the will of the central and state governments.

The winter management of Ladakh and Kashmir offers tremendous scope. Currently, the administrative arrangements for emergent conditions in winter are unprofessional and have seldom received the kind of attention that they need. Vikas mandals of major towns in Kashmir need to be linked with the vikas mandals of towns in the Jammu region. This will contribute to better governance in winter and overcome logistical problems that give rise to negative sentiments, which are in turn annually exploited by the separatists.

A brief analysis of AFSPA is necessary to establish how it has been used to play the perception game. Firstly, this constitutional legislation was mandatory to legitimize the army's deployment in the public order situation in 1989-90. Once it was realized that without the army's robust involvement the counter–proxy war could not be fought, its operations had to be without reference and with a degree of freedom and legal protection of the troops in the face of legitimate mistakes. This protection was afforded by simply empowering only the central government to initiate prosecution, leaving no such powers at the local level.

The law was drafted in the 'context of the times', necessitating the use of some harsh language and delegation of fairly extensive powers. It was partially mellowed down in spirit with the issue of the dos and don'ts of the Supreme Court in 1997. The HQ Northern Command also framed extensive rules of engagement and standard operating procedures, giving a humanizing touch to the conflict. In 1997, the army came out with its path-breaking Operation Sadbhavana (now called only Sadbhavana), the first time that an official military–civic action with an earmarked budget, resources, commitment and programmes was ever drawn up. Yet, two things are important to point out at this juncture.

The nation and the army lost the perception battle in the course of operations. The human rights community on the one hand and anti-national elements on the other whipped up a campaign to brand the army as anti–human rights, and AFSPA as draconian. Little effort was made to fight this accusation. To substantiate allegations, the unmarked graves issue was thrown up. This is an issue harking back to 1989 and the early 1990s when the LoC was violated repeatedly using the notion that Kashmir would soon be separated from India. There were mass interceptions and several deaths because of the inability to differentiate between terrorists, recruits being taken for training and civilians who walked to and fro at will. No system of registration of such deaths and of their ancestry existed at that time, leading to burials in unmarked graves. There are many side effects of sponsored internal conflict. However, it is also true that efforts have to be made to mend the ruptures in society to ensure a semblance of normalcy.

In 2011, efforts were made to rake up the issue of AFSPA under the mistaken notion that it could be abrogated by the de-notification of disturbed areas under the authority of the chief minister. When it was proved otherwise, efforts should have been made to debate the retention of the law or its amendment. The debate must be an informed one, and if AFSPA under a different label is retained, it must have all the provisions and guidelines which humanize its existence within the body of the law. This is the starting point of the perception battle.

The Current Environment

The military situation remains under control with a robust CI grid which has delivered and prevented Pakistan from any capability of surge. However, infiltration will always remain a threat. The hinterland military situation is well in our favour with the extremely low footprint of terrorists and a low-grade leadership. However, the integration of an indeterminate number of surrendered terrorists is as yet suspect. This segment lives dissatisfied and frustrated at the government's inability to fulfil its promises. It can provide the foot soldiers needed for a resurgence. Pakistan's recent efforts in sync with the separatists involve the recruitment of educated but radicalized youth from Kashmir's educational institutions.

Politically, the best situation would be for an empowered Kashmir and an empowered Jammu to exist together in coalition. However, there are contentious factors which will be exploited by Pakistan and the separatists to prevent effective governance and stability. As long as the coalition can display political maturity and not play to the galleries for future political gains, it will be difficult to dislodge or render it ineffective.

With the military space firmly under the army's control and the political space stabilizing with greater understanding between the constituents, it is the social and the psychological space that will be available for competition. It will be Pakistan's intent to strengthen the pro-Pakistan elements among the separatists as against the moderate pro-azadi elements. Induction of finances will be attempted, and despite Pakistan's terrible experience with Islamic radicalism, it is likely to find this the most effective instrument to ensure the loyalty of the youth in the Muslim-majority areas. India's intelligence agencies will have to concentrate on these aspects to dilute Pakistan's effectiveness in interfering in these areas and exercising influence.

The Pakistani strategy is sometimes paradoxical in approach. For example, its aim is to force the Indian Army to reduce its presence so that a resurgence of anti-national activity is quicker and more effective. However, to force out the army or to reduce its deployment, a semblance of stability has to be evident. To allow this, Pakistan would have to shed whatever advantage it has.

Pakistan's Future Strategy

There isn't much need to speculate because, for Pakistan, proxy war is the only option to keep India's racing growth under check and force hyphenation with it. The world has a tendency to hyphenate nations which are on a fast track towards economic development; India's hyphenation is with China and other nations. For Pakistan, proxy war is the way to prevent the world forgetting the existence of J&K as a disputed issue and hyphenate India again with Pakistan. While proxy war has a larger dimension in targeting the whole of India, it is J&K which provides the maximum potential for exploitation. The other aspect emerging loud and clear is that proxy war uses a comprehensive method of exploiting anything which can create schisms in J&K's society and polity, prevent effective governance, keep the streets in turmoil from time to time and play on the minds of the people to prevent the integration that India seeks.

There is bound to be fair resistance within Pakistan's weak civil society and liberal media to the continuance of such a policy. The creation and nurturing of 'lashkars' and 'sipahs' has brought Pakistan to its knees, but the Deep State believes that this is the way to ensure Pakistan's security and the army's prominence in the national pecking order.

The strategy could include the following aspects:

1. The starting point is the belief to be inculcated that Pakistan has succeeded and can further succeed in its War of a Thousand Cuts and no other place symbolizes this better than J&K.
2. Pakistan has withstood international scrutiny and Indian pressure on the international community. There is no serious effort on the part of any important country of the international community to label Pakistan negatively. Pakistan's geo-strategic position will ensure that its requirements to the international community will outweigh the need to curtail its activities in India.
3. With this backdrop, the belief would be that there are enough opportunities every few years which can be exploited to trigger fresh antipathy towards India. At the operational and tactical levels, opportunities have to be sought and even created through networks of over-ground workers (OGWs). There must be every effort made to maintain the networks in the face of the Indian Army and intelligence agencies.
4. There would be a combined effort towards the promotion of separatism, cultivation of the media, flow of finances including counterfeit currency, radicalism, street turbulence, harnessing of youth power, psychological warfare and efforts towards curtailment

of government initiatives and denying the people any benefits of democracy.

5. Sustaining the campaign is contingent upon effective radicalization of the youth, preventing them falling prey to Indian psychological operations and military–civic action. For this, it is necessary that the mosques and the clergy be in the control of Pakistan and the separatists. This can be furthered by promoting divisiveness and crystallizing the thinking that there is actually a Muslim Kashmir and a Muslim Jammu which is temporarily in the control of Hindus. The more miserable Kashmiris are administratively (power, energy, roads, railways), the more will this endure and more will be the antipathy towards India.
6. Innovation is essential to ensure that each time the movement appears to be flagging, a trigger—military, social or psychological—is employed to give impetus and recapture the dwindling space. The milestones of perceived tragedy, such as the calendar days marking incidents of large-scale civilian casualties or like events will be highlighted on a regular basis, as will the funerals of terrorists.
7. In the field of faith, efforts will be towards the promotion of the idea that Indian Muslims have transformed under Hindu influence and are no longer ideal members of the Ummah with whom J&K Muslims can live any longer. They have neither affinity with J&K Muslims nor any sympathy for them. Pakistan will cultivate and promote the idea that India's concept of 'One Nation' is alien to Islam. It is important for Pakistan's psychological warfare machine to keep J&K mired in faith-based issues with which the Indian establishment is uncomfortable. The essence of the doctrine lies in complicating the environment and seeking the support of the worldwide Islamic community based upon global trends of civilizational standoffs.
8. Nothing offers scope for promoting divisiveness more than the issue of the return of Kashmiri Pandits, the nature of the management of pilgrimages and the plethora of Kashmiri Pandit rituals which will be conducted as the community rightly seeks its return.
9. Pakistan has yet to employ social media effectively in its efforts. However, it is a matter of time. Lessons from the Islamic State's model of attracting youth by subtle messaging must already be

under intense scrutiny. A surge in social media activity should be expected any time.

10. Pakistan is aware that India's army is its greatest advantage and asset. Whenever an attempt is made to wrest advantage in the kinetic realm, the Indian Army always responds professionally and restores the situation. However, it can do so only up to a point. An option for Pakistan remains to so structure its proxy war that a low threshold of violence exists for some years, increasing pressure on the Indian government to reduce the army's deployment. A lower army footprint will allow non-military activities to proliferate more effectively. The psychological conditioning of the new generation and emerging generation (two separate entities) will also be much easier without the army's military-civic action schemes such as Sadbhavana.
11. In terms of the military realm, it is not as if the Deep State will allow the Indian Army time for rest and recuperation. The LoC is the symbol of war, but it can also equally be exploited as a symbol of proxy war. Every time Pakistan is in deep trouble internally or externally, the LoC is the release valve. Each time India ignores Pakistan's attempts to engage it without any assurances of delivering on promises or cutting off support to terrorists, the LoC is activated. It is also used to draw the attention of visiting dignitaries to the region but, most importantly, it is across the length of the LoC that Pakistan effects infiltration to sustain the military element of the conflict. The spectrum of operations is wide, from mere shelling and small arms exchanges to the use of 'Border Action Teams' by Pakistan. The choice extends to conducting shallow-depth fedayeen (suicide) type operations against objectives close to the LoC, e.g., the Uri attack of December 2014.
12. Similarly, the attacks at Samba and Kathua are simple to launch because of the shorter time involved and minimal logistics, unlike in the targeting of objectives in the Valley or in the Rajouri–Poonch sector.
13. The activation of the International Boundary sector (which Pakistan refers to as the working boundary) is an innovation on the part of the Deep State. The Indian establishment is as yet wrestling with the reasons that give Pakistan any advantage. In simple terms, the

understanding should be clear. Activating the border in Jammu division would balance the loss of effectiveness in the Valley. A larger segment of population (almost all Hindu) would be affected by border violence, creating more antipathy. Small-scale infiltration would be possible, enabling fedayeen-type attacks to keep turbulence levels at a higher pitch. On these grounds, Pakistan's choice would be wise for its desired ends.

14. Pakistan's experience with intrusions across the LoC has not given much joy to its planners as regards the LoC itself. Kargil, however, was a one-time trigger for effect within the Valley. It did succeed, but repetition of this ploy is unlikely to fetch it any more dividends. However, resorting to the bluff, even if unsuccessful on the ground, could well have indirect effects in the hinterland.

It is important to realize that Pakistan's proxy war against India is a war without end. Pakistan's establishment is well known for its innovative conflict initiation, but equally well known for its inability to terminate a conflict on its terms. Every now and then the war will slide in terms of effectiveness. Seasonally, too, it will be given an impetus. Surprise will remain the biggest factor as much as stamina. The turbulent period of agitation in 2008–10 ran out of stamina. It will always remain a question of how effective an innovation Pakistan can initiate. For India, the answers remain in examining its own past strategy, getting a better understanding of the non-military aspects of the proxy war, especially at the political and bureaucratic levels, and innovating better than Pakistan. Of course, intelligence and monitoring should be the core focus areas.

Contours of India's Response

This necessarily commences with the assumption that in the near future we are unlikely to witness any serious peace process with Pakistan and that J&K will continue to remain a thorny issue. Two crucial aspects need to be outlined in the beginning. First, notwithstanding our ability to stem the Pakistani offensive on J&K on all fronts—diplomatic, military, political and social—there is a severe lack of expertise on the subject. The subject being an ongoing one, and in place for years, still receives perfunctory analyses at the intellectual level, usually dismissed with one-off seminars in Delhi (nowhere else) and almost no recommendations on how to secure ourselves better against Pakistan's designs of irregular warfare. For the last few years, Pakistan has been in the throes of serious internal security problems, forcing its attention away from J&K; Afghanistan has also taken its share of attention. However, the geo-strategic scenario seems to be undergoing a change in the region. The International Security Assistance Force's (ISAF) withdrawal from Afghanistan and Pakistan, the coming of President Ashraf Ghani and his decision to depend on Pakistan to stabilize Afghanistan, the pivotal role that Pakistan is set to play as far as China's proactive entry into the region is concerned and the improving Pakistan–Russia equation have all contributed towards a more confident Pakistan. The US has its own geo-strategic compulsions for supporting Pakistan.

The confidence, in the case of Pakistan, does not emanate from its civil society, but rather from the Deep State itself. It emboldens it to recommence its campaign against India, perceiving itself to be at a relative advantage in comparison to the situation it was in over the last few years. This is in no small measure also triggered by the thought process that the political equations in J&K have dramatically changed post the partnership between the Bharatiya Janata Party (BJP) and the People's Democratic Party (PDP). Viewed as something near impossible in the past, the relationship may well be the harbinger of the type of transformational governance that J&K has always aspired towards.

For Pakistan, this is dangerous, and unless something is done to restore the turbulence which the Deep State seeks, the situation may get out of their control and this will become difficult to reverse. The continuance of proxy war is therefore essential, and it need not be only the type connected to terrorist violence. Sentiments have to be kept alive, the psyche of the new generation has to be manipulated and the effects of India's perception management efforts have to be neutralized. The pro-azadi sentiment is no longer considered to be to Pakistan's advantage. While Hurriyat leader Syed Ali Shah Geelani is still alive, the pro-Pakistan sentiment must be revived.

The level of expertise on the understanding of J&K is minuscule in India, considering that the current phase of proxy war has been going on for twenty-five years. Institutional capacity for intellectual application remains a challenge because there is no core ministry to address the issue. There is a dire necessity for a full-fledged department for J&K affairs working under the national security advisor or the cabinet secretariat. This will enable long-term perspectives to be considered instead of the current summer and winter strategies.

The second issue is that India, as a nation, has rarely articulated its aim while countering the proxy war efforts of Pakistan. There is no clear intent as to where it intends seeing J&K by, say, 2025. There is no focus on the integration aspect. The projection needs to be clear that India intends to overcome the negative effects of the proxy war suffered by the people of J&K, especially the youth, and restore such stability and quality of governance that the people's aspirations will be fulfilled. The people of the Valley in particular suffer from a hurt psyche. The Kashmiri Pandits suffer similar ignominy of being displaced without even being declared internally displaced people. Whatever effort is made, it must create a sense of excitement about the possibility of leading normal lives and replace the sense of doom. Restoration of dignity and self-esteem is one of the greatest challenges in a conflict-termination scenario, because the populace suffers from a sense of victimhood which only generational change will overcome over a period of time.

However, since Pakistan will continue to work overtime to prevent damage control on our part, the change of psyche may not materialize for a couple of generations. Clearly, the deduction is that the efforts of India towards the integration of J&K have to be more energetic and dynamic than the efforts of Pakistan to keep it in a state of turbulence. The periphery has to be held strongly in terms of security by various controls with the involvement of the army, central armed police forces (CAPFs), intelligence agencies and local police, without impinging on liberties and with a perception management system in place. Following is the basic concept of how to offset Pakistan's ongoing and future attempts to embroil India in a proxy war:

1. Intellectual understanding of J&K's internal conflict: The complexities of this proxy war/sponsored internal conflict are barely understood by the managers of conflict. There is a dire necessity to place government officials, politicians, intellectuals, security officials and army officers on a common footing of understanding.

2. Apex-level control: It is recommended that a single department or, better still, a single ministry, should look after the affairs of J&K. It will resolve many of the problems faced in handling day-to-day affairs.
3. Political stability: There is a need to build upon the decision of the BJP and PDP to come together to form the state government. Contentious issues such as Article 370 and AFSPA need to be placed on the backburner even as these are discussed in terms of options. However, an issue likely to prove a game-changer is the potential return of Kashmiri Pandits to the Valley. Proposals have been made towards the creation of settlements, either exclusive or inclusive. A decision on this cannot be hurried as security is the overriding consideration. Experiments have already been carried out with camps for the Pandits. We now need to move beyond by getting them and pro-India Kashmiri Muslims to sit together and chalk out methods of incrementally getting more Pandits back to the Valley, without any reservations. Pakistan's propagandist projection of demographic change must be actively countered in the international environment.
4. We have usually been afraid of triggers which may set off mass agitations. This follows from our experience of the early 1990s and of 2008–10. It restricts options in moving towards any transformational decisions which will alter the status quo. The latter is a victory of sorts for the nexus of the Deep State and the separatists. This mindset has to be overcome. There has to be a bolder approach without political considerations. Whichever regional party from Kashmir is in power will always be under pressure and in danger of losing ground and support.
5. The alternative is to offer the Hurriyat scope for once again entering the political mainstream. It is unlikely that this will be accepted. A second-rung leadership already exists to replace Geelani. This leadership must be engaged separately.
6. Grassroots democracy: J&K has been missing grassroots politics for far too long. The security situation for so many years has been such that politicians have not been able to actually get involved. It is necessary to overcome the legislative hurdles in the introduction

of Panchayati Raj. Successful elections were held in 2011 but empowerment has not occurred. If it does, it will assist in governance and development and wean people away from the negative activities of separatism.

7. Financial control: No separatist movement can survive without financial conduits being available to fund its activities. This has been a major source of weakness and our attempt to cultivate the Hurriyat as a political alternative has not succeeded and is unlikely to. The carrot-and-stick game of finance needs to be played more seriously. Besides, clandestine funds—now available through various conduits like foreign remittances, the Pakistan High Commission and networks which should otherwise be well known to our intelligence agencies—should be blocked to starve the movement.
8. Need for a perception management body: Perception management is necessary to overcome the scars of internal conflict. Efforts have been made by the army in 2011-12 to reinvent its attitude towards the local people. The exercise must commence with a clearer understanding of the conflict itself amongst all Indian stakeholders. A high-level empowered body at the national level must be set up to continuously study the environment of J&K comprehensively from all angles, to include diplomatic, political, socio-economic, military and psychological aspects. It should take inputs from intelligence agencies, think tanks, academia, captains of industry and business-related organizations. It must issue guidance bulletins so that the stakeholders have common base-level perceptions. This body must comprise intellectuals from different walks of life capable of considering national interests and must undertake measures towards the psychological integration of the people of J&K with the rest of India. A similar body at the state level may be considered. The scope of activities must be undefined and open-ended, with strategic guidance from the Prime Minister's Office (PMO) and the Cabinet Committee on Security (CCS).
9. On this count, the emotive landmarks which the separatists never fail to recount—Kunan Poshpura, Pathribal and Handwara—have to be addressed, and the high-level committee must be tasked with erasing these scars.

10. Diplomatic realm: The work by our missions abroad in promoting a positive perception and negating separatist and Pakistani propaganda is as yet insufficiently professional. In the major capitals of the world, the Pakistani diaspora, think tanks, academia and cultivated intellectuals maintain a high pitch of continuous rhetoric on J&K, projecting the Pakistani perception. The fact that Pakistan's sponsored proxy war has been fought for twenty-five years and that it is largely responsible for spawning a large number of radical groups within Pakistan, which in turn spell threats for the rest of the world, has never been prominently projected by our missions. A diplomatic offensive preceding any major initiative towards internal integration is almost mandatory. Once again, India's limited strength of diplomats and its rapidly expanding agenda of economic-related issues are likely to keep the efforts towards diplomatic offensives on J&K extremely limited unless we can expand our important missions without prejudice to only having Indian foreign service officials to handle the responsibility. India's threshold of tolerance in the face of provocation by Pakistan has not been sufficiently projected internationally and this needs to be done proactively.
11. Track two diplomacy: For all its reported perceptions of negativity, track two diplomacy is an excellent instrument of gauging reactions to the measures that we may take to limit Pakistan's options. It is a low-cost, unofficial instrument of engagement without any official label attached to it. It will not reduce tensions but has the capacity to throw up options towards limiting tensions.
12. Tactical handling: In the realm of tactical operations, it must be recognized by the army that its CI efforts have to be taken to an even higher level of effectiveness. These tactical operations at the LoC have broken the back of terror in the hinterland. Even if some redeployment is necessary during summer, it is good to plug the traditional gaps, remembering that infiltration routes are flexible and a pattern emerges each year. This will partially reduce the presence of infiltrators from the urban and semi-urban areas in the hinterland. A word of advice here: the army must lay more emphasis on its conventional operations capability on the LoC. Withdrawal of the reserve brigades from the CI grid and relieving them with

RR sectors/units could be considered. These formations need to be in the hinterland and, in addition to conducting low-level counter-terrorism operations, must continue to train for conventional operations. There will be logistical problems in such a switchover, but these should never be considered obstacles to change. It may also be prudent to observe that the army has shown much dynamism and maturity in its tactical transition in keeping with the times. This must continue with constant internal consultation. It may be advisable at this stage to retract to some extent the control of tactical operations. The army must not try too hard to achieve a zero-terrorist environment in the hinterland. It will open itself up to irreversible mistakes if it gets too ambitious. It will have to rein in its dynamic junior leaders through a system of operational control, which has thus far correctly rested at the lower levels. Tactical control may have to be retrieved to the higher levels progressively even as the lower levels feel disempowered.

13. Kinetic operations: The trans-LoC scope cannot be discussed in an unclassified document. However, India's threshold of tolerance has been extremely high as already discussed. The right to strike across the LoC at terrorist bases remains live and may be demonstrated on a need basis.
14. Possibility of Kargil-like operations: Remembering lessons from Kargil and Pakistan's proclivity to activate the LoC each time the movement flounders within the hinterland, it is important for India to watch for such triggers on the LoC or elsewhere.
15. The army's role in ground-level perception management is continuous and probably the most important and visible intent of the nation as far as its dealings with the local people are concerned. An attitudinal change from conflict progression and conflict stabilization to conflict resolution must be noticeable on the ground. Check post behaviour is crucial in this regard.
16. Handling of youth: J&K's most important ministry should be the Ministry of Youth Affairs. It should be in constant link with the Union Ministry of Skill Development to expand skill development programmes in J&K. The army has shown the path with some well-conceived seminars, where the angst of the youth has been given a

release. Many more of these should be conducted. An exchange of delegations from Jammu, Ladakh and Kashmir should be routine, as must sports competitions for better bonding of the three divisions. The youth of J&K need an outlet from their dreary lives and a chance to compete on an equal footing. Their aspirations cannot be realized without a transformational approach which sees a large segment taking up jobs inside and outside J&K (accepted as members of Indian society, like anybody else).

17. Exploiting social media: The power of social media has yet to be realized within the strategic community of India. It needs extensive study. If the Islamic State model could motivate youth from across the world to take up its diabolical cause, the reverse can also be enabled.
18. De-radicalization: With radicalization as one of the pillars of the Deep State's concept, it is essential to understand the methodology of de-radicalization. Without the assistance of the clergy, this is not possible. It also cannot be restricted to J&K and needs a national-level approach. Major Islamic institutions such as the Dar ul Uloom seminary have been forthcoming with some think tanks of Delhi, but the approach needs formalization. Perhaps this must come within the scope of the high-level body on perception management.
19. Integration of surrendered terrorists: The credibility of any elected government depends on the ability to deliver on the basic promises regarding the integration of surrendered terrorists, which creates hope and negates Pakistan's influence.
20. Media: The role of the media in influencing public opinion is immense. The mainstream national media adopts a nationalistic stance while the regional media of J&K has diametrically opposite stands dictated by the local influences and compulsions. Jammu is in line with the national media. The media of Kashmir has a large array of newspapers in English and Urdu. The personal security of scribes and editors is always at stake. No concerted effort has ever been made to engage the media to adopt at least a bipartisan approach to reporting. The stamp of the separatists is strongly evident. Although efforts have been made towards partnerships with mainstream media houses from the rest of India, these have not flourished. Independent editions of mainstream newspapers do

not find a place in Kashmir, and therefore the citizens of Kashmir do not get a chance to read perceptions and news from the rest of India. As long as this status quo continues, the power of perception will be largely wielded by the separatists. It is not necessary to declare in black and white the ideology of the Kashmiri media because it functions under threat. Measures have to be adopted to secure the media and allow a bipartisan opinion to be expressed even as some mainstream media finds its way to the Valley.

11

Managing Internal Security Challenges

Dr Ajai Sahni

Director, Institute of Conflict Management, New Delhi

Insurgency, Crime and Narcotics

India's internal security has been afflicted by decades of mismanagement, misdirection and drift, resulting in enduring movements of extremism, militancy and terrorism in different parts of the country. These represent the radical tip of an iceberg of potential and enduring conflicts, and of a complex dynamic that mixes in with a range of organized criminal activities. These include the proliferation of small arms, the circulation of fake currency and narcotics trafficking. Difficulties have been enormously compounded by a failure of the security establishment and apparatus to grow and transform itself sufficiently to keep pace with the emerging challenges.

While the Pakistan-backed proxy war in Jammu and Kashmir (J&K) has been the bloodiest single conflict in this context,[1] it lies beyond the purview of this chapter. Outside this theatre, the most significant protracted conflicts, according to 2014 data,[2] include:

1. The Maoist rebellion, which affects—at intensities varying from preliminary political mobilization to full-blown insurgency—some 118 districts in seventeen states of the country, out of a total of 673 districts.
2. Multiple, though degraded, ethnicity-based insurgencies in India's troubled north-east which affect sixty-nine districts in six states.
3. Islamist extremist mobilization and sporadic terrorist attacks at different times virtually across the country.

These visible conflicts are superimposed on a complex structure of diverse and deeply divided societies, with multiple and overlapping stratifications and complex identities—most obviously including caste, religion, ethnicity, class and ideology. These 'identity markers' tend to be the primary basis of political mobilization, increasing social polarization and, at their limits, provoking competitive extremism, insurgency and organized political violence. The consolidation of factionalized elites, the progressive criminalization and delegitimization of the state and its agencies, the suspension or arbitrary application of the rule of law, and the weakening and, in some areas, collapse of governance have created vast 'fault zones' of potential conflict in the country. The disruptive processes of globalization and uneven modernization, as well as the intervention of various external actors, often heighten tensions, creating even greater challenges for the state's enforcement agencies.

These various dangers have, nevertheless, overwhelmingly remained latent. Indeed, trends in various categories of major[3] and low-grade chronic conflict[4]—including violence against scheduled castes and tribes, as well as communal clashes—have broadly been declining and are indeed improving, particularly if increases in population are factored in.

The most direct and obvious connection between major organized criminal activity and extremism/terrorism arises out of the widespread circulation of fake Indian currency notes (FICN) which are printed by state agencies in Pakistan and circulated across India with the twin intent of financing Islamist extremist terrorism and destabilizing the Indian economy. Indian sources contend, on the basis of interrogations of arrested terrorists and couriers, that the FICN recovered was printed at Pakistani Security Presses at the Malir Cantonment in Karachi, and at Lahore, Quetta and Peshawar.[5] Further, India's Ministry of Home Affairs claims that it has confirmed that 'the Inter-Services Intelligence (ISI) has managed to get access to the configuration, specifications and other secret codes of the genuine Indian currency notes from six European companies that supply Indian currency papers fitted with security features, and another company in Switzerland that supplies the security ink used in printing these currency notes in India'.[6]

Exposing the proverbial tip of the iceberg, a total of 3,536,496 counterfeit notes worth Rs 1.71 billion were recovered and seized between January 2010 and 30 September 2014.[7] According to official estimates, FICN worth over $2.2 billion were in circulation in India by 2010.[8] The National Investigation Agency (NIA) observes that 'the quantum of fake currency floating around in the country is enough to keep the terrorist machinery well-oiled and running. The closest that one possibly gets to a figure is the one calculated by a government committee in 2011—over Rs 16,000 crore.'[9] The government has not revised its estimate of the volume of FICN in the economy thereafter, but Indian agencies believe that 'Pakistan is printing and circulating FICN worth an estimated Rs 10,000 crore (Rs 100 billion) every year'.[10]

Other such activities include the misappropriation of funds in the banking sector and capital market, bank robberies, extortion, hawala (illegal money transfers), and funding from various non-governmental organizations (NGOs).[11] Referring to the embezzlement of funds in the banking sector, a Research and Analysis Wing (R&AW) alert noted that Pakistan-based gangs were detected to be running fake lottery rackets through 349 Indian bank accounts. In the country-wide network operated by Indian associates of the Pakistani gangs, at least 133 bank accounts in the State Bank of India, thirty-three in ICICI Bank, eighteen in Punjab National Bank and another twenty-six accounts in Bank of Baroda, Oriental Bank of Commerce, Union Bank of India, Central Bank of India and the United Commercial Bank of India are being operated by Pakistan-based gangs. About 139 accounts are of unidentified banks.[12] Several bank robberies have direct connections with terrorism, and these included at least 346 cases in 2013 alone.[13]

Further, hawala transactions accounted for an estimated 30 per cent of terror funding.[14] The Maharashtra Anti-terrorism Squad (ATS) suspected that the money required to orchestrate the 13 July 2011 Mumbai blasts was sent to Indian Mujahideen (IM) operatives through the hawala route, and came through Pune.[15]

While there have been periodic cries of 'narcoterrorism' in India, the reality is that no clear and significant interdependence between narcotics trafficking and terrorist or insurgent movements has been consistently documented. However, where narcotics production or trade exists in an area of insurgent domination, insurgents invariably find ways to profit from it—either by exercising direct control over the trade or by extorting a 'tax' on the commerce[16]—generating significant revenues to support their underground activities. This has been the case both with the insurgencies in the north-east[17] and with the Maoists.[18] No authoritative estimates are available of the total commerce in illicit drugs in India, but the seizure of 477,850 kg of narcotic drugs was reported to the Narcotics Control Bureau between 2010 and 2013 from across the country.[19] Once again, this is likely to be a tiny fraction of the total volume of trafficking, and while anecdotal evidence of linkages with insurgent groups is available in different regions, there is no convincing case to suggest that such groups have any necessary or inordinate dependence on the trade. Nevertheless, the sheer damage done to society and the economy, and the human misery caused by this scourge make it a critical challenge for enforcement agencies.

There are few authoritative estimates of the availability of small arms in India, but the country is believed to account for a preponderance of the global availability of such weapons according to one 2006 study. According to the International Action Network on Small Arms, there were some 40 million illegal small arms in the country out of an estimated global total of 75 million such weapons. In addition, there is easy access to explosives across the country, and controls are very poorly implemented. For instance, more than 1.5 million kg of industrial explosives was stolen between 2010 and 2013 from carelessly guarded warehouses across the country and made its way into the hands of Maoist guerrillas, illegal miners and others, a report citing the Petroleum and Explosives Safety Organization (PESO) stated. The list of stolen explosives included 850,000 kg of nitrate mixture explosives; 500,000 detonators; 130,000 cartridges for small arms/war rockets; and 30,000 safety fuses/cartridges.[20] Research Department Explosive (RDX), ammonium nitrate fuel oil–based explosives, improvised explosive devices (IEDs) and crude bombs have been extensively used in various theatres of conflict in the country.[21]

This has critical ramifications for national security and law enforcement, since the 'threshold of violence' across the entire range of political tensions and conflicts is directly correlated to the availability and quality of illegal arms and explosives. The intensity of damage in a crisis situation, moreover, is directly proportional to the quantum of illegal arms and explosives in the possession of conflicting parties. India's law enforcement agencies are severely under-equipped to monitor and map the flow of illegal weapons and explosives. Moreover, in the absence of efficacious identification and evaluation methods, information regarding the flow of small arms becomes inaccurate, undermining the state's capacity to neutralize their use in movements of political violence and organized crime.

An elaborate pattern of collusion between criminals, terrorist groups, politicians and the structures of governance in some regions has long facilitated the illegal flow and proliferation of arms and explosives in the country. With the advent of modern tools of violence, a continuous monitoring of weapons, explosives and dual-use technologies available to terrorists and criminal groups is a pre-condition of effective law enforcement and a safeguard against the possibility of the state and society being overwhelmed in situations where a new generation of technologies is illegally introduced into theatres of conflict.

Each of these challenges has its own complexities and demands, and there is a perplexing dynamic of interplay between them. In devising any strategy of response, however, it is crucial to remind ourselves that security is indivisible. National power and security comprise an interlinked, indivisible composite that comprehends every layer, from the defence of the nation to the protection of the individual citizen and her rights. It is obvious that internal threats to national security impact directly on public safety. Somewhat less obvious is the reality that the very structures, institutions and agencies that are mandated to maintain public safety also protect national security interests. If they lack capacity for one objective, they will invariably be found wanting for the other. While special measures, capacities and capabilities may be required to deal with each of the distinct threats to internal security and to elements within these, a system that is vulnerable to, or incapable of dealing effectively with, any one of these is unlikely—on a sustained basis—to be particularly effective or efficient in dealing with others.

Perhaps the most obvious and dramatic example of this is the case of the Dawood Ibrahim gang and the 1993 Mumbai blasts, where the overlap of organized crime, the subversion of the state apparatus and terrorism dovetailed into India's single worst act of terrorism, resulting in 257 killed and another 713 injured. The same patterns, though seldom at the same scale, play out across the entire internal security spectrum. While there is an overwhelming public and policy focus on the 'big bang incidents', it is useful to remind ourselves that terrorism and insurgency are not limited just to the bombing or killing, and counter-terrorism and counter-insurgency responses are not just incident and emergency responses. There are innumerable small and neglected deviations, anomalies, misdemeanours and lesser crimes that culminate in the final act of dramatic violence.

Crucially, the same networks service both petty crime and major crime, including terrorism/insurgency; and the same enforcement agencies fail to cope, or 'look the other way', when such crimes occur. The same hawala networks service corrupt politicians, bureaucrats and businessmen, as well as terrorists. Smuggling channels that bring grey market goods, FICN and drugs into the country also bring in arms, ammunition and explosives. A significant proportion of the networks of terrorism are run on a purely mercenary basis by professional criminals who have no ideological commitment to the purported causes of the anti-state groups they service.

It is, consequently, the general policing and intelligence environment that has direct bearing on the state's capacities to deal with the 'higher order' crimes of terrorism and insurgency. While emergency response capabilities are, no doubt, needed where the terrorist threat actually manifests itself in an act of sensational violence, such an act already represents the failure of the system to detect and pre-empt the succession of lesser acts and conspiracies that culminate in this eventual attack.

Improving Policing and Intelligence

The first and most significant element of a strategy to counter insurgent and terrorist violence, as well the narcotics, arms trade and wider organized crime networks, consequently, is a radical improvement in the currently anaemic general policing and intelligence infrastructure. This is a subject that has been written on repeatedly in the past,[22] but to little effect. Despite the clear demonstrations of vulnerability in the 26/11 Mumbai attacks and the incoherent, uncoordinated and disastrous responses, as well as the tremendous political grandstanding on the issue of internal security threats and response capabilities thereafter, the internal security apparatus remains unequal to the challenges. The first responder to the entire gamut of internal security crises—the police force—is ill-equipped, ill-trained and under-strength. The police–

population ratio remains far from adequate and there are acute deficits in police leadership; insufficient strength and alarming vacancies in the Intelligence Bureau; and institutional deficiencies across the board in the national and state enforcement apparatus.

The technological capabilities of the police, intelligence and specialized enforcement agencies remain insufficient. Crucial projects such as the Crime and Criminal Tracking Network and Systems (CCTNS), global positioning system (GPS)-based surveillance of sea vessels, and other technological upgrades that have been 'under implementation' for years are still to be completed despite the enormous rhetorical emphasis since the 26/11 attacks. Despite repeated policy announcements, the implementation of internal security-related projects and upgrades has been poor, fitful and uncoordinated. Astonishingly, a critical project like CCTNS has now virtually collapsed as the Centre has terminated funding and transferred the responsibility for implementation to the states, ignoring even the crucial central component of the project—the creation of a national hub and database.[23]

No aspect of India's internal security can be adequately dealt with unless police forces across India are made professional, efficient, equipped and accountable. The sad reality is that policing in India is today a 'broken system', overwhelmingly reflecting 'dysfunction, abuse and impunity',[24] and no political formation has demonstrated the will or desire to alter this and raise the country's security apparatus to global standards. A comprehensive modernization of the system would, of course, include a technological overhaul; but modern policing is not the outcome of technologies alone. It is the policeman—his training, orientation, capabilities, and, crucially, mindset—that makes the difference between a modern and an obsolete police force. It is, consequently, the profile of the policeman and also his welfare and status in society that must undergo comprehensive revaluation.

While tremendous emphasis is now rightly placed on police-population ratios, numbers are not everything. This is dramatically borne out by the experience in Andhra Pradesh. In 2005, Andhra Pradesh was among the states worst afflicted by Maoist violence, with all twenty-three of its districts in acute crisis. A focused campaign through 2006 and 2007 decimated the Maoists, reducing the insurgency to a marginal irritant in just eight border districts where Maoists continue to launch occasional attacks, principally against civilian targets. Crucially, the Andhra Pradesh police–population ratio in 2006 was just 98 per 100,000 and in 2007 had fallen to 96 per 100,000, as against an all-India average of 126 and 125 in these years respectively. An undermanned system cannot, of course, maintain exceptional levels of efficiency indefinitely, but the Andhra police have demonstrated what can be achieved even with severely limited manpower.[25]

Every police force in India currently has entrenched inefficiencies built into the existing processes of administration, deployment and operation. Large proportions of police forces are ordinarily wasted in static and unproductive deployments, without clear mandates or objectives within a security, crime-fighting or counter-terrorist framework. It is necessary to make an objective evaluation of current processes and deployments to identify areas of redundancy and waste, and to redeploy the 'recovered' manpower more efficiently. The objective is to operationalize the largest possible proportion of the force and to empower each policeman through reorientation, training and technology to secure the specific purposes for which he is deployed. Greater police efficiency will also change public perception. Both perception and efficiency would, moreover, be significantly improved by addressing the issues of welfare and the skill/education profile of the constabulary.

The world is changing at an unprecedented pace—new techniques, technologies, systems, structures and dynamics evolve on an almost daily basis. Most people in government and in the security system remain insulated from an overwhelming proportion of these transformations. They have little capacity to absorb and adapt to all but the most obvious technological manifestations of these transformations, and to integrate these into the operational structures of their institutions. The training and education of officers and personnel, in these circumstances, must be a continuous and intensive process, must be fully resourced, must be built into the pattern and schedule of their responsibilities, and must produce quantifiable improvements in skills and capabilities. The age of the generalist is past; programmes must now create domain expertise for specialized officers on counter-terrorism and crime-fighting strategy and tactics. Simultaneously, they must create at least minimal awareness of the operational context and environment among all leadership cadres in the force, and define and disseminate, across the force, the strategic and tactical fundamentals of counter-terrorism and crime-fighting responses.

If national security is to be assured, it is now necessary to frame certain consensual minimal standards of policing across the country. These standards need to be applied both across urban centres and rural jurisdictions. In 2009, for instance, the Centre had asked all states in the country to establish and maintain a 'desirable' police–population ratio of 220 per 100,000, 'advice' that has overwhelmingly been ignored.[26] The evolution and maintenance of a range of minimum standards across other quantifiable parameters is an urgent necessity.

An accelerated recruitment programme to address endemic deficits across internal security and intelligence institutions should be the highest priority within a time-bound framework. Sanctioned strengths must also be continuously re-evaluated in the context of emerging tasks and challenges.

The 'virtually unconnected islands'[27] that are our police stations today must be brought into the national CCTNS network at the earliest. Such data networks should have been established in this country decades ago. Unfortunately, the states continue to lag in the execution of the statewide area network (SWAN) and state data centre (SDC) components of the CCTNS project, and the Centre appears now to have washed its hands of all responsibility for execution, even of the central database component.

Each state police establishment must evolve and implement effective 'routines' or protocols for all principal tasks and duties of enforcement. These protocols must, moreover, be translated into efficient practice through intensive training programmes and drills. Every enforcement professional must see himself as being clearly tasked, mandated, trained and equipped to fulfil clear sets of objectives.

Every enforcement professional must have a basic level of fitness and weapons skills to respond effectively in an emergency, if required. The weapons skills of state armed police contingents need dramatic enhancement—with whatever weapons they may possess. Even the antiquated .303 rifle, in the hands of a skilled shooter, can prove to be an extremely effective weapon, especially where the advantages of numbers and initiative are on the side of the police.

The intelligence component of the state police establishment, in most cases, requires exponential augmentation and must have an effective presence in each police station, particularly in the rural and mofussil hinterland. Capacities to gather intelligence of evidentiary value also need to be established, both in central and state intelligence organizations, so that effective prosecutions can be launched and convictions secured against individuals and organizations engaged in enduring criminal operations and pursuits. While CT–CI (counter-terrorism and counter-insurgency) may be regarded as a priority in this context, effective capabilities for all crime are necessary, as these underpin CT–CI ops as well. Intelligence flows generated through the state apparatus must interface in real time with the national databases, including the Multi Agency Centre (MAC) and CCTNS.

Even though no consensus has been reached on a national internal security strategy, it is imperative that the security establishment, even at the level of individual states or within their police departments, defines its own strategic perspectives. Unless this is done, there is little possibility of ensuring coherence in tactical response, technological acquisitions, or institutional and process innovations.

Resolving Centre–State Issues in Managing Internal Security

It is useful here to address some of the red herrings of the strategic discourse in India with regard to internal security. The sheer interconnectedness of the system has raised legitimate concerns regarding the nature and structure of the systems of response, particularly with regard to the purported 'fragmentation' of the country's federal arrangements, and what are thought to be the imperatives of a greater 'coordination' and 'centralization' of responses. There have also been constant calls for new legislation and constitutional amendments, as well as imitative 'architectural flights of fancy' that seek to reinvent the fundamentals of governance and the distribution of power between the Centre and the states.[28] It has, however, been noted that:

> The crisis of governance, today, is not something that afflicts the states alone. All central institutions and agencies are, today, operating at varying levels of dysfunction. Indeed, the rot is as deep at the Centre as it is in many of the states. A restoration of vitality and

> efficiency within the structures of governance across the country is, consequently, the first and most urgent imperative: not a constant, poorly conceptualized, imitative, meddling with the structures themselves. Further, infirmity, both at the Centre and in the states, is, preponderantly, not the outcome of legislative defects, or of structural and 'architectural' vulnerabilities, but of the virtual 'withering away' of state capabilities over the past more than six decades, under successive administrations that have been driven, at best, by misdirected zeal, populism and sloganeering, and, at worst, by sheer incompetence and venality.[29]

In terms of the priorities of necessary transformation, it is content that must be given precedence over form. The crisis in India today is one of capacities, and this cannot be addressed by the reinvention of institutional forms. It doesn't matter if our responses are centralized or decentralized as long as the executing agencies remain infirm, under-manned, under-trained and under-equipped. Issues of mandate and structure will become relevant only after the issue of capacity has been addressed.

The nation state is a single but enormously complex system—and this is more the case for a country with the size and diversity of India. To this extent, a centralized authority is necessary—and already exists in the form of the Government of India. However, since national administration involves complex, multifarious and widely dispersed functions, these can only be addressed through delegation to a progressively decentralized structure, with clear mandate and accountability. No single agency or authority could effectively tackle all aspects of national security management across the length and breadth of the country without turning into a colossal bureaucratic nightmare.

It must be clear, moreover, that there is no ideal configuration or distribution of powers and functions that can produce optimal results—consequently, imitative forays to replicate Western institutions are of little utility and likely to be counterproductive. The crisis is one of efficiency. Governance and administration in India, today, have failed to evolve any systems to maintain efficiency or impose accountability, and are currently operating against the imperatives of even the most rudimentary principles of management or administration. Vast resources are wasted where they produce little positive outcome. Initiatives and structures that could produce the best results are, at the same time, rejected or starved of resources. Even where leakages and inefficiencies have been well documented, these are not corrected. It has not mattered whether this has occurred in centrally administered projects and agencies or in state-administered projects and agencies. Mere structural or constitutional redistribution of powers, functions and responsibility will achieve nothing unless issues of capacity, efficiency and accountability are addressed—*in that order*. It is important to understand why the 'order' is necessary. By definition, an overburdened, under-manned and under-resourced system cannot be expected to fulfil all its obligations with an acceptable level of efficiency; it cannot, consequently, be effectively held to account for its failures.

National security is, of course, a national issue—but that does not necessarily imply that it is a 'central' issue. There is no reason to believe that the states are 'anti-national', or are incapable of tackling issues just because they have trans-state ramifications. This will, once again, bring up the issue of quality of governance. Where the potential for efficient cooperation between states exist, there is no constitutional obstacle to state government agencies acting in concert across state boundaries. Where such cooperation does not exist, it is not clear how central government intervention can significantly alter the equation. If states fail to render effective cooperation to central agencies, the only alternative is to statutorily or constitutionally override the authority of state governments, or to give the Centre paramount powers on certain kinds of issues or in certain situations—e.g., 'federal crimes' or 'national emergencies'. But this is, again, fraught with problems. The Centre is as bereft of effective capacities as are the states. Worse, regimes at the Centre have in the past tended to repeatedly abuse, for partisan political gains, even the very limited provisions that currently exist. Solutions cannot be proposed 'in an ideal world'; systems have to take into account the political and administrative culture that prevails.

Increasingly, what is needed is a well-knit and integrated system of decentralized systems. Modern technologies have created an infinite potential for highly efficient integration within a systems approach. Unfortunately, Indian governance and administration have failed to take advantage of these and have remained trapped in arid debates on 'centralization vs. fragmentation', or over-architectural and legislative transformations. In the meanwhile, as already noted, even the most rudimentary projects have failed to take off. Security-related data across India remains dispersed and inaccessible to any authority beyond the local units responsible for the maintenance of records. Such a situation within the context of the twenty-first century revolution in information technologies is not just intolerable, it is ludicrous for a country with 'great power' pretensions. Integration is the key in any system of systems—and the country is a system of systems, whether it is recognized and administered as such or not.

Various strategies and policies with regard to specific challenges must be reconciled with such an integrated approach. The ad hoc 'resolution' of various insurgencies in India's north-east—through the creation of 'autonomous regions' by introducing elaborate amendments to the Constitution and the inclusion of entire 'memoranda of settlement' with insurgent formations in the VI Schedule—has only created new problems of ethnic polarization. This is even as the constant reiteration of divisive politics is institutionalized through further state formation along purportedly ethnic lines. Thus, an assortment of latent demands for state bifurcation were revived after the creation of Telangana on grounds that were far from consistent or credible.

The sheer inconsistency of approach to insurgencies across states is another case in point. There is a multiplicity of models of extraordinary success within India, and the Ministry of Home Affairs has now acknowledged that the paradigm of police-led counter-insurgency operations that defeated the rebels in Punjab, Tripura and Andhra Pradesh is the template that the country must follow.[30] Unfortunately, little of this has been adequately documented and studied, leave alone actually transformed into policy and practice. As a result, past approaches, with wide variations across states, and incoherence at the Centre, persist.

Addressing External Sources of Internal Threats

India is located in a 'bad neighbourhood', one that is among the most active centres of terrorism, small arms proliferation and drug production and trafficking. Crucially, much of this activity is directly encouraged, supported and often facilitated by established states in the neighbourhood and by their agencies—most prominently Pakistan.

Such states also support, encourage, train, arm, and sometimes direct terrorists, insurgents and criminal groups and exploit such groups for their own geopolitical ends. These activities have resulted both in a flood of sophisticated arms, narcotics and FICN in the region, as well as a significant lowering of the threshold of armed violence. There is an urgent need for India to intensify its efforts to attract global attention to, and secure sanctions against, at least the principal sponsoring state, Pakistan.

Such an effort, however, can only be one of the components of a protracted war strategy against rogue state operations. A comprehensive strategy employing all instrumentalities of state power—but, most significantly, economic and covert instrumentalities—must be evolved and implemented to secure clearly defined end-state objectives over an extended period of time. It is an urgent necessity that such a strategy be articulated to deal with the enduring threat from Pakistan.

Lack or distortion of data and its dissemination across multiple categories has contributed directly to incorrect appraisals of the long-term threat and imperatives of response. In the data maintained by police departments in most of the states, there is no consistent categorization, nor is such data available in an acceptable time frame across state jurisdictions, or to a central database. The CCTNS project was intended to address elements of this urgent deficit, but it appears to be languishing. Several variables not envisaged in the CCTNS project also need to be identified and brought into a coherent database.

Criminal and terrorist activities exhibit tendencies towards consolidation over time. Better crime control mechanisms, supported by a strong and effective intelligence network, and efficient use of information technologies can prevent criminal, insurgent and terrorist groups from becoming a serious threat to national security. The creation of such a strong intelligence enforcement complex spanning the entire country, and including even its most remote and rural hinterlands, is the sine qua non of a national policy on internal security.

12

Financial Support for National Security

AMIT COWSHISH

Former Financial Advisor (Acquisitions), Ministry of Defence, New Delhi

Introduction

The twentieth century was one of global turmoil. The two world wars, the Russian Revolution, the Chinese Civil War, numerous freedom struggles in Asia and Africa, the downward spiral of imperialism, and many other political developments resulted in the emergence of new nations, redrawing of existing boundaries and reshaping of spheres of influence. These developments also redefined the concept of nationhood, which was conventionally seen as the sentiment that bonded conglomerations of people living in a contiguous territory, united by a common descent, history and cultural heritage, including language, customs and beliefs, but not necessarily a common religion.

Though large parts of what presently constitutes India were governed by a single political authority on several occasions in its long history, from the Maurya (322–185 BCE) to the Mughal dynasty (1526–1857 AD), it was the colonial rule which created conditions for the rise of assimilative nationalism in India—till that narrative was disrupted by the two-nation theory. Despite its division, India was largely a territorially satisfied country when it came into existence in 1947.[1] But the invasion of Jammu and Kashmir (J&K) in 1947-48, insurgencies in the north-eastern part of the country in the early 1950s, and the war with China in 1962 gradually made territorial integrity the single most important component of national security.

There are alternative narratives of these developments but these make no difference to the fact that successive legitimately constituted governments perceived them as threats to national security. To a large extent, these cataclysmic developments were—and continue to be—some of the most important factors impacting India's quest for national security.

New Dimensions of National Security

New challenges have appeared since the early years of India's Independence, broadening the concept of national security. It is no more seen primarily in terms of the need for safeguarding territorial integrity from external aggression. Internal threats pose a far more serious challenge.

While it cannot be denied that territorial integrity is the lynchpin of comprehensive national security, its imperatives have to be balanced, with an equal focus on other factors that impact national security. Pakistan's obsession with the real or perceived threats to territorial integrity right from its creation in 1947 has led to its metamorphosis into a national security state and had some disastrous effects on its society, economy and polity.

India always shunned that path but in the process had to strike a balance between allocating enough financial resources for strengthening its military capabilities on the one hand and investing in measures to boost its economy on the other—which is a sine qua non for raising financial resources required to ensure national security—mostly with unsatisfactory results on both fronts.

It is beyond the scope of this chapter to go into the non-military aspects of national security. The discussion, therefore, is limited to three aspects of its military dimension: the basis of financial outlays for defence, constraints faced by the government in augmenting defence budgets, and the impact of these two factors on defence preparedness.

Part I: Basis of Allocation for Defence

It is difficult to discover the basis on which budgetary allocations are made for defence as very little information is available in the public domain. The primary sources for such information are the budget speeches, budget documents, reports of the Standing Committee on Defence[2] and various Finance Commissions, occasional Parliament questions and some other government publications, though these sources too mostly reveal only the raw data related to budgetary allocations rather than the basis for allocation. The analysis that follows is based on these sources.

1947-48 to 1949-50

Given its munificent worldview, the government that assumed political power in 1947 adopted a pro tempore approach to allocating financial resources for defence. In the budget for 1947-48, a sum of Rs 92.74 crore was earmarked for defence out of the total central government revenue expenditure (CGE) of Rs 197.39 crore. This accounted for almost 47 per cent of the total CGE. In addition, a sum of Rs 14.97 crore was allocated for capital expenditure on works projects for the three services and for the purchase of plant and machinery for manufacturing establishments.[3]

In percentage terms, this was a substantial allocation. But it was more out of compulsion than by choice, and certainly not for financing any long-term defence plan. In fact, while presenting the budget, the Union finance minister told Parliament that the 'defence expenditure is ... considerably inflated due to the slowing down of demobilisation following the partition of the country and the necessity to maintain larger forces than would normally be necessary'.[4]

During the next two years, before the Constitution was adopted on 26 January 1950, budgetary allocation for defence accounted for 47.05 per cent and 48.79 per cent respectively of the CGE.[5] However, these allocations were not made in pursuance of any strategic roadmap for building up India's military capabilities. They were primarily pro tempore, prompted largely by the circumstances unfolding in J&K.[6]

1950-51 to 1957-58

India adopted central planning as the primary vehicle for building its economy. A Planning Commission was set up in March 1950 to formulate five-year plans. The first plan was formulated for the period 1951–56. The commission was tasked with the responsibility of assessing the resources of the country, suggesting ways of augmenting the scarce resources, setting priorities and formulating plans for the efficient utilization of resources to achieve the objectives of each five-year plan. The military dimension of national security, however, did not fall in the commission's remit.

Consequently, the earlier practice of allocating a high percentage of revenue expenditure for defence, more on account of the government's response to the prevailing circumstances than with a view to systematically building up India's military capability, continued at least till 1957-58, albeit with a downward trajectory. From a possibly all-time high of 49.72 per cent in 1950-51 it slid to 40.43 per cent of CGE in 1957-58, remaining above 40 per cent except in 1956-57 when it fell to 37.40 per cent.[7]

The following excerpt from the 1950-51 budget speech of the then finance minister, John Mathai, reveals continuity in the pro tempore approach to defence expenditure:

> Our policy, as the Prime Minister has declared more than once, is to contribute in every way we can to the maintenance of peace and to the employment of peaceful methods to the settlement of international disputes. As anybody who knows the Prime Minister will appreciate that declaration has been made from the highest of motives and with the completest [sic] sincerity of purpose. If, however, contrary to our expectation events so develop that the peace and security of this country are endangered, Government will have no hesitation in raising whatever finance may be required for meeting the situation. Government will not hesitate to call upon the people to make whatever sacrifices may be necessary for safeguarding the vital interests of the country.[8]

Seven years later, another finance minister, T.T. Krishnamachari, was to echo the same sentiment when he informed Parliament while delivering the budget speech for 1957-58 that 'the increasing demands being made on our resources by Defence requirements cannot be lightly passed over' and that 'the increase under this head … is the major element in widening the deficit'. 'Defence,' he said, 'is hardly an item on which we should like to spend more either in terms of domestic currency or of foreign exchange,' adding that 'if, however, the exigencies of the situation make such increases inevitable, the necessary sacrifices have to be made'.[9]

All this while, the People's Republic of China had been strengthening its stranglehold over what now constitutes the Tibetan Autonomous Region (TAR), but the strategic thinking in India remained inward-looking and reactive, with no long-term planning for capacity building or modernization of the armed forces. This did not change even after the Dalai Lama crossed over to India in March 1959 following the Tibetan uprising that saw China upstaging his government.

1958-59 to 1963-64

The events of March 1959 also brought China to India's doorsteps. India and China thus came to share a disputed border. India's response by way of the 'Forward Policy', which involved setting up military outposts in areas claimed by China and launching aggressive patrols,[10] was not backed by budgetary allocations required to sustain that policy. In fact, the revenue allocation for 1959-60 was Rs 24.19 crore less than the revised estimates for 1958-59. The finance minister saw this as an 'improvement' resulting from a reduction in the gross expenditure and an increase in receipts and recoveries.[11]

The allocation for defence expenditure, which accounted for 34.94 per cent of the total expenditure in 1958-59, fell to 17.87 per cent by 1961-62.[12] It rose marginally to 24.88 per cent of the total expenditure the next year, ostensibly because of the situation on the border with China. Delivering the interim budget speech for 1962-63 on 14 March 1962, the then finance minister, Morarji Desai, informed Parliament that this marginal increase 'reflects the cost of measures taken to strengthen the armed force ... intended to safeguard the territorial integrity and security of the country'.[13]

It was too little and too late. India had a disastrous war with China in October 1962. As was to be expected, following the war there was a substantial increase in the allocation for defence for 1963-64. Of the total revenue expenditure of Rs 1,852.40 crore for 1963-64, a sum of Rs 708.51 crore was earmarked for defence, which works out to 38.24 per cent of the total expenditure. Out of the total central government capital outlay of Rs 827 crore, representing an increase of Rs 234 crore over the previous year's revised requirements, defence capital outlay accounted for an increase of Rs 106 crore.[14]

The finance minister also talked about 'the need to build up the defence potential of the nation' as the 'paramount consideration in framing the Budget for 1963-64'[15] but in the same breath announced that 'it would not be prudent ... to provide for the paramount claims of defence by sacrificing the claims of development'.[16]

1964-65 to 1972-73

The total defence budget for 1964-65 (revenue and capital) was Rs 854 crore. Though it was a little more than 30 per cent of the central government expenditure,[17] it represented a negative growth over the previous year's budget. When the budget for 1965-66 was presented, the share came down further and the growth vis-à-vis the previous year fell below 10 per cent.

The 1965 war between India and Pakistan was triggered by Operation Gibraltar launched by Pakistan to infiltrate its forces into J&K to foment insurgency. While misjudgement of the situation in the state was an important factor behind this operation, it is a no-brainer that Pakistan's military leadership would have also been encouraged by its military alliances, growing closeness to China and the moderate spending by India on building up its military capabilities even after the 1962 war.

In 1966-67, following the war with Pakistan, the revenue budget was increased by Rs 29 crore but there was 'practically no increase in the defence Capital outlay'.[18] While presenting the budget, the then finance minister, Sachindra Chaudhuri, told Parliament that it had 'always been our policy to restrict expenditure on defence to the maximum extent possible so as to conserve all possible sources [sic] for securing the well-being of our people, we cannot afford to take any chances with the security of the nation, devoted though we are to the cause of peace'.[19]

The annual growth in allocation remained below 10 per cent per annum between 1967-68 and 1971-72. The year-on-year increase in the defence budget for 1971-72 was 7.82 per cent. This was before the war broke out between India and Pakistan yet again towards the end of 1971. On account of this war and its consequences, the actual expenditure on defence for that year witnessed a jump of 27.19 per cent over the previous year's actual expenditure.[20]

As in the aftermath of the 1965 war, the government did not contemplate any paradigm shift in its approach to defence and security. The budget for 1972-73 was marginally less than the revised estimates for 1971-72, with the then finance minister, Y.B. Chavan, expressing the hope while delivering the budget speech that 'out of the anguish and agony of the recent past will emerge a new spirit of peace and harmony in this great sub-continent so that all its 700 million inhabitants can devote their entire energies against their common enemies of hunger, want, disease and exploitation of man by man'.[21]

1973-74 to 1979-80

Although the allocation for 1972-73 was less than the revised estimate for 1971-72, it was an increase of 13.43 per cent over the previous year's budget estimate. This momentum was maintained by the government from 1973-74 to 1976-77 by increasing the defence budget by more than 13.61 per cent in 1973-74, followed by 19.69 per cent, 18.75 per cent and 11.87 per cent respectively in the following three years.[22] But the increase in 1974-75, as also in the following year, was largely on account of the implementation of the recommendations of the third central pay commission.

A state of Emergency was declared by the government on 26 June 1975 under the provisions of Article 352 of the Constitution. It was lifted on 21 March 1977, and on 24 March 1977 a non-Congress government took charge at the Centre for the first time in India's history. This government lasted less than three years before the Congress came back with a thumping majority in January 1980. This interregnum did not bring about any palpable change in the approach to the issue of national security. During this three-year period, the year-on-year growth of the defence budget remained below 10 per cent.

The erratic trend of budgetary allocation is significant from another point of view. While India had adopted central planning in 1950, it was not until 1964 that the first five-year defence plan was formulated for the period 1964–69. The second plan was formulated for 1969–74 but it was soon converted into a roll-on plan for 1970–75 (third plan) and then reformulated for the period 1974–79 (fourth plan). The fifth plan covered the period 1979–84 but this too was soon converted into the sixth plan for 1980–85 to make the defence plans co-terminus with the national five-year plans.[23]

Very little is known about these plans: what did they seek to achieve;[24] what was the budgetary support sought by the planners; whether the financial outlay was based on any commitment of funds by the Ministry of Finance (MoF); whether the funds were actually released as per the requirement projected by the Ministry of Defence (MoD) or as agreed to by the MoF; and, last but not the least, what impact these plans had on national security. If making defence plans co-terminus with the national plans was intended to strengthen national security in a planned and systematic manner, it was not borne out by subsequent developments.

1980-81 to 2001-02

The sixth five-year defence plan (1980–85) was not only the first that was co-terminus with the national plan but also the first to have received the approval of the Cabinet Committee on Political Affairs (CCPA) on 15 April 1982. Like the earlier plans, very little is known about this one too. What is known, however, is that between 1980-81 and 1986-87, the annual growth was robust and consistent, the lowest being 13.03 in 1985-86 and the highest being 21.43 per cent in 1982-83.

It is unlikely that this comparatively good run of the defence budget was on account of the sixth five-year defence plan being approved by the CCPA. For one thing, it was approved at the start of the third year of the plan period. Second, it seems improbable that the sixth defence plan was predicated on an uneven flow of financial support as evident from the annual growth rate, which plummeted during the last two years of the plan period after peaking in 1982-83. Most importantly, no analytical account is available to show what impact, if any, the sixth defence plan had on defence preparedness and national security.

The seventh five-year defence plan was made for the period 1985–90 and approved by the CCPA in August 1988, well into the fourth year of the plan period. Its impact on defence preparedness cannot even be of any academic interest because of its belated approval.

While this plan was still being formulated, or was in the process of being approved, the allocation went up by 13.56 per cent in 1986-87, which was marginally higher than the increase in the previous year's budget. In 1987-88, the financial support grew by a whopping 43.35 per cent because of the implementation of the recommendations of the fourth central pay commission. During the next two years (1988-89 and 1989-90), the budgetary allocation remained static at Rs 13,000 crore, though the actual expenditure exceeded the allocation.

The eighth five-year defence plan for the period 1990–95 did not reach the stage of CCPA approval but, based on the recommendations of the Arun Singh Committee, the MoD and MoF agreed upon annual budgetary ceilings. The Gulf war soon upset that agreement. The commencement of the national plan was deferred to 1992 because of the war, with the intervening periods being declared as plan holidays. Accordingly, the defence plan was also deferred to keep it in sync with the national plan. In the event, the eighth national as well as the defence plan covered the period 1992–97.

During the two-year plan holiday, and after the stagnation in financial support for two consecutive years, the budget grew by 21.15 per cent in 1990-91, declined sharply the next year, rose marginally over the next two years, peaked at 19.92 per cent in 1994-95 and plummeted to 9.01 per cent in 1996-97.[25] No authentic account of the impact of the eighth plan on national security is available, but judging by the chinks in the state of defence preparedness revealed by the Kargil war in 1999, either the plan was not well conceived, adequately financed or well executed.

This could also be said of the ninth five-year defence plan for the period 1997–2002, which was approved by the Cabinet Committee on Security (CCS) in December 1997. The allocation for 1997-98 was increased by 28.14 per cent, followed by a 15.67 per cent increase the next year. But these increases were largely for implementing the recommendations of the fifth central pay commission. In 1999-2000, the allocation grew by 10.91 per cent, but the Kargil war later during the year resulted in the actual expenditure exceeding the initial allocation.

In 2000-01, the allocation went up by 28.22 per cent, mainly on account of the war. Presenting the budget for 2000-01, the then finance minister, Yashwant Sinha, informed Parliament that the increase of nearly Rs 13,000 crore in the defence budget over the budget estimates of the previous year represented the largest ever increase in the defence budget in a single year and that more funds would be provided whenever needed. [26]

However, once the war was over, the growth in 2001-02 was back to a sedentary 5.83 per cent.[27] There was no account given in the budget speech of what had been achieved as a result of the substantial increase in the previous year's budget or whether the government had any long-term and financially sustainable plan to build up the military capability. No explanation was given for cutting down the growth in the allocation for defence so drastically for 2001-02.[28]

2002-03 to 2013-14

In a way, this period is a microcosm of the previous history of budgetary allocation for defence since Independence. There were troughs (0.46 per cent increase in 2003-04), apparently because of the poor state of the government's finances, and peaks, as in 2009-10, when the budget grew by 34.19 per cent on account of the implementation of the recommendations of the sixth central pay commission.

Year	*Budget (in Rs crore)*	*Increase (per cent)*
2001-02	62,000	5.83
2002-03	65,000	4.84
2003-04	65,300	0.46
2004-05	77,000	17.92
2005-06	83,000	7.79
2006-07	89,000	7.23
2007-08	96,000	7.87
2008-09	105,600	10
2009-10	141,703	34.19
2010-11	147,344	3.98
2011-12	164,415.49	11.59
2012-13	193,407.29	17.63
2013-14	203,672.12	5.31

(Table 1: Defence budget since 2001-02. Source: Defence Services Estimates of the relevant years.)

This period also coincides with the tenth (2002–07), eleventh (2007–12) and the beginning of the twelfth (2012–17) defence plans, which were never brought before the CCS for approval. The tenth plan remained under discussion between the MoD and MoF, and it was probably in the third year of the plan period that the financial support package was mutually agreed to.

The eleventh plan also remained in a loop because the MoD and MoF could not come to an agreement on the financial outlay for the plan. Finally, it was decided by the MoD not to bring the eleventh plan before the CCS. In keeping with this decision, the twelfth plan (2012–17) was also not taken to the MoF/CCS. Instead, it was approved by the Defence Acquisition Council, presided over by the defence minister, on 2 April 2012.

As in the case of the previous plans, there is no official report on the objectives of these plans and the extent to which these objectives were achieved. The reports of the Standing Committee on Defence also do not throw much light on this. The focus of the committee has instead been, among other things, on the non-finalization or non-approval of the defence plans, inadequacy of allocation, and delays in the procurement of equipment and weapon systems.

2014-15 to 2016-17

The National Democratic Alliance (NDA) came to power in the general elections held in May 2014, ending the ten-year rule of the Congress-led United Progressive Alliance (UPA) government. Several promises were made in the election manifesto of the Bharatiya Janata Party (BJP), which led the NDA government, with regard to external security and defence production. More specifically, the manifesto promised that the party will:[29]

- Address the issue of reforms with regard to defence equipment, support services, organizational reforms and other related matters.
- Address the increasing shortage of commissioned and non-commissioned officers in the defence forces.
- Implement one rank, one pension.
- Take measures to make Short Service Commission more attractive.
- Set up a National Maritime Authority.
- Modernize armed forces and increase research and development in defence, with the goal of developing indigenous defence technologies and fast-tracking of defence purchases.
- Deal with cross-border terrorism with a firm hand.

- Introduce punitive measures to check illegal immigration.
- Set up four dedicated defence universities to meet the shortage of manpower.
- Appoint a Veterans' Commission to address the grievances of veterans.

As for defence production, the manifesto promised that the BJP will strengthen the Defence Research and Development Organization (DRDO), encourage private sector participation and investment, including foreign direct investment (FDI), in select defence industries and encourage technology transfer in defence manufacturing to the maximum. The manifesto also promised to continue to pursue the nuclear programme for civilian and military purposes, review the nuclear doctrine to make it more relevant to current challenges, and invest in the indigenous thorium technology programme. These were, and continue to be, important elements in the security calculus.

The new government started on a promising note by raising the FDI cap in defence production from 26 to 49 per cent and increasing the defence budget for 2014-15 by 12.44 per cent over the previous year's budgetary allocation. In fact, Finance Minister Arun Jaitley dwelt at some length in his budget speech not just on the need for the modernization of armed forces and encouraging defence production but also on other issues such as One Rank, One Pension and constructing a war memorial. He also talked about the development of rail infrastructure in the border areas and promised to set up a defence technology fund.[30]

These audacious promises were not backed by adequate funds, as was evident from the fact that the budgetary allocation for 2014-15 was Rs 79,362.72 crore less than the requirement projected by the MoD. Ironically, the MoD was not able to utilize the funds, resulting in the allocation being brought down by Rs 6,630 crore at the revised estimate (RE) stage.

In the event, it turned out to be a flash in the pan as the very next year (2015-16) the year-on-year growth fell to 7.74 per cent, followed by a measly 0.96 per cent increase in 2016-17. The saving grace is that, because of the likely underutilization of funds, the RE for 2015-16 has been slashed by Rs 22,091 crore and, therefore, if the increase in the budget estimates (BE)/allocation of 2016-17 is reckoned with reference to the RE 2015-16, it works out to a more respectable 10.89 per cent.[31] Quite evidently, the trend of budgetary allocation and utilization since 2014-15 is a continuation of the past trend since 1947-48.

Inferences about the Basis of Budgetary Allocation for Defence

The history of budgetary allocation for defence over a period of almost seven decades constitutes a fairly reliable basis for drawing informed, though perhaps arguable, inferences.

First, the building up of military capabilities was not a critical factor in the worldview of the political elite in the wake of India's Independence. The focus was more on economic development and welfare. For better or worse, budgetary allocations were seen as a zero-sum game. The allocation for defence accounted for a fairly high percentage of the total central government expenditure for a long time in the initial years but this was more on account of the prevailing circumstances than a desire to finance any long-term defence plan with a view to consolidating military capabilities. The wars in 1947-48, 1965 and 1971 did not change this template.

Second, although attempts at defence planning started in the 1960s, it was not until the sixth plan for 1964–69 that defence plans were made co-terminus with the national five-year plans in what appears to be more of a symbolic gesture. As brought out earlier, only three of the twelve five-year plans were brought before and approved by the CCPA/CCS. But apparently even these approvals made no significant impact either in terms of assured and sustained funding during the plan period or building up military capabilities.

In any case it made little sense to go to the CCS for approval of the five-year plans considering that the Long Term Integrated Perspective Plans (LTIPP), which form the basis of the five-year plans, require the approval of only the Defence Acquisition Council (DAC). With the dissolution of the Planning Commission by the NDA government that came to power in 2014 and the consequent discontinuation of national five-year plans, defence planning faces an uncertain future, though it also provides a good opportunity to evolve a new pragmatic model of defence planning.[32]

Third, the occasional surge in the defence budget was always either in the wake of different wars that India had to fight with Pakistan and

China or on account of the implementation of the recommendations of various pay commissions. There were some other short spells of comparatively robust increase in the defence budget, as from 1980-81 to 1986-87. Since this period partially overlaps the period of the sixth five-year defence plan (1980–85), it would be tempting to conclude that this surge was the result of the approval of this plan by the CCPA. But the fact that this plan was approved in the third year of the plan period, by which time allocation had already been made for the first three of the five-year period, does not support this conclusion.

There is another fact which does not support the inference that there was a direct link between the approval of plans and the surge in defence budgets. The seventh plan (1985–90) was also approved by the CCPA. In the first two years, the growth in the defence budget was the same as in the preceding year. In the third year it went up drastically because of the pay commission. But thereafter the growth plummeted to below 4 per cent in the fourth year and to 0 per cent in the final year of the seventh plan. It is unlikely that this trend of allocation was in keeping with the trend of allocation envisaged in the plan. Thus, the empirical evidence does not support the inference that these surges were part of any systematic attempt at consolidating military capabilities.

Fourth, while the defence budget as a percentage of the central government expenditure varied from 40 to almost 50 per cent during the first ten years after Independence, it has remained in the 12 to 16 per cent band during the last twenty-five years.[33] This could well be seen as the basis for determining the size of the defence budget, though there is little evidence that it is indeed the official policy of the government to peg the defence budget at this level in terms of its percentage to the total central government expenditure.

Fifth, though it is conventional wisdom that a higher allocation for defence is contingent upon the state of the economy, empirical evidence does not support this view. It can be seen from Table 2, which reflects the data for sixteen years selected at random, that there is no co-relation between the increase in the gross domestic product (GDP) at market price and the increase in the defence budget. For example, while the GDP at market price increased by 15.7 per cent in 1996-97, the defence budget increased by 9.01 per cent. In contrast, while the GDP at market price increased by 7.63 per cent in 2000-01, the defence budget increased by 28.22 per cent. As Table 2 would show, these are not aberrations.

The foregoing analysis only indicates the pro tempore approach to fixing the annual allocation for defence. The MoF, which is responsible for providing funds, is surely driven by its internal assessment of how much can, and should, be allocated for defence in a given year. And although it is known that at least for the eleventh plan it had indicated the likely availability of funds for defence expenditure for the entire duration of the plan (2007–12), the basis on which this decision was made is not known.

Year	*GDP at Market Price (Rs crore)*	*Increase (%)*	*Defence Budget (Rs crore)*	*Increase (%)*	*% of GDP*
1996-97	1,419,277	15.7	27,798.48	9.01	1.96
1997-98	1,572,394	10.79	35,620	28.14	2.27
1998-99	1,803,378	14.69	41,200	15.67	2.28
1999-00	2,023,130	12.19	45,694	10.91	2.26
2000-01	2,177,413	7.63	58,587	28.22	2.69
2001-02	2,355,845	8.19	62,000	5.83	2.63
2006-07	4,294,706	16.28	89,000	7.23	2.07
2007-08	4,987,090	16.12	96,000	7.87	1.92
2008-09	5,630,063	12.89	105,600	10	1.88
2009-10	6,477,827	15.06	141,703	34.19	2.19
2010-11	7,784,115	20.17	147,344	3.98	1.89
2011-12	9,009,722	15.74	164,415.49	11.59	1.82
2012-13	10,113,281	12.25	193,407.29	17.63	1.91
2013-14	11,355,073	12.28	203,672.12	5.31	1.79
2014-15	12,503,122	10.11	229,000	12.44	1.83
2015-16	14,247,410	13.95	246,727	7.74	1.73

(Table 2: Increase in GDP and Defence Budget, 1996-97 to 2001-02. Source: Based on the data contained in the Statistical Handbook on Defence Expenditure)

Part II: Constraints faced by the Government

The MoD, or the National Security Council Secretariat, does not bring out any report on strategic defence and security review. But even in its absence, plenty of credible reports are available that portray a worrisome picture of India's defence capabilities. Stalled modernization of the Indian army, falling squadron strength of the air force and depletion in the number of operational submarines are some of the well-known problems besetting India's defence establishment.

The reports of the Standing Committee on Defence have been routinely highlighting these problems. A 2015 report by the Comptroller and Auditor General of India (CAG) talks about an inadequate war wastage reserve of ammunition to sustain a forty-day intense war, which is the norm followed by the Indian Army.[34]

There are financial and non-financial factors that have led to this situation. The non-financial factors, such as those related to defence planning and the higher defence management structures, are beyond the scope of this chapter. Purely from the financial point of view, however, the problem is two-fold: real or perceived inadequacy of budgetary allocation and its efficient utilization.

Financial resources are always going to be limited no matter what the state of the economy because of serious limitations on the government's ability to raise money beyond a certain limit. This problem has got compounded because of the disconnect between defence planning and financial realism. The budgetary support sought by the MoD during the past several years has far exceeded the MoF's ability to meet the demand. Ironically, year after year, the MoD has also failed to fully utilize the allocated funds, mostly for capital expenditure.

For the tenth five-year defence plan (2002–07), the MoF had agreed in principle to the MoD's projection of Rs 418,101 crore. But while agreeing to this figure in December 2004, the MoF also informed the MoD that 'it was an indicative figure' and that 'actual allocation for defence services would depend largely on resources available with the government at that point of time, capacity to utilize the funds, pace of expenditure, contractual agreements and other committed liabilities'.[35]

At Rs 379,300 crore, the actual allocation during this period was Rs 38,801 crore less than what had been agreed upon. But even the reduced budgetary allocation was not fully utilized. The actual expenditure during this period was Rs 358,145.56 crore only. Of the total under-utilization of Rs 21,154.44 crore, a sum of Rs 17,704 crore was under-utilized under the capital segment, which bears the expenditure on infrastructure development and modernization of the armed forces.[36]

History repeated itself during the eleventh five-year defence plan (2007–12) also. As in the past, while indicating the likely availability of funds, the MoF also added that 'the actual allocation would depend, *inter alia*, on availability of resources with the Government at the relevant point of time, capacity of the Ministry to utilize the funds, pace of expenditure, contractual agreements and other liabilities'.[37] This remained a matter of academic interest only as the MoD anyway wanted much more than what the MoF was prepared to agree to.

Unlike the tenth five-year defence plan, however, the actual expenditure during the eleventh plan period exceeded the total annual allocation by Rs 18,165.85 crore. But this was on account of excess expenditure under the revenue segment, which dissembled under-utilization of the capital budget.[38]

Challenges of Meeting the Requirement

Meeting the MoD's requirement in full is a huge challenge. The gap between the projection and allocation increased from Rs 12,453.42 in 2009-10 to Rs 79,362.72 in 2014-15. For 2015-16, the gap between projection and allocation was Rs 40,659.33 crore.[39]

As in the past, the defence outlay for 2016-17 formed the second largest chunk of expenditure in the non-plan segment of the Union budget after interest payment and ahead of subsidies. In the capital segment of the non-plan segment, defence capital budget accounted for almost 90 per cent of the total capital expenditure. This had been the pattern for the past several years.

The enormity of the problem of resource allocation can be understood better if it is taken into account that until now the expenditure on defence pensions and other organizations, such as the Coast Guard, was not included in what was commonly referred to as the defence budget. While the reorganization of the MoD's Demand for Grants for 2016-17 might change this narrative, the expenditure on other paramilitary forces will continue to be not included in the defence budget.

The government has to generate more income to be able to allocate more money for defence and other sectors. As observed earlier, there are serious limitations in doing so. According to a 2013 report, only 2.89 per cent of the Indian population paid income tax as compared with 45 per cent in the United States.[40] Political and socio-economic compulsions prevent the government from widening the tax base in any substantial measure. Indirect taxes, the burden of which anyway eventually gets passed on to the consumers, also cannot be raised beyond a certain point and, therefore, cannot make up for inadequate revenue generated through direct taxes.

The Fiscal Responsibility and Budget Management (FRBM) Act 2003 adds another dimension to this problem. It requires the central government 'to ensure inter-generational equity in fiscal management' and manage its debt 'consistent with fiscal sustainability through limits on the Central Government borrowings, debt and deficits'. Section 4 required the revenue deficit to be brought down to nil by 31 March 2008.[41] Besides this, it required the fiscal deficit to be brought down to not more than 3 per cent of the GDP by the same date.[42]

Successive governments have been struggling to achieve these targets. In his budget speech for 2016-17, Finance Minister Arun Jaitley set the target of 3.5 per cent for fiscal deficit. The revenue deficit target of 2.8 per cent for 2015-16 was reduced to 2.5 per cent in RE 2015-16. It is not clear what the target for 2016-17 is, but there is little doubt that the target of nil revenue deficit will remain elusive for a long time to come.[43]

Part III: Impact on Defence Preparedness

While these factors have affected the overall allocation for defence, the impact has been more acute on the revenue segment of the defence budget, which caters to obligatory expenses on pay and allowances, ration, clothing and so on. Since this expenditure cannot be curtailed, the funds available for operational requirements, such as ordnance stores, transportation, maintenance of equipment and infrastructure, training—all of which is financed from the revenue budget—are becoming increasingly limited.

The share of pay and allowances in the revenue budget is increasing rapidly. In 2005-06, this accounted for 46.99 per cent of the revenue budget and 27.53 per cent of the total defence budget. In 2015-16, this rose to 65.56 per cent and 40.43 per cent respectively.[44] Between 2008-09 and 2009-10, the bill for pay and allowances almost doubled from Rs 26,587.44 crore to Rs 52,975.94 crore. Its share jumped from 46.16 per cent to 60.86 per cent in the revenue budget and from 25.18 per cent to 37.31 per cent in the total defence budget. This was primarily on account of the implementation of the recommendations of the sixth central pay commission. A similar jump after the recommendations of the seventh central pay commission are implemented in 2016-17 could take the share of the pay and allowances well beyond three-fourths of the revenue budget and half of the total defence budget.

The capital segment of the defence budget, on the other hand, presents a strange paradox. The capital acquisition budget is a sub-set of the capital budget. All expenditure on the acquisition of equipment, weapon systems, platforms and other capabilities meant for the modernization of the armed forces (excluding the Coast Guard) is incurred from this segment of the budget. Since 2001-02, there is a dedicated capital acquisition organization in the MoD which handles this task. Between 2002-03 and 2014-15, a total sum of Rs 542,812.47 crore was allocated for capital acquisitions but only Rs 491,344.76 crore could actually be utilized.[45]

While these figures do not indicate that funding of capital acquisitions is presently a problem, the fact remains that this segment of the capital budget could also come under great strain as and when capital acquisition programmes start getting executed with greater speed than has been the case so far. These figures also show that the problem besetting capital acquisition and infrastructure development, which are funded from the capital budget, are not on account of paucity or inadequacy of outlays but other non-fiscal reasons.

Contrary to the common perception that the gap between the allocation and the actual expenditure is on account of the MoF unilaterally reducing the allocation at the RE stage, the reduction is the result of a very detailed assessment made by the MoF in consultation with the MoD some time in the month of December or early January. The amount likely to remain unspent is then withdrawn by the MoF.

Be that as it may, from the financial point of view, demands being based on unrealistic assumptions about the likely availability of funds, inaccurate costing of the projects/other activities, and inefficiency in the utilization of the allocated funds is an area of great concern as it impacts the efficient management of the overall financial resources of the nation.

There are many other demands on the nation's financial resources apart from those that are met through the defence budget, defence pensions being one of them. The actual expenditure on defence pensions has gone up from Rs 2,312.76 crore in 1992-93 to Rs 60,449.75 crore in 2014-15. The BE for defence pensions for 2015-16 was pegged at Rs 54,500 crore but had to be increased to Rs 60,238 crore in the RE. For 2016-17, the allocation has been increased to Rs 82,332.66 crore. This steep increase is on account of the impending implementation of the decision on One Rank, One Pension and the recommendations of the seventh central pay commission.[46]

Till 2014-15, the Demand for Grant for MoD[47] (also referred to as the civil estimates) provided for the budgetary requirements of the secretariat of the MoD, Defence Accounts Department, Defence Estates Organization, Armed Forces Tribunal, Coast Guard, Jammu and Kashmir Light Infantry (JAKLI), Canteen Stores Department (CSD) and the Chief Directorate of Purchase. The allocation under this Demand, which also did not form a part of the defence budget, grew from Rs 4,106.92 crore in 2001-02 to Rs 16,577.87 crore in 2014-15.[48]

The budgetary allocation for the Coast Guard, which also formed a part of the MoD's civil estimates, grew from Rs 500 crore to Rs 2,680.26 crore during the same period. In 2015-16 it was reduced to Rs 2,514 crore, but it has been increased to Rs 3,124.41 crore for 2016-17.[49]

The budgetary allocation for the Border Roads Organization used to form a part of the Demands for Grant of the Ministry of Road Transport and Highways till 2014-15. In 2015-16 it was included in the Demand for Grant for MoD (Civil). The budgetary allocation of this organization, which is responsible for developing road infrastructure along India's borders, increased almost four times from Rs 1,220.25 crore in 2002-03 to Rs 4,813.24 crore in 2014-15 but it came down to Rs 3,480.57 crore in 2015-16; for 2016-17 it is Rs 3,075.73 crore, a good Rs 1,332.67 crore less than the BE 2014-15.[50]

The moderate roller-coaster rate of growth of these outlays exhibits the financial constraint faced by successive governments. This constraint has been compounded by the rising budgetary allocation for defence research and development and the ordnance factories. The time and cost overrun of the research and development projects, the quality and productivity issues with the products manufactured by the ordnance factories, and the stagnation of the defence public sector undertakings have resulted in India emerging as the largest importer of defence equipment. This is anathema both to the efficient utilization of the limited budgetary allocation and the positive spin-offs for the Indian economy.

Four inferences that can be drawn from these facts: (a) the MoF has not been able to meet the requirement as projected by the MoD in full, (b) the long-term commitment of funds for the defence plans has always been conditional; (c) the MoD has not been able to synchronize the plan with the likely availability of funds; and (d) the conditional commitment of funds or even the mismatch between the projection and allocation of funds has not adversely affected capital acquisitions as the MoD has repeatedly failed to fully utilize the funds allocated for capital expenditure (which also raises questions about the accuracy of the requirement projected by the MoD).

The simple picture that emerges from these facts is that while the government faces serious constraints in raising financial resources, there are huge demands on the limited resources it is able to generate, which apparently makes it difficult for the government to strike a balance between the demands from various sectors to everyone's satisfaction. The situation has been exacerbated by ubiquitous cost inefficiencies. This may possibly be true of other sectors also but the growing budgetary demand of the defence sector, based on unrealistic assumptions about the availability of funds and the burgeoning revenue expenditure, is an important constraining factor in this financial calculus, the complexity of which is seldom fully appreciated by those not responsible for the generation and allocation of financial resources.

Conclusion

The ultimate objective of all defence spending is to ensure that the armed forces remain at the highest level of preparedness at all times. There is no MoD report that throws any light on this crucial aspect of national defence. The Standing Committee on Defence had submitted a report to

Parliament in February 2014[51] on the threat perception and preparedness of the armed forces. While this report and the subsequent action-taken report[52] submitted in August 2015 go into the details of the problem, the MoD's response to a query by the Standing Committee on Defence in December 2014 sums it up succinctly.

As noted by the Committee, when asked about the compromises made, or likely to be made, because of the reduced budgetary allocation, the MoD responded as follows:

> Under the revenue segment, provision is first made for salary and other obligatory expenses. The balance allocation available is distributed to meet the requirement of stores (including ordnance), transportation (of personnel and stores), revenue works and maintenance, etc. These areas are likely to be impacted by the reduced allocation. In so far as the capital segment is concerned, funds are first set aside to meet the projected Committed Liabilities likely to materialize during the year. The remaining allocation is distributed to meet the projected requirement for other items. The procurement plan for capital modernization schemes may have to be reviewed and reprioritized, based on available funds. Budget for high value acquisitions like MMRCA is not available under the current allocation. However, these schemes will continue to be processed and additional funds will be sought if approval for these schemes is likely to be forthcoming.[53]

Though this statement does not reveal much and fails to give a credible account of the state of defence preparedness, it is as close as the MoD has ever got to admitting the implications of the financial constraints on defence preparedness. This statement, when seen against the background of the foregoing analysis in this chapter, surely lends itself to the following prognosis.

One, if inadequacy of the revenue budget is impacting the expenditure on stores, transportation, revenue works and maintenance, etc., there is no question that the day-to-day normal operations of the armed forces are getting adversely affected. This explains, though not fully, the chronic deficiency of ammunition, low serviceability levels of the equipment and weapon systems, poor maintenance of the infrastructure, tardy implementation of measures such as raising of the mountain strike corps,[54] depleting numbers of aircraft and submarines, non-procurement of artillery guns, and so on.

Two, while it is not a problem as of now, at the present level of funding it would be impossible to acquire all capital assets and capabilities envisaged in the defence plans within the desired timeframe.

Three, the constraint in raising the level of funding beyond 10 to 15 per cent on a sustained basis over a long period of time may or may not have stymied the rapid modernization of the armed forces but it is undoubtedly one of the fundamental reasons why ideas like raising of aerospace and cyber commands are not even on the drawing board as of now. Thus, financial constraints have a far-reaching impact on the future development and expansion of the armed forces both in quantitative and qualitative terms.

Four, it goes without saying that if the pace of certain activities, such as the development of infrastructure along India's borders, is to be increased, it would require the infusion of huge sums of money beyond the present level of funding. While there are various other reasons for it, the insignificant budgetary allocation cannot but be a significant constraining factor for rapid infrastructure development in the border areas.

Five, certain objects of expenditure, not germane to the core function of defence but nevertheless important on account of the impact they have on the morale of the troops, are also likely to get adversely affected. The Ex-servicemen Health Scheme (ECHS) is an example. The budget allocation for ECHS increased from Rs 150 crore in 2004-05 to Rs 2,639 crore in 2015-16. At Rs 2,363.64 crore, the allocation for 2016-17 was less than the RE of 2015-16 (Rs 2,609 crore). Going by past experience this may turn out to be grossly inadequate. Except for 2004-05, the actual expenditure on ECHS has always been more than—in some years, far in excess of—the initial budgetary allocation.[55] This is also true of the outlays for defence pensions.

Six, since the source of funding of all the activities is the same, resource allocation will continue to be a zero-sum game. This is a serious challenge that calls for realistic solutions rather than simplistic prescriptions like insistence on the defence budget being increased to the level of 3 per cent of the GDP. This is an impractical idea. As conveyed by the MoD to the Standing Committee, co-relation of defence expenditure with GDP is just an indexation and other than that it has no bearing on defence preparedness or ability to safeguard the interests of the country.[56] After all, GDP is not income in the hands of the government.

Though that is not the only requirement, defence and other components of comprehensive national security require a huge infusion of funds. Within the defence component, more funds are required not just for the armed forces but also for the Coast Guard and the Border Roads Organization, not to speak of the other paramilitary and central police forces.

This is where the rub lies. The situation arising from the constraints in raising enough financial resources to meet the requirements has been made more complex by the absence of financially viable long-term planning and a variety of other non-financial factors, such as the glitches in the defence production, complexity of procurement policies and procedures, and tardy decision-making. The challenge of finding a long-term solution lies in recognizing these realities and infusing realism in policymaking, evolving a new paradigm of defence planning, integrating it with a comprehensive national security strategy, and improving the MoD's track record on quick decision-making.

13

India's Space Programme: The Need for a Techno-Military Orientation

LIEUTENANT GENERAL DAVINDER KUMAR

Former Signal Officer-in-Chief, Army HQ, New Delhi, and CEO and MD, Tata Advanced Systems

The international security environment continues to be uncertain, dynamic, complex and dangerous. An international 'disorder' seems to prevail, with an ever-increasing economic, technological and digital divide accentuated by globalization, rising aspirations, greater unemployment and the related challenges of climate change, terrorism, national and human security. An absolutely different security paradigm is evolving with economic, energy and food security taking prime position, and the emergence of outer space and cyberspace as new arenas of competition and conflict due to their vital impact in determining the comprehensive combat power of a nation.

In the twenty-first century, sovereign nations must be able to deter and, if necessary, fight and win wars in multiple domains (land, sea, air, outer space and cyber space) and modalities (irregular, conventional, asymmetric and nuclear). Accordingly, the nations are competing and concentrating on the development of capabilities that exploit the global commons, viz., sea, air, space and cyber space. In this race, space, nuclear and cyber security have emerged as the vital strategic capabilities for national security.

India needs to hasten further development of its capabilities in these three fields and integrate those with other elements of national power. This chapter deals with what India needs to do to develop world-class and India-specific capabilities in the spheres of outer space and cyber space. Both are highly contested, congested and competitive 'global commons'.

Outer Space

Space has emerged as the new strategic high ground for positioning assets like satellites and space stations for intelligence, surveillance, target acquisition, reconnaissance (ISTAR), communication, navigation, weather forecasting, broadcast services for entertainment, education, disaster management and so on. From a military perspective, space is mainly used for communication, observation and positioning.

1. The communication function covers data transfer, such as command-and-control dissemination, voice, video, data (email, Internet) and unmanned aerial vehicle (UAV) operations.
2. The observation function deals with intelligence, surveillance and reconnaissance systems such as geographic intelligence, signals intelligence, electronic intelligence, monitoring of own and enemy forces, support to electronic warfare, missile warning and environment monitoring (mission planning, munitions loading decisions, weather forecasting).
3. Positioning is determined by time distribution and today is a fundamental task in the use of precision-guided munitions, navigation for all services, support to friendly force tracking and UAV operations.

The first military revolution in space (1957–1990) was marked by the communication and reconnaissance satellites that provided added stability with the elimination of surprise attacks.

The second revolution (1990 onwards) is marked by the integration of advanced digital information and communication technology with orbiting assets not just for enhanced command, control, communication, intelligence, surveillance and reconnaissance (C3ISR) capabilities but also for the precision targeting and weapons guidance that have high priority in modern warfare.

An important aspect of this revolution is the emergence of the technology–anti-technology spiral, with the development of electronic, communications and global positioning system (GPS) jammers, anti-satellites and directed energy weapons (DEW) to defeat or reduce the space advantage of the adversary.

The technological and political developments of the past decade have, thus, heightened the concerns of the space technology threshold being crossed by the advanced space-faring nations, because further the militarization of outer space will certainly lead to a new race for space weapons technology and space control strategies. Trends indicate that space has the potential to become an over-contested domain, particularly in the continuing absence of integrated policy and the promotion of best practices and behaviours.

It is perhaps only a matter of time before the next transformation in outer space takes place with the introduction of weapons in space for missile defence, anti-satellite operations and even for extended force projection from 'earth orbits' to achieve 'full spectrum dominance'. As access to sophisticated technologies becomes cheaper and easier, adversaries will attempt to deny or degrade the use of space.

Space and Satellite Systems

Space is an extremely harsh and inhospitable environment featuring solar radiation, extreme temperature gradient, micro gravity and absence of external pressure, transfer of heat only by conduction, ultra violet radiation, space debris and meteoroids, all of which directly impact the design, useful life and survivability of satellites and other space assets. The net effect is that a space system is very fragile and vulnerable.

A satellite system consists of two major components: a space segment comprising the satellite and the launch vehicle and a ground segment consisting of the earth station and the telemetry and tele-command (TT&C) systems for satellite, payload and network management. Hence, a satellite system is vulnerable on ground, during launch, through the TT&C system, and in space. To ensure 'technological sovereignty', a nation must not only have inherent capabilities in all these spheres and their integration but also in international agreements for TT&C and deep space communications.

The Indian Scene

India is one of the very few developing countries that made an early investment in space technology and has sustained it over five decades. The very nature of the beginning of the Indian space programme fundamentally differs from some of its counterparts. The Indian government has typically taken a stand on the utilization of outer space for civilian benefits and the development of a national space infrastructure that can independently serve the vision of facilitating the civilian benefit programme. This particular stand has eventually created a vibrant space programme that has indigenously developed capabilities in space, launch and ground systems on the upstream and specific civilian programmes (resource monitoring, earth observation, education, broadcast services, communications, meteorology and disaster management) on the downstream.

The Indian Space Research Organization (ISRO) adopted a twin approach wherein communication, broadcast and meteorology services were provided by the Indian National Satellite System (INSAT) series of satellites and Earth observation services were engineered on the Indian Remote Sensing (IRS) satellites.

India's Military Space Programme

Most nations have adopted 'dual-use' technologies and systems to build their space assets and capabilities. The powerful among them, like Russia, the US, the UK and China, also have dedicated military satellite programmes.

Essentially, a military space programme will consist of a national space vision and policy; a space doctrine and an associated roadmap for its implementation; technology for designing, launch, monitoring, survivability and maintenance of space systems; organization including skilled manpower; a robust industrial, engineering and manufacturing infrastructure; research and development (R&D) and testing facilities; and a large system integration capability backed by strong political will and assured budgetary support.

Based on these, the nation develops its strategies for space control, space power, space situational awareness and counter-space capabilities.

The Development of Indigenous Technology

The Indian military had a very modest start in engineering voice communication on hired satellite channels in the 1990s followed by the hiring of full transponders and the provision of triple play services. Concurrently, the Earth observation satellites were used to provide very rudimentary surveillance capabilities. The first military satellite, Radar Imaging Sattelite-2 (RISAT-2), was launched in April 2009 to provide radar imaging all-weather, day-and-night surveillance capability. This was followed by RISAT-1 (2011), an indigenous radar imaging satellite of world-class capabilities. This is in addition to the new, higher-resolution daylight imaging spacecraft launched in 2008 and the existing low- and medium-resolution remote sensing satellites already being utilized by the Indian intelligence organization for the state and the military. It is believed that India has a substantial satellite surveillance capability.

GSAT-7/INSAT 4F, launched on 30 August 2013 on board French rocket Ariane, is the first dedicated Indian military communication satellite, built specially to meet the strategic and operational requirements of the Indian Navy. Built by ISRO, GSAT-7 is the most advanced communication satellite capable of providing a wide range of service spectrum—from low-bit-rate voice-to-video to high-bit-rate data transfer. It has great potential to integrate warships, submarines, aircraft and shore-based installations through a highly encrypted data network. With this launch, India has joined the club of the top five countries—the US, Britain, Russia, China and France—that have a satellite customized for defence communications. A dedicated air force communication satellite, GSAT-7A, was scheduled for launch in 2016.

On 27 August 2015 the Geosynchronous Satellite Launch Vehicle (GSLV), with an indigenous cryogenic engine, successfully placed in geosynchronous orbit the strategic communication satellite GSAT-6/INSAT-4E. The satellite has an unfurlable antenna of 6 metres in diameter that would be utilized for five spot beams over the Indian mainland, and very small handheld devices would be required to be used for data, video or voice transfer. The spot beams would exploit the frequency reuse scheme to increase the frequency spectrum utilization efficiency.

Satellite-based navigation is another important arena which has significant military utility. ISRO is developing a programme called the Indian Regional Navigation Satellite System (IRNSS) to provide accurate position information services to civilian and military users. A position accuracy of better than 10 metres is expected to be provided to military users. The IRNSS would have seven satellites, out of which five have already been placed in orbit and the system is expected to become operational shortly.

India also has a strategic tie-up with the Global Navigation Satellite

System (GLONASS), Russia's GPS and navigation system, facilitating accuracy to within half a metre for our missiles, including those fired from the nuclear submarine Chakra. Also, a strategic tie-up has been made with the EU Navigation and Positioning System Galileo, which will become available by 2020.

All these satellites together constitute India's military space investments.

Organization

Subsequent to China's anti-satellite test in 2007, the Space Security Coordination Group (SSCG) was set up in 2010 under the chairmanship of the former national security advisor, Shivshankar Menon. The SSCG had representation from the Defence Research and Development Organization (DRDO), the Indian Air Force (IAF) and the National Technical Research Organization (NTRO). Its main task was stated to 'guide India's response to the Chinese threats'. Not much is known about the activities of this group in the open domain.

In 2012, the then DRDO chief, V.K. Saraswat, emphasized a defensive strategy for India in the space domain. Following the trial of the Agni V intermediate-range ballistic missile (IRBM), Dr Saraswat declared that the DRDO would field a full-fledged ASAT (anti-satellite) weapon by the end of 2014 based on Agni and the AD-2 ballistic missile interceptor without resorting to actual testing. He projected the view that space security entailed the creation of a 'gamut of capabilities' without weaponizing. These capabilities included the protection of satellites, communications and navigation systems and denying the enemy access to its own 'space systems'. He further stated that India has mastered technical expertise over all the components of ASAT capabilities without actually testing an ASAT weapon.

Integrated Space Cell

An Integrated Space Cell has been set up to utilize more effectively the country's space-based assets for military purposes and to look into threats to them. It functions under the Integrated Defence Services headquarters of the Ministry of Defence. It envisages cooperation and coordination between ISRO, DRDO as well as the civilian agencies dealing with space.

The cell was the first step towards the coordination and protection of India's space assets and may, in the near future, provide the basis for an Indian space command. The CARTOSAT-2A, a dedicated satellite of the Indian armed forces, would also fall under the jurisdiction of this nodal agency.

Launch Vehicles

India has proven launch capability in the polar and elliptical orbits. It has launched seventy-five satellites since 1975 of all types, including nano and pico satellites. Satellites have been launched from various vehicles, including American, Russian and European satellite launch rockets. India has multiple launch capability in the form of the Multiple Independently Targetable Re-entry Vehicle (MIRV). The Polar Satellite Launch Vehicle (PSLV) launched ten satellites in a single launch in 2008. India has also demonstrated its strategic capability of launching a satellite in the geosynchronous orbit successfully with an indigenous cryogenic engine.

A previous DRDO chief is on record to state that with the successful launch of Agni V, India has all the components of a viable ballistic missile defence capability, as also the capability to launch low-earth satellites in case of an emergency.

Along with GSLV-Mark III, ISRO has been working on another critical technology programme: the development of a semi-cryogenic stage, which is expected to double the lifting power of the GSLV. Such vehicles could carry 6 to 10 tonnes of weight (heavy communication satellites). They could also be used for a human space mission, or the development of a space station.

India is also building a hyper plane, AVATAR (Aerobic Vehicle for Hypersonic Aerospace Transportation). It is a single-stage, reusable space plane capable of horizontal takeoff and landing, being developed by the DRDO along with ISRO and other research institutions. It could be used for cheaper military and civilian satellite launches. When operational, it is planned to be capable of delivering a payload weighing up to 1,000 kg to the low-earth orbit. It would be the cheapest way to deliver material to space at about $67/kg. Each craft is expected to withstand 100 launches.

Allied Facilities

India, over the years, has developed a satellite system R&D, manufacturing, testing and human resource development ecosystem. It has top-of-the-line telemetry and tele-command facilities spread across the world, including those on board ships. It also has international tie-ups for deep space communications. Besides, ISRO is engaged in a number of 'technical demonstrator projects'.

Moreover, the DRDO is involved in developing necessary counter-space, ballistic missile defence (BMD) and directed energy weapons (DEW) capabilities. It has, however, a long way to go.

The Need for a Techno-military Orientation

To begin with, India must review its space vision in the light of emerging global threats, particularly in view of China's enormous space capabilities; the strategic imperative to protect its space assets; and the militarization and an impending weaponization of space.

India must exhibit political will and promulgate its national space policy and space doctrine without any further delay. It is essential to ensure a focused and systematic development of capabilities in space and integrating the same with other components of national power.

With the doctrinal guidance, the armed forces must formulate a strategy for the development and employment of space forces, formulate a roll-on plan, draw a roadmap and implement the same in a time-bound manner. Concurrently, they must develop the supporting strategies for organizing, training, equipping and employing space forces, and build requisite capabilities and the right force mix of offensive and defensive forces required to negate any threat. They must also discuss and formulate India-specific tenets of space power and the operational art of employing space forces.

These would require an empowered and dedicated organization and assured budgetary support. Concurrently, ISRO and DRDO must ensure the development and availability of necessary technology and assistance in the training and skill development of officers and men of the armed forces. They must continue with their respective missions and programmes. Together with the armed forces, they must assist in the techno-military transformation of India's capabilities in outer space to include counter-space capabilities such as missile defence and a new class of DEW and anti-satellite capabilities. Passive capabilities like physical and electronic hardening; anti-jam technologies; satellite manoeuvrability; redundancy at system and sub-system levels; quick launch facilities; and mini, micro and nano satellites both for the restoration of facilities and as weapons to destroy satellites must be developed concurrently to ensure greater survivability of our space assets.

The government must declare the immediate raising of a space command. In the absence of a clear vision, doctrine and dedicated organization, any build-up of space forces would be ad hoc and not integrated with the national security apparatus.

The militarization of space took place immediately after the launch of Sputnik, the first artificial Earth satellite, by the Soviet Union in 1957. The weaponization of space is likely in the next decade. India has to make haste in promulgating its space doctrine and developing requisite capabilities both for offensive and defensive space operations.

The critical importance of space for both national development and national security has made space a highly contested, congested and competitive domain. Nations are talking about space power, space control and space situational awareness as parameters of capability development for space security and exploitation. These, accordingly, are the three pillars which India needs to build on to acquire overall space capability.

Space Power

Space power can be defined as 'the total strength of a nation's capabilities to conduct and influence activities to, in, through, and from space to achieve its objectives'. The definition of space power is expanding to claim 'the aggregate of a nation's abilities to establish, access, leverage, and sustain its orbital assets to further all other forms of national power.'

Simply put, space is inherently a medium, as with air, land, sea and cyber, and 'space power is the ability to use or deny the use by others of that medium'. Space power is a precondition to control the sea, land or air. It provides the ability of continuous awareness of terrestrial events and has become the concern of all organizations regardless of their technical sophistication. It is based on the following conjectures:

1. Space forces are necessary to enhance war-fighting capabilities.
2. Space forces can target sea, land and air forces.
3. Adversaries must be deprived access to space to gain a decisive advantage.
4. Space power is perishable and must be protected.

Space Control

Space control supports freedom of action in space for one's own forces, and, when necessary, defeats adversary efforts that interfere with or attack one's space systems, and negates adversary space capabilities. It consists of:

1. Offensive space control (OSC): Measures taken to prevent an adversary's hostile use of space capabilities or offensive operations, and to negate an adversary's space capabilities that are used to interfere with or attack one's own space systems.
2. Defensive space control (DSC): Operations conducted to preserve the ability to exploit space capabilities via active and passive actions, while protecting one's own space capabilities from attack, interference or unintentional hazards.

Space Situational Awareness (SSA)

SSA involves characterizing, as completely as necessary, the space capabilities operating within the terrestrial environment and the space domain. SSA is dependent on:

1. Integrating space surveillance.
2. Collection of and processing data in real time.
3. Environmental monitoring.
4. Status of own and cooperative satellite systems.
5. Collection of own space readiness.
6. Analysis of the space domain.
7. It also incorporates the use of intelligence sources to provide insights into the adversary's use of space capabilities and its threats to one's space capabilities with a view to understanding the adversary's intent.

Besides the creation of the above-mentioned capabilities, other related activities that India needs to undertake as part of the techno-military orientation of its space programme are:

1. So far we have a limited space-based communication and surveillance capability. We need to enhance it in multiple domains and orbits.
2. A scheme for the sharing of transponders and facilities both within the defence forces and with civilian resources must be evolved and rehearsed for greater survivability and redundancy.
3. Defence forces must get involved in the planning and execution of national satellite plans; design, development and manning of Earth stations; TT&C facilities; and launching of micro and nano satellites in low-earth orbits both from fixed and transportable launch facilities.
4. India must have more launching facilities with services earmarked for quick launch by defence forces and transportable launch stations on a variety of platforms.
5. Defence forces need to be involved and trained in measures for the passive protection of satellite systems like electronic hardening, virus protection, redundancy and orbital measures.
6. Missile defence, satellite communication, navigation, earth observation, ocean monitoring and surveillance, weather monitoring, and electronic intelligence systems should be operated jointly to start with and handed over to defence forces gradually.
7. A space command should be raised without further delay and should have a well-trained space force to undertake the above-mentioned tasks.
8. Training must be conducted with sister services and friendly forces in exploitation and survivability of satellite systems.
9. It is essential to set up a high-powered Space Defence Agency authorized to pool the resources, expertise, talent and infrastructure available in the country, cutting across the private–public sector barriers for realizing space-based assets for the exclusive use of defence forces in a fast-track mode with minimal bureaucratic interference.
10. A synergy between the technologies developed by ISRO and DRDO

could prove a win-win development for putting in place a platform for developing and launching a range of defence satellites.

11. The Government of India has recognized space as a priority sector of its Make in India campaign. There is an urgent need for the government to give practical shape to this statement in accordance with the reviewed space vision.
12. The MoD's 'Technology Perspective and Capability Roadmap' till 2025 has also identified space warfare as a priority area. The roadmap identifies, in unambiguous terms, the development of an anti-satellite capability based on 'electronic or physical destruction of satellites in both low and geostationary orbits'. This needs to be translated into a time-bound implementation plan executed in a 'mission' mode and monitored at the highest level.
13. For India, there is an imminent need to develop a robust system to protect space assets that are critical to every aspect of military operations on the ground, in the air and on the sea. DRDO has hinted that it is working on putting in place the building blocks of an Indian anti-satellite system to neutralize hostile satellites moving in low-earth and polar orbits. The focus of DRDO would be on laser-based sensors and exo-atmospheric killer vehicles (EKV), the technology of which could be derived from its missile development programme. Technologies developed for India's long-range, nuclear-capable Agni V missile must be profitably exploited for boosting India's space defence and space warfare capabilities.
14. It is incumbent upon the current Government of India to take this issue seriously, for once, in a proactive manner, instead of reacting to international demands. There is still time for India to test and demonstrate the technology, acquire the capability and thereby safeguard our long-term strategic interests. The window of opportunity for India will not last very long in case the US decides to force the issue of an internationally verifiable space weapons regime.

In conclusion, it is imperative for India to address the above concerns by adding to its civilian space capabilities the necessary techno-military components to address national security concerns and to protect the space security interests of the country. Space is clearly emerging as the new dimension of any future warfare on Earth. Like nuclear weapons, space capabilities are likely to emerge as the currency of power in the future and impact on international equations. Space also serves as a major catalyst for socio-economic development and techno-economic competitiveness. Space capabilities are, therefore, indispensable for the aspirations of a progressive country like India that is on the fast growth curve. India needs to have a well-calibrated outer space policy that would not only enhance the civilian space profile but also enable the development of suitable counter-space capabilities to protect its own security concerns. Such an integrated approach alone will enable India to claim its rightful place among the advanced space-faring nations.

14

Cyber Security: Status and Imperatives

LIEUTENANT GENERAL DAVINDER KUMAR

Former Signal Officer-in-Chief, Army HQ, New Delhi, and CEO and MD, Tata Advanced Systems

Introduction

The rapid and unprecedented growth of information and communication technology and media, with their speedy and all-pervasive penetration, has ushered in the digital age. Not only has it brought the world together through globalization, but it has also become the driver for economic growth. Technology and information have become the new mantras of this digital transformation. We are witnessing a connected world with new business and cultural orientations. Business is being transacted at the speed of light, with billions of dollars transferred every day across the globe. This transition from an industrial to an information era has also ushered in a new security paradigm, with new threats to both national and human security. With large-scale automation, technology and connectivity, the developed nations are enjoying a much better quality of life. There exists a definite digital divide between the developed, developing and poor nations. This digital divide, coupled with the rising aspirations of the people and total dependence on technology, has created serious security issues wherein new threats by way of cyber crimes, cyber terrorism, cyber espionage and even cyber war have emerged, making cyber security a strategic imperative at the national, regional and international levels.

Environmental Scan

India lives concurrently in three ages—agrarian, industrial and information. The Indian society is, therefore, in constant transition. While India has made considerable progress in the last decade or so towards the establishment of ICT infrastructure, enhancing the reach of the electronic media and extension of e-services in the finance, health and education sectors to ensure better governance, the development has been differential. The situation, however, is changing rapidly with the mobile telephone revolution which is under way and through the greater penetration of the Internet. Projects like National Broadband Network, Make in India and Digital India would change the digital landscape substantially, with a direct impact on governance, transparency and accountability. While there is a definite requirement of greater penetration of ICT for development and better governance, this rapid change towards a digital environment has brought to the fore the challenge of cyber security. A cyber-insecure digital India initiative can turn from a strategic asset to an unaffordable liability and a direct threat to national security. India, like other countries, needs and must ensure safe navigation through cyberspace—a global commons—for its prosperity and national security.

It is paradoxical that as nations and societies transit from the industrial to the information age, through the deployment and exploitation of ICT, their vulnerability to cyber threats increases. These vulnerabilities could result from weaknesses in technology, because of improper design implementation, use of pirated software, oversight of technological products, software coding, or malware planted deliberately or via smartphones with options of millions of applications to be downloaded.

Consequently, each level of the cyber realm—physical infrastructure, operational software, information and people—is susceptible to security breakdown, whether through attack, infiltration or accident. Cyberspace is thus inherently not secure and requires consistent efforts, technology, trust, international cooperation and innovative measures to ensure its security, which at best could be 'relative'.

With the rapid expansion of cyberspace, emergence of new threats and the exponential advances in technology, this will remain a 'work in progress' and hence present an ongoing challenge.

The Threat Scenario

Cyber threats are a function of technology and related vulnerabilities. These exist 24x7 and manifest themselves along the full spectrum, starting from cyber crime and cyber espionage to cyber terrorism and cyber war.

This is due to some unique characteristics of cyberspace, namely, offence dominance, difficulty in attribution of attacks (thus providing anonymity to the attacker), attack at the speed of light, no direct collateral damage and relatively low cost of development of cyber weapons by state and non-state actors.

In 2015 alone, the number of cyber attacks worldwide grew by 48 per cent and the cost of each incident increased by 92 per cent.

The Indian ICT Landscape

India has the second largest telecommunication infrastructure in the world, second largest number of Internet users and nearly a billion mobile users, with about 30 per cent having smartphones, registering a growth of 165 per cent in 2014. Unfortunately, almost 80 per cent of the phones are imported, which entails risks and vulnerabilities.

Mobiles have already overtaken fixed Internet access, and mobile marketing is the latest business model. Mobile applications are the drivers of this growth, with 64 billion applications downloaded in 2012 across all platforms (iOS, Android, Windows Mobile, etc.) in the world. India's share of this was 1.56 billion. It was likely to be 9 billion by the end of 2015 (a yearly growth of 75 per cent). Most of these applications are not tested and certified and are a major source of vulnerability propagation and cyber security threat. Interestingly, the highest number of downloads was in the age group of sixteen to thirty years, which tends to be more adventurous than risk-averse.

India has the dubious distinction of the following:

1. According to the Computer Emergency Response Team-India (CERT-In), 4.2 million computer systems including mobile phones were infected with the botnet virus in India by June 2013.
2. Thanks to botnet viruses of the kind of CUTWAIL, India is the leading generator of spam in the world.
3. India figures third in the list of countries targeted by phishing attacks, with more than 23 per cent of online users facing these attacks in 2014. So, there is a huge possibility that employees could reveal crucial information to rivals by mistake since they would be unable to differentiate between phishing emails and legitimate ones.
4. Ramnit Botnet virus infected about 3.2 million computers across

the world and has been in existence for nearly five years. The worst affected countries in recent times have been India, Indonesia, Vietnam and Bangladesh.

5. India has the third largest number of computers infected by the Zero Access botnet virus. It is a sophisticated, very virulent and resilient botnet active since 2011.

India faced 60,000 reported cyber attacks in 2014. It is estimated that the actual number would be five to ten times this since most attacks are not reported. The Nuclear Power Corporation of India faces ten cyber attacks per day on average.

Emerging Contours of Cyber Security

Cyber crimes have changed the nature of conflict by blurring the line between state and non-state actors. These are a real threat today and are proliferating very rapidly, both in intensity and complexity, with the spread of Internet and smartphones. About 80 per cent of cyber attacks are related to cyber crimes. The quantum of cyber crimes is dependent on the number of people connected. There are 3.125 billion Internet users today and that is 41 per cent of the world population. These are increasing at the rate of 100 connections per second and would cover 70 per cent of the world population by 2017. By 2020, there would be six devices per person connected to the Internet on an average. By 2025, there are likely to be 50 billion people/things connected to the Internet. The extent of availability of malware is mind-boggling. Nearly 27 per cent of all malware variants were created in 2015 alone. Panda Security collected 84 million new malware samples over the year. This amounts to 230,000 new malware samples a day!

Cyber crimes are likely to increase exponentially with the fielding of virtual currency, Internet of Things, big data, cloud technology, drones, robotics and so on. Capabilities of hijacking a car, taking over the controls of an aircraft, cyber murder and remote injunction of viruses through drones and aircraft have already been demonstrated.

The dark net and deep web are already being exploited for the sale of vulnerabilities, weapons, recruitment of people in terrorist groups, drugs and so on. The latest entrant on the long list of cyber crimes is the installation of 'Ransom Ware' to cripple a network or facility and demand ransom to restore the same. This is an extremely scary scenario and demands a collective response for its mitigation.

Cyber Espionage

Nations, industries and organizations across the world are involved in cyber espionage. It is estimated that more than 90 per cent of open-source intelligence is being obtained from the cyber world. It is economical and safe. Cyber espionage is also being used for technology theft and for launching probing missions on critical infrastructure for possible exploitation later. The extent of threat can be gauged from the fact that Japan alone had 25.6 billion cyber attacks in 2014, mostly for technology exfiltration. That is 900 cyber attacks per second. The fact that attack vectors for cyber espionage and cyber war are the same makes cyber espionage a major threat. The Internet has thus become a very powerful source of intelligence in support of national, diplomatic, military, technology or economic objectives.

Cyber Terrorism

Coincidence between the physical and virtual worlds, as demonstrated by the Stuxnet virus attack on Iran's nuclear facility at Natanz in 2010, has put the complete category of infrastructure at risk. Targeted attacks on a nation's critical infrastructure like military installations, power plants, air traffic control, surface transport traffic control and telecommunication networks would be considered cyber terrorism. These are low-level, 'short of war' attacks which would cripple part of a critical infrastructure or adversely affect the functioning of a business. These attacks are not large enough to warrant a military response but have the potential to inflict enough damage so that numerous attacks over a long period of time could harm an economy, complicating a policymaker's calculus for determining an appropriate response. Cyber terrorism is an attractive option for modern terrorists. Many nations have publicly stated that an attack on their critical infrastructure would be considered an act of war and would attract a strong response. Attribution, however, remains a major issue.

Fear of such attacks, particularly in the developed nations, is so pronounced that they are trying to manage the threat through bilateral or regional agreements related to non-interference in each other's critical infrastructure.

Social Media

Social media sites like Facebook, Twitter and LinkedIn have emerged as very powerful tools for perception management, social engineering and open-source intelligence gathering. They have emerged as major instruments of waging asymmetric warfare through the exploitation of the aspirations of people, differential development, varying religious beliefs and cultural leanings. They have also become attractive sources for recruitment and radicalization by terrorist organizations.

Nations across the world are putting in place legal frameworks, infrastructure and human resource for monitoring this media. The major dilemma they face is the issue of privacy vs. human/national security.

Cyber Warfare

It is universally acknowledged that a twenty-first century war will be highly 'cyber-centric' if not fully led by the cyber theatre. Cyberspace has been accepted as the fifth domain of war that nations need to protect and exploit for offensive operations. The militarization of cyberspace and development of cyber weapons are raising the spectre of a cyber war. Cyber weapons are being equated with nuclear weapons and are being termed as 'weapons of mass disruption'. Strategic thinkers are debating issues like 'cyber deterrence'.

Military planners across the globe are at an inflection point, taking far-reaching decisions which include the ushering in of cyber weapons fully integrated into military operations and kinetic warfare. Nations like the US, Russia, China and the UK have already pronounced their respective cyber warfare doctrines, created appropriate organizations and policies to implement the same and tested cyber weapons on a limited scale.

China has developed 'full spectrum' capabilities in cyber warfare, has announced a major organizational transformation and integrated kinetic and information warfare in accordance with its national doctrine. It has a powerful 'cyber militia' which can operate both as non-state actors and as part of the state machinery. Chinese cyber capabilities will have to be factored in any decisions or policy formulations made by India.

Insider Threat

Insider threat and non-state actors represent extreme dangers. Their involvement in any major cyber attack or intervention is almost certain, resulting in the loss of crucial technical or human intelligence. These threats raise the question of cyber security's direct impact on national, economic and human security, and reinforces the urgency of capacity building in this field. India needs to quickly build its capacity across the full spectrum of cyber security and ensure safe navigation through cyberspace for its prosperity and national security. Ensuring complete cyber security of our assets and national information infrastructure is thus both a national strategic imperative and an urgent national mission.

In pursuance of this objective, the Government of India released the National Cyber Security Policy in July 2013 with the declared vision 'to build a secure and resilient cyberspace for citizens, businesses and government' and mission 'to protect information and information infrastructure in cyberspace, build capabilities to prevent and respond to cyber threats, reduce vulnerabilities and minimize damage from cyber incidents through a combination of institutional structures, people, processes, technology and cooperation'.

It is a very comprehensive document which was formulated over a period of two years after extensive deliberations with the government, industry, academia and research and development (R&D) organizations. Inputs were also taken from the NASSCOM-DSCI (the National Association of Software and Services Companies and the Data Security Council of India) document 'Securing Our Cyber Frontiers'. It not only lays down the objectives but also includes the corresponding strategies for implementation. The objectives spelt out are:

1. To create a secure cyber ecosystem in the country, generate adequate trust and confidence in information technology (IT) systems and transactions in cyberspace and thereby enhance adoption of IT in all sectors of the economy.
2. To create an assurance framework for the design of security policies and for the promotion of and enabling actions for compliance to global security standards and best practices by way of conformity assessment (product, process, technology and people).

3. To strengthen the regulatory framework for ensuring a secure cyberspace ecosystem.
4. To enhance and create national- and sectoral-level 24x7 mechanisms for obtaining strategic information regarding threats to ICT infrastructure, creating scenarios for response, resolution and crisis management through effective predictive, preventive, protective, response and recovery actions.
5. To enhance the protection and resilience of the nation's critical information infrastructure by operating a 24x7 National Critical Information Infrastructure Protection Centre (NCIIPC) and mandating security practices related to the design, acquisition, development, use and operation of information resources.
6. To develop suitable indigenous security technologies through frontier technology research, solution-oriented research, proof of concept, pilot development, transition, diffusion and commercialization, leading to the widespread deployment of secure ICT products and processes in general and specifically for addressing national security requirements.
7. To improve the visibility of the integrity of ICT products and services by establishing infrastructure for the testing and validation of the security of such products.
8. To create a workforce of 500,000 professionals skilled in cyber security in five years through capacity building, skill development and training.
9. To provide fiscal benefits to businesses for the adoption of standard security practices and processes.
10. To enable the protection of information while in process, handling, storage and transit so as to safeguard the privacy of citizens' data and for reducing economic losses due to cyber crime or data theft.
11. To enable the effective prevention, investigation and prosecution of cyber crime and enhancement of law enforcement capabilities through appropriate legislative interventions.
12. To create a culture of cyber security and privacy, enabling responsible user behaviour and actions through an effective communication and promotion strategy.
13. To develop effective public–private partnerships and collaborative

engagements through technical and operational cooperation to enhance the security of cyberspace.

14. To enhance global cooperation by promoting shared understanding and leveraging relationships to further the cause of security of cyberspace.

Towards this end, the policy recommends the adoption of a prioritized approach to implementation so as to address the most critical areas in the first instance. It also suggests that this policy shall be operationalized by way of detailed guidelines and plans of action at various levels, such as national, sectoral, state, ministry, department and enterprise, as may be appropriate to address the challenging requirements of securing the cyberspace. It also emphasizes the absolute necessity of public–private partnerships and international cooperation.

Surprisingly, the policy is silent on capacity building for cyber warfare and the development of cyber offensive capabilities. The then national security advisor, Shivshankar Menon, however, when talking about cyber security architecture, mentioned that it would also involve capacity and authority for operations in cyberspace. It is presumed that this would be taken up by the National Technical Research Organization (NTRO), the Defence Research and Development Organization (DRDO) and the Integrated Defence Staff of the Ministry of Defence. The proposed coordinating structure for cyber and information warfare is given in Appendix 1.

Cyber Security Status

The last decade has witnessed a slow but steady realization within the Indian government and industry that the threats of the future will come from cyberspace. Unfortunately, while the realization exists, the Indian security establishment has not been jolted into action in the manner in which the Kargil war or the 26/11 terrorist attack on Mumbai galvanized the nation to adopt a series of corrective measures. India was one of the first few nations to promulgate an IT Act as early as 2000. It detailed a legal framework against cyber crimes. It is creditable that India could foresee the threat to its critical information infrastructure and introduced appropriate sections, 70A and 70B, in the year 2008. It is sad that such a landmark and proactive legal provision went largely unnoticed in policy circles.

While the announcement of the National Cyber Security Policy was a very welcome step, its implementation has been rather slow. Nevertheless, the government has given a fillip to capacity building in cyber security by bringing online major projects and appointing a national cyber security coordinator under the Prime Minister's Office.

Now, India is setting up its own 'cyber security architecture' that will comprise the National Cyber Coordination Centre (NCCC) for threat assessment and information sharing among stakeholders; the Cyber Operation Centre that will be jointly run by the NTRO and the armed forces for threat management and mitigation for identified critical sectors and defence; and the National Critical Information Infrastructure Protection Centre (NCIIPC) under the NTRO for providing cover to 'critical information infrastructure'.

Concurrently, the government is also coming up with a legal framework to deal with cyber security, has launched a drive for creating greater awareness to this threat and is creating necessary human resources with requisite skills. Major cyber security projects under implementation are mentioned in the succeeding paragraphs.

National Cyber Coordination Centre (NCCC)

The government has approved the setting up of a National Cyber Coordination Centre at an outlay of Rs 770 crore. The NCCC is a critical component of India's cyber security against hackers and espionage, as well as to track terrorist activity online. It is likely to start operations by the end of 2016. A group of cyber security professionals and experts will look after the functioning of the centre and track illegal and terror activities online. It will run on similar lines as in the US, UK, France and Germany.

The setting up of the NCCC is the responsibility of the CERT-In. It will function under the National Information Board (NIB). Some of the components of the NCCC include a cyber crime prevention strategy, cyber crime investigation training, review of outdated laws, etc. It is expected to coordinate between intelligence agencies, specifically during network intrusions and cyber attacks. Its mandate may also include cyber intelligence sharing. Indian and US intelligence agencies are also working together to curb the misuse of social media platforms in the virtual world by terror groups.

Botnet Cleaning and Malware Analysis Centre

To obviate and limit the threat due to botnets, the government is setting up a Botnet Cleaning and Malware Analysis Centre at an envisaged investment of Rs 90.5 crore. The project is being implemented on a fast track. It is part of the Digital India programme and aims to create a safe and secure cyberspace. It will automatically detect botnets that trigger various cyber crimes and suggest the device owner to remove them from his device with the centre's help.

Central Monitoring System (CMS)

The Central Monitoring System is the Union government's ambitious electronic intelligence monitoring system. According to Ministry of Home Affairs (MHA) officials, the high-tech unit, which will provide unhindered access to phone calls, text messages, and social media conversations to law enforcement agencies in real time, will have two units in the inaugural phase, in Delhi and Bangalore.

The CMS was conceptualized by the Department of Telecom after Shivshankar Menon decided to put in place a robust system for monitoring calls. It aims to stop the leakage of information from the service providers' end. As per the government's strict norms for the interception of calls, violation by any private agency or individual can result in a jail term of five years and fine of Rs 1 crore.

The total cost of the project would be approximately Rs 590 crore. The entire monitoring system, which is being designed and integrated by Telecom Enforcement, Resource and Monitoring (TERM) and the Centre for Development of Telematics (C-DoT) will be supervised by the Intelligence Bureau. All telecom platforms, including PSTN (public switched telephone network), GSM (global system for mobile communications) and CDMA (code division multiple access) technologies, will be easily intercepted as CMS would provide convergence of all lines at one location.

National Critical Information Infrastructure Protection Centre (NCIIPC)

Article 70A (2008) mandated the need for a special agency that would look at designated critical information infrastructure (CIIs) and evolve practices, policies and procedures to protect them from cyber attacks. But the then United Progressive Alliance government took another six years to create such an agency. On 16 January 2014, the Department of Information Technology (DIT) issued a notification announcing the creation of a specialized body to protect India's CIIs. The NCIIPC was created and placed under the NTRO to roll out countermeasures in cooperation with other security agencies and private corporate entities that man these critical sectors.

A 'critical sector' has been defined under the notification as 'sectors that are critical to the nation and whose incapacitation or destruction will have a debilitating impact on national security, economy, public health or safety'.

The government has identified twelve sectors that fit the bill and can be covered under the NCIIPC project as mandated by Section 70A. These range from energy to power, law enforcement, aviation, banking, critical manufacturing, defence and space. While several of them are housed within the government, sectors such as energy and power are manned by the private sector. Hence, protection of CII is a joint responsibility of both the public and private sectors and demands synergy and mutual trust. They must jointly develop appropriate plans, adopt requisite standards, share best practices, and refine procurement processes. This will mean sitting together to conduct joint exercises, map vulnerabilities, build countermeasures and achieve a synergy that it is currently lacking.

Protection of Power Sector

In December 2010, the Ministry of Power constituted CERTs (computer emergency response teams) for the power sector, i.e., CERT-Thermal (nodal agency: National Thermal Power Corporation), CERT-Hydro (nodal agency: National Hydroelectric Power Corporation) and CERT-Transmission (nodal agency: Power Grid Corporation of India Limited) to take necessary action to prevent cyber attacks in their domains. The state-run power utilities have also been advised to prepare their own sectoral crisis management plans and align themselves with the nodal agencies for the necessary actions.

Grid Security Expert System (GSES)

The Grid Security Expert System was proposed to be developed in March 2015 and it involves the installation of the knowledge-based Supervisory Control and Data Acquisition (SCADA) system, numerical relays and remote terminal units of up to 132 kV stations, and the reliable optical fibre ground wire (OPGW) communication system at an estimated cost of around Rs 1,200 crore. The objective of the GSES is the implementation of the automatic defence mechanism to facilitate reliable and secure grid operations.

The Government of India has also prepared a crisis management plan for countering cyber attacks and cyber terrorism and for preventing a large-scale disruption in the functioning of critical information systems of the government, public and private sector resources, and services. The Crisis Management Plan for Countering Cyber Attacks and Cyber Terrorism outlines a framework for dealing with cyber-related incidents for rapid identification, swift response and remedial actions.

Network Traffic Analysis System (NeTRA)

This is a monitoring and electronic surveillance project being executed by the DRDO. It will intercept and examine communication over the Internet for keywords like 'attack', 'blast', 'kill', etc. It appears to be the Indian government's first attempt at mass surveillance rather than individual targets. It will scan activities over social networking websites and scan emails and chat transcripts and even voice transmitted over the Internet.

It would be seen that these efforts are aligned towards developing a cyber defence capability. There is no information in the open domain regarding the development of cyber offensive capabilities and their integration. Cyberspace is offence-dominant because of technical characteristics that undermine deterrence and defence and because the defender has to defend all the time. Cyber power includes both defensive and offensive capabilities backed by appropriate organizations, technology, skilled human resources and a well-developed defence electronic manufacturing and components base. It is reported that more than 140 nations are busy developing cyber offensive capabilities and about forty have some modicum of organization for cyber war.

As India moves further into a digital world, it becomes increasingly vulnerable to cyber interventions. The irony is that India has practically no technological, semi-conductor and electronic manufacturing base and limited human resource with skills, particularly in system and large system integration. Consequently, technology, products, operating software, system engineers and integrators have to be imported with their attendant impact on security, finance and dependency for maintenance and upgradation. In short, India has serious strategic inadequacies impacting on its 'technological sovereignty'. India needs to develop full-spectrum cyber capabilities without any further delay, particularly in light of major national projects like Digital India, National Broad Band Network, Make in India and the emergence of China as a cyber superpower.

Imperatives

India needs a national-level effort supported by political will, adequate funding, contemporary technology and skilled people to realize the necessary cyber security capability. These imperatives would require synergy amongst various ministries and agencies through appropriate policy frameworks and organizations and must be executed concurrently. Some of the essential imperatives are given in the succeeding paragraphs.

Establish a National Cyber Security Commission (NCSC): A fully empowered body with its own department, on the lines of the Space Commission and Atomic Energy Commission. The country needs to build thought leadership and bring together India's potential in cyber security under one organization. The NCSC will have the onerous task of creating synergy amongst various stakeholders through an enabling policy framework, and of developing technology, manpower, industry clusters, education standards and certification, intelligence and counter-intelligence mechanisms, cyber forensics, security standards, and undertaking policy research. It will also coordinate with all ministries for the National Critical Information Infrastructure (NCII) in their areas. It will play a catalytic role for the requirements of the military in cyber warfare.

The NCSC must be headed by a technocrat with the position of a cabinet minister. It should have two secretary-level officials, one responsible for the cyber security of all civilian sectors and assets and the other a defence forces officer, chartered with the responsibility of creating top-of-the-line, full-spectrum information warfare capabilities, including cyber offensive capability and their integration with other components of national power. These capabilities will have to be developed in accordance with the information warfare doctrine of the armed forces, which obviously would be based on the national doctrine. All central agencies like NCIIPC, CMS, NCCC should be placed under this organization. The states must have a separate and dedicated set-up for cyber security on the lines of disaster management, fully integrated with the NCSC; their CERTs must be linked up with the CERT-In, with emphasis on information sharing and incident reporting.

The National Cyber Security Policy 2013 needs an urgent review to include the development of full-spectrum capabilities; synergy amongst various organs of the government, industry, R&D establishments and academia; organization; technology, R&D, standards, testing facilities and a vibrant electronic industrial base; availability of necessary skilled resource, and their constant training and retention; assured budgetary support; international cooperation; and a legal framework. This policy should be translated into a time-bound action plan, a national cyber doctrine, and specify clearly the responsibility for its execution and accountability. The policy, action plan, organization and assured budgetary support must be discussed and approved by Parliament.

Develop Cyber War Capability: India urgently needs to develop policies and capabilities in this 'fifth' domain of war. These cannot wait and must be taken up on top priority by the services. The situation and threats to India are unique and hence there is the necessity of developing an indigenous solution in consonance with the doctrine to include organization, technology, skill sets and R&D as per a very tightly monitored time schedule.

Within the overall structure, time-bound action is needed for raising an Indian Cyber Command with a mission to ensure the operations and defence of information networks and prepare to, and when directed, conduct full-spectrum military cyberspace operations to enable actions in all domains; ensure freedom of action in cyberspace and deny it to our adversaries.

India announced its ***National Electronic Policy (NEP) in 2012*** with a view to establish an electronic system design and manufacturing (ESDM) ecosystem in the country. It also proposed establishing semiconductor fabrication plants (fabs) for making semiconductor chips in the country. Unfortunately, the scheme did not take off in spite of the fact that it offered attractive financial and taxation terms. This scheme has now been given a push under the Make in India programme. The establishment of fabs, however, is lagging behind and needs immediate intervention. It may be appreciated that the absence of an electronic manufacturing base and fabs in the country is a strategic deficiency. These are absolutely essential and fundamental prerequisites for cyber security and need immediate attention at the highest level.

Cyber Policy Research Centre: There is no think tank that is studying policies and documents being produced by groupings of governments, industry, civil society, academia, interested organizations and established key entities like the International Corporation of Assigned Names and Numbers (ICANN), Internet Society (ISOC), Internet Engineering Task Force (IETF), World Wide Web Consortium (W3C), United Nations Government Group of Experts (UNGGE), Internet Governance Forum (IGF), International Telecommunication Union (ITU), Global Commission on Internet Governance, Asia Pacific Network Information Centre (APNIC), Regional Internet Registries (RIRs), European Union (EU), North Atlantic Treaty Organization (NATO), International Chamber of Commerce (ICC), and many others. Thousands of pages are being churned out which require a deeper understanding through analyses and discussions to decide what is in India's interest. We are unable to address policy as well as operational issues due to the lack of focused studies. Numerous NGOs created at the behest of foreign governments are obfuscating policy discussions to derail national positions. Also, as technology evolves, a large amount of cyber security research and policies require timely revision.

Cyber Threat Intelligence Centre: We do not have cyber analysis centres which may collect tonnes of attack data on various infrastructures, and correlate 'big data' generated from the government with financial and commercial data to create patterns and suggest anomalies for advance preventive actions. The capability to develop semantics and ontology libraries of globally spoken languages for cyber analysis is an important imperative.

Cyber workforce development: There is an urgent requirement to have a national plan to develop a security workforce and an associated cadre. The NCSP 2013 has set up a target of half a million skilled cyber resources in the non-formal sector for cyber security, and also to exploit the business opportunity of providing services to global customers by 2018. We also must lay emphasis on developing the science of cyber security.

R&D for product development: There is no focused R&D with a well thought-out plan to develop cyber security technology, products, email and social media platforms in the private sector. Funding in universities with no accountability for outcomes has not led to any innovation in any dimension of cyberspace. We need focused R&D in the development of safe products, discovery and analysis of vulnerabilities, fixing attribution and designing cyber weapons.

Security Standards, Frameworks and Audit: India needs to develop and promulgate the cyber security standards and frameworks for the development and audit processes for the assurance of protection of our NCII. Enabling policy measures are required to encourage the establishment of testing labs for managing ICT supply chain risks.

Cyber-crime investigations: There is an urgent need for the development and continual upgrade of cyber forensics capabilities and investigating skills for our law enforcement agencies (LEAs) to handle cyber crimes, given the proliferation of devices, platforms, big data, Internet of Things, mobility and social media.

Assurance Framework, Test & Certification: There is an immediate requirement to set up a national cyber test facility providing for network emulation, monitoring and audit, vulnerability analysis, simulated attacks, graduated response, performance analysis and security assurance modelling.

Build Thought Leadership, Executive/Political Sponsors: There is a need to build cyber security–savvy leadership, subject matter experts, solution architects and system engineers so as to address the inadequate comprehension of the lack of cyber security capability and its bearing on national security, including the military dimension. Fostering systems thinking—strategic, ahead of times, at the national scale—about cyber warfare as replacement for co-existing with components of kinetic energy weapons (KEWs) in the country will keep us in step with the rest of the world. There is also a need to build operational requirements and articulate and validate a cyber doctrine as a standalone option or in tandem with KEWs in training exercises and war games.

Leveraging Diaspora: The Indian diaspora is at the forefront of building security technologies, platforms and solutions across world-class institutions and industry in the US and Europe. They can be the biggest catalysts in building cyber security capability. Proactive and aggressive steps should be taken to leverage the diaspora.

Outreach Programme to Attract Industry: The government needs to make it attractive for the private sector to invest in capability building through innovative mechanisms, such as by funding the development of new technologies, committing to buy from partner companies, etc. Both the government and the industry must recognize the multi-billion-dollar opportunity in cyber security–related products and services and cash in on this through a focused and proactive approach, as was done for IT.

Establish a Cyber Policy Research Centre: This will constitute a think tank funded by the government for studying all facets of cyberspace and making policy recommendations to the government. Its mandate would be to resolve differences amongst different wings of the government and develop international consensus on issues like ICANN, intellectual property rights, cyber security, content regulation, freedom of expression, cyber crimes, and law enforcement agencies' access to data, mutual legal assistance treaties, etc. This think tank's mission will include understanding the emergence of transnational institutions like ICANN and their role in the future of Digital India, and the role of multinational corporations like Google, Amazon and Facebook that are the new Internet monopolies with a potential to control the economic, social and political life of India. Examining the possibility and the need for an 'Indian Internet' to ensure India's technological sovereignty is also a priority.

Cyber security is going to become a major concern amongst people and nations in the next ten years. One would think that cyber security would be dealt with at the same level as terrorism and climate change. India needs to expedite capacity building in cyber security and implement measures to ensure its economic development, and national and individual security. This is a strategic imperative and India cannot afford to delay or neglect it.

15

A Defence R&D Strategy for India

Professor Amitav Mallik

Founder Director, DRDO Laser Science and Technology Centre, New Delhi, and former member of the National Security Advisory Board

Technology and Security

Perceptions about India's military might and defence preparedness are changing significantly as compared to the Cold War decades of the past century. Today, the decisive impact of technology on defence and security is much more pronounced than ever before. Nuclear weapons, missile technology advances, satellite technology and precision weapons delivery technology were the major components of defence strategy that determined the power balance of the past century. The twenty-first century, however, will likely be dominated by technologies that can either defeat or reduce the strategic importance of these existing winner technologies. In the international system of power play, while strategy, doctrine and tactics represent the key ingredients, technology has been and will be the lowest common denominator. Hence, mature technology and research and development (R&D) strategies will be crucial for the future.

Since World War II, hundreds of regional wars have been fought, with thousands of casualties, almost all in the territories of the developing nations. This is ample proof that the technologically developed nations are not only superior in terms of economy and quality of life but also enjoy better levels of security and stability with sound techno-military strategies. The importance of modern technology in security and world affairs has never been so convincingly demonstrated as in the Iraq operations of 2003. The overwhelming techno-military dominance of the US-led coalition was on vivid display on millions of television screens across the world, setting new benchmarks for future warfare, where the main strategy would be to weaken the enemy in the technology dimension so that actual war fighting can be short, decisive and affordable.

The 'shock and awe' strategy was successful because of the vastly improved technology of satellite imagery, with unprecedented levels of intelligence and targeting details, while the global positioning system (GPS) provided instant and reliable support to every pilot and foot soldier. The C3I (command, control, communications and intelligence) network was made versatile for easy integration, leading to high situational awareness, which could then effectively support military strategies for the 'digital battlefield'. A kind of revolution in military affairs (RMA) was achieved by using 'network-centric' strategies and operations that dramatically reduced the 'sensor to shooter' time gap. This was an impressive demonstration of the maturity of the technologies for real-time global operations. Yet another new strategy, that of using remote-controlled 'unmanned air vehicles' (UAVs), has evolved successfully for surveillance as well as for combat-mode operations. These represent the new technologies and strategies that are changing the nature of war or means of conflict resolution in future.

In the emerging new world order dictated by core techno-economic strengths, India is still hesitating or unable to take bold strides to prove itself truly competitive with the best in the world. While the advanced Western nations are forging cooperative security and risk reduction programmes, and China is fast catching up with the US in terms of comprehensive national power, India continues to be perceived by the world as a country unable to resolve its regional disputes as well as its internal disorder. One can indeed blame it on a lack of governance or political will, but in actual tangible terms it is the lack of techno-economic capability and professional values in the society that has been compounding the problems and holding India down. This chapter presents a brief discussion on the core issues of technology and strategy in the context of India's defence and security discourse.

Technology and Strategy: Changing Perceptions

The challenge of modern defence planning is about dealing with today's threat while preparing for tomorrow's conflicts, and the armed forces that are better equipped with superior technology, training and strategy have always been more successful. Galloping advances in technology and the growing influence of globalization are transforming the very definition of war and peace. Threat perceptions are undergoing paradigm shifts, and the tools and techniques for the future of warfare are changing significantly. The changing environment of global interdependence demands radically new approaches for the control and management of sensitive technology. The future will demand a new culture of responsible conduct among nations, and societies must learn to cooperate and compete at the same time.

The technological revolution of the past few decades has created a paradigm change in techno-military doctrines and overall security perceptions. Most critical technologies for defence are now dual-use in nature, and enabling technologies such as information and communication technology (ICT), advanced computing, robotics, biotech, nanotech, and so on, are transforming the spectrum of defence capabilities. Advances in sensors and simulation technology, technologies for instant global reach, counter-space technologies, energy weapons and cyber warfare capabilities offer a range of new options today for offence and defence strategies for the resolution of future conflicts and for war prevention objectives.

Diffusion of technology has become unavoidable in all international transactions, and technology control regimes are becoming diluted. This may be one of the main causes of the growing asymmetric threat perceptions, since potent technologies are becoming increasingly accessible to rogue states, non-state entities and terrorist groups. The traditional methods of technology denial through export controls are fast losing effectiveness, and there is an urgent need for a new strategic approach to prevent the misuse of high-end, dual-use technologies while promoting constructive cooperation in the same technology areas for security, development and progress.

The US–India cooperation in civilian nuclear technology has brought out many of the complexities of such challenges, and the move towards evolving an international code of conduct is indeed a welcome one. Such trends seem to indicate the way forward for future strategies of technology management, particularly for sensitive technologies with a potential security impact. India must analyse the changing patterns of technology development in different parts of the world in the context of security and achieve clarity on how the Indian defence R&D strategy may be fine-tuned in its pursuit of modern defence technology. India's security strategy should strengthen international cooperation for the common good (cyber security or space security) and also for action against common threats (terrorism or global warming). All the while, India must sharpen its own indigenous capability to build the techno-military power to sustain and improve its deterrence capacity to prevent any military adventurism in the neighbourhood and prevent the misuse of technology by militants and terrorists against India.

The globalizing world today is going through a unique transformational phase where the very premise of future conflict or future war is being re-defined. The deterrence value of sophisticated technology is increasing significantly with every new development, and the world power equations of the future will certainly be decided more by techno-economic capabilities than by the mere size of military force and the numbers of weapon systems. There is an overall sense that the likelihood of full-scale conventional war between major powers is diminishing significantly, and the real conflicts between major states would be about the scarcity of resources such as water or energy, or about a fair playing field for economic competition. The major emerging international concern today is about global warming and climate changes that can have very grave security implications on all of mankind in the future, particularly in the poor developing nations.

Regional conflicts over territory or religion continue to remain unresolved in many parts of the world, and the states involved in such circumstances continue to remain vulnerable to conventional military strengths. The information revolution has transformed the level of awareness in the world, and there exists a peculiar mix of expectations and aspirations among the developing and progressive nations. In such regions, aspirations are very alive for new cutting-edge technologies and yet one cannot neglect the older, proven technologies and weapon systems that are better suited for the kind of regional conflicts that remain relevant. Therefore, techno-military supremacy on the ground continues to remain as important as before in such regions, until and unless they can mature towards a cooperative security strategy.

The use of military force and technological power to bring about regime changes in distant countries is setting new trends in the international power game, and the techniques of preventive military strike are gaining international acceptance. While these are reshaping global perceptions of military threats and risk-reduction measures against asymmetric or terrorist threats, new technological requirements for 'low-intensity warfare' may influence India's future defence and security strategies. Information superiority is becoming very critical for future conflicts that may be settled in outer space or cyberspace. Such new dimensions of defence and security may offer India an opportunity to quickly catch up with the world leaders through robust R&D efforts. For the routine military modernization requirements, the 'Buy and Make' strategy involving private Indian industry capacities can help India gain impressive indigenous capabilities in defence systems to reduce import dependence and emerge as an important player in the global defence and security calculus.

Indian Defence R&D: Potentials and Impediments

Historically, conventional defence technologies and weapon systems have always provided the military superiority needed for defending sovereignty and national interests. But now there is a subtle shift to newer classes of technologies that are becoming more relevant for national security as well as for power projections beyond sovereign boundaries. India's rapid techno-economic progress, as well as the nuclear tests of 1998, has helped to create a major shift in the global perception of India as a potential emerging global power. This, along with the market forces of globalization, has changed the basic precepts of defence, offence and security for India. India's defence technology architecture in the future may, therefore, be quite different from the traditional approach to defence modernization of the past.

Enabling technologies such as infotech, data fusion, artificial intelligence, robotics, nanotech, biotech and so on are transforming the spectrum of technology capabilities. Advances in sensors, precision guidance, missile defence, satellite systems and energy beam weapons are offering a range of new capabilities for offence and defence. While these would indeed represent the universal wish list of modern defence forces, India's actual architecture of defence technology will be governed by factors such as threat perceptions, the indigenous techno-industrial base, the country's economic strength, and of course its defence strategy and security doctrines. Chances are that future defence and security requirements will demand a new set of sophisticated technologies and a substantially revised strategy for the future imponderables in the multiple possible dimensions of future conflicts.

For India, the 1962 war with China brought about a major change in defence policy by which defence R&D and defence production got the much-needed importance in the overall national defence planning process. Starting with modest efforts towards import substitution and product upgrades, the indigenous defence R&D gained real momentum only after a restrictive technology embargo was imposed on India by the West as a reaction to the 1974 peaceful nuclear test. Interestingly, this actually helped fuel the urgency to achieve a high degree of self-reliance in the technologies critical for defence and development. However, due to the competing priorities of economic development, India's defence budgets were very modest. Defence modernization typically got only about 10 to 15 per cent of the total defence budget, and defence R&D got an even smaller share of about 2 per cent. The teething problems, the faltering progress, the heavy dependence on imported Soviet equipment, as well as the struggle to compete with the other modernizing forces of the world—all that is history that is well documented and well known.

The introduction of computers and digital electronics received a major political boost in the 1990s, and the opening of the Indian economy in 1991 was a major milestone that saw foreign investments flow into the country. The 'Y2K' push for software expertise at the turn of the century saw impressive performances by Indian engineers and software professionals, and India started emerging as a powerful international player in ICT and business process outsourcing (BPO). This began to change India's image in the global marketplace.

By 1995, India was already surrounded by a nuclear-capable China that helped Pakistan acquire nuclear weapons for itself to counter India's conventional military superiority. Given the grave nuclear threat from sworn adversaries with a history of war on both sides, it was imperative for India to end its long nuclear ambivalence and declare itself a nuclear power. This was achieved in May 1998 with a series of nuclear tests—Pokhran-II—to establish its nuclear credentials. Pakistan was quick to follow with its own tests to go overtly nuclear, albeit with help from China. India's indigenous development of a credible nuclear deterrence was indeed a shining example of self-reliance in a critical defence capability. This was achieved by the combined R&D strength of Indian scientists and engineers in the atomic energy establishment as well as the defence R&D laboratories.

India's defence R&D potential is very impressive, as has been demonstrated in the nuclear, missiles and electronic warfare fields, where imported options are just not available, or even acceptable. But in the area of conventional defence modernization, the performance of the same defence R&D apparatus has been very disappointing, mainly because of organizational weaknesses and misplaced priorities. In technology development terms, the Defence Research and Development Organization (DRDO) evolved rapidly, with many pockets of excellence in the fields of missiles, radar, sonar, avionics, electronic warfare, fast computing, robotics and system software technologies. But most of its successes remained in the laboratories as 'pockets of excellence' because defence public sector undertakings (PSUs), with their culture of 'licence production', could not convert the lab success into user acceptable systems within the cost and time framework. The users—the armed forces—had little motivation to accept indigenous products when competing imported systems were aggressively marketed by global defence industrial giants.

The net result was that India became one of the largest importers of defence systems, paying for yesterday's technology at tomorrow's prices. The much-talked-about hallowed principle of 'self-reliance' remained a topic for periodic parliamentary discussions without any action. The system was designed to fail, with the DRDO having no control on the defence production process and defence PSUs having no real motivation to convert R&D prototypes into success. There was no convergence of motivation for indigenous success or any real priority for self-reliance, except for critical systems that were not available via the import route. Deficiencies in the Indian defence procurement system are well known to all, and hence, even for conventional defence imports, the defence services often remained starved due to indecisions and delays.

India's defence technology strategy, including R&D, production and acquisition, thus needs to be completely re-designed, with R&D

laboratories concentrating only on new cutting-edge technologies, much along the lines of the US's Defense Advanced Research Projects Agency (DARPA). Defence production has to be totally revamped with robust capacities to meet the nation's critical defence production requirements. For all other defence modernization requirements, Indian industry must compete or tie up with overseas suppliers to satisfy user requirements at globally competitive prices. Several committees have recommended close variants of the above wisdom, but not much has changed because the whole process has fallen victim to electoral compulsions and the lack of political priorities. The situation can change only if the entire process of defence planning, budgeting and procurement can be totally institutionalized and insulated from the ad hoc nature of the discretionary powers of the bureaucratic and political leadership.

Challenges for the Future

India's future defence R&D strategy will have to be based on a mature recognition of the changing nature of threats and the need for new ways of smart planning to acquire new techno-military capabilities. The twenty-first century priorities must focus on countering asymmetric threats at home and dealing with strategic threats at the international level. India must indeed become a world-class power as soon as possible, but first it has to earn recognition as a decisive and major power in the neighbouring Asian region. Comprehensive national power will be the key to having a credible deterrence capacity to exercise robust influence in the region.

In the future, advances in surveillance capabilities will be vital for maintaining a sharp 'situational awareness' across the full spectrum of threats to national interests. The real deterrence capacity will probably depend not just on nuclear-missile capability but also largely on India's comprehensive power, as perceived by others. The capacity for punitive precision strikes with remote-controlled combat UAVs is rapidly gaining international acceptance, and India must quickly master such technologies. Simultaneously, India must also develop technologies to counter enemy UAVs and other surprise-attack scenarios, and the applicability of light-speed energy weapons may rise very steeply in the future. The security of the outer space assets of the nation will become increasingly urgent, and the development of counter-space technology and micro-satellite systems must assume a very high priority for India. Cyberspace is becoming increasingly active for international security management, and artificial intelligence (AI), robotics and fast computing may become very critical for countering the wide spectrum of threats of the future.

In the Indian scenario, the technologies for 'low-intensity conflicts' will remain important for a long while for countering internal militancy as well as for eliminating cross-border terrorism. Addressing border disputes will require strong political will and a suitable deterrence capacity to support hard negotiations. The Indian military apparatus will have to get meaner and thinner for quick reaction to meet unpleasant surprises. The globalizing world of the future will require different sensitivities for defence and security, and future planning must start with the clear recognition that incremental changes will not do any more for India. A clear and honest assessment of India's strengths and weaknesses would help realize its full potential in the defence and security arena. Only then can a fifteen-year plan define aggressive milestones for all the sectors of the Indian defence establishment—R&D, defence PSUs and the armed forces, as well as the intelligence apparatus that must become a smart and flexible force for the many surprises of the future.

India urgently needs proactive and professional governance capable of taking fast decisions on important issues to change its image of being a risk-averse and indecisive nation. Indian defence headquarters must grow out of the insecurity of fractious departmental acrimonies to rise as an integrated entity capable of combining various core strengths in India's supreme national interest. India has no dearth of talent or intelligence. Given the right opportunity and professional environment, India's demographic dividend can make a huge difference to its R&D and professional defence capabilities, which will not only improve India's defence and security capabilities but also strengthen its economic power.

By 2030, global power, prestige and capability may well shift to China, India and other Asian giants, whose combined strengths in economy and political influence would be greater than those of the US and the Western powers. This could lead to unforeseen responses from them since they are not used to being less powerful, resulting in new conflicts and uncertainties in the cyberspace, outer space or maritime trade arenas. Information warfare will take centre stage, and the adverse impact of climate change may emerge to be the main cause of global-level disturbances. The nature and intensity of asymmetric threats may grow due to the deepening religious and economic divide in the global society. On the other hand, the technological edge of the West and the human potential of Asia may combine for greater world peace if they can avoid working against each other.

These would be the major challenges for humanity. For India, an ambitious and prudent technology strategy, including defence R&D, will be a critical asset in preparing for the future.

16

Economic Warfare to Support National Security

Sanjay Pulipaka

Senior Consultant, East Asia Research Programme, Indian Council for Research on International Economic Relations, New Delhi

Understanding Economic Warfare

The developments of 2015 in Nepal brought into relief the role of economic instruments to promote foreign policy objectives. As the parliament in Nepal promulgated the constitution in September that year, there was discontent in some ethnic groups, such as the Madhesis, that their legitimate political aspirations had not been factored in. The Madhesis, who populate the India–Nepal border areas, went on an agitation and blocked border trade and transit routes. Nepal, a landlocked country that depends on India to ensure supply and transit of essential commodities, experienced severe economic distress because of the blockade.

While the Indian government denied that it had any role to play in the economic blockade of essential commodities, including fuel supplies, there was a strong perception in large sections of Nepal that the Indian government had aided and abetted the blockade. These developments, irrespective of the veracity of perceptions, compel us to critically explore economic warfare as a possible tool of India's foreign policy. The intent of this chapter is not to advise the Indian government to deploy economic warfare measures. Rather, it is to demonstrate the complexity involved in deploying economic warfare measures as a tool of foreign policy.

The liberal theories of international relations often argue that enhanced economic interactions will result in peaceful relations between countries. Therefore, economic relations, in this perspective, enable the emergence of conditions for peace to prevail. On the other hand, certain developments in East Asia have demonstrated that enhanced economic interactions might not be sufficient for the emergence of peaceful relations between countries. Sometimes, as in the case of Pakistan's approach towards India, countries may refuse to have enhanced trade and economic relations with other countries. These experiences do not necessarily mean that economic interactions cannot be an effective tool for foreign policy. Countries can deploy economic warfare measures to achieve various political, economic and security objectives. Economic warfare involves a country with superior economic capabilities and/or tactics inflicting significant pain on the adversary by impairing its economy to prevent it from acquiring war-making capabilities, or reduce the adversary's morale, or prompt the adversary to either come to the negotiating table to sort out differences or alter policies, or quickly conclude the battle by accepting defeat. Economic warfare measures are used for varied other purposes, such as to bring about a leadership change within a given regime, to ensure that there is a peaceful transition to democracy, to promote human rights, to prevent the acquisition of weapons of mass destruction, or to compel a state/regime to alter its foreign policy. They are seen as significant instruments either to prevent armed intervention or to at least delay the prospect of armed intervention to achieve certain political objectives.

There are various kinds of economic warfare measures such as 'trade embargoes, boycotts, sanctions (financial sanctions and trade sanctions),[1] tariff discrimination, freezing of capital assets, suspension of aid, prohibition of investment and other capital flows, and expropriation.'[2] They can be applied with varying degrees of intensity, namely, full sanctions or partial. They are based on certain assumptions, for example, that the hardships generated by such measures will compel the regimes to look at demands made by other external actors more favourably. They also assume that economic hardships may propel the social base that supports a regime in a given country to withdraw its support in favour of alternative political/economic policies.

Determining the effectiveness of economic warfare measures becomes challenging in cases where they precede military intervention. The extent to which economic pain played a role in determining the outcome of military intervention tends to be difficult to ascertain. As American political scientist Robert A. Pape succinctly sums up, 'Economic sanctions could be employed in war, but the expected coercive mechanism would have to be [such] that the target state would make concessions because of its unwillingness to bear the economic pain, not because its economic weakness would lead to military defeat.'[3]

What kind of impact will the structure of international politics have on the efficacy of economic warfare measures? According to Stephen D. Collins, a professor of political science at Kennesaw State University in the US, American sanctions or economic warfare measures seem to have achieved their stated objectives more in the post–Cold War era than during the Cold War phase.[4] In a bipolar context, it is possible for the targeted state to move closer to one of the powers and thereby reduce the negative consequences of external punitive economic measures. One of the major powers in a bipolar context can also actively aid and assist the targeted country to discredit the other. There is great possibility of such balancing or assistance in case of a multipolar context as well. However, it must be noted that even in a bipolar context, there is a possibility of economic warfare measures becoming effective in achieving their intended objectives. For instance, a targeted country can become an area of agreement for the implementation of sanctions. On the other hand, in a unipolar context, the efficacy of the sanctions may be more as the targeted state often finds itself isolated without any substantive help coming from the others.

The nature of the economy of the targeted state will also determine the effectiveness of the measures. If it is dependent on a few natural resources, then economic warfare measures on the movement and procurement of those natural resources will have strong effects on the behaviour of the targeted state. On the other hand, if the sender country is heavily dependent on the resources supplied by the targeted country, then the sanctions may be difficult to sustain. Drawing on the works of Professor James Mayall of the University of Cambridge, the following factors will determine the effectiveness of economic warfare measures:[5]

1. Universality of application.
2. High degree of dependence in the target state resulting in high costs for the targeted state if punitive economic measures are imposed.

3. The impact that such measures will have on the political processes in a country, viz., the role sanctions may have in generating a siege mentality or national cohesion/determination.
4. The capacity of the sender to convince its allies that they should also subject the targeted state to economic warfare measures.
5. Policing procedures for the implementation of economic warfare measures.

Imposition of Economic Measures in India's Neighbourhood

By the above criteria, there are very few states in South Asia other than Nepal that can be subjected to punitive economic measures by India. With the high peaks of the Himalayas on the north and India on three sides, any economic embargo/blockade will have a telling effect on Nepal as long as the alternative all-weather northern routes into China do not get operationalized. If such a possibility materializes, the returns from an economic blockade will be minimal. Further, the absence of a significant hydro-electricity collaboration has ensured that Nepal has a very minimal capacity to retaliate with punitive economic measures of its own. However, it should be noted that sustained and/or frequent economic blockades will further alienate large sections of the population in Nepal. It may also contribute to a 'siege mentality or national cohesion/determination' in substantial sections of Nepal's population.

On the other hand, Bhutan, compared to Nepal, has greater leverage to fend off punishing economic measures from India because of growing interdependence between the two in the hydropower sector. Currently, 1,416 MW of hydropower is exported to India from Bhutan, and both governments have decided to increase hydropower generation capacities to 10,000 MW by 2020.[6] With Indian companies working in Bhutan, and given the significant hydropower exports, implementing tough economic measures such as sanctions on Bhutan will be a difficult enterprise. Bhutan can retaliate by cutting off power supply, plunging parts of India into darkness.

In terms of total formal trade, in 2013, India was the third largest trading partner of Bangladesh.[7] India amounted to 9 per cent of Bangladesh's total trade. On the other hand, the European Union (with 22.2 per cent) and China (with 11.6 per cent) were the first and second largest trading partners of Bangladesh in 2013.[8] In the case of Sri Lanka, while India was the largest trading partner, accounting for 16.1 per cent of total trade, the EU (with 13.3 per cent) and China (with 12.1 per cent) were the second and third largest trading partners.[9] In case India has to deploy economic warfare measures against Bangladesh or Sri Lanka, it will have to factor in the impact of such policies on the EU and China and their possible responses. However, this does not preclude India from reducing its trade with these countries in the anticipation that such unilateral measures will inflict significant economic pain on them to compel them to bring about the desired policy change.

Moreover, such unilateral measures will have to surmount significant challenges to yield positive outcomes. Any economic blockade/sanctions against Bangladesh or Sri Lanka will require a significant naval deployment and round-the-clock policing of maritime trade routes. Given the important role that Colombo port plays in India's external trade, it will be very difficult for India to indulge in economic sanctions/blockade against Sri Lanka. It has been reported that more than half of the cargo that goes in and out of India has been handled by the Colombo and Singapore ports.[10]

Pakistan's economic dependence on India is minimal. Therefore, unless India compels others countries to join the sanctions framework, its ability to inflict significant economic pain will be minimal. However, given Pakistan's porous border with Afghanistan and Iran, and with its improved connectivity with China, ensuring a successful sanctions regime will be a difficult enterprise for India. Nevertheless, Pakistan is not in sound financial health. In 2013, it had cash to pay for only one month of imports.[11] In September 2013, the International Monetary Fund (IMF) approved a loan of $6.6 billion to be disbursed over a three-year period.[12] In February 2014, 'Saudi Arabia loaned $1.5 billion to Pakistan to help Islamabad shore up its foreign exchange reserves [and] meet debt-service obligations'.[13] In April 2014, the World Bank approved a $12 billion loan to Pakistan to be disbursed over a span of five years. The Asian Development Bank, in August 2015, approved a loan of $6 billion to be invested in the transport and energy sectors.[14] Pakistan has been the recipient of approximately $20 billion in financial assistance (economic and security) over the past fifteen years.[15] The US figures as the top destination for Pakistan's exports (approximately $3.7 billion).[16] Given these developments, if the US and other international organizations get on board, punitive financial measures may then be explored as one of the tools to compel Pakistan from giving up its policy of state-sponsored terrorism.

At the moment, it appears that India has very few levers of economic warfare with China. This is because India is not as dominant an economic player as the US. For instance, in terms of gross domestic product (GDP), the US economy is at $17.4 trillion, China's economy is at $10.3 trillion and India's is at $2.06 trillion.[17] China's economy is much more integrated in global production networks compared to India's. As a consequence, India's capacity to inflict economic pain on China is limited. At the most, India can indulge in market denying tactics with China. However, such tactics may cause disappointment but not severe economic distress in China. While in theory India has the option of disrupting Chinese trade through or around the Strait of Malacca, in practice it will be difficult to operationalize.

India has a 1,600-km-long border with Myanmar. Myanmar has endured a sustained sanctions regime imposed by Western countries led by the US, up to 2010. However, due to Myanmar's access to multiple resources that generated significant finances, its porous borders and the absence of universality in the application of sanctions, it is difficult to conclude that the democratic transition in Myanmar was a consequence of the rigorous economic sanctions that were imposed on it. Given the meagre bilateral trade, the relations between India and Myanmar, porous borders, and Myanmar's relations with China and other South-East Asian countries, India's capacity to successfully implement sanctions and/or blockade of Myanmar is very limited.

Conclusion

As can be seen from the above analysis, deploying economic warfare measures requires a nuanced understanding of the political economy of various countries. There is a need to develop something like a National Intelligence Council that will monitor the economies in India's neighbourhood and those of a few other important countries on a regular basis. Such monitoring should result in a comprehensive

SWOT (strengths, weaknesses, opportunities and threats) analysis with suggestions for possible areas of interventions, including smart sanctions. Developing a dependency on India in the economies of other countries in the immediate neighbourhood and countries of vital importance should also be factored in when designing external economic interactions.

There is also a need to develop area studies departments in various universities and think tanks which focus on the political economies of countries that are of critical importance to India. Scholars should be encouraged to briefly live and study in some of these countries to better understand the functioning of these economies. There is also a need to study the business interests of important players in various countries and the nature of economic interactions that should be deployed to ensure that the respective national interests are promoted harmoniously. It should be noted that, until not too long ago, India was at the receiving end of various punitive economic measures. Hence, the planning for offensive economic warfare and measures to protect the Indian economy from similar strategies of others should go hand-in-hand.

17

Challenges and Strategy for Energy Security

Shebonti Ray Dadwal

Senior Fellow, Institute for Defence Studies and Analyses, New Delhi

Growing Energy Needs

Given that energy is one of the major drivers of any economy and an essential building block of economic development, India's demand for energy can only grow. A combination of burgeoning population and strong economic growth, together with the ever-growing aspirations of people for a better standard of living, has led to the growth in the country's energy demand, so much so that today India is the fourth largest consumer of energy worldwide and is still perceived as energy deficient.

On the face of it, India has added a huge amount of generation capacity over the past few decades, and its installed capacity currently stands at around 260,000 megawatts (MW), the majority of which consists of thermal power (180,000 MW), and the rest nuclear power (5,780 MW); hydropower (40,867 MW) and renewable energy (RE), including solar, wind, bio-power and small hydro (31,692 MW).[1] In fact, in 2013, India became the third largest producer of electricity with a 4.8 per cent share in global electricity generation. Interestingly, its peak power deficit has come down and currently accounts for only 3.1 per cent.[2] Yet, several parts of the country are often subjected to blackouts that last anywhere between four and sixteen hours a day. Moreover, around 300 million people, particularly in the rural areas, are not connected to the grid, and many of the people residing in remote areas are dependent on wood and biomass, which in turn have a deleterious impact on the environment, both in terms of carbon emissions as well as depletion of forest cover.

No doubt, much of the problem lies in poor management of the power distribution infrastructure as well as other technical issues, such as transmission and distribution (T&D) losses—the official figure of which is pegged at around 24 per cent—caused by illegal tapping of lines, faulty electric meters, poor payment collection from certain sections of consumers, and tariff subsidization of some sectors. This in turn leads to the financial distress of state utilities and low load factor (PLF) of power plants. At the same time, bottlenecks in fuel chains, such as coal and natural gas, and inadequate domestic energy infrastructure, both for fuel and power supplies as well as gas pipeline grids, further create shortages.

Nevertheless, while many of these problems can be resolved by better management as well as regulation, as long as India remains heavily dependent on hydrocarbons, it will remain fuel deficient and hence import dependent. Despite having huge coal reserves, and potentially large natural gas reserves, demand far outstrips supply. As a result, the country's energy import basket has been growing year-on-year, which in turn has seen its hydrocarbon import bill take up a substantial portion of its overall import bill.

In the case of coal, imports were expected to rise to around 200 million tonnes (MT) in 2015 from around 180 MT a year before, as the coal ministry took advantage of the sharp drop in international coal prices. In fact, some analysts forecast that imports could rise to 250 MT over the next three to four years if prices remain depressed due to an oversupplied market.[3]

With regard to natural gas, India's output is around 90 million metric standard cubic metres per day (MMSCMD) against consumption of 134 MMSCMD. According to official data, India has been unable to meet its natural gas production target, with production down by over 8 per cent. On the other hand, demand has escalated, and the balance has been met with imports of liquefied natural gas (LNG) to meet the demand, which has risen by almost 46 per cent.[4]

Hydrocarbons: Import Substitution Measures

However, it is the rise in India's oil imports that is perceived as a major challenge, with crude imports accounting for about 34 per cent of the country's total import basket. Part of the reason for this growth is the stagnant production from domestic fields while demand is growing exponentially, particularly in the transport sector, which accounts for around 51 per cent of the overall consumption of petroleum products.

Worse, demand is expected to grow at 6 to 8 per cent over the coming years due to the rapidly expanding ownership of vehicles. Moreover, although the demand for oil for the grid-based power sector remains low—less than 1,200 MW in 2014—demand for power from generator sets is growing at a rate of 5,000 MW to 8,000 MW annually due to the absence of reliable and quality power supply from distribution utilities.[5]

Hence, given the huge dependence on imported hydrocarbon and the impact on the country's exchequer for procuring the same, and in keeping with its goal of 'least cost to the environment', the current National Democratic Alliance (NDA) government has devised a strategy which will focus on some key areas, aimed at enhancing the country's energy security while ensuring sustained economic development and poverty eradication.

First on the government's list of priorities is cutting the dependence on imports by ramping up the domestic production of hydrocarbons. In the case of oil, as enunciated by Prime Minister Narendra Modi, the goal is to cut oil imports by 10 per cent by 2022 and by 50 per cent by 2030. This will be replaced by enhanced domestic production. For this, the New Exploration Licensing Policy or NELP, which has not been very effective in attracting the requisite foreign investment and technology over the last nine rounds, is being revised. It is expected to offer better terms to interested firms, both domestic and foreign, including in the private sector, to invest in the country's upstream basins by providing a more level playing field.

Several steps are also being taken to augment the production of natural gas, such as intensification of domestic exploration and production (E&P) activities through the NELP rounds, giving final shape to the shale gas policy framework, development of gas hydrate resources in the country, the import of LNG, as well as exploring the possibility of constructing transnational natural gas pipelines. According to the petroleum ministry, India's natural gas production is expected to rise 52 per cent over the next three years.[6]

Second, the government is also actively pursuing the acquisition of overseas oil, natural gas and coal assets. To that end, a more sharp focus is being placed on enhanced energy diplomacy in order to gain preferential access to asset acquisition opportunities, particularly in

African and South American countries. According to Petroleum Minister Dharmendra Pradhan, a paradigm shift has taken place in the ministry's asset acquisition policy, with a strong system connecting the Ministry of Petroleum and Natural Gas with the Prime Minister's Office (PMO), Ministry of Finance (MoF) and the Ministry of External Affairs (MEA) being put in place. This will focus on better aligning India's interest with the target countries' national agendas, somewhat akin to the policy pursued by rival national oil companies.[7]

Third, a decision has been taken to commission over 5 MT of strategic (crude) petroleum reserves (SPRs) to be stored in underground storages to ensure uninterrupted oil supply for about two months in case of disruptions in imports due to geopolitical reasons. The first SPR of 1.33 MT in Visakhapatnam is ready, and two more facilities—in Mangalore (1.5 MT) and Padur (2.5 MT)—will be ready soon. The second phase of capacity expansion in Bikaner (Rajasthan), Rajkot (Gujarat) and Chandikhol (Odisha) has also been initiated and is expected to be complete by 2020. Once complete, the SPRs are targeted to store crude oil to last ninety days.

Fourth, in keeping with its agenda of self-sufficiency and bringing down the country's carbon footprint, the government has put renewable energy (RE) at the top of its agenda, with a target to generate 15 per cent of its energy from renewables by 2020. Central to this initiative is the solar energy sector. Accordingly, while earlier the target was to install 20,000 MW of solar energy capacity by 2022, this has now been raised five-fold to 100,000 MW. The government also wants to put in place 60,000 MW of wind power capacity. Although this appears ambitious, given that the current output from solar energy is under 3,000 MW, there are reports that the government has already secured pledges from several public and private companies to set up RE capacity of 266,000 MW (266 GW) over the next five years.

Given that a major drawback for the RE sector is its lack of price competitiveness vis-à-vis coal-based power, the government will be focusing on the acquisition of cheaper equipment to ensure lower tariffs. It is expected that in the next three to four years solar power will achieve grid parity, the goal being to provide RE-based power at less than Rs 4.50 a unit.

The government is also pursuing greater use of biofuels, with ethanol and biodiesel emerging as the preferred options for the transport sector. The objective is not only to cut down the use of and dependence on imported oil but also to address the issue of climate change by increasing the use of greener fuels to reduce greenhouse gas (GHG) emissions, as well as provide new employment opportunities. According to reports, the government has been considering a blend of over 10 per cent of ethanol as against the earlier 5 per cent in order to reduce the import of petroleum by $3 billion a year. However, given the debate surrounding the issue of using land for food versus for fuel, second generation or advanced alternatives, such as blending petrol with cellulosic ethanol produced from biomass such as switch grass, paper pulp, sawdust, municipal waste, and non-edible parts of plants, are also being looked at.[8]

Nuclear Energy and Hydropower

Despite the focus on RE, the government is also pursuing the development of nuclear energy, with PM Modi declaring that nuclear power would be an essential part of India's energy security and calling for the tripling of nuclear power to 10,000 MW over the next decade from the current 5,780 MW. A few important developments in the nuclear sector have taken place. In September 2014, India signed a nuclear cooperation deal with Australia. In April 2015, an agreement was signed with Comeco of Canada for the supply of uranium for the reactors placed under international safeguards. Moreover, the clearance of some roadblocks has also been expedited, such as the civil liability for nuclear suppliers, which proposes the setting up of an insurance pool with a liability cap of Rs 15 billion ($240.91 million) to indemnify international and domestic nuclear suppliers in case of an accident.

Hydropower is perceived to have tremendous potential, which has been pegged at 148,000 MW. However, at the end of January 2015, installed hydropower share stood at only 17 per cent—down from 46 per cent in 1966—with generation capacity at only 36,000 MW. But now, with its emphasis on clean energy, the NDA government is looking at augmenting the share of hydropower by adding around 13,000 MW of installed capacity in the near future. Much of the new development will be focused in the north-east region, where 93 per cent of the potential capacity has yet to be developed.

Some of the factors that have led to the slow pace of development of hydropower include environmental concerns, rehabilitation and resettlement issues, land acquisition problems, long clearance and approval procedures, financial challenges and capability of developers. Furthermore, these problems have been compounded by the fact that hydropower development has largely remained under the ambit of state governments, with varying policies adopted by the states, although the sector was opened up to private sector participation as far back as 1991.[9] For example, several projects with common river systems between states are held up due to disputes on water sharing.

The challenges in developing hydropower projects are far less in the case of smaller projects (SHP). As a result, the focus is now on pursuing projects that are under 25 MW station capacity, which are under the purview of the Ministry of Renewable Energy (MNRE), while projects above this capacity are under the ambit of the Ministry of Power. The estimated potential for power generation in the country from SHPs has been pegged at about 20,000 MW, with the goal being set at harnessing at least 50 per cent of the potential in the next ten years. Furthermore, the SHPs are essentially driven by private investment as they are more economically viable.[10]

Structural Reforms

Apart from augmenting fuel supplies, both from renewable and non-renewable resources, steps are being taken to reorganize the energy sector. One of the biggest problems was that the entire energy sector was divided between several ministries, with each operating in separate silos, often in conflict with one another. This is now being tackled, and an attempt is being made to formulate a more integrated energy policy in order to tackle the country's energy challenges in a holistic and comprehensive manner. An important step in that direction was initiated by bringing three ministries—the ministries of coal, power and renewable energy—under the charge of one minister.

Although several measures have been taken to address the challenges prevailing in the energy sector, and many have begun showing results, several challenges still remain to be addressed. The most formidable one is to attract investment and technology in the various energy sectors, given that the energy sector is hugely capital- and technology-intensive. This would require reforms to be implemented and expedited.

First, the subsidy regime that prevails across the energy sector should be phased out, and prices must be allowed to reflect market realities. Second, the tax administration should be simplified and continuity of policies should be ensured to encourage greater interest and involvement of the private sector. Third, the national and regional grid capacities need to be enhanced and upgraded in order to absorb capacity additions, both from renewable and non-renewable fuels. The pricing of retail power will have to be rationalized, particularly to resolve the contradictions in augmenting capacity from cleaner and greener fuels as against the cheaper but more polluting ones. A way out could be introducing carbon taxes, but this would require deft and intelligent handling due to the likely social and political fallout.

Finally, there should be better clarity and transparency on fiscal, pricing, operational and regulatory issues across the energy spectrum, the lack of which has prevented the induction of investment as well as technology in various sectors. A beginning has been made and the results have been positive thus far, as can be seen from the changes in the coal and power sectors, reflected in the drop in the power deficit. However, much is left to be done before India can embark on the path of being energy secure.

18

Indigenization of Defence Production

Commodore Shridharan Shekhar

Regional Director,
National Maritime Foundation, Chennai

Background

Since Independence, defence production has largely remained in the hands of the public sector—in the form of defence public sector undertakings (PSUs) and ordnance factories. The share of the private sector has been minimal. This has largely been the reason for India's defence inventory still being predominantly imported. Even the so-called 'indigenized' inventory held with all the three services has a significant percentage of imported content. If we go down to the component level in critical items like weapons and sensors, the picture is still starker. And if we take into account the material content for strategic characteristics like stealth, the situation is dismal.

One of the prime reasons for this sorry state of affairs is that there is no 'strategy' at the national level for the indigenization of defence production. Indeed there is not even a commonly accepted definition of the term 'indigenization', much less a common understanding of how to go about it.

This is because a communication gap exists between the four pillars of the defence establishment in India: the users or the armed forces; the designers, primarily the Defence Research and Development Organization (DRDO); the defence industry, predominantly consisting of the defence PSUs and ordnance factories; and last but not the least academia, which needs to produce the human capital with educational and vocational competence and the necessary skills at the functional, supervisory and managerial levels.

Figure 1 shows the current conventional institutions engaged in the Indian defence establishment. The private sector, where it is engaged in any of the three domains other than the armed forces, needs to be

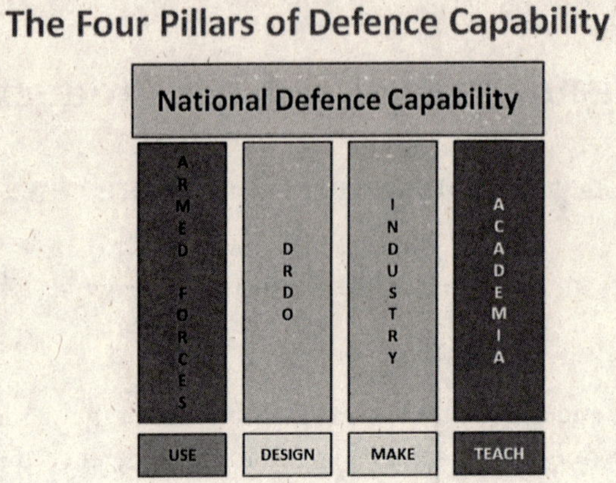

The Four Pillars of Defence Capability

National Defence Capability

ARMED FORCES	DRDO	INDUSTRY	ACADEMIA
USE	DESIGN	MAKE	TEACH

FIGURE 1

interpolated into the design, make and teach functions, to a greater degree.

An even more critical reason is that in our current system for strategy formulation in the defence domain, restricted to the political and bureaucratic elements, there is limited knowledge, as well as continuity of such knowledge where it does exist, of all the three components of what is being discussed in this chapter—indigenization, defence and production.

In public perception, 'defence' and 'military' are synonymous. As can be well argued, this is not so. 'Military' pertains to the armed forces and includes men, materiel and morale of all the three services: the army, navy and air force. On the other hand, 'defence' is an omnibus word and includes amongst its many components one of the 'tasks' which is assigned to the military. It includes not only the whole gamut of all forces engaged in the defence of the country but also the complete range of weapon systems and ordnance required to wage war, as well as the wherewithal to support the military and paramilitary establishment.

'Indigenization' is a term that is used in a variety of ways depending on the context. It is the act of making something more native: the transformation of some service, idea, etc. to suit a local culture. In the defence context, it has been taken to mean import substitution of components of defence equipment at one end of the spectrum, and the manufacture of a complete weapon platform at the other. It is also not clear, at the strategic level, as to whether we are referring to the 'indigenization' of every nut, bolt and washer of every component of every system of every weapon platform.

When it comes to the term 'production', the confusion is certainly confounded. Where does production start and where does it end? Does it include the design stage and extend to the delivery-acceptance trials stage? Or does it go beyond the product lifecycle, for example, to include upgrades and modernizations? Also, we are surely missing the wood for the trees by concentrating on issues such as defence procurement procedures, considering the prevalent system of the majority of defence 'production' being the responsibility of the Ministry of Defence—either through its public sector undertakings or through its ordnance factories. It involves complex procedures and myriad agencies operating virtually in silos. It is this complex process of production that must be our focus, not just procurement procedures.

Strategy for Indigenization

A strategy for indigenization must, therefore, stem from a holistic appreciation of the need gap which exists between what the troops on the ground—or in the air or at sea—require, and what they actually get from 'indigenous' sources, and more importantly the quality, cost and timeframe in which they get it.

Since indigenization and production are inseparable, we need to go back to the three 'M's of production, viz., manpower, materials and money, and evolve a policy for a successful and meaningful indigenization of defence production. Currently, these issues are not being looked at, at the strategic level, and are being addressed piecemeal by various sectors without a cross exchange of data and information.

Skill Development

Addressing the 'manpower' issue first, let us take a look at the critical issue of skill development. As a generalization, 'skill' is taken to mean a functional ability at the lower levels of production as in welding, machining, carpentry, electrical wiring, etc. Skills at the supervisory and managerial levels are developed, if at all, in a haphazard manner and by in-house institutions, often overridden by shop floor pressures to meet production targets. Skills at the higher levels as in design, development, project management, etc. are presumed to have been acquired at the academic institutions.

Thanks to the Make in India programme and the thrust on skill development as evidenced by the creation of a separate Ministry for Skill Development, a certain degree of clarity has indeed emerged in this area. However, strangely enough, while as many as seventeen Sector Skill Development Councils have been set up, covering sectors as varied as agriculture, beauty and wellness, media, and even security (incidentally this covers security guards), there is no mention of defence. Also while the National Skill Development Corporation (NSDC) website outlines the ministries with which it coordinates, the Ministry of Defence (MoD) is conspicuous by its absence.

Ship Building as a Case Study

There is no doubt that warship building is a shining example of the transition of the Indian Navy from a 'buyer's navy' to a 'builder's navy'. This has not happened overnight or singlehandedly, but due to a well-thought-out strategy involving the MoD, the Indian Navy headquarters (HQ) and the industry, in this case the five public sector shipyards and their vendor chains.

If we strip any one of the component elements of ship building—say, the weapons and sensors—down to systems, equipments and components, we can understand the enormity of the indigenization effort. We only need to extrapolate this example to other platforms to grasp the complexity of the indigenization of defence production, the non-availability of a 'one size fits all' solution, and the need for a strategic approach.

It is a fact that our educational institutions—for higher technical learning, undergraduate studies in various engineering disciplines and our vocational training institutes—simply do not have a clue about the skill sets needed. So the manufacturing organizations are currently forced to engage in their own skill development.

Material Aspects

Once again, let us take a leaf out of the warship building industry and consider as mundane an activity as the manufacturing of pipes. Pipes on board a warship, numbering tens of thousands, come in various shapes, sizes, fitted out with different types of flanges, and are made of various materials, requiring various types of coating, finishing, annealing, tempering, etc. While pipe manufacturing is the responsibility of the shipyard, one can imagine the complexity of the myriad other components which make up the equipment and sub-systems of a modern weapon platform, be it an armoured fighting vehicle, light combat aircraft or submarine. And when we move on to the strategic material requirements such as for electromagnetic compliance, stealth, noise reduction, etc., we are convinced that the acquisition and development of strategic materials cannot be left to individual manufacturing organizations in isolated domains of the defence sector, but can be met only by an equally strategic and holistic approach.

At the strategic level, at the core of all three—defence, production and indigenization—is technology: its acquisition, development and deployment. Thus the starting point of the indigenization of defence production really is evolving a strategic policy for technology acquisition. By this it is meant that in addition to looking at a strategy for weapon platform acquisition, we need to in fact look at a strategy for technology acquisition if we are to seriously address the indigenization of defence production.

Obviously we need to include all the stakeholders, particularly the four pillars in the policy formulation process. This policy needs to be deployed as suggested in the next figure.

The Cost Factor

Unfortunately, our defence strategists are not financial experts, and neither is the reverse true. So we get bogged down by the ambiguities in the various clauses of the defence procurement procedures and the inability to reap the benefit of the offset clauses.

The devil is obviously in the detail, and the questions to be posed strategically are not of the 'price' but of the 'cost'. What, for example, is the opportunity cost of buying equipment from foreign sources? This can be

Strategic policy for technology acquisition

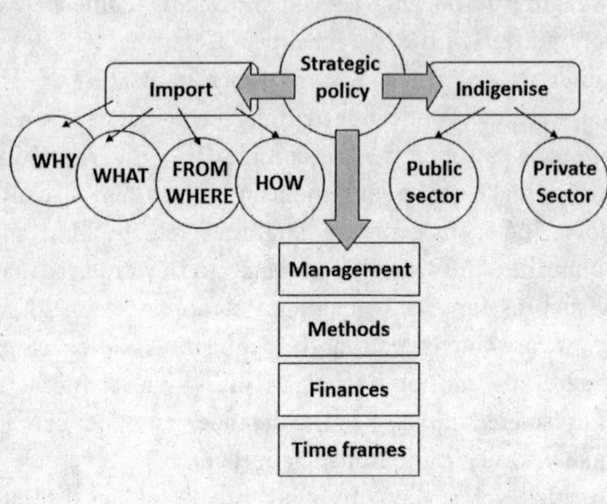

FIGURE 2

What next?

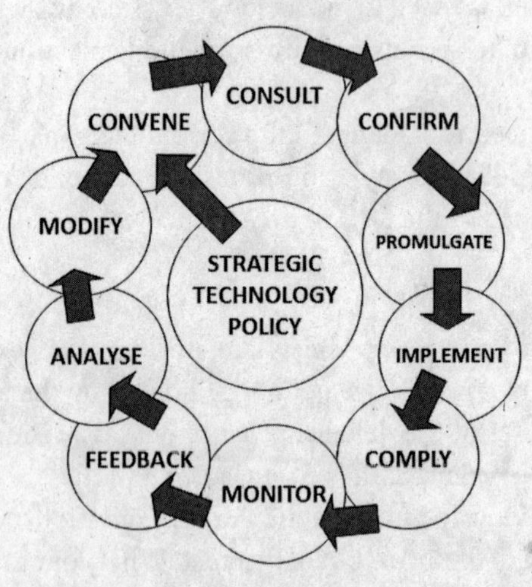

FIGURE 3

considered equal to the benefits that we would derive out of indigenizing a particular component or material, or can be considered the cost of denial, if a specific system or technology or material was denied to us due to political reasons.

What is the cost of the intellectual property involved in the transfer of technology (TOT) of a specific item? What is the cost of the human resources needed to imbibe the TOT even when it is offered? While we are perhaps one of the largest importers of military hardware in the world, can we honestly say that we have a system or templates to work out the costs of all these factors?

More importantly, as has been brought out in various reports available in the public domain, what is the cost of an item not being available to the armed forces in the timeframe that has been promised by those responsible for indigenous development, be it the DRDO, or the defence PSUs or the ordnance factories?

Strategy for the Indigenization of Defence Production

Of all the definitions of the word 'strategy', the one that is the most appropriate is: an implementable long-term plan for achieving tangible and intangible objectives, with a clear understanding of who is to do what, how, why and in what timeframes.

It would also be desirable that the concept of SMART goals be applied to this process, viz., specific, measurable, achievable, reviewable and time-bound. If we apply this to the indigenization of defence production, the following possible solutions emerge:

Who: The objective should be to engage all the stakeholders at the decision-making level in generating an actionable national policy document on this theme. In fact, there is no dearth of policy documents originating from various authorities which are often at cross purposes. There are also innumerable position papers by reputed consulting organizations, defence analysts, et al dealing with the subject.

Also, many of these policy statements and position papers are outdated in the light of current initiatives like Make in India, creation of skill development sectors, revisions to defence production policy, raising of the cap on foreign direct investment (FDI) in defence, and so on.

The first step would be to constitute a panel of experts who would carry out an in-depth analysis of the gap between what is needed and what is available.

What: Stemming from the above, the primary charter of the expert panel should be to elaborate on the steps which need to be taken to liquidate the need gap. The time-tested method of analysis would be to draw up a multi-dimensional matrix of technology needs, hardware and software needs, sources from where these needs could be met and changes which need to be incorporated into existing policy frameworks.

How: As in all domains of human endeavour, this is the tricky bit. Finding the resources to achieve self-sufficiency in the defence domain is difficult even in a resource-rich economy. Doing so in the Indian context, where there is a permanent debate on 'guns versus butter' or defence versus development, the problem is even more acute.

The policy would need to discriminate between the various types of technologies required for indigenous production, simplifying from the platform level to components and materials, and would need to consider the role of the private sector, the need for human resource and skill development, the design and development effort, and economies of scale.

The strategy should also address the complaints now being expressed, particularly by the private sector, of the complex bureaucratic processes, lack of financial incentives, lack of a 'level playing field' for all players, with regulations loaded in favour of the public sector, insufficient involvement of the micro, small and medium enterprises (MSME) sector and more.

Why: This is an equally important issue to be addressed in the strategy for indigenous defence production. As suggested in the proposed strategy for technology acquisition, it is important to substantiate why a particular sub-system, equipment, component or material needs to be indigenized, and then allocate the necessary resources to accomplish the objective, irrespective of the cost of doing so.

The SMART methodology advocated for generating the strategic plan envisages two areas which are time-specific. In the first, the emphasis is on when specific actions need to be taken and will form the yardstick for an effective monitoring system. In the second, the accent is on timeframes for various phases of the action plan to be achieved, and will be useful in the review mechanism.

Strategy Formulation

While defence capability requires the four pillars of user, designer, industry and academia, strategy formulation needs the four pillars of purpose, people, process and product.

Purpose is what drives the strategy. It could consist of one or more of the following:

- Vision and mission
- Functional objectives
- Societal objectives

People at various levels convert the vision of an organization into reality. People operate at various levels:

- Conceptual
- Directional
- Functional

Processes are the means available to 'people' to convert thought into action. They could be:

- Intellectual
- Technological
- Financial

Products are the end result of efforts put in by the people in an organization. They could be:

- Concepts
- Physical entities
- Services

Purpose

It would be stating the obvious that the strategy for indigenization of defence production should stem from an overarching national strategy for taking India into the higher echelons of the comity of nations of the twenty-first century. An element of that would be the national security strategy, an approach for which is outlined in the other chapters of this book. From this should evolve the national defence strategy, in turn encompassing the four pillars of defence capability. Enough of this has been elaborated upon in the earlier sections of this chapter, including the need for a strategy for technology acquisition.

People

Earlier paragraphs throw light on one of the aspects of the complexity of ship building as an example of a domain where indigenization of defence production would be required. Delving deeper both literally and figuratively into the world of submarines, it is believed that funds to the tune of Rs 60,000 crore have been allocated for the indigenous submarine programme P75 I. Having had the experience of building submarines of our own of both German and French origin, not to mention the pathbreaking design and construction of our own nuclear submarine with appreciable assistance from the Russians, should not P75 I be a cakewalk?

But do we have the people at the conceptual, directional and functional levels to launch and deliver this programme in a time-bound manner not only at the construction yard but also at the myriad indigenous units of Tier 1, 2 and 3 equipment manufacturers, system integrators, vendors, and so on? How about the fifth generation fighter aircraft programme? And what of the advances made in the integrated guided missile development programme? Do we have the people? Do they have the skills? Are we retaining them? Most importantly, are we motivating them to deliver at their optimum? Does each of this require a separate strategy? Or should this be part of the national strategy?

Processes

Reams of material are available commenting on the efficacy or otherwise of the defence procurement policy, and stemming from this, the defence procurement procedures. Special focus has also been directed towards the offset clauses. Critics of the defence procurement policy bring out various lacunae:

- The policy document is too verbose and voluminous. This makes it too difficult to understand for the organizations and individuals who are expected to make it work.

- The document looks at the 'procurement' process purely from the perspective of the 'procurer' and not the 'supplier'.
- The policy is highly loaded on the side of the government and the public sector.
- The Defence Procurement Rules are highly subject to interpretation and thus hard to implement.
- Stakeholders including MSMEs must be involved in the policy formulation process.
- The above are particularly applicable to the offset clauses.
- Specific issues pertain to the vagueness of the offset policy pertaining to 'training' and the methodology of computing the eligibility of claiming offsets through training, especially by original equipment manufacturers.

Products

And finally, the 'products' of 'indigenization' range from the complete weapon platform, as in ships, submarines, aircraft, armoured fighting vehicles, etc., through the whole gamut of systems, sub-systems, equipment, components, right down to nuts, bolts, washers, cables, material and so on. A look at the following news item that appeared on defenseindustrydaily.com makes for interesting reading:

> Huntington Ingalls Industries (HII) delivered the submarine John Warner (SSN-785) to the navy on Thursday, with this marking the twelfth Virginia-class sub to be delivered. The boat's keel was laid in March 2013 and the sub was christened in September last year; the five-year, $17 billion deal will build ten Virginia-class Block IV fast attack submarines for the US Navy, with production split between HII and General Dynamics Electric Boat, with the latter designated as the design authority.
>
> Commissioning for the newly delivered boat is set for August.
>
> 1. Sub keel laid: March 2013.
> 2. Christened: September 2014.
> 3. Delivered to navy: June 2015.
> 4. Commissioning: August 2015.

When can we expect our public sector shipyards like Mazagon Dock Limited (MDL), Garden Reach Shipbuilders and Engineers (GRSE), etc. to deliver comparable results? While these two organizations have indeed delivered ships and submarines of comparable class, and with a fair amount of indigenous content (let us for a moment ignore time and cost overruns), can we say the same of the other PSUs under the department of defence production, or the myriad ordnance factories under the Ordnance Factory Board? Can all this be achieved without a comprehensive strategy for the indigenization of defence production and a critical re-look at the very functioning of our defence PSUs? Can the formulation of this strategy be left to the MoD performing the roles of prosecutor, defence and judge?

Conclusion

We live in a complex world, in complex times. National security is of paramount importance to a nation with a burgeoning population, expanding economy and a not-too-friendly neighbourhood. One of the components of the national security apparatus is the defence establishment.

As repeated in many forums, ad nauseum, it ill behoves a nation of our demographic mass, economic strength and military might to import 70 per cent of its military requirements. On the contrary, we must leverage our intellectual property, financial muscle, manufacturing capacity, and purchasing power for military equipment to imbibe and harness technology in such a manner as to make the transition from an importer to an exporter in the defence domain. Indigenization of defence production is a must, and a comprehensive strategy for this needs to be evolved. There are no short cuts.

19

Contours of India's Grand Strategy

Major General Raj Shukla

*Commander, Higher Command Wing,
Army War College, Mhow, and former General Officer Commanding
of an infantry division in Kashmir*

'All states have a grand strategy, whether they know it or not.'
—Edward Luttwak

Introduction

The quote above is prescient—it tells us that grand strategizing is simply not a choice; it is as essential for effective statecraft as it is challenging to pull off in the messiness of our democracy. While written articulation may be hugely helpful, it is not a sine qua non. Grand strategizing is an activity that often takes place in a nation's subconscious. The processes of intellectualization, introspection and contemporization that accompany the formulation of a grand strategy add value; the associated debates and discussion help in refining thoughts and in imparting direction. In the US, the RAND (Research and Development Corporation) has a Grand Strategy Advisory Board that indulges in grand strategy formulations on an iterative basis, as have a couple of US Armed Service Senate Committees constituted for the specific purpose. Even though successive US governments have never formally adopted these formulations, they are known to have engaged actively with the processes. Renowned futurist Andrew Marshall, who was instrumental in planning the demise of the Soviet Union, in propounding the Revolution in Military Affairs, in authoring the Air–Sea Battle Doctrine, and who is revered even in China's strategic circuit, headed the Pentagon's Office of Net Assessment from 1973 till his retirement in January 2015. In the process, he helped to structure a continuous grand strategic frame for the US for well over four decades—through the Cold War, numerous military conflicts and ten presidential elections.[1]

Much of China's military transformation was also inspired by Marshal. General Chen Zhou of the PLA Academy of Military Science at Beijing and the principal author of China's four defence white papers acknowledged as much when he said, 'We studied RMA exhaustively. Our great hero was Andy Marshall in the Pentagon. We translated every word he wrote.' Closer home, about 2,300 years ago in the fourth century BCE, the Arthashastra—one of the world's most incisive treatises on statecraft,[2] was a wise, if somewhat rudimentary, grand strategy. The rigorous Constituent Assembly debates and the process of drafting a constitution for independent India was perhaps a persuasive essay in grand strategy making. More recently, our draft nuclear doctrine was inspired in large measure by freewheeling debates and a Combat Paper on the subject written by General K. Sundarji as Commandant, College of Combat.

The value of grand strategizing, therefore, is apparent, irrespective of whether it is given a formal veneer or not; governmental thought and actions are often inspired, if not driven, by such strategies, often without owning up to the same. This chapter seeks to delineate the possible contours of a Grand Strategy for India, in three parts as under.

- To begin with, the design framework of a grand strategy in the Indian context has been explored.
- Subsequently, the need to chisel out a contemporary worldview for a new and resurgent India has been expounded.
- Finally, an attempt has been made to draw up the possible contours of a Grand Strategy for India.

Design

Grand strategy may be defined as a nation's view of itself, based on a deep understanding of its unique circumstance and the play between its highest interests and its relationship with the world.[3] It could also be described as an interdisciplinary conversation about a nation's power and its purpose—the thought and methodology of a nation grappling with questions of its destiny. A word about the salience of India's proposed grand strategy may be pertinent. The essential point in the Indian context is that the Indian grand strategy should not be mimetic of Western responses; it should be a thoughtful product—one that is tailored to our unique circumstance, as also one that delineates how India's power could be deployed purposefully in pursuit of a very benign purpose. Such a strategy would enable Indian policymakers in that they would not simply be reacting to events or be handling them on a case-by-case basis;[4] it would also provide a contemporary and coherent idea of what the Indian nation should seek to accomplish in domestic and international affairs. A grand strategy for a confident, new and resurgent India would be far more than merely a mechanical exercise of matching means to ends. It would be less about adapting purpose to reality and more about moulding reality to purpose, while aspiring to creatively shape the environment in the light of our values, aspirations and deemed interests.

Grand strategy is as much an execution challenge as it is a blueprint issue—it must therefore neither be unduly grandiose nor be overly prescriptive. It must, on the other hand, for the sake of wider acceptability, be flexible and pragmatic. Yet, in order to be of utility, it must be brutally honest and speak truth to power. Two additional caveats may be in order. One, we are neither Singapore nor China; execution timelines, therefore, crafted in the mould of India 'becoming a global power by 2050' et al do not suit the Indian genius and are best avoided. Putting together a bouquet of persuasive, cogent, well-thought-through ideas may be more appropriate, while leaving the nitty-gritty of execution to the government of the day. Two, the objectives of an Indian grand strategy should be modest, in the realization that grand strategy is neither a transformative project to remake the regional order nor a panacea that will wipe away all challenges. At best, a grand strategy can provide an intellectual reference point for dealing with multiple complexities, and a process by which policymakers can seek to bring our resources and our day-to-day actions into better alignment with our enduring interests. Achieving this much would be good enough, expecting anything more would be quixotic.

A Worldview for a Resurgent India

> 'I look forward to a great future for America—a future in which our country will match its military strength with its moral restraint, its wealth with its wisdom and its power with its purpose.'
>
> —John F. Kennedy, 1963

We Indians are indeed proud of the remarkable experiment in democracy and nation building that we have nurtured over the last seven decades, one that has belied the grim forebodings of Winston Churchill, who, deeply sceptical of India's unity holding in the face of its monumental diversity, said on the eve of our Independence, 'India is a mere geographical term. It is no more a united nation than the Equator.' A raw and fractured vision of India in the 1940s and 1950s, captured by the very earthy Punjabi expression, 'Sutlej ke niche dilli, baki sab tambhi' (Below the Sutlej river is Delhi; the rest are all Tamilians), has over the years metamorphosed into one of indelible physical unity, federal equipoise and considerable sophistication.

Our achievements thus far have been stupendous; amongst our many successes, the achievement of political integrity in the broadest sense and institution building are perhaps the most significant. An India, thus empowered and enabled, is critically poised, even as it faces a new reality—that of a breakout nation—one that could flourish or disappoint in equal measure, depending on the trajectory that it adopts in the years to come. Today's India is not tentative, it is robust enough to innovate and experiment even as the popular mood is one of a deep yearning for change. While Lutyens' Delhi may yet be caught in the classical clichés of 'the old civilization, young nation' kind to justify the status quo, the frenzy for change is visible across India's earthy heartlands—the streets, gullies and mohallas of Bahraich, Trichur and R.K. Puram,[5] where the urge to shake off economic shackles is acquiring momentum. There is a new confidence and willingness to experiment. Our electoral democracy, for example, which has for long been set in a stereotyped web of caste and community equations of this or that stronghold, has seen these fundamental assumptions being challenged. The traditional metrics for electoral success, such as community, class and pedigree, seem to be making way for virtues like merit, ability, sincerity, integrity and grass-root connect.

India is still a developing society, with a host of challenges to be overcome. When Indians think about themselves and their role in the world, their first question is not about how they can shape the universe but rather how they might cope with it. Success in navigating the world still stems from success in political, economic and social management at home.[6] This fundamental premise, however, may be altering in significant ways for three reasons. One, rising, youthful aspirations at home cannot be addressed in old-fashioned ways. Two, in a globalized world, coping may no longer suffice, shaping may be more useful. And three, modern India perhaps realizes that 'the power of the argument' must now be complemented by 'the argument of our power'. Our grand ideology of Nehruvian ideas, arguments and moralpolitik must be complemented by the realities of realpolitik as also by our enhanced leverage in the power dynamic. The India of today is critically poised—a robust political union awaiting transformation into a modern nation state in every sense of the term. The grand strategy that we seek should create the transition that lies at the intersection of India's moment of destiny and the rising crescendo for change.

The Possible Contours of a Grand Strategy for India

'There is nothing new to be discovered in physics now.'
—Lord Kelvin, 1900

Overview

What should the framework of such a grand strategy be? It could be predicated, possibly, on the principles of continuity, evolution and change. Our core values—democracy, secularism, pluralism, liberalism, inclusive nationalism and internationalism—have stood us in good stead domestically and internationally. We must continue to abide by them. We remain steadfast in our fundamental orientation—that of ensuring the economic well-being and equity of our billion-plus people. We are also clear that we are not like the US or Pakistan, not a national security state. The power that we seek is only for benign purposes. Equally, we must be aware that calibrated military strength is essential to secure our economic aspirations, to spread equity and to defend our core values—we need perhaps to become so strong that war is not worth inflicting upon us.[7] We must recognize that defence and development constitute the sagacious way forward. Defence versus development was the false debate.

Conceptualization to Delivery

The Nehruvian worldview was wise, but it was crafted for a different era. It grappled with and successfully addressed the great intellectual questions of nation building—whether or not India should be a Hindu state, issues related to the mechanics of federalism and the linguistic character of states, the challenges of strengthening our democratic institutions, et al. In fact, an apt critique of the Nehruvian vision is that, while it was in many ways a wise and grand ideology, it was resourced in some manner by a bland strategy; its sheer loftiness led to a disconnect with extant realities, resulting in the reverses of 1962. We now need a different orientation: a strategy that marries conceptualizing with delivery.

Transforming the Edifice

The edifice of India's democracy—the executive, judicial and legislative pillars—are creaking under the weight of the economic spiral and aspirational change. The former has huge implications for the Indian state—both in the manner in which it looks at itself and the way in which the world looks at us. Our GDP in 1995 was $300 billion. Fifteen years later, in 2010, it grew four times to $1.24 trillion. As a global business opportunity (measured by the sum total of money flows), in the same period, India grew ten times from $132 million to $1.36 trillion. Economic and governance theorists tell us that each doubling of GDP requires a fundamental reorganization of the state in terms of laws and structures—in the US, where the GDP doubles only once in twenty years, the government has twenty years to reinvent itself. In India, where the GDP is expected to double every nine years, the period to reform[8] will naturally be far shorter. The need to transform the fundamental structures of the Indian state expeditiously, therefore, is compelling—in order to optimize the quality of our global engagement as also to meet rising aspirations at home. A 'mai-baap sarkar' has to metamorphose into one that is a diligent service provider, accountable, focused on the deliverance of public good, one that embodies multidisciplinary talent through a calibrated revolving-door policy and one that allows a diffusion of power across capacities and competencies instead of being concentrated in any one service.

Modern India merits a bureaucracy that governs and does not reign. The poor performance of our premier services contributes to India's governance deficit—political interference is only a partial explanation. The elite bureaucracy must square up to the idea of devolution and put an end to the mindless accumulation of power, if it is to regain the nation's trust.[9] We also need comprehensive judicial reforms to complement the surgery of our public administration. Consider these facts—80 per cent of Indians cannot even access the judicial system on account of complicated procedures and legal costs. Of the remaining 20 per cent, 18 per cent are denied timely justice on account of interminable delays. Thus a bare 2 per cent get justice from India's judicial system.[10] In numerous countries, for very basic justice, citizens can argue their own case without the facility of lawyers.

There is a compelling need, therefore, to informalize or simplify our judicial system so as to improve access, as also to surgically reduce delays. Our legislative processes, similarly, need a qualitative upgrade in terms of sagacity and oversight with a single-minded focus on implementation and deliverance—one needs to rummage through the proceedings of parliamentary committees in the House of Commons, for instance, to get a feel of their great utility. Unless the edifice of our governance—the administrative, legal and legislative mechanisms—is transformed, India will remain caged in the status quo, our growth will not translate adequately into development, our much-vaunted human resource capital will not be able to take us to excellence, and India will remain a caged phoenix—unable to fly.[11]

Growth and Equity

The debate between growth and equity needs to be rationally harmonized. While equity must remain the nation's primary focus, it must be realized that growth is the essential enabler. It provides the financial foundations for the welfare state, for the funding of social welfare schemes and facilitates the bestowing of legal rights through employment, education and food. The relationship between economic growth and poverty reduction is empirically positive. Growth has allowed government spending to triple since 2004-05 to the current fiscal estimate of Rs 16.65 trillion.[12] The headcount ratio of poverty has also declined substantially during the high growth period—from 37.2 per cent in 2004-05 to 29.8 per cent in 2009-10, whereas over a longer period of two decades, the decline has been about 1 per cent a year.

If the growth trajectory is to be sustained or given a fillip, in deference to changing times, autarky and governmental control must increasingly make way for globalization and a far greater acceptance of market forces. Governance has to get more sophisticated. There is a need for a simple, transparent, pro-market system and a need to transit governance out of a discretionary approval regime to one of smaller government and calibrated regulation. The state must emerge as the lubricator of natural human enterprise and as an enabler for the generation of wealth. It must focus more resolutely on equity while increasingly letting business and the market take care of growth. It must be emphasized that what is at stake is not a stark choice between good and evil, between the visible hand of the state and the invisible hand of the market, but more a question of nuanced prioritization. We will do well to remember that it was the visible hand of the state rather than the invisible hand of the market that helped India catch up with the industrialized world.[13] But in our current stage of development and economic reality, it may be wise to accord greater salience to markets. A pro-market philosophy is quite distinct from a pro-business approach, which has connotations of promoting crony capitalism. If a June 2013 World Bank Report ranks India at 134, below even Pakistan and Bangladesh, in terms of ease of doing business, there is some cause for worry and introspection.[14]

There is a concurrent need to refrain from resorting to Robin Hood politics to fund populist economics. One, however, cannot rely on growth alone for poverty reduction. Inclusive policies pertaining to education, access to credit and other resources are as critical—a thoughtful integration of bazaar, samaaj and sarkar to take India to the next level.[15] It is also important not to get paralysed by poverty. While we should tackle it squarely, it should not come in the way of the concurrent realization of other dreams. Consider this: if India had not set up ISRO in the 1960s, when we were poorer, we would not have had the ability to track cyclones in real time and save thousands of lives today. The Taj Mahal was built at great public expense—Rs 3.2 crore in the seventeenth century—but today it brings in Rs 20 crore annually (figures not adjusted for inflation) by way of revenue for India.[16] We also need to take a careful look at the growth model that we need. It may not be wise to ape or replicate the high-energy and resource-intensive Chinese model, simply because the world cannot accommodate another China.[17] What that precise growth model should be could form a major plank of our envisaged 'Grand Strategy'.

New Thinking and Instrumentalities

Economic growth and affluence, it must be realized, are not our manifest destiny. We need to pursue a long-range economic policy as also create the necessary fiscal space and reserves to create cushions for the natural cycles of economic boom and bust, for sustained growth. The future will also need the creation of new thinking and instrumentalities. If we are to address our poverty challenge, reap demographic dividends and bring about regional equity, the locus of our growth will need to shift northwards—from the development hubs of Pune, Hyderabad and Chennai to the hitherto neglected spaces of Uttar Pradesh and Bihar. From reservations we need to transit to empowerment, as also place far greater emphasis on skill development and put in place financial leadership and governance structures to create 11 million jobs if social tensions are to be contained. As the Indian economy becomes more capitalist in the decades to come, we will need to devise and structure an elaborate social security administration infrastructure to take care of unemployment, health care and old-age needs, particularly for the left out regions and groups.[18] Current politics and developments in the US and Europe benchmark the enormity of the challenge. It will be wise for us to get down to the hard work right away.

Ascending the Knowledge Hierarchy

For too long we Indians have prided ourselves on our 'jugaad'. If we wish to be leaders in wealth creation in the years to come, 'jugaad' will not suffice. Indians will need to evolve from 'jugaad' to 'innovation'—cultivated brilliance that could transform science fiction into fact and socio-political dreams into everyday reality. Innovation, in turn, is driven by the spirit of entrepreneurship and knowledge. What takes nations really ahead of the pack is their status in the knowledge hierarchy. We need to give a significant boost to intellectual greatness by fostering a liberal immigration culture, a well-endowed university system with generous funding for fundamental research, a culture for individualism and an ingrained respect for against-the-grain thinking.

The scourge of 'an open society with a closed mind' must give way to 'an open society with an open mind'. India needs to evolve from a high decibel, argumentative democracy to one that is respectful and appreciative of the contrarian view. We must significantly upgrade our ratio of Nobel laureates to living population and cultivate talent irrespective of source. By way of illustration, it should be a matter of some concern for us that the emerging global hub for strategic studies should be at the S. Rajaratnam School of International Studies in Singapore and not in India. That a country with no significant security threats should find the energy, time and resources to facilitate the growth of such an institution of excellence, while think tanks in India (with far greater threats and challenges) should be relatively moribund, calls for some reflection. There is also a case perhaps for a concerted drive to leverage high-technology capabilities, such as those in the space, atomic energy, defence and information technology domains, to create an ecosystem of innovation and marketization. In the absence of an indigenous effort, these capabilities are instead being leveraged by foreign entities, several of whom have set up large research and development centres in India, to generate cutting-edge technologies, innovations and products, which are then patented and commercialized beyond Indian shores.[19]

Internal Security

The principal mechanism for conflict resolution must continue to be political and socio-economic initiatives, dialogue, accommodation and grievance redressal. Concurrently, we need to realize that our democratic ethos and way of life necessitate that we invest greatly in the creation of sophisticated policing capacities across the internal security spectrum—to meet challenges from basic policing through heightened law and order to insurgencies—thus unburdening the armed forces and leaving them free to grapple with the rather considerable external challenges. To dub policing as non-plan expenditure is fine as an accounting metric, but as a philosophical vision it is hugely misplaced, if not downright illiterate. In the counter-terror domain, we need to invest and create conjoint capacities in our diplomatic, military, intelligence and policing instruments. What we need is integrated skills and not turf-infested silos that we continue to nourish.

International Engagements

The foreign policy 'sagacity' demonstrated by the Modi government in the first year of office has won widespread applause. Yet, if the quality of our international engagements is to acquire further acuity, the proposed grand strategy may like to revisit two critical aspects of our orientation and practice: the tone and tenor of our strategic outlook and the calibration of force and diplomacy.

Strategic Outlook

The proposed grand strategy may like to take a hard look at the contours of India's strategic outlook—the drivers of our power and purpose. National security has always been an ambiguous concept. Security is often seen as a burden; nations are, therefore, inclined to keep it at the lowest level considered adequate for protection.[20] This level will often be lower than what military leaders or other security-minded participants in the decision-making process believe it should be. A discrete middle ground needs to be found between a realist policy guided solely by the national security interest and the exercise of self-restraint in the pursuit of national interest, as advised by American diplomat and historian George Kennan.

What has helped greatly in recent times is the proliferation of the understanding in India that national security is a much broader concept than merely defence and military affairs. The focus has evolved appropriately to that of integrating all possible strands—political, economic, social and military—in building the comprehensive strength of the nation. Concerns are, however, voiced regarding whether or not we are striking the right balance in our strategic outlook. In the broadest sense, of course, the primary objective of India's strategic policy would continue to be to create a secure internal environment and external periphery so that the country can grow and bring prosperity to its people in an equitable manner. It may also be wise to advance our foreign and strategic policy objectives with varying combinations of soft and hard power in tune with our natural appeal, while always underlining the sagacity of the message that we radiate: that our hard power is directed at nobody else, except to secure our own interests.

The worry, however, is that there continues to be an inadequate understanding of hard power and its numerous stabilizing uses—that it can be wielded for soft purposes; it can, through military engagements, help to secure peace; and leadership contacts can be leveraged to defuse crisis. We must recognize hard power's utility as a tool for deterrence as also for hedging, its value in increasing the elbow room for diplomacy, and in the final analysis as a resort to win conflicts. The lack of expertise to optimally leverage hard power in pursuit of national security outcomes remains a fundamental weakness in India's national security system.

There are two accompanying assertions that are also a cause for some worry. One is the belief that national security in the modern world is much more than the military, which is true, provided we do not miss the substantive import of such an assertion. The national security pie is of course growing in size and diversity, but it is concomitantly leading to the growth of an unfortunate premise that national security is about everything else—energy, technology, pandemics, development, cyber security, climate change, organized crime, et al, everything except hardcore military and defence issues, which is not only erroneous but may also be dangerous. There is no evidence to suggest that military concerns are shrinking even though they may be changing hugely in form and nuance.

Second is the widely bandied wisdom that since the prospect of state-on-state conflict is decreasing, hardcore military capacities are unimportant.[21] This is not true. The wise inference may be to examine how hard power must be reconfigured conceptually and structurally to enhance deterrence and make it more sophisticated, precise and utilitarian, instead of drawing the somewhat erroneous conclusion that military power has become unusable. It may also be useful to take a hard look at globalization—the new reality in the international discourse. While it brings with it the many obvious blessings, it is also not without burdens that will need to be borne in blood and treasure. We must carefully think through the challenges posed by the latter and work towards creating the necessary geopolitical tools: appropriate regional and global poise, business relationships, aid mechanisms, funding structures, expansion of the Foreign Service, necessary force capacities, etc.

In doing so, the one question that one needs to ask and answer in the Indian context is about the purpose of India's power. Is it only to defend our critical national security interests at home? Is it to protect those friends in our neighbourhood who cannot protect themselves? Is it about making astute adjustments to a changing regional and international order, about calibrated engagement, about responding meaningfully to the overtures of prospective friends, and about putting in place a web of interlocking relationships? A nuanced set of military capabilities is required to meet each of these challenges. If we continue to muddle along by not seeking answers to these critical questions, there is every possibility of developing unusable military capacities and, worse, using the wrong set of capabilities in contingencies they are not configured for, with possibly grave consequences. The proposed Grand Strategy must help us steer clear of the trap.

Calibration of Force and Diplomacy

Our foreign policy lacks the robustness and military dynamic so essential to the addressing of external security challenges. In fact, if the successful practice of foreign policy is about the skilful calibration of force and diplomacy, India is in the Jurassic period. While strategic restraint is indeed the hallmark of wisdom in statecraft, we may like to distinguish it from the strategic muddle that seems to have defined many of our responses to crisis situations in the past, reducing in the process our strategic restraint to a forced choice as against a carefully chosen alternative.

India's image is not only that of a reluctant power but also one of a responsible power with a benign purpose and unparalleled moral restraint. If such power, however, is not to appear like a lot of hot air, it must be encased in strategic wisdom and usable military strength. It makes little sense to spend $40 billion annually if in response to threats to our sovereignty and even in the face of grave provocation all we have to offer is 'strategic restraint'. Some new thinking is called for. While the world acknowledges the value of defence diplomacy as a core driver in shaping the regional and international security architecture, India has not gone more than a couple of baby steps down the road. This is yet another consequence of the lack of fusionism in our crisis management discourse.

The advent of meaningful defence diplomacy in India's strategic framework is long overdue. One can say this on the basis of the realization that such diplomacy furthers military-to-military cooperation not only with allies and partners but even with potential rivals, as also the fact that globally the military today is a more engaged institution in the practice of diplomacy and foreign policymaking alongside other institutions that have traditionally dominated the process. But for that to happen, we will first need to trust and empower our military—something that is anathema to the Ministry of External Affairs (MEA) and something national security advisors (NSAs) have been hesitant to push.

China was slow to get off the blocks in so far as military diplomacy was concerned, because for long it was unsure of its military's capabilities and was, therefore, more inclined to conceal than engage. The US, of course, has been the foremost exponent of its military in the pursuit of diplomacy—the US secretary of state has a permanent three stars as a military advisor and is christened the senior military assistant or SMA to constantly advise and drive the effort. Why India, which has always had a very professional and apolitical military to boast of, should choose to so disadvantage itself[22] could perhaps be attributed to the absence of a secure and integrated politico-military-bureaucratic dispensation that understands and is adept at leveraging force to preserve the peace. We would do well to make amends.

National Security

In India's grand strategic instrument, the most neglected, and therefore perhaps the weakest link, is that of 'National Security'. The subject therefore needs some very tender caring if it is to be nursed back to health. The reform agenda could perhaps be structured around intellectual & structural reforms as also doctrinal calibration.

First and foremost there is an urgent need to upgrade the quality of our national security discourse. We must abandon false premises and deepen the quality and oversight of our security debates. The day our security debates acquire the depth of our economic ones, our national security discourse and actions will acquire greater prescience. It also needs to be appreciated that in matters of national security, relative progress is poor consolation. The obtaining adversarial threat is the pertinent metric. And in the stated context, the growing architecture of the Chinese military juggernaut and the consequential threat that it emanates is hugely worrisome. Through continued neglect we are perhaps deceiving ourselves yet again. We need to act wisely and quickly. While a lot needs to be done, the critical issues are outlined hereafter.

Given the nature of our security environment, the political class must urgently address the foremost cause of our strategic debility, namely, their ignorance of complex national security issues and their consequent detachment. A natural corollary is that India's politicians have deliberately chosen to assign responsibility for national defence and security to the bureaucracy. In this bizarre paradigm, bureaucrats make policy, while strategy is crafted by diplomats and even policemen, and grand strategy, in matters like nuclear deterrence or ballistic-missile defence, remains the exclusive domain of scientists and technocrats. Uniquely among major powers, India's armed forces remain excluded from any formal role in national security decision-making.[23] There is an urgent need to fix this debility and the perilous lack of integration between the various institutions dealing with national security, as also amongst the armed forces themselves.

We also need a paradigm shift in our civil–military relations model. It needs to be infused with modernity and rationality, as also brought in line with models in liberal democracies.[24] There is a crying need to make our instruments of force more utilitarian, ready, relevant and strategically balanced. In so far as defence industry reform is concerned, we need to embrace indigenization as a diligent and conscious rationale and not as distorted humbug; we perhaps need to return to the Nehruvian concept of self-reliance in high-end, critical strategic areas, with calibrated diffusion of responsibility elsewhere: DRDO, public sector, FDI, private sector and select strategic relationships. We also need to bring the user and customer (armed forces) to the centre of the paradigm, with a positive say in matters of procurement as against the squeaky voice that they are currently accorded. In our defence relationship with our strategic partners, we need to move increasingly from a buyer–seller relationship to co-production and development. Our acquisition structures need a comprehensive overhaul,[25] even as there is a need to institutionalize professional military education.[26]

Doctrinal Calibration

Along with intellectual and structural reform, there is a concurrent need for doctrinal calibration. The nation can no longer afford to continue on an indolent roll without an incisive survey of the dangers and opportunities in its security path. The process of forward planning must, therefore, be subjected to far greater rigour. While the future will always surprise us, forward-looking reviews are essential to minimize risks. Doctrinal calibration as recommended will help us create a usable hard power capability that provides viable strategic options in crisis situations while allowing national security to move from flaccidity to greater strategic purpose.

The first step in the process should be the formulation of a National Security Strategy (NSS) which will help sketch a whole-of-government approach to security. It should challenge legacy assumptions about the nature of the security environment encompassing threats from the immediate to the distant—terrorism, conventional threats from our adversaries in the neighbourhood, the prospect of destabilizing wars in places that matter to us, the possible loss of political influence in regions from where we source our energy, the nature of military competition, the emerging threat of state-on-state cyber attacks, the manner in which we should address threats and opportunities in the global commons, and the fact that there can no longer be a distinction between home and abroad. The need to integrate external and internal threats in a seamless fabric is also one of the issues that the proposed NSS must address. Having defined the threats and explored ways to manage risks, the NSS must seek to link the missions of the armed forces to the government's wider foreign and security policy and help deduce the military–strategic tenets of planning and direction. In sum, the NSS will try and establish the contours of the evolving strategic context.

The Strategic Defence Review (SDR), after drawing from the NSS, should attempt to take the process further and arrive at the precise capabilities we need to invest in so as to ensure effective delivery of our national security policy. Such a review must seek to bring defence policy, plans, commitments and cross-governmental resources into balance, while identifying the capabilities that the nation should build in the future. To appreciate the criticality of the need, consider this: in the period 2009–13, the country spent Rs 300,000 crore on capital acquisitions. Just two projects, the Rafale and the Mountain Strike Corps (in their original forms), could cost the exchequer as much as Rs 240,000 crore over the next decade. And where would that leave other critical purchases like the

P-75I submarine project, artillery guns, heavy lift and attack helicopters, the second aircraft carrier, et al?[27]

Clearly, the defence budget is out of balance. The NSS and SDR are urgently required in order that we arrive at the precise capabilities we need in light of the prevalent threats and the risks that we are prepared to take. The SDR in turn will drive transformation in the management, structure, organization, processes and work culture in the MoD, with the specific purpose of delivering the precise capabilities outlined in the SDR. It will also entail a paradigm shift from 'bureaucracy' to 'empowerment and discretion'. Key decision makers (service chiefs and vice chiefs) will need to be empowered to take decisions, allowed greater discretion to make these decisions, while being held responsible and to account for their decisions—both for the choices they make and the choices they defer. Accountability for the correctness of choices made must be determined not by the strength of processes but by the viability of outcomes. To be properly accountable, one also needs the power to act; accountability must, therefore, be matched with commensurate decision-making powers. Amendments to the Rules of Business, by empowering service vice chiefs with secretarial powers, is called for.

Conclusion

A concluding comment on how we could possibly develop a new grand strategy is in order. We could toss thoughts like these to think tanks and forums like the National Security Council Secretariat and the National Security Advisory Board for critiques. A more robust version could then be taken to a parliamentary committee constituted for the sole purpose. For those of us who think that parliamentary committees do nothing, may I say that is a sweeping generalization and commend to you the reports of recent standing committees on defence. The unanimity, deep insight, perspective and strategic outlook of a motley political gathering as diverse as Satpal Maharaj, Kamal Kishor 'Commando', Varun Gandhi, Kalyan Singh, Asaduddin Owaisi, Prof. P.J. Kurien and Shobhana Bhartia appears to be superior to that of turf-infested South and North Blocks. Should the strategy get through the portals of the parliamentary committee, we may push it through to the Cabinet Committee on Security. It is a tall order for sure and may not ultimately see the light of day. The utility of the endeavour, however, lies in the fact that while governments are loath to formally adopt grand strategies, they often refer and consult. The benefits lie greatly in the related processes and associated debates, not so much in the visible outcomes.

The author has expressed views and made recommendations in this chapter in his personal capacity and they do not have any official endorsement.

20

The New Arthashastra: A Security Strategy for India

Brigadier Gurmeet Kanwal

Distinguished Fellow, Institute for Defence Studies and Analyses, New Delhi, and former Director, Centre for Land Warfare Studies, New Delhi

'Cheshire puss,' she began rather timidly …
'Would you tell me, please, which way I ought to go from here?'
'That depends a good deal on where you want to get to,' said the cat.
—Lewis Carroll, *Alice in Wonderland*

Ends, Ways and Means

The Cheshire cat made its point perfectly well. All national-level endeavours must be based on a clear sense of purpose. The idea is elemental, but one that is little appreciated and often ignored. Does India have a comprehensive, clearly enunciated national security strategy? Does India need such a strategy in its nuclear weapons–dominated, unstable external security environment, with its internal security vitiated by foreign-sponsored insurgencies? The answer to the first question is definitely 'no'; and, to the second, an unambiguous 'yes'.

There can be no doubt that India's approach to national security issues has been shaped by certain broad objectives, principles and policies since Independence. These have varied from time to time depending on the prevailing security environment. However, they have never amounted to a well-conceived national security strategy that is an integrated whole and has specific objectives with a clear operational linkage. In the absence of a formally stated long-term national security strategy tied to viable operational plans, policymaking tends to be driven by knee-jerk responses based on emerging situations and is, hence, mainly reactive.

The ministries of defence (MoD), external affairs (MEA) and home affairs (MHA) have different planning cultures and processes.

Their strategies and plans must be based on shared assessments of environmental conditions, appropriately aligned and prioritized and moderated by the constraints imposed by the availability of resources. In view of the extreme complexity and interdependence of the various elements of national security and the multiple organizations responsible for the implementation of plans, there is an inescapable need to draw up holistic, time-bound plans of action with an inter-ministerial, inter-departmental and inter-agency approach to safeguard India's national interests and have relatively clear, well-defined objectives. India must state its national security interests, derive the national security objectives necessary to meet those interests, formulate a national security strategy to achieve those objectives and then pursue it relentlessly.

The most appropriate method for the formulation of a national security strategy is to follow the 'ends, ways and means' approach. However, it is first necessary to evaluate the threats and challenges confronting India over the mid and long terms. Threats and challenges have a dynamic of their own and are never easy to assess or predict with any certainty. They appear, disappear and reappear when least expected and in a form and manner that invariably come as a surprise. Hence, the strategies once drawn up can never be treated as sacrosanct and need to be reviewed periodically to fine-tune them in line with the changes occurring on the geo-strategic landscape. The progress of implementation needs to be monitored on a regular basis so that mid-course corrections can be applied when necessary.

The aim of this concluding chapter is to summarize current and emerging threats and challenges to India's national interests in the prevailing geo-strategic and regional security environment, identify the national security objectives, and recommend a comprehensive national security strategy for India that is dynamic in design. The national security strategy recommended here is based on and draws from the policy options recommended by the authors of previous chapters but is not necessarily limited to or constrained by those recommendations.

Polycentric World Order: Era of Strategic Uncertainty

The twentieth century was perhaps the bloodiest in history. Two world wars, the spectre of nuclear weapons, numerous small wars and insurgencies and many ethnic conflicts in the past few decades ensured that the last century of the second millennium remained mired in violence. The peace dividend that was expected to accrue after the Cold War ended in 1991 failed to materialize. Instead, numerous small wars and insurgencies broke out all over the world, such as those in Bosnia–Herzegovina, Kosovo, Somalia, Rwanda, Kampuchea, Chechnya and East Timor, and then in West Asia. In a world that continues to be in a state of transition after the collapse of bipolarity, new challenges and threats to national security are emerging constantly. While conventional war is becoming increasingly unviable as an instrument of foreign policy, sub-conventional conflict and armed violence have become more prevalent.

The end of the Cold War has led to what may be characterized as an era of strategic uncertainty. Almost three decades later, the world order is once again in the process of transition; this time from America's 'unipolar moment'[1] to a polycentric future. The global balance of power is shifting gradually but inexorably from North America and Europe to the Indo-Pacific region that is poised to become the new strategic centre of gravity in international politics. 'Brexit', Britain's impending exit from the European Union, has jolted the foundations of globalization and brought nationalism once again to the fore.

Some commentators have declared that the twenty-first century will be an Asian century.[2] For the first time since the commencement of the Industrial Revolution, the single largest concentration of economic power will be found not in Europe or the Americas but in Asia. However, despite its growing economic clout, the Indo-Pacific region will remain a relatively turbulent region—beset by internal conflicts and political transitions and subject to continuing instability due to a contested external environment and increasing militarization.

Though national security is still essentially an amalgam of political, economic and military components of national power, there has been a gradual erosion of the primacy of the state as the predominant player in international geopolitics. While, at one level, regional groupings like the European Union have subsumed some of the functions of the state—now being contested by movements like Brexit—at another, terrorist warlords like Abu Bakr al-Baghdadi of the so-called Islamic caliphate and ethnic chieftains are emerging as powerful entities. Some armed forces have begun to outsource limited security functions to private entities. For example, the North Atlantic Treaty Organization (NATO) employs Blackwater (now called Academi) for ancillary security duties in Afghanistan and Iraq. In January 2015, the US Central Command had 54,700 private security guards under its jurisdiction.[3] Mercenaries have been hired by both sides in the ongoing war in south Yemen between the Houthis and the coalition led by Saudi Arabia. Large multinational corporations (MNC) are increasingly taking protective measures to guard their commercial interests across national boundaries and may soon raise their own private armies. International non-governmental organizations (NGO) are also gradually becoming a force to reckon with in eroding the sovereignty of nation states. Paradoxically, despite all these changes, nuclear weapons and ballistic missiles have continued to remain central to international politics as the predominant currency of military power, though the reliance on other weapons of mass destruction (WMD) has declined.

While many old territorial and boundary disputes are yet to be resolved, some of these are latent and are unlikely to be the cause for a sudden conflagration. The more potent emerging challenges to security stem from cyber attacks on military and civilian infrastructure, radical extremism and fundamentalist terrorism, the proliferation of small arms, narcotics trafficking, socio-economic disparities and ethnic tensions. All of these need to be addressed with vigour. In fact, narcoterrorism will be a primary concern in the next few decades.

Like China, India will soon emerge as a major economic and military power. India will continue to seek cooperative and constructive engagement with all major powers. A closer economic linkage between the South Asian Association for Regional Cooperation (SAARC) and the Association of South-East Asian Nations (ASEAN) and a shared interest in peace and stability will drive maritime cooperation as trade across the Indian Ocean increases rapidly. The architectural framework of security of the global commons in the Indo-Pacific region will work satisfactorily only if, despite being driven by strategic competition, it is encased in a matrix of cooperative security.

Threats, Challenges and Vulnerabilities

Regional Security Environment

India's neighbourhood in South Asia is the second most unstable region in the world and is competing closely with West Asia for the number one spot. In the Arabian Peninsula, Yemen's Houthis backed by Iran are holding their own against the forces of Saudi Arabia and the UAE and the mercenaries employed by both. Further west, in the perpetually strife-torn West Asian region, the virulently radical Sunni militants of the Islamic caliphate (also called Daesh, the Islamic State of Iraq and Syria—ISIS—or the Islamic State of Iraq and the Levant—ISIL) proclaimed by Abu Bakr al-Baghdadi is engaged in a vicious fight with the armed forces of Iraq and Syria and the Peshmerga—forces of the Kurdistan Regional Government (KRG) from the Kurdish belt along the Iraq–Turkey border. The ISIS has captured territory in Iraq and Syria and has demonstrated its ability to defend its gains despite having lost the central city of Fallujah to Iraqi forces in 2016. In the civil war that has been raging in Syria since 2011, almost 250,000 people have been killed and thousands of refugees have migrated to Europe; many hundreds have perished in the attempt.

Despite Russia entering the fight against the ISIS and the formation of a coalition of thirty-four Islamic nations by Saudi Arabia, the terror group has consolidated its hold on the territory it has gained across the Iraqi and Syrian borders. In its cyber and word-of-mouth outreach, it has begun propagating its future plans to extend the caliphate to the east to Khorasan (Afghanistan, Iran and Pakistan) and to then fight the Ghazwa-e-Hind—the last battle for Hindustan. It even managed to capture and temporarily hold a few districts in the Nangarhar province of Afghanistan, appointed a regional head for South Asia and declared Bangladesh as a new battleground.

After the completion of the hasty NATO–ISAF (International Security Assistance Force) draw-down in Afghanistan, the Taliban are once again showing signs of resurgence. They control a large swathe of territory in the Sangin district of Helmand province in southern Afghanistan and elsewhere and have succeeded in launching several terrorist strikes in Kabul. Pakistan-sponsored reconciliation talks with the Taliban broke down in July 2015, when President Ashraf Ghani got tired of Pakistan's double games. Rahmatullah Nabil, the head of the National Directorate of Security, Afghanistan's intelligence service, resigned saying Pakistan cannot be trusted. President Ghani has called the Pakistan Taliban the greatest threat facing Afghanistan. A gradual descent into civil war appears to be the most likely outcome in Afghanistan.

The Pakistani army is still struggling to complete operation Zarb-e-Azb to eliminate the Tehreek-e-Taliban Pakistan (TTP) in North Waziristan. Pakistan's internal turbulence is a major cause of regional instability. The instability along the Hindu Kush mountains on the Af-Pak border; the Pakistani army's prolonged operations against home-grown Taliban like the TTP and the Tehreek-e-Nafaz-e-Shariat-e-Mohammadi (TNSM); fissiparous tendencies in Balochistan; continuing radical extremism and creeping Talibanization that has reached the Punjabi heartland; ethnic tensions, including protracted violence against the Shias and the Ahmadiyyas; and the floundering economy signal the nation's gradual slide towards becoming a 'failed state'. Pakistan's pursuit of 'full-spectrum nuclear deterrence', particularly its quest for the acquisition of tactical nuclear weapons (TNW) for battlefield use, is a major cause for instability at the strategic level.

Almost all the countries in South Asia are beset by socio-economic disparities, political tensions, radical extremism and ethnic challenges. Sri Lanka continues to struggle to find a lasting solution to its ethnic tensions. The rise of Islamist fundamentalism in Bangladesh could trigger new forces of destruction if left unchecked. The government of Sheikh Hasina and the Narendra Modi government in India are cooperating to neutralize organizations like the Harkat-ul-Jihad-e-Islami (HuJI) and the Jamaat-ul-Mujahideen Bangladesh (JMB).

The political situation in Nepal remains fragile. The Madhesi stand-off in protest against the promulgation of a flawed constitution continues in one form or another. Nepal's desire to seek neutrality between India and China is a setback to what has historically been a stable India–Nepal relationship. Simmering discontent that is gathering momentum in Tibet and Xinjiang against China's repressive regime has the potential to snowball into a full-blown revolt. The long-festering insurgencies in Myanmar may destabilize the government despite its post-election confidence. Iran's nuclear deal with the US and its strategic partners has provided a rare silver lining in a strife-torn region.

External Threats and the China–Pakistan Nexus

India has major territorial and boundary disputes with Pakistan and China in Jammu and Kashmir (J&K) and with China over Arunachal Pradesh and, to a limited extent, on the Uttarakhand–Tibet border. For almost seven decades now Pakistan has been fighting a low-intensity limited war with India on the Line of Control (LoC). The proxy war of the Pakistan army and the Inter-Services Intelligence (ISI) against India, now in its third decade, poses a serious threat to India's territorial integrity even though there has been a gradual reduction in the number of infiltration attempts across the LoC in J&K and in the incidents of violence over the ten years up to 2016.

In 2014-15, the Pakistan army repeatedly violated the mutually observed ceasefire agreement of 25 November 2003 on the LoC, but a stronger-than-usual Indian response quickly neutralized these efforts. Because of terrorist strikes at Gurdaspur, Udhampur and Pathankot, sponsored by Pakistan's 'Deep State' (the army and the ISI), ties between India and Pakistan remain stuck in a groove despite the initiative taken by the two prime ministers to revive stalled negotiations through a twelve-point Comprehensive Bilateral Dialogue.

China is in physical occupation of 38,000 sq km of Indian territory on the Aksai Chin plateau in Ladakh and claims the entire state of Arunachal Pradesh (approximately 93,000 sq km), which it calls Southern Tibet. The Line of Actual Control (LAC) on India's border with Tibet has not been demarcated on the ground and on military maps, and perceptions about where it runs vary on both sides. Though no shot has been fired in anger for several decades, transgressions, stand-offs and face-offs on the LAC are common. One of these could flare up and escalate into a local border skirmish with the risk of further escalation. While several confidence-building measures (CBM) are in place, these do not work very well during moments of crisis. Hence, the early resolution of the territorial dispute should be a national priority.

The Indian and Chinese worldviews are widely divergent. India recognizes China's military power and economic strength, but it is itself a country with a rapidly growing economy that will be a close second to China's in fifteen to twenty years and a population that will overtake China's in the same timeframe—with a much younger workforce. India sees itself as a co-equal Asian power and accepts that competition for influence and markets is inevitable between the two Asian giants. In the interest of peace and stability in the Indo-Pacific, India is willing to work cooperatively with China.

However, Chinese thinking is driven by a different calculus. According to a Chinese saying, one mountain cannot accommodate two tigers. China thinks of itself as the only tiger on the Asian mountain and is reluctant, even unwilling, to cede any strategic space to India. China's grand strategy is to confine India to the backwaters of the Indian Ocean as a subaltern state. It is engaged in the encirclement of India on land through inroads into each one of India's neighbours and in the Indian Ocean through its 'String of Pearls' strategy, wherein each pearl is a naval port at present and a potential naval base.

China is seeking to team up with Russia to pursue a joint strategy against the US and its strategic partners, even though Russia's response has been lukewarm so far. The China–Pakistan strategic partnership is a de facto military alliance. The friendship between the two has been described by senior leaders on both sides as being 'higher than the mountains, deeper than the oceans, stronger than steel and sweeter than honey. China … sees a strong, capable Pakistan as an asset … An India that is forced to look nervously over its shoulder at its western neighbour is easier for China to manage.'[4] China has 'guaranteed' Pakistan's territorial integrity.

Pakistan's proxy war against India is China's proxy war too, as Pakistan would be in no position to sustain a protracted sub-conventional conflict with India without Chinese backing. The growing nexus of nuclear warheads, ballistic missiles and military technology between China and Pakistan is adding to regional instability. By gifting to Pakistan nuclear warhead designs; testing Pakistan's nuclear warheads in the Lop Nor range—as is widely believed; by transferring crated M-9 and M-11 ballistic missiles to Pakistan; and facilitating the transfer of Nodong and Taepo Dong missiles from North Korea, China has irrevocably changed the geo-strategic equation in South Asia. It has pulled Pakistan up to India's level and it cannot now be undone.

China has made a commitment to spend $46 billion to link Xinjiang with Karachi and Gwadar under the China–Pakistan Economic Corridor

(CPEC) programme, which is part of China's One Belt, One Road (OBOR) or Silk Road initiative. India objects to the northern portion of the road-cum-oil pipeline project passing through Gilgit–Baltistan, an area that is part of the disputed territory of J&K. Despite all the negatives, the India–China relationship is stable at the strategic level, but politically, diplomatically and militarily unstable at the tactical level. China's objection to India's membership of the Nuclear Suppliers Group (NSG) is an example of instability at the tactical level. As long as the territorial and boundary disputes with China and Pakistan are not resolved, the possibility of conflict cannot be discounted, even though the probability is low. And if there is conflict with either one of them, given their deep nexus, both may be expected to come to each other's aid, though in varying degrees.

Clearly, India is confronted with a 'two-front' threat from China and Pakistan. However, while a border skirmish can never be ruled out in view of the competition along unsettled borders, the probability of large-scale conflict with either China or Pakistan will remain low for a decade or so. China is engaged in consolidating its economic gains and is undertaking major military reforms even as it modernizes its armed forces and strives to bring them to RMA (Revolution in Military Affairs) standards.[5]

China's key security concerns are limited to the merger of Taiwan with the mainland and the peaceful resolution of dissidence in Tibet and Xingjian. Pakistan is involved in fighting the demons within, demons of its own creation. Its armed forces are fighting radicalization and creeping Talibanization even as they have been bruised by the counter-insurgency campaign Zarb-e-Azb in Khyber Pakhtoonkhwa. It would not be in Pakistan's interest for the army to initiate hostilities with India. This gives India a ten-year window to modernize its armed forces and upgrade combat capabilities while undertaking socio-economic development and remaining prepared for a short, sharp border skirmish.

Internal Threats

Though it is an ancient civilization, India is a young nation state that is still engaged in the process of nation building. This process has been marked by ethnic tensions, fissiparous tendencies and socio-economic challenges.

India has been saddled with a long-drawn low-level insurgency in J&K due to its inability to fully integrate all parts of the state with the national mainstream. Several of India's north-eastern states have been in turmoil for many decades due to political and economic neglect, poor governance and, consequently, inadequate socio-economic development.

However, the insurgencies in the north-east are now waning, and it is time to launch a major drive aimed at providing good governance and stepping up socio-economic development. The rising tide of left-wing extremism (LWE) or Maoist/Naxalite terrorism has engulfed large parts of central India. Former prime minister Manmohan Singh had called the Maoist threat India's number one internal security threat on several occasions. The state governments have been unable to cope successfully with the challenge posed by these raiders of the night.

Emerging Threats and Challenges

Even as India grapples with diverse external and internal threats to its security, many new challenges are emerging on the national security horizon. These include cyber and information warfare threats to critical infrastructure and military command and control systems; the threat of mass migrations from neighbouring countries due to extreme poverty, natural disasters and political instability; the dangers inherent in the proliferation of small arms (light weapons); difficulties inherent in providing energy security as fossil fuels will become more and more inadequate for the nation's increasing energy needs; successive droughts hampering efforts to achieve water security; exponential increase in threats to India's maritime security and resources in its exclusive economic zone (EEZ); security of the environment and the preservation of the ecological balance; and the security of the Indian diaspora, especially in the Gulf region.

Besides these, still newer challenges that are emerging on the horizon include those from organized crime and narcoterrorism as India is flanked by two of the most notorious narcotics-producing regions in the world: the Golden Crescent (Afghanistan, Iran and Pakistan) to the west and the Golden Triangle (Laos, Myanmar and Thailand) to the east. Money laundering and the issue of fake currency by inimical neighbours are new problems to contend with. The Asian financial crisis demonstrated that a nation's currency can be undermined through external intervention and its economy can be destabilized. Pakistan's ISI has been engaged in circulating fake currency notes as part of its efforts to systematically destabilize India's currency and also fund its sponsorship of terrorist activities in India. The Ministry of Defence Annual Report of 1995-96 listed several other non-military 'pressures' on the national security environment which cannot be ignored. These include 'those relating to trade, intellectual property rights, environment, human rights ...'[6] (Strategies for dealing with the non-traditional threats and challenges to national security have been covered in detail in previous chapters.)

National Security Objectives

The character of conflict has been gradually changing, particularly since the end of the Cold War. The incidence of conventional conflict between states or groups of states has been steadily declining. Sub-conventional conflicts, ranging from intra-state conflict to proxy wars using terrorism as a tool, as also civil wars, are gaining prominence. Non-state actors are engaged in what Israeli military historian and theorist Martin van Creveld has called 'crummy little wars'—fought by terrorists, bandits, guerrillas, drug cartels and criminal networks.[7] To the two old categories of 'wars of interest' and 'wars of conscience', a new category of 'wars of intervention' has been added.[8] These changes have led to a reappraisal of the strategies to be adopted to safeguard national interests and achieve national security objectives.

Grand strategy is 'the art and science of employing national power under all circumstances to exert desired degrees and types of control over the opposition through threats, force, indirect pressures, diplomacy, subterfuge and other imaginative means, thereby satisfying national security interests and objectives.'[9] It goes well beyond the narrow domain of military strategy as it encompasses the coordinated employment of all the instruments of national power to achieve the national aim. According to British military historian and theorist Captain Basil H. Liddell Hart:[10]

> The role of grand strategy—higher strategy—is to coordinate and direct all the resources of a nation ... towards the attainment of the political object ... Grand strategy should ... develop the economic resources and manpower ... the moral resources ... fighting power is

> but one of the instruments of grand strategy ... the power of financial pressure ... ethical pressure ... grand strategy looks beyond the war to the subsequent peace ... (for) security and prosperity.

The primacy of national interests in the formulation of national security strategy is well recognized. According to Hans J. Morgenthau, one of the major twentieth-century figures in the study of international politics, 'The meaning of national interest is survival—the protection of physical, political and cultural identity against encroachments by other nation states.' National interests may be defined as 'the claims, objectives, goals, demands and interests which a nation always tries to preserve, protect, defend and secure in relations with other nations'. These are classified as vital or survival interests and other interests. The US defines 'vital interests' as 'those of broad, overriding importance to the survival, safety and vitality of our nation. Among these are the physical security of our territory and that of our allies, the safety of our citizens, the economic well-being of our society, and the protection of our critical infrastructures—including energy, banking and finance, telecommunications, transportation, water systems and emergency services—from paralysing attack. We will do what we must to defend these interests, including, when necessary and appropriate, using our military might unilaterally and decisively.'[11]

Clearly, vital national interests must by definition be defended by applying military force if it becomes necessary. India's vital national interests would include the following: the security of Indian territory on land and sea and that of Indian airspace; the protection of Indian citizens; the security of India's energy sources, refining facilities and merchant vessels engaged in transporting oil and gas and trade; a peaceful and stable internal and external security environment for unhindered socio-economic development; and the protection of critical infrastructure against physical disruption and cyber attacks.

Other major national interests comprise the following: an egalitarian world order that is rules-based and promotes free trade and security of the global commons through international cooperation; and the promotion of democracy and respect for universal values at home and around the world.

The national security objectives must be carefully drawn up if the national security strategy is to be achievable. As a country's national security objectives are normally derived directly from its national interests, India's major national security objectives should comprise the following:

- Maintaining the territorial integrity of India's borders on land, sea and air, as defined by law and enshrined in the Constitution, including the defence of India's island territories.
- Defending India's coastline against aggression and infiltration, and ensuring the security of Indian personnel and assets such as ships and oil rigs operating in the Exclusive Economic Zones (EEZ).
- Resolving the territorial and boundary disputes with China and Pakistan on favourable terms through negotiations in an early timeframe. (In this context, as large chunks of territory have been occupied by the Chinese on the Aksai Chin Plateau in Ladakh and by the Pakistanis in Pakistan-Occupied Kashmir (POK), building a national consensus to resolve both territorial disputes through a negotiated settlement should be an important political objective.)
- Protecting the lives and property of India's citizens, including during insurgencies and against acts of terrorism.
- Maintaining effective nuclear deterrence against the use or the threat of use of nuclear weapons against India.
- Protecting critical infrastructure and military command and control systems against cyber attacks from state and non-state actors and developing offensive cyber operations capabilities to deter such attacks.
- Ensuring the security of India's energy sources, refining facilities and modes of transportation, especially the security of oil and gas fields, ships transporting oil and gas and, where necessary, oil and gas pipelines within India and abroad.
- Undermining the China–Pakistan nexus and reducing the salience of the Pakistan army in the country's polity.
- Ensuring through diplomatic means and in conjunction with strategic partners that India will not be required to fight a simultaneous two-front war with China and Pakistan.
- Providing a stable and peaceful external security environment in India's area of strategic interest to facilitate unimpeded socio-

economic development and the free flow of trade. (This may involve military intervention, singly or in conjunction with strategic partners, when India's vital national interests are threatened.)

- Creating and sustaining an effective capability for out-of-area contingency (OOAC) operations through military intervention, when necessary, to ensure peace and stability in the Indo-Pacific and the security of the global commons (freedom of navigation in the sea lines of communication, air space, cyberspace and outer space).
- Being prepared to provide security and other assistance to the Indian diaspora, especially in West Asia and the Arabian Peninsula.
- Preventing narcotics trafficking and the smuggling of small arms and disrupting the linkages of the smugglers with terrorist organizations.
- Bringing to speedy justice both overseas and local perpetrators of terrorist strikes in India and against Indian assets anywhere.
- Preventing the destabilization of friendly countries in India's area of strategic interest extending from the South China Sea in the east to the Horn of Africa in the west, and providing military and other assistance when requested by them. (In this context, stability in Afghanistan, Bangladesh, Bhutan, Nepal, Pakistan and Sri Lanka is a major national interest.)
- Developing balanced relationships with strategic partners, including through defence cooperation, to deter conflict and manage crises, and engaging with organizations such as the ASEAN Regional Forum (ARF) and the Shanghai Cooperation Organization (SCO) to launch cooperative security initiatives while preserving India's strategic autonomy.
- Promoting cooperation and understanding with neighbouring countries and implementing mutually agreed CBMs to prevent crises through miscalculation.
- Pursuing security and strategic dialogues to address key challenges before the international community.
- Following a consistent and principled policy on nuclear disarmament and international security issues based on universality, non-discrimination and equal security for all.
- Working dynamically to achieve the goal of self-reliance (70 to 80 per cent indigenous content) in defence procurement by 2025. (The

indigenous manufacture of microchips, the basic building block of ICT—information and communications technology—products, must be a national priority.)

- Investing appropriately in the development of high-end defence technologies in conjunction with strategic partners to gain an edge in combat capabilities over military adversaries.
- Developing a proactive strategic culture.

Strategic Vision: Extending India's Influence and Reach

At no other time since its independence from colonial rule in 1947 has India been better poised as a strong and confident nation to shape its security environment with a view to promoting peace and stability and exploiting the available opportunities to its advantage for the economic development and prosperity of its people. A growing and resurgent India faces four major strategic challenges: managing the rise of China and its collusion with Pakistan; dealing successfully with Pakistan's proxy war; ensuring peace and stability in the South Asian region to enable unfettered economic growth; and maintaining a stable internal security environment. Besides ensuring that India's national interests are protected, the country's national security strategy must focus on meeting these four challenges successfully.

National security strategy overlaps with foreign policy and includes the employment of diplomatic and economic means to achieve the desired ends. In the rapidly globalizing, interdependent and wired world, isolationism is no longer a viable option. A peaceful and stable neighbourhood and a secure internal environment are essential prerequisites for unhindered socio-economic development and national prosperity. India must strike the right balance between brandishing the primacy of its comprehensive national power in its immediate neighbourhood—the muscular 'Indira Doctrine' of the 1980s—and engagement on a mutually beneficial basis—the conciliatory 'Gujral Doctrine' of the mid-1990s. Both should be backed by deft military diplomacy and defence cooperation. In its area of strategic interest, the best course of action for India is to take the lead to work towards the establishment of a cooperative security framework in conjunction with its strategic partners and stakeholders in the Indo-Pacific even if some littoral countries are unwilling to join the effort and prefer to go it alone.

For far too long—certainly since the Pallava and the Chola empires—India has been inward-looking, and strategic restraint has been a key feature of its foreign and security policies. India's reactive strategic culture—exemplified by the Panipat Syndrome[12]—has guided the political leadership to remain within a self-imposed Lakshmana Rekha.[13] There is an instinctive tendency to preserve the past. Jawaharlal Nehru, India's first prime minister, had advocated an 'Asian' Monroe Doctrine that was actually intended to keep foreign powers out, but also resulted in insulating India.

Resurgent India is now at a breakout moment in its history. It must reassert its primacy in South Asia, particularly in the Indian subcontinent. It should broaden its strategic outreach by looking and acting outwards in ever-growing concentric circles. In keeping with its growing comprehensive national power (CNP), India must use 'smart power'—a combination of hard and soft power—to fulfil its responsibility to provide leadership in South Asia and the Indian Ocean Region (IOR), in particular, and the larger Indo-Pacific region, in general. India should do this by seizing diplomatic and economic opportunities and, in conjunction with its strategic partners, contribute to stability and security, uphold the rule of law, promote democracy and human rights.

Though power projection should not be an end in itself, the ability to intervene is a handy tool for ensuring peace and stability in the neighbourhood. The Andaman and Nicobar Islands in the Bay of Bengal and the Lakshadweep and Minicoy islands in the Arabian Sea provide natural springboards for power projection and must be developed accordingly. The Indian Navy and the Indian Air Force will need base facilities for power projection, coercion and contingency operations. Agalega in Mauritius and Ayni in Tajikistan would be suitable.

As a status quoist power that has shunned military alliances and maintained its strategic autonomy, India is being gradually propelled by China's military assertiveness to hedge its bets. Many would argue that non-alignment served a useful purpose as a foreign policy tool during the era of bipolarity. However, since the end of the Cold War, non-alignment (version 2.0 or in any other form) is no longer relevant.

India should enter into and, where necessary, upgrade its strategic partnerships to undertake multi-nation contingency operations. The real test for Indian statecraft over the next few decades would be to balance India's engagement with China with its growing strategic partnership with the US. India must remain fully conscious of the reality that while China is a large trading partner, it will continue to be a military adversary as long as the territorial and boundary disputes with it are not resolved and, given its nexus with Pakistan, perhaps even later. The US may in the future be a strategic competitor but is extremely unlikely to ever become a military adversary.

In the decades ahead, India's national security paradigm and its influence in the Indo-Pacific region and beyond will be underpinned by its strong economic growth. After many decades of being stuck in the quagmire of what was pejoratively called the Hindu rate of growth, India is growing at an annual rate of 7 to 8 per cent—the highest among the world's large economies. It is the responsibility of the government to shape a peaceful and stable security environment so that even more rapid economic growth can take place unhindered.

A double-digit annual increase in the country's GDP should be the target. The entrepreneurial spirit of India's youth, its proclivity for innovation and its capacity to grapple with the complexities of design and development will provide the impetus for the rapid growth of India's economy. The economy will be increasingly knowledge-based, driven by research and development, technology and manufacturing, rather than being predominantly dependent on the growth of the service sector. To optimize the benefits of India's demographic dividend—the largest youth cohort in the world—adequate time and effort must be invested in 'skilling' the youth and providing opportunities for growth.

It is India's manifest destiny to play a leading role in shaping the emerging polycentric world order with the confidence that comes from a growing economy, rising military power, unique demographic dividend and deep civilizational values. India must be unwavering in safeguarding its territorial integrity, ensuring the security of its citizens and contributing proactively to stability in the Indo-Pacific. Even while coping with the threats of today, India must take the long view and plan to face up to the challenges of tomorrow through a strategy of national renewal. The national security mantra should be to deter future adversaries through the acquisition of overarching military capability backed by technological superiority and, if deterrence fails, to fight and win comprehensively on battlefields in every domain—land, sea, air, space and cyberspace—by conventional or sub-conventional means.

India's military power should be sufficient to ensure favourable outcomes each and every time, i.e., the achievement of India's strategic objectives. Only then will India count as a trustworthy regional power capable of providing leadership in moments of crisis and contributing positively to conflict resolution; and only then will India's aspirations of playing a global role be viewed favourably by the international community. If India continues to grow economically at a brisk pace and begins to act proactively to shape the environment and provide stability, there will be no need to hanker after 'great power' status or a permanent seat in the United Nations Security Council—both are destined to come India's way.

External Security Strategy

Given the uncertainty prevailing at the strategic level, defence planning has become more difficult in several ways. The sources and types of conflicts for which planning must be carried out have become more diverse and less predictable even as the number of potential adversaries continues to grow. The range of missions that armed forces need to undertake is expanding to include those likely to be assigned in sub-conventional conflict, including low-intensity border wars and insurgency fuelled by foreign powers. And the global security agenda has expanded in functional terms. Yesterday's peripheral challenges, such as the security of energy sources and the threat of mass migrations, now compete with conventional threats for a share in the defence pie. Systemic changes in the structure of the global economy, the information revolution and emerging military technologies are likely to alter the strategic landscape. These changes in the security paradigm are changing the strategic terms in which policymakers, military leaders and defence analysts must address long-term defence planning so as to evolve capabilities that will be relevant to the emerging threats.

Ensuring Territorial Integrity

The territorial and boundary disputes with China and Pakistan are unlikely to be resolved in the short (five to ten years) to mid term (ten to fifteen years) as it suits the vested interests of both China and Pakistan to keep the pot simmering. While the LAC with China and the LoC with Pakistan are contested to varying degrees due to disagreements about their alignment, the probability of large-scale conventional conflict is low as war will not suit any of the players over the next ten to fifteen years.

India must maintain a continuous vigil over the frontiers and carefully observe Chinese and Pakistani activities across the disputed boundaries. The capabilities of modern surveillance technology should be exploited to add to human vigilance. From the efforts being put in to develop infrastructure along the borders on land, including the refurbishment of advance landing grounds (ALGs) in Arunachal Pradesh and Ladakh, and the raising of new forces, it is clear that the army and the air force are gradually pivoting to the mountains.

The raising of potent forces like 17 Corps, popularly called the Mountain Strike Corps, will help to upgrade the quality of India's deterrence. Two additional divisions (56 and 71 Mountain Divisions) have been raised recently for defensive operations in Arunachal Pradesh. Similarly, one Strike Corps out of three in the plains and one additional infantry division with high altitude air assault capability need to be placed on high alert to counter aggression. The addition of new combat capability in the mountains, particularly the ability to launch and sustain offensive operations across the LAC, will send an appropriate signal to China. The ability to launch offensive operations into Chinese territory will upgrade India's military strategy against China from dissuasion to deterrence.

Deterrence in the maritime domain should also be enhanced so as to be prepared to confront the Chinese and Pakistani navies and, if necessary, even their merchant shipping as a counter strategy to exploit the weaknesses of the adversaries in the maritime domain should a war break out on the LAC or the LoC. The essence of India's military strategy should be to deter war, but if war is thrust on India, to fight synergized tri-service operations and ensure that conflict termination takes place on favourable terms. The military aim in a future conflict, if it cannot be avoided, should be to cause maximum damage to the adversary's war-waging capability by kinetic means and to capture a limited amount of territory as a bargaining counter.

Nuclear Deterrence

With a pacifist strategic culture steeped in Gandhian non-violence, India is a reluctant nuclear power. India believes that nuclear weapons are political weapons, not weapons of warfighting. Their sole purpose is to deter the use and threat of use of nuclear weapons by India's nuclear-armed adversaries. India's nuclear doctrine professes 'credible minimum deterrence' and is built around a 'no first use' posture. As a corollary, India is willing to absorb a 'first strike' and has declared its intention of launching a massive retaliation to cause unacceptable damage. Consequently, India follows a policy of 'deterrence by punishment' through a 'counter value' targeting strategy aimed at inflicting unacceptable damage, as against a 'counter force' strategy aimed at destroying the adversary's nuclear forces.

India's nuclear force structure is based on a triad: Prithvi I and II surface-to-surface missiles (SSM) and Agni I to IV intermediate-range ballistic missiles (IRBM) manned by the Missile Group of the Indian Army; nuclear glide bombs under-slung on Mirage 2000 and SU-30 MKI fighter-bomber aircraft of the Indian Air Force; and, in due course, submarine-launched ballistic missiles (SLBM) on ballistic missile submarines (SSBN) with the Indian Navy. India has willingly abjured the use of 'tactical' or 'battlefield' nuclear weapons as these are mainly employed against targets in the tactical battle area (TBA) and lower the threshold of use due to the proclivity to 'use them or lose them'. These also involve complicated command and control mechanisms, enhance the risk of unauthorized and accidental launches and are complex and costly to manufacture and maintain.

Unlike in China, which has an authoritarian regime, and in Pakistan, where the army calls the shots on key policy issues, India's nuclear weapons are firmly under civilian control. The Nuclear Command Authority (NCA) is the apex body of India's nuclear command and control system. The Political Council of the NCA is chaired by the prime minister. All policy decisions, including the decision to employ nuclear weapons, are vested in the Political Council. The Executive Council is headed by the national security advisor. It provides inputs to the Political Council for nuclear decision-making and executes its directives.

India has consistently been a strong advocate of total or universal nuclear disarmament. This policy, enunciated by the Nehru government after Independence in 1947, did not change even after the Pokhran tests of May 1998 as nuclear disarmament is seen to be in India's interest. Despite not having signed the Non-Proliferation Treaty (NPT) and the Comprehensive Test Ban Treaty (CTBT), India has complied with all of their provisions and supports the early conclusion of discussions on the Fissile Material Cut-off Treaty (FMCT). India has always complied with the provisions of the Missile Technology Control Regime (MTCR) and was admitted as a full member on 27 June 2016. India views these treaties as important enablers of non-proliferation, arms control and disarmament measures that are necessary for regional and international peace and stability. India has voluntarily renounced further nuclear testing and has an unblemished non-proliferation record among the nuclear powers.

India has invested deeply in strategic stability; this is reflected in the nuclear doctrine, the no-first-use posture, the force structure and the arrangements for command and control. India has never flaunted its nuclear weapons and has exercised immense strategic restraint despite grave provocation, particularly from Pakistan by way of a quarter-century-old proxy war being conducted through state-sponsored terrorism. India's conduct as a responsible nuclear power was recognized in the US–India Civil Nuclear Cooperation Agreement of July 2005. Ten years down the line, India is waiting to be given membership of the Nuclear Suppliers Group (NSG),[14] the Australia Group and the Wassenaar Arrangement as a state armed with nuclear weapons. China still does not recognize India as a nuclear power and has been doing the best it can to block India's entry into the four nuclear groups listed here.

The following policy imperatives would enhance the effectiveness of India's nuclear deterrence and merit the government's consideration:

- *Review of India's Nuclear Doctrine*
  - As almost twenty years have elapsed since India declared itself a state armed with nuclear weapons, it would be prudent to undertake a review of the nuclear doctrine.

- While the no-first-use posture continues to be appropriate, the reference in the doctrine to massive retaliation and retaliation with nuclear weapons for chemical and biological strikes against India need to be reconsidered.

- *Effectiveness of Delivery Systems*
  - India must step up efforts to acquire missiles with a range between 5,000 and 10,000 km for better long-range deterrence against China. The Agni-VI/Surya programme, which can benefit from the PSLV and GSLV—polar and geosynchronous—series of satellite launch vehicles, needs to be given high research and development (R&D) priority.
  - For a nation that follows a no-first-use nuclear doctrine and is willing to absorb a nuclear strike that may cause large-scale destruction and cripple its nuclear forces, genuine deterrence can be provided only by a robust, infallible and potentially insuperable nuclear deterrent capability including SSBNs armed with nuclear-tipped SLBMs. It is imperative for India to make all efforts to acquire and operationalize its SSBNs as early as possible.
  - Till such time as SSBNs enter service with the Indian Navy, a small number of surface combatants in both the eastern and the western naval fleets must be equipped with nuclear-tipped missiles to add to the uncertainties of the direction of launch that an adversary must consider.

- *Testing of Warheads and Missiles*
  - As only six nuclear tests have been conducted by India, the country's nuclear warhead designs are based on only a small database. Hence, despite the availability of sophisticated computer simulation and modelling techniques for improved warhead design, India must retain the option to carry out further nuclear tests as and when it is considered technically necessary by scientists of the Atomic Energy Commission (AEC) and is politically feasible to do so, and signing the CTBT is not a viable policy option in the near future.
  - Similarly, India's IRBMs have been inducted into service after only a limited number of flight tests. Additional tests of the Agni

series of missiles should continue—both to inspire confidence among the users manning these missiles as well as to enhance the credibility of India's nuclear deterrence by showcasing their technological maturity and accuracy of delivery. Meanwhile, India's diplomacy must endeavour to add value to credible deterrence through appropriate interventions in international fora.

- *Technological Developments*
  - The deployment of effective ballistic missile defence (BMD) systems to defend value targets and provide point defence to important installations will considerably enhance the quality of India's deterrence. Endeavours must continue to acquire this capability ex-import as well as through indigenous R&D as early as possible. However, actual deployment will be subject to whether China and Pakistan opt for BMD systems.
  - In view of the developments related to the multiple independently targetable re-entry vehicle (MIRV) in China, it would be prudent to make India's research programme on MIRV technologies public but maintain its status as a technology demonstrator.
  - India is faced with a continuing nuclear warhead and missile technology nexus between China and Pakistan. As no nation can go it alone in an endeavour as complex as nuclear deterrence, it is in India's interest to seek out strategic partners who might stand by India diplomatically and, where possible, by providing technological support that does not violate treaty obligations.

- *Need for Nuclear Signalling*
  - In view of the doubts raised over India's nuclear tests in May 1998, tangible measures need to be adopted by way of signalling to enhance the credibility of India's nuclear deterrence.
  - Similarly, nuclear signalling must be conducted to convince India's adversaries about the resolve of the political leadership to order 'massive retaliation'.

- *Non-proliferation Measures and Treaty Obligations*
  - New nuclear weapons states, especially those in India's neighbourhood such as Iran, are not in India's national interest.

India should, therefore, cooperate with the international community in furthering non-proliferation efforts even while remaining outside the NPT.

- India must continue to make efforts to enhance nuclear CBMs and nuclear risk-reduction measures (NRRM) with Pakistan so as to reduce the risk of accidental and inadvertent nuclear detonations and must extend these efforts to negotiating similar CBMs and NRRMs with China as well.
- It is not in India's interest to sign the CTBT at present, as it is important to keep the option of further nuclear testing open for political purposes, even though it may not be critical to test again in the near future for technological reasons.
- India should consider joining the FMCT only after sufficient fissile material has been stockpiled for producing the number of warheads considered adequate for credible minimum deterrence. However, India should continue to participate in the negotiations which are likely to go on for five to ten years.
- For counter-proliferation efforts to succeed, international support is needed for the Proliferation Security Initiative (PSI) and Container Security Initiative (CSI) launched by the US. India should join these initiatives as an equal partner after ensuring that Indian interests are safeguarded.

- *Deterrence and Diplomacy*
  - India's nuclear deterrence policy should work along twin tracks: continue to enhance the quality of India's nuclear deterrence while simultaneously working to achieve total nuclear disarmament in as early a timeframe as possible. Total nuclear disarmament is in India's national interest as it will eliminate the risk of nuclear war and also provide a level playing field.
  - India must strive to achieve this goal through vigorous diplomacy by mobilizing all its strategic partners and friends in the United Nations. This should be an important foreign policy objective.
  - The political leadership and the senior bureaucracy must be regularly briefed and sensitized about the complexities of nuclear deterrence so that they can make realistic assessments of military options during crises.[15]

Managing the Rise of China and Its Collusion with Pakistan

India's foremost national security challenge in the 2020–30 timeframe will be to manage the rise of a militarily assertive China that is seeking to achieve a 'favourable strategic posture'. It will also have a bearing on the ability of India and its strategic partners to ensure peace and stability in the Indo-Pacific region.

Now that China has completed its 'four modernizations',[16] it has discarded Deng Xiaoping's twenty-four-character strategy[17] to 'hide our capacity and bide our time' and has begun to flex its military muscle. China senses the emergence of a security vacuum in the Indo-Pacific and is rushing to fill it.

With its growing military power and preference for resolving territorial disputes through coercion and the use of military force, the probability of China displaying militarily irresponsible behaviour in the Indo-Pacific region, including against India, cannot be ruled out. China could decide to intervene militarily in the South China Sea to establish its presence on some of the disputed Spratly or Paracel islands (it has already been engaged in building air strips on reclaimed land), or to occupy one or more of the disputed Senkaku/Diaoyu islands or decide to resolve the remaining territorial disputes, like that with India, by using military force.

Also, China has deep internal fault lines. Its rapid economic growth, now slowing, has been fairly uneven and non-inclusive. There is a growing sense of resentment among the people against the leadership of the Communist Party for the denial of basic freedoms. The discontentment simmering below the surface could boil over and lead to a spontaneous implosion that may be uncontrollable. The crash of Chinese stock markets in July 2015 and again in January 2016 and their continuing volatility also point to the possibility of a meltdown.

Both the contingencies—implosion and military adventurism—have a low probability of occurrence, but will be high-impact events with widespread ramifications around the Indo-Pacific should either of them come to pass. Both contingencies will shake up the markets, result in millions of refugees and lead to a bloodbath. India and its strategic partners will need to cooperate closely to deal with the fallout and to manage the disastrous consequences if either of these contingencies unfolds.

Closer home, in South Asia, China is engaged in the strategic encirclement of India by making deep inroads into each of India's land neighbours. As mentioned earlier, as part of its 'String of Pearls' strategy, it is acquiring port facilities from which its navy can operate in the northern Indian Ocean.

The growing China–Pakistan nexus for nuclear warheads, ballistic missiles and military hardware is a matter of concern not only for India but also for the region. In a grossly unfriendly act, in June 2016, China virtually vetoed India's application for the membership of the Nuclear Suppliers Group (NSG) on the specious grounds that the criteria for membership needed to be established first.

China is now engaged in developing the China–Pakistan Economic Corridor (CPEC) to link Xinjiang with Gwadar on the Makran coast as part of its OBOR initiative. Involving an investment of $46 billion, the project is designed to give a fillip to the Chinese economy, create an alternative route for oil and gas supplies and counter US influence in the Indo-Pacific.

India must join the US and other strategic partners, such as Australia, Japan, Singapore, South Korea and Vietnam, to establish a cooperative security framework for peace and stability in the Indo-Pacific, for the security of the global commons and to deal with contingencies like those described above. If China is willing to join this security architecture, it should be welcomed. However, as China still suffers from the Middle Kingdom syndrome,[18] it is unlikely to do so.

In this context, the India–US strategic partnership makes eminent sense as a hedging strategy for both countries. In more senses than one, it is India's 'principal' strategic partnership, as former prime minister Manmohan Singh had once described it. His predecessor, Atal Bihari Vajpayee, had gone further and said that India and the US were 'natural allies'.

Whichever term is used to describe the relationship, clearly, the US cannot be expected to pull India's chestnuts out of the fire, and vice versa. Only when the vital national interests of both are simultaneously threatened will the two countries come together and act in concert.

Defence cooperation, a key component of the strategic partnership, must be taken to the next higher trajectory to enable the two countries to undertake joint threat assessment; contingency planning for joint operations; sharing of intelligence; simulations and table-top exercises—besides training exercises with troops; coordination of command, control and communications; and planning for operational deployment and logistics support. All of these activities must be undertaken in concert with India's strategic partners in Asia.

Because of its exaggerated claims over the South China Sea, China has been objecting to India's Oil and Natural Gas Corporation (ONGC) prospecting within Vietnam's territorial waters. Future ONGC operations should be backed up with support from the Indian Navy by way of providing point defence to offshore oil installations and conducting maritime patrolling in the South China Sea jointly with the US and other strategic partners.

Vietnam has often expressed an interest in Indian weapon systems. These must be provided on soft loans, including ballistic missiles that do not violate MTCR guidelines such as the BrahMos supersonic cruise missile, Prithvi I and II and Prahar SSMs. The indigenously designed and manufactured Pinaka multi-barrel rocket launcher (MBRL) should also be provided. Initial batches of these weapon systems could be gifted and training teams sent to provide in situ training assistance. Notably, in May 2016, the US lifted its fifty-year-old embargo on the sale of arms to Vietnam.

Afghanistan has given India a wish list of weapons and equipment in accordance with the provisions of its strategic partnership with India. So far India has given only non-lethal defence equipment, including a few utility helicopters. The other items required by the Afghan National Security Forces (ANSF) in order to improve combat capability should also be provided. The training assistance being provided to the ANSF should be stepped up by an order of magnitude.

If invited to do so by the Afghan government, India should be prepared to train ANSF personnel inside Afghanistan. The Indian training teams should be self-sufficient and capable of organizing their own local security, including limited counter-terrorism measures.

The trilateral agreement with Iran and Afghanistan for India to develop the Chabahar port and link it with the Zaranj–Delaram highway, built by India in Afghanistan, to gain access to the Central Asian republics and beyond to the countries part of the Commonwealth of Independent States (CIS) is a positive development.

It will also provide a suitable route for logistics support should India be called upon to send an infantry division to Afghanistan to support operations of the ANSF if it becomes necessary. Similarly, India should reach out to Bangladesh, Bhutan, the Maldives, Myanmar, Nepal and Sri Lanka and the countries on the Indian Ocean littoral in order to minimize the negative impact of the overtures being made by China to them.

China is too large to be contained effectively, but India can and must raise the cost for its pursuit of its grand strategy to confine India to the backwaters of the Indian Ocean as a subaltern state. India should do this through astute diplomacy and proactive defence cooperation with its strategic partners.

Fostering an Interdependent Neighbourhood

India has had good relations with almost all its neighbours over several millennia and deep cultural ties bind the region. However, India has allowed these linkages to weaken over the past few decades as it was looking inward while it was engaged in undertaking socio-economic reforms. This must change in the larger interest of national security and economic growth. Roads, rail lines, coastal transport—all of these must be extended to the countries around India as part of its 'neighbourhood first' policy.

Deepening India's outreach to the neighbours will help to improve trade in the long run and to move towards the establishment of free trade areas (FTA), including a SAARC FTA. Similarly, the 'Look East' engagement with the ASEAN countries should be upgraded to 'Act East'. India should work towards joining multilateral trading arrangements like the Trans-Pacific Partnership (TPP) and the Regional Comprehensive Economic Partnership (RCEP) when it suits India's interests. India's strategic outreach will lead to the faster integration of South Asia and its assimilation into a rapidly globalizing world.

At the same time, India's red lines should be clearly spelt out. While India does not seek primacy and respects its neighbours' sovereignty and autonomy, that is, their right to develop relationships as they deem fit, they should also ensure that India's national interests are not hurt. For equilibrium to prevail in a region with one large nation, referred to by the smaller neighbours as the 'big brother', all the neighbours must be equally mindful of each other's interests. In turn, the big brother should reach out to its smaller neighbours in every possible way without making it contingent on reciprocity. Efforts made to deepen India's strategic outreach must necessarily be complemented by military force. At least two Rapid Reaction Divisions (RRDs) will need to be raised over a period of ten to fifteen years.

Dealing with Pakistan's 'Deep State' and Its Proxy War

Despite facing seemingly insurmountable internal security challenges, the Pakistani army and the ISI—together constituting the 'Deep State'—have been engaged in a low-intensity limited war against India for almost three decades. The Pakistani army believes that the balance of terror must be in its favour, especially when the balance of power is not. Through low-key terrorist strikes, the Pakistani army is keeping the machinery of its proxy war well oiled so that levels of violence can be ratcheted up whenever necessary.

Pakistan's Deep State is continuing to sponsor terrorist attacks not only in India but also against Indian assets in Afghanistan through extremist organizations like the Lashkar-e-Taiba (LeT) and the Jaish-e-Mohammed (JeM). Incidents like the terrorist strike at the Pathankot airbase in January 2016 and Pakistan's proclivity to remain in denial, even though hard evidence of the involvement of the organs of the state is given to it, are exhausting Indian patience. A single miscalculation could lead to conflict between the two nuclear-armed neighbours. While India is willing to discuss the resolution of the Kashmir dispute, it cannot do so with a gun held to its head.

India's carefully calibrated strategy to fight Pakistan's proxies within its own borders and on its own side of the LoC, in order to keep the level and the intensity of conflict low and maintain a stable environment for rapid economic growth, has not yielded the desired dividends. While the security environment within J&K is stable, sporadic incidents of terrorism continue unabated. Large-scale riots and incidents of stone pelting, as seen in the summer months of 2010 and 2016, can be triggered by seemingly small incitements. These are symptomatic of the people's continuing sense of alienation, especially in the Kashmir Valley. Also, the proxy war has slowed down efforts to integrate J&K with the national mainstream.

For the Pakistani army it is a low-cost, high-payoff option to keep several divisions of the Indian army and a large number of units of the central armed police forces (CAPFs) embroiled in conflict. For India the opportunity costs have been prohibitively high in terms of the strain on the defence budget and slowing down of the rate of growth; for example, the negative impact on the economy of the decline in tourism in J&K.

The remaining roots of Kashmiri militancy—control stations, training camps and logistics bases—now lie across the LoC in POK. An attempt to eliminate these through military means would not be a viable option. A long-drawn-out conflict, especially one predominantly limited to the mountainous terrain of J&K, is not in India's interest. Also, large-scale hostilities run the risk of escalation to a conflict in the plains with nuclear overtones.

India should pursue a four-pronged strategy to gradually force Pakistan to stop waging a proxy war against India. First, India should continue to engage the elected civilian leadership of Pakistan with a view to gradually resolving the seemingly intractable disputes between the two countries and reducing the salience of the Pakistani army in the country's polity. India should also engage members of Pakistan's civil society and senior veterans of its armed forces who are amenable to seeing reason as they wield considerable influence with the generals in command. Efforts to further liberalize the visa regime, encourage people-to-people contacts and enhance trade should continue.

Second, India should simultaneously 'hit to hurt' the Pakistani army on the LoC where it is deployed in large numbers and can be easily reached. For every act of terrorism on Indian territory for which there is credible evidence pointing to the involvement or sponsorship of the Pakistani army and the ISI, carefully calibrated military strikes must be launched against the Pakistani army. These should include artillery strikes with guns firing in the 'pistol gun' mode to destroy bunkers on forward posts with minimum collateral damage; stand-off precision-guided munition (PGM) strikes on brigade and battalion headquarters, communications centres, logistics infrastructure, ammunition dumps and key bridges; and raids by Special Forces and Border Action Teams (BAT).

During the Kargil conflict in 1999, the Indian artillery had fired 250,000 rounds of ammunition in fifty days. If half that quantity is fired in one year on the Pakistani army's forward posts, it will have a sobering effect on it. The Pakistani army will retaliate and cause extensive collateral damage. This is likely to lead to hundreds of people leaving their villages near the LoC, but that is a factor that has to be vectored into the calculations.

Third, if Pakistan continues to drag its feet on bringing to justice the leaders of terrorist organizations against whom hard evidence has been provided by India, covert operations should be launched against them. These should be based on hard 'actionable' intelligence and should be sanctioned at appropriate levels. Covert operations are certainly a game that two can play, but the Deep State leaves India with few other options. In any case, Pakistan's ISI has been conducting covert operations in India for long. Since Pakistan is not inclined to bring to justice the leaders of terrorist organizations like the LeT and the JeM—terrorists whom they call 'strategic assets'—they must be neutralized through covert operations.

Finally, along with overt military measures and covert operations, India's growing diplomatic clout must be harnessed to influence the outcome by isolating the Pakistani army internationally as a rogue army due to the acts of terrorism that it perpetuates along with the ISI. The international community, which is already tiring of Pakistan's shenanigans in Afghanistan, will not need too much convincing to accept that the time has come to stop mollycoddling the Pakistani army on the grounds that it must be supported in order to ensure that its nuclear weapons do not fall into jihadi hands. Instead of wining and dining with the military leadership, Indian diplomacy must ensure that the international community censures the Pakistani army in the strictest possible terms and gives it six months to stop destabilizing its neighbours.

Failing satisfactory progress, the United Nations Security Council (UNSC) should be approached to approve an embargo on the sale of arms, ammunition and military equipment to Pakistan. If the UNSC resolution is vetoed by China, as it well might be, India should use its buyers' clout in the military industrial complex to ensure that arms manufacturers that supply weapons and defence equipment to Pakistan stop doing so. India should lobby extensively with the US political leadership and the members of the US Congress to apprise them of the fact that continuing US support for the Pakistani army is hurting the growing Indo-US strategic partnership because military aid strengthens the Pakistani army and gives it greater confidence to destabilize its neighbourhood with impunity. It also casts a shadow of doubt over the long-term intentions of the US in the region. In order to develop some leverage, India should launch a sustained campaign to exploit Pakistan's fault lines in Balochistan, POK and Gilgit–Baltistan. India should do this by providing political, diplomatic and moral support to the people of these areas whose human rights have been crushed under the military jackboot. Also, India should support the Afghan position on the Durand Line and on sharing the waters of the Kabul river.

This four-pronged strategy will make it extremely costly for Pakistan to continue to wage a proxy war, even if it does not force Pakistan to bring it to an end in one to two years. If it does not, it would be time to raise the ante and consider tougher measures such as the abrogation of the Indus Waters Treaty, as has been recommended by some analysts, but such a drastic step may not be necessary. While this strategy will enable India to raise Pakistan's cost for waging a proxy war, lasting solutions for the vexing issues plaguing Indo-Pak relations can only be found through diplomacy. As has been widely reported, the then Indian prime minister Manmohan Singh and Pakistani president General Pervez Musharraf had come close to accepting a four-point formula for resolving the Kashmir dispute through painstaking negotiations undertaken by trusted back-channel negotiators. Such efforts must continue. In fact, India should take the lead in engaging the Pakistani army to institute military-to-military CBMs to reduce the risks of large-scale conflict.

Border Management Strategy

Surveillance measures, both physical and electronic, as well as intelligence acquisition need to be enhanced along all land borders to ensure that territorial integrity is not compromised and that state-sponsored and non-state elements inimical to Indian security do not gain entry. In order to reduce infiltration and prevent the smuggling of fake currency, small arms and narcotics, a more cohesive border management strategy needs to be drawn up than is the case today. Border-guarding forces must not only intercept intruders and smugglers but also deter them from making the attempt.

While border-guarding forces like the Border Security Force (BSF), the Indo-Tibetan Border Police (ITBP) and the Sashastra Seema Bal (SSB) should be under the operational control of the MHA and given the responsibility to guard all 'settled' borders, like they do at present, the MoD should be responsible for managing unsettled and disputed borders. Consequently, operational control over the forces deployed on these borders should be with the MoD. The responsibility for managing the LoC in J&K and the LAC on the Indo-Tibetan border should be that of the Indian Army. Battalions of other forces deployed on the LoC and the LAC (BSF, Assam Rifles and ITBP) should be placed under the army's operational control. The principle of 'single point control' must be followed if the borders are to be effectively managed.

The early resolution of the territorial and boundary dispute with China should be a priority for the government. As prolonged negotiations will be required to reach a settlement, as a first step, India should propose to demarcate the LAC on the ground and on military maps as a CBM without prejudice to each other's claims. The exercise to exchange maps showing each other's perception of the LAC was abandoned in 2002 due to Chinese intransigence.[19] This should be taken up in earnest again.

The LoC with Pakistan was demarcated after the Shimla Agreement of 1972. It stipulates that no attempt should be made by either side to unilaterally alter the LoC. Yet, experience has been that the LoC continues to be contested. Pakistan's intrusions across the LoC in the Kargil district of J&K, which led to the fifty-day conflict in the summer of 1999, are an example. Maintaining the integrity of the LoC should remain a primary responsibility of the army. The Actual Ground Position Line (AGPL) at the Saltoro Ridgeline west of the Siachen Glacier must also be demarcated jointly with Pakistan, especially if an agreement to demilitarize the Siachen Conflict Zone is to be signed between the two countries. Development of the necessary border infrastructure to enable the induction, deployment and sustenance of offensive operations by corps-level forces along the LAC and the LoC by 2025 should be a key border management priority.

To a limited extent, the advances in surveillance technology, particularly satellite and aerial imagery, can help to maintain a constant all-weather, twenty-four-hour vigil along the LAC and the LoC and make it possible to reduce physical deployment as and when modern surveillance assets can be provided on a regular basis to the formations deployed forward. Similarly, the availability of a larger number of helicopter units will enhance the quality of aerial surveillance and the ability to move troops to quickly occupy defensive positions when it becomes necessary, provided 'acclimatized' troops are available. However, these are both costly ventures and need to be viewed in the overall context of the availability of funds for modernization.

The Task Force on Border Management, appointed by the Group of Ministers that had reviewed the recommendations of the Kargil Review Committee in 2000-01, had recommended lateral induction from the army to the CAPFs to enhance their operational effectiveness. This important recommendation must be implemented in letter and spirit. Appropriate measures must be taken to establish closer linkages with the people living in border areas to protect them from subversive propaganda to prevent unauthorized settlements and to initiate special developmental programmes.

Internal Security Strategy

In stark contrast to the difficulties of conflict resolution on the external front, the past few years have witnessed substantial progress in resolving internal conflicts. The militancy in J&K is at a low ebb though the state is still far from being fully integrated into the Indian Union. The central government's ceasefire with the Nagas held fairly well for over a decade even while internecine quarrels among the Nagas continued unabated. The ceasefire led to tangible progress in negotiations with both the Issak-Muivah and the Khaplang factions of the National Socialist Council of Nagaland (NSCN). There was cause for optimism about the early resolution of the long-drawn conflict until the Khaplang faction broke the ceasefire in March 2015 and opted out of the peace talks.

The United Liberation Front of Asom (ULFA) in Assam—except

for the break-away military wing led by Paresh Barua, who is said to be taking shelter in Myanmar and is getting covert support from the Chinese—has begun negotiations with the central government without any pre-conditions. The ULFA leadership should be incentivized to act in a statesman-like manner for the good of the people of Assam rather than continue to pursue power for its own sake.

Left-wing extremism in almost 220 districts of the central states has settled down to sporadic acts of violence that are directed mainly against the security forces. The fightback of the security forces has improved since the Central Reserve Police Force (CRPF) was nominated as the country's primary counter-insurgency force in 2001. However, only enhanced quick reaction capability, better weaponry, modern surveillance equipment for operations at night and improved standards of training and junior leadership will allow the security forces to begin dominating the ground. The initiative must be seized from the Naxalites before the tide begins to turn.

Need for Broad-based National-level Strategy

The management of internal security, particularly the long-term resolution of an insurgency, must follow a three-pronged approach: the delivery of governance and justice; the socio-economic development of the area; and ensuring a safe and secure environment in which development and governance can be delivered. All three must go hand-in-hand. Simultaneously, sound perception management must ensure that the message goes home that insurgency does not pay off in the long run and that it is better to join the national mainstream and enjoy the fruits of development. It is axiomatic that there cannot be a military solution to an insurgency. The army and other security forces can only achieve temporary military control over the security and law and order situation. The elimination of the root causes of insurgencies requires sensitive political handling and long-term politico-economic strategies that are not based on vote bank politics.

The present strategy of employing the army for counter-insurgency operations in the hinterland, and the CRPF and the state armed police in the urban areas has yielded good results. The army's ethos of conducting operations with an 'iron fist in a velvet glove', implying the use of minimum force and people-friendly operations with an emphasis on 'winning hearts and minds' (WHAM), must be replicated by all other security forces deployed for internal security duties. Experience has shown that large-scale operations like 'cordon and search' are counter-productive as they yield little by way of tangible gains and succeed in further alienating the people. The best results are obtained by launching surgical strikes based on accurate intelligence. The clearance of roads before convoys ply on them has proved to be extremely useful as it helps to recover improvised explosive devices (IED) and reduces the probability of ambushes.

A coordinated approach involving all organs of the state is necessary to formulate and implement a broad-based national-level strategy to fight internal security challenges to national security. The internal security function of the MHA should be hived off into a separate ministry headed by a cabinet minister as it requires full-time ministerial attention. The government must draw up a comprehensive internal security strategy that is inter-ministerial, inter-agency and inter-departmental in character. Only then will various stakeholders feel empowered to take ownership of the strategy and work unitedly to achieve its aims and objectives. Such a strategy must also balance the interests of the central and the state governments.

In the Constitution, law and order is a subject on the state list; the term 'internal security' does not find mention. The Constitution must be amended to introduce the term. Internal security must be added to the concurrent list so that the central government can act on its own initiative when necessary, particularly in the case of externally aided insurgencies and terrorism, or when a state government drags its feet due to vote bank politics. The establishment of unified commands in states affected by militancy has been only partially successful. While a unified approach with a clear sense of direction, the sharing of intelligence at all levels and the coordination of operations between different security forces are essential objectives, unless the chief ministers take personal interest in providing directional guidance, the true potential of unified commands will not be realized. Internal security is a civilian responsibility and the political leadership must accept that it has a role to play. When things go wrong, as they sometimes will, the political leaders must also take the rap.

Counter-terrorism Strategy

The menace of terrorist strikes in urban areas, which stems mainly from radical extremism, continues to remain unchecked. Though terrorist strikes have been sporadic and spaced out in time, the overall impression is that of an unstable internal security environment as the terrorist organizations appear to be able to strike at will. Indian Muslims have mostly remained detached from the ultra-radical ISIS and its aims and objectives, except for a handful of misguided youth who are reported to have signed up to fight. They are being approached by ISIS recruiters mostly through social media. Carefully drawn up counter-radicalization and de-radicalization plans must be made to wean the youth away from the lure of joining the ISIS.

Despite the lessons learnt from the terrorist strikes from the sea in Mumbai in November 2008, coastal security continues to be weak. The Marine Police are too few in number to effectively patrol the vast area entrusted to them; they are ill-equipped and inadequately trained; and there is poor coordination between them and the Coast Guard, which is an armed force of the Union under the MoD. Far better Centre–state coordination is necessary to improve coastal defence, including surveillance and early warning of intended terrorist strikes through national technical means.

Effective early warning and accurate intelligence assessments are a prerequisite for success in counter-terrorism operations, especially preventive measures. The National Counter-terrorism Centre (NCTC), first proposed by former home minister P. Chidambaram in 2009, has not been set up so far. It was expected to draw up and coordinate counter-terrorism plans, integrate intelligence gathering and coordinate with all existing investigating and intelligence agencies, including the National Investigation Agency (NIA), the National Technical Research Organization (NTRO), the Joint Intelligence Committee (JIC), the National Crime Records Bureau (NCRB) and the National Security Guard (NSG). The National Intelligence Grid (NATGRID), which was approved by the Cabinet Committee on Security (CCS) in June 2011, will provide a data bank of twenty databases such as travel records, immigration details and income tax records as inputs to the NCTC.

Unless the NCTC is empowered to conduct counter-terrorism

operations like its US counterpart, on which the Indian version was expected to be based, urban terrorism will continue to remain a cause for concern. Without an effective NCTC or a similar organization, the planning and execution of India's counter-terrorism policies will remain mired in systemic weaknesses.

International Cooperation

As terrorism has become a major international threat, it is becoming increasingly necessary to develop counter-terrorism linkages with friendly powers so as to fight the menace together with synergized capabilities. Since the threat is transnational in nature, cooperation in intelligence sharing is crucial for successful counter-terrorism operations. India's strategic partners like the US can provide India with sophisticated counter-terrorism technologies and surveillance equipment to help India upgrade its capabilities.

India should also provide full diplomatic support to and work with the UN to formulate a consensual approach in the fight against the ISIS. It should cooperate closely with the international community by way of sharing information and intelligence and providing logistics support. India's neighbours who plead helplessness and express their inability to prevent attacks on India from their soil must be persuaded through firm diplomacy to act decisively or through joint operations.

If this option fails to elicit the right response, India must reserve its right to launch proactive operations against terrorists and terrorist organizations, including 'hot pursuit' operations by the Special Forces. This was done twice across the India–Myanmar border, in June 2015 and May 2016, with the concurrence of the Government of Myanmar. If necessary, trans-border air-to-ground strikes may also be launched. It needs to be impressed upon neighbouring countries through deft diplomacy that cooperation with India is in their own national interest as the prolonged harbouring of terrorists and other militants may ultimately lead to full-blown insurgencies on their own soil, as has clearly happened in Pakistan.

Building Combat Capability for Future Conflict

Threat-cum-Capability–based Forces

The combat capabilities that will be required to influence outcomes on future battlefields form an important pillar of the national security strategy. As long as the territorial disputes with China and Pakistan remain unresolved, it will be necessary to continue with threat-based forces. However, in this era of strategic uncertainty, future threats and challenges are not entirely predictable. Hence, it would be appropriate to configure a mix of threat-based (70 to 80 per cent) and capability-based (20 to 30 per cent) forces.

The Indian armed forces are still, mostly, 'Second Wave', industrial-age armed forces—lumbering formations and battalions that lack both firepower and mobility and are equipped with obsolescent command and control systems. In order to undertake the defence of Indian territory and provide stability and security in India's area of strategic interest, the armed forces must be strengthened and modernized. However, before all else, attitudinal reform is necessary so that the armed forces do not prepare to fight yesterday's wars. They must transform themselves into light, lethal and wired 'Third Wave' forces with precision strike and stand-off kinetic capabilities and C4I2SR (command, control, communications, computers, intelligence, information, surveillance and reconnaissance) relevant to both the contact and non-contact battles. They should be capable of conducting joint effects–based operations (EBOs) in a network-centric battlefield environment. State-of-the-art defence technology, partly acquired from strategic partners and partly developed indigenously, must be integrated with the weapon platforms to gain a decisive edge over India's military adversaries.

Firepower Asymmetry

The army and the air force must pivot to the mountains as that is where the territorial disputes are and the probability of conflict is the highest. As large-scale manoeuvre is not possible in the mountains due to the limitations of the terrain and large-scale offensive operations are likely to threaten nuclear red lines in the plains, the army and the air force must upgrade their capability to engage targets and destroy them. Only overwhelming asymmetry of firepower will help to achieve military aims in the future. Massive doses of accurate strikes from the army's guns, rocket launchers and missiles using terminally homing PGMs; from fighter ground attack aircraft and attack helicopters; and, when within range, from ship to shore, will tilt the balance in India's favour. Combat drones—unmanned combat aerial vehicles, or UCAVs—firing PGMs should be introduced into service as early as possible.

High priority must also be accorded to addressing the 'critical hollowness' hampering defence preparedness, particularly ammunition and equipment shortages. It would be prudent to prepare for a thirty-day war and maintain reserves for another twenty to thirty days. It has been reported that 17 Corps, being raised as a Mountain Strike Corps, is being equipped from the WWR (war wastage reserves), i.e., without acquiring new weapons and equipment due to budgetary constraints and the slow pace of weapons acquisition. This type of risk taking assumes that the probability of conflict is extremely low in the near term. As had been the case during the Kargil conflict in 1999, when the nation had been taken by surprise by the Pakistani army's perfidious intrusions across the LoC, such an assumption may prove to be dangerously optimistic.

Strategic Air Force, Blue Water Navy

The IAF's combat power has dwindled considerably over the past two decades. Not only must the shortfalls be made up for expeditiously, the air force must graduate to a truly 'strategic' air force capable of dominating the air space over India and its immediate neighbourhood, supporting the operations of the army and the navy and participating in Indian interventions abroad. The Indian Navy will soon have to contend with the Chinese navy and must acquire genuine blue water capability.[20] Maritime security has been neglected for long and an immediate course correction is necessary. Like in the past, the armed forces will also be required to undertake humanitarian assistance and disaster relief (HADR) operations, including jointly with strategic partners as had happened during the South-East Asian tsunami in December 2004.

Developing Capacities for Military Intervention

High priority must be accorded to the creation of combat capabilities for military intervention beyond India's shores singly or in concert with

India's strategic partners. Both for intervention as part of contingency operations and as a force multiplier for conventional conflict, it is necessary to acquire air assault and amphibious operations capability. The minimum requirement is to raise a division-size rapid reaction force by the end of the 13th Defence Plan (2017–22). Two brigades of the Rapid Reaction Division (RRD) should be air assault brigades that are armed, equipped and trained to secure threatened islands, seize an air head and capture an important objective inside the adversary's territory such as a key bridge that is critical for further operations in depth. These brigades should have integral firepower, combat service support and logistics support units and should be based on Chinook CH-47 and MI-17 transport helicopters. Besides fighter ground attack aircraft, these brigades should have the firepower support of two to three flights of attack and reconnaissance helicopters and one flight of UCAVs. The third group should be an amphibious brigade with the necessary transportation assets being acquired and held by the Indian Navy, including landing and logistics ships. All the brigade groups and their ancillary support elements should be capable of transportation by land, sea and air.

The RRD should be logistically self-contained for an initial deployment period of fifteen to twenty days with limited daily replenishment. The infrastructure for such a division, especially strategic airlift, attack helicopters, heli-lift and landing ship capability, will entail heavy capital expenditure to establish and fairly large recurring costs to maintain. However, it is an inescapable requirement and funds will need to be found for such a force by providing additional budgetary support. Another RRD should be raised over the 14th and 15th defence plans by about 2032, when India's regional responsibilities would have grown considerably. The RRDs should also be equipped and trained to operate as part of international coalition forces for speedy military interventions. Unless planning for the creation of such capabilities begins now, the formations will not be available when these are required to be employed.

Internal Security Capabilities

The army's internal security, counter-insurgency and counter-terrorism capabilities also need to be modernized as most of the emerging challenges will lie in the domain of sub-conventional conflict and operations other than war. The Indian Army's performance in counter-insurgency operations over the past fifty years has been outstanding and is regularly studied by all modern armies, particularly its concept of the use of minimum force—fighting insurgents with one hand tied behind the back.

However, its prolonged, large-scale employment for counter-insurgency operations has considerably eroded the army's conventional deterrence capability as it has affected operational preparedness, hampered training for conventional operations and slowed down the army's modernization plans. This has emboldened Pakistan to continue and, occasionally, even step up its proxy war against India as it perceives the Indian Army to be unprepared to fight and win a conventional war. It is imperative that the involvement of the army in such operations is gradually reduced to manageable limits so that India's conventional deterrence can again be made potent enough to thwart Pakistan's proxy war designs.

Although the concept of raising the Rashtriya Rifles as the army's counter-insurgency force has proved to be useful, in view of the army's continuing commitment for internal security duties, the time has come to seriously consider constituting a more cohesive 'Third Force' that is specially equipped and trained for internal security operations. Adopting this course of action will reduce the negative effects of prolonged employment of the regular army for counter-insurgency operations. The Force and Sector HQ and the 63 battalions of Rashtriya Rifles that have been raised so far could form the nucleus of the Third Force. Such a force would naturally be available as additional reserves for conventional conflict by temporarily scaling down its deployment for counter-insurgency operations.

The CAPFs have performed creditably in meeting the challenges of internal security confronting the country. However, with their present organizational structure, organic weapons and rudimentary surveillance capabilities, they are not adequately equipped to effectively counter nearly full-blown insurgencies with secessionist tendencies supported by inimical foreign powers. A bipartisan National CAPF Commission needs to be appointed to take a hard look at the organizational structure and equipment profile of all CAPFs and recommend viable practical measures to revamp and prepare them for the tasks at hand. As a first step, the CAPFs must begin to operate as cohesive battalions and not in isolated companies. An experienced commanding officer must be in charge of counter-insurgency operations, perhaps the most complex of all types of operations.

Technological Superiority

Appropriate investments need to be made to enhance cyber security and to acquire cyber-attack capability—to deter state actors and to cripple non-state actors tinkering with India's command and control networks and critical infrastructure. The technologies of tomorrow, including hypersonic missiles, ramjet propulsion, non-nuclear electromagnetic pulse (EMP), directed energy weapons, robotics and artificial intelligence, must be suitably exploited. Special Forces operating in conjunction with the intelligence agencies will play a major role in shaping the battlefield.

Conflict in the twenty-first century requires an 'all of government' approach. The operational synergy that comes from 'jointmanship' must drive future force structures and the upgradation of combat capabilities. Doctrinal concepts, organizational structures and training methodologies must keep pace with technological advancements. Suitable doctrinal guidance must be developed for joint operations as well as multi-nation intervention operations. Hard power cannot be applied successfully unless its 'software'—vision, will, capacity, doctrine—is in place. The armed forces must train their personnel for certainty and educate them for uncertainty.

Developing a Proactive Strategic Culture

A fundamental element of CNP that all great powers have in common is a proactive strategic culture. India's reactive strategic culture is a national failing. It must be gradually transformed to a proactive one through a conscious effort at all levels of government. The almost complete absence of the discussion of national security–related issues in the political discourse in India needs to be corrected.

Institutions like the National Defence University, which is yet to see the light of day, and strategic studies think tanks must be given greater prominence in consultations involving decision making. National security issues must be included in the syllabi of all schools and colleges to enhance the understanding of students about basic threats and challenges to national security and the measures necessary to overcome these.

The government should consider introducing compulsory military service for three to five years as a prerequisite for entry into all officer-grade posts of the central government, i.e., IAS, IFS, IPS and allied services. It will be a win-win situation all round. The armed forces will get many more bright young officers than they do at present, even if some of them leave after short tenures. As more candidates will apply, it will gradually reduce the shortage of officers in the armed forces. Candidates for the central services will benefit immensely by serving in the armed forces for three to five years. All government training institutions must educate their trainees about national security issues by devoting a portion of the syllabus to the subject. Many other pragmatic steps will need to be taken, particularly relying on proactive responses when a crisis unfolds.

Concluding Observations

The ambit of national security strategy extends well beyond the defence of the country and the non-traditional facets of security. In the prevailing socio-economic environment, where the tensions generated by the inadequacies in governance and widespread extreme poverty could lead to situations that pose serious challenges to security, the armed forces and the CAPFs cannot be expected to deal successfully with the complex, multiple and diverse threats and challenges to national security all by themselves. It has to be a national-level endeavour that follows a 'whole-of-government' approach and includes all the organs of the state as well as all the citizens of India.

In this context, the concept of comprehensive national power (CNP) has gained currency in the last two decades. The CNP of a nation is a product of its strategic culture; its economic strength; its military power, including the state of its preparedness for war; its foreign policy clout and diplomatic influence; its internal cohesion; its ability to deliver good governance and justice; the capability of its human capital; its advancement in science and technology and innovation; its knowledge and information base; its advantages of geography and natural resources;

the firmness of its national will; the resolve of its leadership; and the attractiveness of its soft power.

While India is gradually moving up the ladder in almost all other parameters of CNP,[21] the lack of internal cohesion is decidedly dragging the country down. Political divisiveness; social inconsistencies like the inequalities inherent in the caste system, which is a relic of a feudal past, and varying personal laws; sectarian differences; religious intolerance; ethnic tensions; fissiparous tendencies; inter-state issues like tensions over the sharing of river waters; and corruption in public life and electoral politics are all factors that contribute to the internal cohesion fault line. The popular catchphrase of 'unity in diversity' has not quite played out the way it was intended to. Instead, vested interests, encouraged and supported by inimical foreign powers, have for long been fanning the flames of disunity.

Another major fault line has been created by the inequities that have crept into India's economic growth. Elitist education and haphazard economic development have created some islands of excellence, but have resulted in numerous cesspools of mediocrity and extreme poverty. This has happened as the reliance that had been placed on the trickle-down benefits of growth has not worked as well as the ruling elites had hoped it would. Meanwhile, the phenomenal reach of television and the social media is fuelling the desire of families across the country to possess the full range of consumer goods. However, the lack of employment opportunity in many economically backward areas makes it impossible to meet these desires. The growing anger due to unfulfilled desires could eventually lead to the advent of a revolution triggered by rising expectations.

India's huge 'demographic dividend' (the country has the youngest workforce in the world) that economists exult so much about is likely to turn into a demographic disaster if additional opportunities for employment are not forthcoming at the required rate. While India's growth rate has been more than 7 per cent per annum, much of it has been 'jobless growth'—growth in the manufacturing sector that does not create new jobs in keeping with the investment.[22] Ten to twelve million young women and men will join the workforce every year over the next twenty years. Unless the requirement of 100 million new jobs every year is met, the country will have a major challenge to contend with.

The lack of internal cohesion coupled with rising expectations and a high rate of unemployment, in addition to the ongoing internal security challenges, could lead to instability of an unimaginable magnitude. All the CAPFs (BSF, CRPF, ITBP, SSB, CISF, et al), numbering over 1.5 million—more than the combined personnel strength of the army, the navy and the air force—will be inadequate to maintain internal security in such a situation. Dealing with these challenges will require astute political leadership and a dynamic inter-ministerial, inter-departmental and inter-agency strategy that is multi-disciplinary in nature.

Various other facets of national security have been lucidly covered in the preceding chapters and are not repeated here. There are also the responsibilities that are placed on a nation as a member of the international community. For example, it is incumbent on great nations to abide by the 'just war' doctrine[23] that is based on the principles of 'distinction, necessity and proportionality' and the need to observe the 'Responsibility to Protect'.[24] A comprehensive national security strategy must include plans to deal with all of these in appropriate measure.

The armed forces will be willy-nilly drawn in to meet some of the emerging challenges. They must analyse the nature of engagement and the type of tasks that they may be called upon to undertake. Only then can they prepare to squarely face the future with confidence and professionalism. The modernization of the armed forces, including the acquisition of force multipliers, and the creation of rapid reaction capabilities for conventional conflict and intervention operations are capital-intensive ventures that require large budgetary outlays. The present defence budget that is less than 1.75 per cent of the country's GDP is grossly inadequate to support the force structures that will be required to deter future wars and to fight and win if deterrence fails. As has been repeatedly recommended by Parliament's Standing Committee on Defence, the government must progressively raise the defence outlay to 2.5 per cent of the GDP in five to seven years and 3 per cent by 2025.

Unlike in the past, when the practice was to leave the armed forces to themselves to identify the threats that they were likely to confront, the government must give them a clear directive and provide the necessary wherewithal to prepare them for future threats and challenges. In fact, the government should appoint a National Security Commission to undertake a holistic review of all major issues impinging on national security. Following such a review, the government should publish India's National Security Strategy as a statement of intentions and to reassure the Indian public as well as friends and strategic partners.

India's standing as a regional power that has global power ambitions has been compromised by its inability to ensure peace and tranquillity and successfully manage ongoing conflicts in its neighbourhood, singly or in concert with its strategic partners. These conflicts are undermining South Asia's efforts towards socio-economic development and poverty alleviation by hampering governance and vitiating the investment climate. It appears inevitable that the South Asian region and its extended neighbourhood in the Indo-Pacific will see the continuation of ongoing conflicts without major let-up. In fact, the situation in Afghanistan and Pakistan could deteriorate beyond the ability of the international community to control it effectively.

Perhaps the National Security Strategy recommended here is ambitious, but then India is a country that is resurgent and marching forward with rapid strides in this Asian century and can afford to dream big. An increasingly more self-assured India must lead from the front and reassert its primacy in South Asia and the Indian Ocean Region. While being mindful of its own security interests, India must join its strategic partners to contribute to a stable and peaceful regional security environment that enables the free flow of trade and security of the global commons. Inimical elements among India's neighbours must not be allowed to interfere with the achievement of the country's national interests.

Finally, the Indian government, the strategic community and India's teachers must give the Panipat Syndrome that has plagued the country's strategic culture for over half a millennium a quiet burial. Backed by its growing national power, a self-assured and resurgent India must graduate from a passive to a proactive strategic culture. India's National Security Strategy must reflect the transformative change in India's circumstances. It is time for the government to emulate Kautilya and write a new Arthashastra.

APPENDIX 1

Proposed Coordination Structure for Cyber and Information War

NSA with the NSCS should be the national controlling and coordinating agency for CIW. An omnibus board could be created in the NSCS along with a CIW Executive Committee (CIWEC). These could be established by the NIB. Recommended composition and roles of these two bodies in brief is given in the succeeding paragraphs.

CIW Board

Composition, amongst others:

(a) Chairman: NSA
(b) Members (Government): Cabinet Secretary, Director-General (DG) Research and Analysis Wing (R&AW), Secretary DIT; representatives from MHA, Ministry of External Affairs (MEA), Ministry of Information and Broadcasting (I&B), and the Ministry of Power
(c) Members (Ministry of Defence): CDS (when created) and DG DRDO
(d) Private Sector: Chairman of NASSCOM
(e) DG CIW
(f) Member Secretary: Deputy NSA

Notes

1. Representatives of ministries should be of a status in keeping with other members of this committee.
2. The board may invite or co-opt technical or other experts as required.
3. The board should meet at least once a quarter or as required.

Charter

(a) Overall review and policy for CIW.
(b) Formulation of strategy for meeting emerging threats.
(c) Ensure necessary coordination between all public and private agencies at the national level as also monitor implementation of all aspects of CIW.
(d) Ensuring all international treaties and agreements are vetted in keeping with needs of national security.

CIWEC

The deputy NSA, who is the secretary of the apex body, could chair the CIWEC, DG CIW will be the secretary with support from the NSCS. He will be responsible to ensure day-to-day coordination and follow up on all CIW issues and report to the apex body through deputy NSA.

The composition of this CIWEC could include:

(a) Members (Public Agencies): Chairman NTRO, DG CERT, representatives from MHA, R&AW, Council of Scientific and Industrial Research (CSIR), DIT, public IT-related services, i.e., the Ministries of Finance, Railways, Telecom, Civil Aviation, Power, Human Resources (HR) and I&B. Also, a representative from MEA who is an expert on international agreements.
(b) Members (Ministry of Defence): Representative of Integrated Defence Staff, representatives of cyber command (when formed) & DRDO.
(c) Private Sector: Representatives from NASSCOM representing different spheres of the IT industry.
(d) Academic Institutions: At least three.

Charter

CIWEC will be a coordinating agency which will issue policy guidelines and monitor all activities on a regular basis. Its organization will be flexible to ensure representation of all agencies. Sub-groups could be formed for specific aspects such as proactive defence or protection of critical infrastructure. The CIWEC will meet at least once a month to oversee and report progress on all issues which include:

(a) National Cyber Security Policy, as also international cooperation in this regard, and all agreements on IT with respect to the needs of national security. This will also include recommendations for simplifying and laying down flexible procedures to meet requirements of the IT domain.
(b) Technology development for protection of networks and systems, as also proactive defence.
(c) Installation of systems, monitoring and response management, especially for emergencies.
(d) Development of HR and public awareness. Recommendations for funding in this regard both in the public and private spheres.
(e) Standardization and certification. This will include creation of test beds.

Organization and Functioning

CIWEC should be an empowered body. The DG CIW should be of appropriate level to ensure executive action and compliance by agencies. All public agencies like the DRDO, HQ IDS, NTRO, DIT, national CERT, CSIR, and the National Informatics Centre (NIC) are represented and could constitute its executive arms. For necessary coordination and follow-up, the office of DG CIW in NSCS must comprise security, legal and technical experts. It could be a small body to start with. Allocation of business rules must formalize functioning. Policy and conduct of offensive cyber operations could also be coordinated by a sub group drawn from the above.

Source: IDSA Task Force report, March 2012

APPENDIX 2

A Defence Industrialization Strategy[1]

SMITA PURUSHOTTAM

India's ambassador to Switzerland

'There are no shortcuts for obtaining technology.' —Rees Ward

As the largest arms importer in the world, India is exporting not only foreign exchange but also the ecosystems that a thriving defence industrial complex could have generated for India. India has fortunately resolved to discard its 'Import with Benefits' model and usher in a 'Make in and by India' re-industrialization strategy to produce its own high-tech defence, telecommunications, electronics and aerospace equipment and other advanced manufactures. Because in the twenty-first century, the single most decisive factor in the race for global domination is going to be technological superiority. According to McKinsey, disruptive technologies deployed in this century will increase the gap between 'Technology Haves' and 'Technology Have-nots' by an estimated $33 trillion annually, which is why China wants to overtake the US in R&D spending by 2019.

Both for national security and national welfare reasons, India must catch up with the technologically advanced nations. A successful plan has to dig practically into every aspect of our nation's functioning. For this, India can learn from the strategies of other countries. For example, China has followed a four-phased Techno-Nationalist Strategy to build its scientific and technological capabilities:

- First phase : Technology imports
- Second phase : Massive reverse engineering of foreign technologies
- Third Phase : Developing capabilities and ecosystems for indigenous innovation
- Fourth Phase : Delivering disruptive technologies

India has not even mastered the reverse engineering stage, being stuck in the licensed production mode, which entails export controls and de-incentivizes indigenous innovation. The Forum on High-tech Defence Innovation has,

[1]Report of the 5th Meeting of the Forum on High-tech Defence Innovation, 26 November 2014.

therefore, for the last few years been calling for a Defence Industrialization Strategy (DIS)—based on an indigenous innovation ecosystem; a proactive state; and R&D-intensive smart manufacturing. It can capture maximum value addition in India; reverse our huge import dependence in arms, aircraft, IT and telecom hardware; stimulate a massive demand for scientists, skilled technicians and entrepreneurs; and accelerate many virtuous cycles for our country. At its 5th meeting on 26 November 2014, the forum, therefore, proposed a holistic Defence Industrialization Strategy based on the four 'RISE Pillars', as follows:

- Massive R&D investment, discarding the dead end of licensed production: R
- Innovative Indian industry: I
- A proactive science state supporting the innovation ecosystem and advanced manufacture: S
- Education as the foundation for all the above: E

'R' for R&D

India's R&D infrastructure requires drastic reform because only R&D investment will help it kick its reliance on licensed production. India must:

- Increase R&D investment to 2.5 per cent of GDP by 2020 to boost the competitive advantage of key sectors as a cornerstone of industrial policy.
- Industry must take on a greater share of R&D funding as it does in advanced countries; in the US, industry funds about 67 per cent of all R&D; in the EU, 55 per cent; in Germany, 70 per cent; and in China, Singapore and Taiwan, above 60 per cent (2010 US S&E Indicators).
- Extend R&D co-funding to technology start-ups along Israel's OCS model of matching government funds.
- Introduce India-specific standards in key sectors.
- Actively prioritize indigenous technologies in domestic procurement. Israel has provisions for price preferences for indigenously innovated products and China supports indigenous innovation in many ways.
- Support strategically vital indigenous technologies and fend off attempts by vested interests to scuttle these. WTO provisions do not apply to strategically vital industries.
- Make the existing R&D public sector infrastructure more accountable, radically transform the management structures of government-funded laboratories and make the commercialization of technologies and working in partnership with industry mandatory.

- Replicate in India the dynamic US compact between state, industry and the world famous research universities and federally funded R&D centres (Los Alamos, Livermore, Sandia, Oak Ridge, Jet Propulsion Laboratory, the NIH, etc.).
- Reform the Patent Office to incentivize indigenous innovation.
- Ensure a flexible approach to ensure the viability of the indigenous pharmaceutical and software product industries.
- Prepare a compendium of India's vast R&D and technology capabilities so that indigenous capabilities can be identified and prioritized in national development plans.

'I' for Strengthening Domestic Industry

The government has already prioritized removing the multiple burdens on domestic industry, historically hampered by irrational rules in a rentier economy. The situation was so bad that SMEs and large industry players were forced to establish branches abroad to bid for domestic tenders. Many took their investments out of India in despair. The prime minister's Make in India programme and initiative for improving India's ranking from 142 to 50 in the World Bank's 'Ease of Doing Business Index' and the plans of the ministries of defence, railways and power and the Department of Electronics and Information Technology to boost domestic high-tech manufacturing are manifestations of the government's resolve to reverse this state of affairs. This should be speeded up and a unified, national transparent market established.

Offsets

Many countries[2] have chosen to leverage defence and aerospace Offsets to boost high-tech manufacturing rather than turn to majority FDI. Despite its huge market leverage and status as the eleventh most industrialized country in the world, India has been unable to leverage Offsets for industrial benefit like South Korea, Brazil, China, Israel, UAE and even Canada. This is surprising as India has one of the weakest Offsets policies in the world[3] and should, therefore, attract massive Offsets (Table 1). Some of the reasons are poor negotiating capacity due to a lack of training and a weak implementation mechanism. Rafale agreed to 100 per cent Offsets with Canada on a much

[2]Israel has an economy-wide National Offsets Policy; Turkey, South Korea, Brazil and now Canada and the central European countries have leveraged Offsets successfully. Today Brazil and South Korea supply 75 to 80 per cent of their defence requirements. South Korea, China and Brazil's Offsets policies created an aircraft industry, while India frittered away Civil Aviation Offsets.

[3]The most liberal FDI caps, the highest thresholds and the lowest quotas.

lower aircraft order than 66 MMRCAs. SAAB gave generous Offsets to several countries and is predictably winning many orders in Brazil, Indonesia, etc., which are serious about developing indigenous capability. But OEMs still complain about strict Offsets and run down Indian industry, their views getting gratuitous and copious coverage in India.[4]

Country	*Quota (per cent)*	*Threshold ($)*	*FDI ceiling (per cent)*	*Direct/Indirect Offsets*
Brazil	100	5	Controlled	Defence, aerospace, government decides others
Canada	100	—	—	—
Malaysia	100	15	—	Direct & Indirect
South Korea	>50	10	40 of offset contract	Direct & Indirect
UAE	50-70	10	49 but flexible	Direct & Indirect
Turkey	60	0	Encouraged. Exit strategy	Direct & Indirect
China	Own regime	Own regime	Own regime	Own regime
Israel	50 (defence)	5	Requirement for government approval	All sectors
India	30	50	49	Direct/aerospace & Internal security

(Table 1: Comparison of Offsets Regimes in Different Countries. Figures are approximate, but depict a clear pattern: India's Offsets regime is the weakest of them all.)

The Forum heard passionate pleas from India's top high-tech companies—Bharat Forge, Tejas Networks, Zen Technologies, Hycator, HAL, GRSE, L&T, Saankhya Labs, Sankhya Infotech Ltd, Shyam Telecom, Tatas, CBS Technologies, iSPIRT/ Product Nation and many others—to recognize and feel pride in domestic high-tech capabilities. India must seize the golden opportunity for Indian firms in defence, aerospace, telecom, electronics, railways and much else to create its own Defence Industrial Base (DIB) by strengthening its Offsets policy. India should:

1. Strengthen Offsets:

- Raise Offsets quotas from existing 30 per cent to 70 to 100 per cent. With 100 per cent Offsets, defence imports estimated at $100 billion to $200 billion in the next few years could boost the Indian economy by a similar magnitude.
- Reduce the minimum threshold to $5 million.
- Ensure full export, production rights and TOT including of source codes.

[4]'The case for Indian Industry', https://vistasbharat.wordpress.com/2014/06/20/the-case-for-indian-industry.

- If strong oversight and audit over Offsets is successfully established, permit indirect Offsets on at least 50 per cent of the quota, with 50 per cent still devoted to defence manufacture. For example, use Offsets to develop science and technology education and the high-tech vocational skills ecosystem as skilled human resources are as crucial to the success of the DIS as hardware.
- Institute the National Offsets Policy for imports of aircraft, telecom equipment, electronic hardware, etc. Israel's National Offset Policy has greatly boosted its economy. Service behemoths in IT, telecommunications and aerospace must offset their huge hardware imports through investments in domestic R&D and manufacturing before they are given permission to invest abroad.
- Promptly reactivate Civil Aviation Offsets, following the Chinese and Brazilian examples, to leverage huge military/civilian aircraft purchases. Many countries have inserted themselves into the global aviation production chain by exploiting Offsets. Thus, Offsets should apply on Indigo's purchase of commercial jets worth $35 billion. The MRO market must be exploited, reversing the unilateral grant of air seats under bilateral ASAs to make India an aviation hub, and ensuring that Indian taxation rates do not make domestic MRO uncompetitive.
- Train MOD officials as the real bottleneck in implementing a strong Offsets policy lies not in Indian industry but in the inability of the government mechanism to handle large flows of Offsets projects.
- Institute a strict oversight and audit mechanism to prevent fraud and monitor progress towards targets.

2. Support Industry

- Designate Indian firms or consortia as lead integrators for defence offsets and manufacturing projects. JVs formed with OEMs for defence contracts should have the Indian partner in majority control, as per the Brazilian pattern. Indian firms will select their joint venture partner.
- Address the issue of financial viability for Indian firms and give tax incentives (Brazilian model) and price preferences (Israel model) to Indian industry successfully indigenizing high-tech production. Fix the inverted tax/duty structure to encourage local value addition/ high-tech manufacturing, and remove foreign exchange uncertainty for Indian industry bids.
- Devise better tendering policies to ensure quality in procurement.

3. Apply Civil Military Integration

Many countries see defence industrialization as a way to increase employment and indigenous high-tech capabilities, developing their economies in the process. Pursuing a Civil Military Integration Strategy is a crucial component of this plan. The 'spin-on' advantages of Civil Military Integration are huge, as most innovations and new technologies are produced in the civilian sector today. In order to shift to a post-industrial, dual-use economy, India should classify electronic, ICT and telecom products as strategically important sectors. WTO provisions will then be easier to handle. Recommendations are given in our more detailed report, but a few are given here.

- Fully restore Preferential Market Access (PMA) in the CMI sectors and defence. The PMA is a misnomer; preferential access means access of a foreign product to another country's market as pointed out in an ICRIER report.
- Formulate a good Defence Export Policy with time-bound clearances and a simple negative list of destinations. Indian firms winning contracts may be given deemed export status. In foreign policy, hi-tech exports rather than low-tech exports should be prioritized in bilateral aid programmes.

4. Formulate the RDA: Research, Development and Acquisitions System

India is the only major power that does not have an integrated Defence Production Manual or what advanced countries call the RDA: Research, Development and Acquisitions system. It only has a Defence Procurement Procedure (DPP), which stepmothers R&D and domestic production and facilitates an import-oriented culture. If India wants to be considered a modern manufacturing nation, we must have an RDA which focuses on indigenous development from the R&D stage to productionizing the technology and final acquisition. The RDA must:

- Give clear procurement preference to indigenously innovated products and maximize local content across all DPP categories.
- Reform Procurement/CVC Guidelines to facilitate procurement from start-up/innovative firms with new, pioneering technologies for which there may be no competitor. At present, Indian procurement procedures do not have any guidelines for innovation, which especially disadvantage high-tech SMEs, crucial sources of innovation. No one ever thought Indian companies could innovate!
- The best should not be an enemy of the good. RDAs are extremely complex. The first iteration of the RDA can be developed from the

current 'Make' procedure in the DPP while a comprehensive new one is being drafted by domain experts.

5. Demonstrate Inclusiveness and commitment to employment creation

The government should announce a quarterly employment report to demonstrate its commitment to increasing gainful high-value high-skilled employment, as in advanced nations.

'S' for the Science State

The US's stunning technological achievements were made possible with active state intervention and funding. The state plays a key role in all advanced countries with major defence production capabilities: the US, Russia, China, UK, France, Germany, and now even Turkey, the UAE and South Korea. India too needs a proactive 'Science State' infused with the mandate to transform India into a high-tech nation and encourage economic growth through every means at its disposal. For this:

- The country's top leadership must provide oversight for implementing the DIS, as in the US and China.
- The Parliament must conduct hearings and ask for reports on every aspect of the national S&T base, and its relative international performance, like the US Senate and Congress do.
- At every level, the state must prioritize the development of indigenous capabilities. Economic and other relevant policy must promote indigenous industrial capabilities and innovation ecosystems.
- CEOs should be appointed along the lines of the Delhi Metro/Space Commission for executing strategically important projects, and indigenization must be made a criterion for promotions.
- Every government department/private or public sector company should carry on its website a list of (a) projects to be awarded for indigenization, (b) imports and (c) proactive officials in charge of indigenization.
- State power should be used to leverage imports against exports with many countries which will expand the market for our manufactures including defence industrial base.
- Just as the Chinese state subsidizes massive infrastructure, the Indian Science State must also invest in infrastructure aggressively. Fortunately the 2014-15 Budget focuses on infrastructure, in recognition that government funding is really the best option, since FDI isn't going yet into infrastructure and PPPs aren't doing that well.
- An exclusively Indian Security Manufacturers Association must

be established for strategic interaction with MOD, related strategic departments and the armed forces.

In fact, this last recommendation is already being acted upon, with the emergence of the Defence Innovators and Industry Association (DIIA).

'E' for Education

Defence industrialization will require an enormous supply of scientists, skilled technicians and operators. Only 0.3 per cent of the Indian population has access to high quality education. The system is still oriented towards rote and not to inculcating critical thinking skills, accounting for India's low PISA scores and university rankings. India should:

- Make massive investment in primary, secondary and university education and reform teaching methods and the exam system to test understanding and critical thinking and not just memory.
- In secondary/skilled manpower, new funding sources, for example, defence offset funds or the proceeds of disinvestment, can be tapped to create new educational and vocational training institutions. The German vocational education system and applied science universities which feed its high-tech industrial sector can be applied in this regard.
- At the university level, world-class defence technology and research-oriented universities must be established, with international best practices, curricula, faculty and applications-based education. The US has a Defence Acquisitions University. China has a vast infrastructure of Defence Technology Academies, such as on Aerospace Aerodynamics, the Chinese University of Defence Technology, etc.
- India should also allow the best foreign universities to open up branches to introduce international best practices and enable massive savings and earnings of foreign exchange as Indian students stay in India and foreign students come to India to study.
- Provisions favouring endowments to educational institutions, like the American inheritance tax laws, should be incorporated in tax law.

If the entire country focuses on developing indigenous capabilities, India can reach its goal of becoming a high-tech nation speedily.

Notes

Preface: The Conceptual Underpinnings of National Security Strategy

1. Charles A. Beard, *The Idea of National Interest* (London: Macmillan, 1934).
2. Joseph Frankel, *National Interest* (London: Macmillan, 1970), p. 20.
3. Ibid, p. 21.
4. Norman Padelford and George Lincoln, *The Dynamics of International Politics* (London: Macmillan, 1967).
5. Robert E. Osgood, *Ideals and Self-Interest in America's Foreign Relations* (Chicago: 1953).

1. Introduction: Defence Policy and Management of National Security

1. Lord Hastings Ismay was Secretary of the Chiefs of Staff Committee in the United Kingdom, Chief of Staff of Winston Churchill during World War II, and also Secretary of the War Cabinet. After World War II, he was invited by the US to advise on its defence organizational set-up. He came to India in 1947 as Chief of Staff to Mountbatten.
2. Walter Lippmann, *Foreign Policy: Shield of the Republic* (Boston: Little Brown, 1943), p. 5.
3. 'GoM Report on National Security', p. 1, www.vifindia.org/sites/default/files/GoM%20Report%20on%20National%20Security.pdf
4. Ibid, p. 73.
5. It is learnt that Prime Minister Narendra Modi has started meeting the service chiefs every month, but individually and not collectively.
6. Rajat Pandit, 'Govt develops cold feet over General No. 1', *Times of India*, 18 June 2013, http://timesofindia.indiatimes.com/india/Govt-develops-cold-feet-over-General-No-1/articleshow/20640396.cms?
7. During the India Today Conclave in March 2015, Defence Minister Manohar Parrikar stated that 'a Chief of Defence Staff is a must'.
8. N.N. Vohra recommends the establishment of a separate National Security Administrative Service cadre, whose members should be selected from among the best civil servants in the country.
9. The US, UK and several other countries publish National Security Strategy papers in the public domain. China issues White Papers on National Security Strategy regularly.
10. Arvind Gupta, 'A National Security Strategy Document for India', IDSA Comment, 20 October 2011, Institute for Defence Studies and Analyses, http://www.idsa.in/idsacomments/ANationalSecurityStrategyDocumentforIndia_arvindgupta_201011.

11. Shyam Saran, 'Revamping India's National Security Architecture for Optimum Synergy in the Use of Its Instruments of National Power', 18th Colonel Pyara Lal Memorial Lecture 2014, United Service Institution of India, http://usiofindia.org/Article/?pub=Journal&pubno=598&ano=2748.
12. K. Natwar Singh, *One Life Is Not Enough* (New Delhi: Rupa & Co, 2014).
13. Kanti Bajpai, 'Be Civil with the Military', *Times of India*, 6 March 2010, timesofindia.indiatimes.com/edit-page/Be-Civil-With-The-Military/articleshow/5648165.cms.
14. At one stage, in consultation with the national security advisor, we prepared a list of essential weapons and equipment required urgently by each service and sent it to the Ministry of Defence. We were assured that the material would be procured within two to three months. Nothing could be procured during the ten weeks of war.

2. International Experience: The Defence Policies of Major Powers

1. In a speech delivered in Bruges, Belgium, in 1988.
2. 'National Security Strategy, May 2010', https://www.whitehouse.gov/sites/default/files/rss_viewer/national_security_strategy.pdf, accessed on 2 April 2015.
3. Department of Defense, United States of America, Quadrennial Defense Review 2014, http://www.defense.gov/pubs/2014_Quadrennial_ Defense_Review.pdf, accessed on 10 April 2015.
4. Ibid.
5. Ibid.
6. Ibid.
7. 'Emergent Strategy: How Does the Government Define the UK's National Interests?', http://www.publications.parliament.uk/pa/cm201012/cmselect/cmpubadm/1625/162506.htm.
8. 'Securing Britain in an Age of Uncertainty: The Strategic Defence and Security Review, October 2010', https://www.gov.uk/government/uploads/system/uploads/attachment_data/file/62482/strategic-defence-security-review.pdf, accessed on 1 April 2015.
9. 'A Strong Britain in an Age of Uncertainty: The National Security Strategy, October 2010', https://www.gov.uk/government/uploads/system/uploads/attachment_data/file/61936/national-security-strategy.pdf, accessed on 1 April 2015.
10. Ibid.
11. 'Securing Britain in an Age of Uncertainty: The Strategic Defence and Security Review, October 2010', https://www.gov.uk/government/uploads/system/uploads/attachment_data/file/62482/strategic-defence-security-review.pdf, accessed on 1 April 2015.

12. Ibid.
13. Ibid.
14. Ibid.
15. Scott Erb, *German Foreign Policy: Navigating a New Era* (London: Lynne Rienner Publishers, 2003), pp. 19-20.
16. Stefan Collignon, 'Germany's Strategic Interest', 12 May 2011, *Social Europe*, http://www.socialeurope.eu/2011/05/germanys-strategic-interest/.
17. The German constitution is called Basic Law.
18. Hans-Peter Schwarz, 'For German National Interest', *IP Journal*, Spring 2005, https://ip-journal.dgap.org/en/ip-journal/topics/german-national-interest
19. Ibid.
20. Article 56 of the Basic Law contains the oath under which the German president, chancellor and ministers are solemnly sworn into office (with or without religious affirmation). It states: 'I swear that I will dedicate my efforts to the well-being of the German people, promote their welfare, protect them from harm, uphold and defend the Basic Law and the laws of the Federation, perform my duties conscientiously, and do justice to all. So help me God.'
21. Lutz Unterseher, 'German Defense Planning: In a Crucial Phase', October 2001, Project on Defense Alternatives, Commonwealth Institute, http://www.comw.org/pda/0110gerdef.html.
22. Patrick Keller, 'German Hard Power: Is There a There There?', 8 October 2013, American Enterprise Institute for Public Policy Research, https://www.aei.org/publication/german-hard-power-is-there-a-there-there/.
23. Ibid.
24. Ibid.
25. Claudia Major and Christian Mölling, 'German Defense Policy: Is the Change for Real?', June 2014, German Marshall Fund of the United States, www.gmfus.org/file/3413/download.
26. The English version of the document 'National Security Concept of the Russian Federation', approved by Presidential Decree No. 24 of 10 January 2000, http://www.mid.ru/ns-osndoc.
27. The document 'National Security Strategy of the Russian Federation to 2020', approved by Decree of the President of the Russian Federation No. 537 on 12 May 2009, in Russian is available at http://www.scrf.gov.ru/documents/99.html. An English translation is available at http://rustrans.wikidot.com/russia-s-national-security-strategy-to-2020.
28. Extracted from 'National Security Concept, 10th January 2000' and 'National Security Strategy 2009'. Also see, 'Russia and US National Interests—Why Should Americans Care?', prepared by the Center for the National Interest, Belfer Center for Science and International Affairs, Harvard University, October 2011.

29. Vladislav Inozemtsev, 'Russia's National Interest: What Does It (and What Should It) Mean for Post-Soviet Countries?', 22 August 2014, Center for Post-Industrial Studies, http://www.postindustrial.net/en/?p=33.
30. Ibid.
31. Victor Pirozhenko, 'Russia's National Interests and Foreign Policy', 5 March 2012, Strategic Culture Foundation, http://www.strategic-culture.org/news/2012/03/05/russia-national-interests-and-foreign-policy.html.
32. Extracted from 'National Security Concept, 10th January 2000' and 'National Security Strategy 2009'.
33. Ibid.
34. Ibid.
35. 'The Georgian Campaign as a Case Study', 12 February 2009, https://www.stratfor.com/analysis/part-4-georgian-campaign-case-study; and 'Russia', *The Military Balance*, International Institute of Strategic Studies, 3 February 2010, p. 211.
36. Jim Nichol, 'Russian Military Reform and Defense Policy', 24 August 2011, Congressional Research Service, https://www.fas.org/sgp/crs/row/R42006.pdf.
37. Ibid.
38. Ibid.
39. Ibid.
40. Caitlin Campbell et al, 'China's "Core Interests" and the East China Sea', US–China Economic and Security Review Commission Staff Research Backgrounder, 10 May 2013, http://www.uscc.gov/sites/default/files/Research/China's%20Core%20Interests%20and%20the%20East%20China%20Sea.pdf.
41. 'China's Peaceful Development', Information Office of the State Council, the People's Republic of China, September 2011, http://english1.english.gov.cn/official/2011-09/06/content_1941354.htm, accessed on 11 April 2015.
42. Caitlin Campbell et al, 'China's "Core Interests" and the East China Sea', US–China Economic and Security Review Commission Staff Research Backgrounder, 10 May 2013, http://www.uscc.gov/sites/default/files/Research/China's%20Core%20Interests%20and%20the%20East%20China%20Sea.pdf.
43. Rukmani Gupta, 'National Interests and Threat Perceptions: Exploring the Chinese Discourse', IDSA Monograph Series No. 17, April 2013, Institute for Defence Studies and Analyses, http://www.idsa.in/system/files/Monograph17.pdf.
44. Deng Xiaoping, *Collected Works Vol. 2* (Beijing: People's Publishing Press, 1993), p. 168.

45. Jian Yang, 'China's Security Challenges: Priorities and Policy Implications', available at http://www.baraka.consulting/uploads/China_s%20Security%20 Challenges%20Priorities%20and%20Policy.pdf, accessed on 14 April 2015.
46. Dennis J. Blasko, 'The 2007 Report on the Chinese Military: The Top 10 List of Missing Topics', *Joint Force Quarterly*, Issue 47 (December 2007), p. 53.
47. Jian Yang, 'China's Security Challenges: Priorities and Policy Implications', available at http://www.baraka.consulting/uploads/China_s%20Security%20 Challenges%20Priorities%20and%20Policy.pdf, accessed on 14 April 2015.
48. Dean Cheng, 'China's View of South Asia and the Indian Ocean', 31 August 2010, Lecture No. 1163 on China, http://www.heritage.org/Research/Lecture/ China-s-View-of-South-Asia-and-the-Indian-Ocean.
49. Lu Fanghua, 'An Analysis of US Involvement in the South China Sea Dispute', *Contemporary International Relations*, Vol. 6, No. 20 (2010), pp. 133-34.
50. 'The Diversified Employment of China's Armed Forces', Information Office of the State Council, the People's Republic of China, April 2013, http://www. wantchinatimes.com/UploadFiles/The%20Diversified%20Employment%20 of%20China's%20Armed%20Forces.pdf, accessed on 13 April 2015.

4. National Security Objectives

1. 'Report to the Nation 2006-2009', National Knowledge Commission, http:// knowledgecommission.gov.in/downloads/report2009/eng/report09.pdf.
2. National Knowledge Network, nkn.gov.in, accessed 23 July 2016.
3. Arvind Gupta, 'A National Security Strategy Document for India', IDSA Comment, 20 October 2011, Institute for Defence Studies and Analyses, http:// www.idsa.in/idsacomments/ANationalSecurityStrategyDocumentforIndia_ arvindgupta_201011.

5. Beyond Non-Alignment: New Imperatives for Defence Diplomacy

1. For an account of all Indian expeditionary operations from the late eighteenth century to the end of the nineteenth century, see Intelligence Branch, Army Headquarters, *Frontier and Overseas Expeditions from India*, Vol. VI (Government of India: Simla, 1907); reissued by Mittal Publications, Delhi, 1983.
2. For a brief overview, see D.P. Marston and C.S. Sundaram, eds., *A Military History of India and South Asia: From the East India Company to the Nuclear Era* (Praeger: London, 2007).
3. For a discussion, see Stephen P. Cohen, *The Indian Army: Its Contribution to the Development of a Nation* (Berkeley: University of California Press, 1971), pp. 88-113.
4. Michael Brecher, 'India's Decision to Remain within the Commonwealth',

The Journal of Commonwealth & Comparative Politics, Vol. 12, No. 1 (1974), pp. 62-90.

5. P.R. Chari, 'Indo-Soviet Military Cooperation: A Review', *Asian Survey*, Vol. 19, No. 3 (March 1979), pp. 230-44; see also, S. Nihal Singh, *The Yogi and the Bear: The Story of Indo-Soviet Relations* (New Delhi: Allied Publishers, 1986).
6. C. Raja Mohan, 'India's Regional Security Cooperation: The Legacy of the Nehru Raj', *ISAS Working Paper*, No. 168 (March 2013), Institute of South Asian Studies, Singapore.
7. See, for example, David Axe, 'Why South Asia Loves Peacekeeping', *The Diplomat*, 20 December 2010, http://the-diplomat.com/2010/12/20/why-south-asia-loves-peacekeeping/?all=true, accessed on 14 February 2012.
8. Satish Nambiar, *For the Honour of India: A History of Indian Peacekeeping* (New Delhi: Lancer, 2009).
9. For a discussion of the concept of the 'India Centre', see Peter John Brobst, *The Future of the Great Game: Sir Olaf Caroe, India's Independence and the Defence of Asia* (Akron: University of Akron Press, 2005).
10. Srikant Dutt, 'India and the Himalayan States', *Asian Affairs*, Vol. 11, No. 1 (1980).
11. Devin T. Hagerty, 'India's Regional Security Doctrine', *Asian Survey*, Vol. 31, No. 4 (April 1991), pp. 351-63.
12. For a review, see John H. Gill, 'US–India Military-to-Military Interaction', in Sumit Ganguly, Brian Shoup, and Andrew Scobell, eds., *Beyond Words: US-Indian Strategic Cooperation into the 21st Century* (New York: Routledge, 2006), pp. 113-30.
13. For a broad survey, see Brian K. Hendrick, *India's Strategic Defence Transformation: Expanding Global Relationships* (Carlisle, PA: Strategic Studies Institute, 2009).
14. US Department of Defense, 'Report to Congress on US–India Security Cooperation', November 2011. See also Gil Plimmer and Victor Mallet, 'India becomes biggest foreign buyer of US weapons', *Financial Times*, 24 February 2014, http://www.ft.com/intl/cms/s/0/ded3be9a-9c81-11e3-b535-00144feab7de.html#axzz3oOxQtxRA.
15. For the text of the agreement, see Embassy of India, 'New Framework for the US–India Defence Relationship', Washington DC, 28 June 2005, http://www.indianembassy.org/press_release/2005/June/31.htm, accessed on 14 February 2012.
16. For a review, see David Brewster, *India as a Pacific Power* (New York: Routledge, 2012).
17. See R.N. Das, 'The Sino-Indian Defence Dialogue: Addressing the Persistent Security Dilemma', IDSA Comment, 7 December 2011,

Institute for Defence Studies and Analyses, http://www.idsa.in/idsacomment/TheSinoIndianDefenceDialogue_rndas_071211, accessed on 10 February 2012.

18. For a review, see Michael Krepon, 'Prospects for Nuclear Risk Reduction in South Asia', *Strategic Analysis*, Vol. 33, No. 3 (2009), pp. 426-32.
19. For a discussion, see Ali Ahmed, 'India–Pakistan Relations: Military Diplomacy vs. Strategic Engagement', *Journal of Defence Studies*, Vol. 5, No. 1 (January 2011), pp. 147-54.
20. For a review of these agreements, see C. Raja Mohan, 'Modernizing the Raj Legacy', *Seminar*, No. 629 (January 2012).
21. Ibid.
22. For a brief overview, see David Scott, 'India's "Extended Neighbourhood" Concept: Power Projection for a Rising Power', *India Review*, Vol. 8, No. 2 (April-June 2009), pp. 107-43.
23. Pankaj Kumar Jha, 'India's Defence Diplomacy in Southeast Asia', *Journal of Defence Studies*, Vol. 5, No. 1 (January 2011), pp. 47-61.
24. Iskander Rahman, 'Keeping the Dragon at Bay: India's Counter Containment of China in Asia', *Asian Security*, Vol. 5, No. 2 (May 2009), pp. 114-43.
25. See David Brewster, 'An Indian Sphere of Influence in the Indian Ocean?' *Security Challenges*, Vol. 6, No. 3 (Spring 2010), pp. 1-20.
26. Sudha Ramachandran, 'India Airbase Grounded in Tajikistan', Asia Times Online, 10 December 2010, http://www.atimes.com/atimes/South_Asia/LL01Df02.html.
27. R.V.R. Chandrasekhara Rao, 'The Brezhnev Plan and the Indo-Soviet Treaty', *Economic and Political Weekly*, Vol. 8, No. 46 (17 November 1973), pp. 2059-65.
28. Elizabeth Wishnick, 'Soviet Asian Collective Security Policy from Brezhnev to Gorbachev', *East Asia*, Vol. 7, No. 3 (1988), pp. 3-28.
29. Pankaj Kumar Jha, 'India's Defence Diplomacy in Southeast Asia', *Journal of Defence Studies*, Vol. 5, No. 1 (January 2011), pp. 47-61, n. 23.
30. For a discussion, see Yogesh V. Athawale, 'The IONS Initiative and the Prospects for Security Cooperation within the IOR', *Maritime Affairs*, Vol. 6, No. 1 (2010), pp. 98-115.
31. Pankaj Kumar Jha, 'India's Defence Diplomacy in Southeast Asia', *Journal of Defence Studies*, Vol. 5, No. 1 (January 2011), pp. 47-61, n. 23.
32. See P.K. Ghosh, 'Maritime Security Trilateralism: India, Sri Lanka and the Maldives', *Strategic Analysis*, Vol. 38, No. 3 (May 2014).
33. For a comprehensive account of the construction of the excessive civilian dominance over the military and its many negative consequences, see Steven I. Wilkinson, *Army and the Nation: The Military and Indian Democracy since Independence* (Cambridge: Harvard University Press, 2015).

34. Sourabh Gupta, 'US–India Defence Ties: Limits to Interoperability', East Asia Forum, 31 July 2011, http://www.eastasiaforum.org/2011/07/31/us-india-defence-ties-the-limits-to-interoperability/.
35. A notable exception is Military Affairs Centre, *Net Security Provider: India's Out-of-Area Contingency Operations* (New Delhi: Institute of Defence Studies and Analyses, 2012).
36. For a review of the advances under the Modi government, see Sylvia Mishra, 'India and the United States: New Directions in the Defence Relationship', Occasional Paper No. 72, Observer Research Foundation, September 2015.
37. Franz-Stefan Gady, 'Confirmed: Japan will permanently join US–India naval exercises', *The Diplomat*, 13 October 2015, http://thediplomat.com/2015/10/confirmed-japan-will-permanently-join-us-india-naval-exercises/.
38. For a summary of the first trilateral ministerial meeting between India's external affairs minister Sushma Swaraj, Japanese foreign minister Fumio Kishida and US secretary of state John Kerry, see the press release, 'Inaugural US–India–Japan Trilateral Ministerial Dialogue in New York', 29 September 2015, http://www.mea.gov.in/press-releases.htm?dtl/25868/Inaugural_USIndiaJapan_Trilateral_Ministerial_Dialogue_in_New_York.
39. For an assessment, see Danielle Rajendram, *India's New Asia-Pacific Strategy: Modi Acts East*, Lowy Institute, Sydney, 2014; on Indian Ocean, see C. Raja Mohan, 'Modi and the Indian Ocean', ISAS Insights, Institute of South Asian Studies, Singapore, 2015.
40. Jon Huntsman Jr and Bharath Gopalaswamy, 'Transforming India from a Balancing Power to a Leading Power', *The National Interest*, 14 April 2015, http://nationalinterest.org/feature/transforming-india-balancing-leading-power-12624.

6. The Future of Intelligence

1. Matthew M. Aid, *Intel Wars: The Secret History of the Fight against Terror* (London: Bloomsbury Press, 2012).
2. Sun Tzu, *The Art of War* (London: Harper Press, 2011).
3. Marc Goodman, *Future Crimes: A Journey to the Dark Side of Technology—and How to Survive It* (London: Bantam Press, 2015).
4. Ibid.
5. Vikram Sood, 'Patriot Games', *Hindustan Times*, 19 April 2007, http://www.hindustantimes.com/india/patriot-games/story-EV5p9yXyOZ0hkJ3t7HYFJJ.html.
6. 'US Military Unveils Swarm of Mini-Drones', *Newsweek*, 16 May 2015, http://newsweekpakistan.com/u-s-military-unveils-swarm-of-mini-drones/.
7. Ray Kurzweil, *The Singularity Is Near: When Humans Transcend Biology* (New York: Penguin, 2006).

8. Marc Goodman, *Future Crimes: A Journey to the Dark Side of Technology—and How to Survive It* (London: Bantam Press, 2015).
9. Ibid.
10. Ibid, p. 36.
11. Ibid.
12. Ibid.
13. Christoph Reuter, Raniah Salloum and Samiha Shafy, 'Digital Jihad: Inside Islamic State's Savvy PR War', *Der Spiegel*, 8 October 2014, http://www.spiegel.de/international/world/the-professional-pr-strategies-of-isis-in-syria-and-iraq-a-995611.html.
14. Vikram Sood, 'Intelligence: How Not to Reform', 7 August 2011, http://soodvikram.blogspot.in/2011/08/intelligence-how-not-to-reform.html.
15. Vikram Sood, 'A Spy's Lament', 3 February 2009, www.rediff.com.
16. Vikram Sood, 'Intelligence: Reform or Perish', 1 June 2007, http://soodvikram.blogspot.in/2007/06/intelligence-reform-or-perish.html.
17. Vikram Sood, 'The Art and Business of Spying', *Mid-day*, 11 December 2014, http://www.mid-day.com/articles/the-art-and-business-of-spying/15834155.
18. Frank Konkel, 'How the CIA Partnered with Amazon and Changed Intelligence', 11 July 2014, http://www.defenseone.com/technology/2014/07/how-cia-partnered-amazon-and-changed-intelligence/88555/.
19. Vikram Sood, 'Intelligence Reform', 9 February 2009, http://soodvikram.blogspot.in/2009/02/intelligence-reform.html.
20. Vikram Sood, 'Patriot Games', *Hindustan Times*, 19 April 2007, http://www.hindustantimes.com/india/patriot-games/story-EV5p9yXyOZ0hkJ3t7HYFJJ.html.
21. Ibid.

7. Nuclear Deterrence and India: Doctrine, Strategy, Force Structure and Operationalization

1. Suo motu statement by Prime Minister Atal Bihari Vajpayee in Parliament on 27 May 1998, as reproduced in *Strategic Digest*, July 1998.
2. Kenneth Waltz as quoted by Gen. K. Sundarji, *The Blind Men of Hindoostan* (New Delhi: UBPSD Ltd, 1993), p. 68.
3. External Affairs Minister Jaswant Singh's speech in Parliament on 16 December 1998, downloaded from http://www.meadev.gov.in.
4. Barry R. Posen, 'The Sources of Military Doctrine', in Robert Art and Kenneth Waltz, eds., *The Use of Force: Military Power and International Politics* (Boulder, Colorado: Rowman and Littlefield Publishers, 2004), p 24.
5. As learnt during many discussions on the subject with Air Commodore Jasjit Singh, who was one of the authors of the doctrine as part of the first NSAB.

6. Jonathan Schell, *The Abolition* (Stanford, CA: Stanford University Press, 2000), p. 54.
7. Robert McNamara, 'Apocalypse Soon', *Foreign Policy* (May–June 2005).
8. For a comprehensive list of incidents until 1996, see Jasjit Singh, 'Why Nuclear Weapons', in Jasjit Singh, ed., *Nuclear India* (New Delhi: Knowledge World, 1998), pp. 12-13.
9. Steven P. Lee, *Morality, Prudence and Nuclear Weapons* (Cambridge: Cambridge University Press, 1993), p. 16.
10. Robert McNamara, *Blundering into Disaster: Surviving the First Century of the Nuclear Age* (London: Bloomsbury, 1987) pp. 13-14.
11. Manpreet Sethi, *Nuclear Strategy: India's March towards Credible Deterrence* (New Delhi: Knowledge World, 2009), p. 134.
12. 'India tests new underwater nuclear missile', *Times of India*, 26 March 2014, http://timesofindia.indiatimes.com/india/India-tests-new-underwater-nuclear-missile/articleshow/32694060.cms.
13. Statement made by Lt Gen. Khalid Kidwai, then director general of the Strategic Plans Division, a pivotal organization in Pakistan's National Command Authority, in an interview in 2001.
14. James J. Wirtz, 'Deterring the Weak: Problems and Prospects', *Proliferation Papers*, IFRI Security Studies Centre (Fall 2012), p. 7.

9. Crafting a Strategy for India's Maritime Security

1. Captain A.T. Mahan, *The Influence of Sea Power upon History: 1660–1783* (Boston: Little Brown, 1905), p. iv-v.
2. K.M. Panikkar, *India and the Indian Ocean: An Essay on the Influence of Sea Power on Indian History* (London: George Allen & Unwin, 1945), p. 23.
3. Paul M. Kennedy, *The Rise and Fall of British Naval Mastery* (London: The Ashfield Press, 1983), p. 17.
4. Captain A.T. Mahan, 'The Persian Gulf and International Relations', *National Review* (September 1902), p. 249, cited in Jon Tetsuro Sumida, *Inventing Grand Strategy and Teaching Command: The Classical Works of A.T. Mahan*, (Washington, DC: Woodrow Wilson Centre Press, 1999), p. 93.
5. 'Freedom to Use the Seas: India's Maritime Military Strategy', Indian Navy, Integrated Headquarters, Ministry of Defence, May 2007.
6. George K. Tanham, *Indian Strategic Thought: An Interpretive Essay* (Santa Monica: RAND, 1992), p. 13.
7. Chanakya (also known as Kautilya), an advisor to Emperor Chandragupta Maurya (322–298 BCE), is credited with having crafted the influential text *Arthashastra* that described, among much else, how princes acquire, maintain and enhance power in a predatory environment. Chanakya's policy

formulations (or 'Chanakya-niti') relating to statecraft derived from a concept of the mandala theory, which envisaged concentric circles of states, alternately hostile and friendly. He advocated the dictum that 'my enemy's enemy is my friend'.

8. Ashley Tellis, *Non-Alignment Redux: The Perils of Old Wine in New Skins* (Washington, DC: Carnegie Endowment, 2012), pp. 5-7.
9. Asle Toje, 'Strategic Culture as an Analytical Tool: History, Capabilities, Geopolitics and Values', *Western Balkan Security Observer*, No. 14 (July–September 2009).
10. George K. Tanham, *Indian Strategic Thought: An Interpretive Essay* (Santa Monica: RAND, 1992), p. 60.
11. US Department of Defense, http://www.defense.gov/home/features/2014/0314_sdr/qdr.aspx, accessed on 15 May 2015.
12. 'Freedom to Use the Seas: India's Maritime Military Strategy', Indian Navy, Integrated Headquarters, Ministry of Defence, May 2007, p 1.
13. Rear Admiral Raja Menon, *Maritime Strategy and Continental Wars* (London: Frank Cass, 1998).
14. Ibid, pp. 182-83.
15. Ibid, pp. 202-04.
16. 'Maritime Doctrine', Indian Navy, pp. 23, 109-10.
17. 'Freedom to Use the Seas: India's Maritime Military Strategy', Indian Navy, Integrated Headquarters, Ministry of Defence, May 2007, pp. 99-106.
18. Ibid, pp. 108-09.
19. Chinese president Hu Jintao is reported to have said in 2010, 'Certain major powers have attempted to dominate the Malacca Strait, which could constitute a major crisis for China.' Statements such as this helped in constructing a hypothetical scenario in which the US and/or India could cripple China by blocking its Indian Ocean energy supply sea routes.
20. Admiral Arun Prakash (retd), 'Charting a Course for India's Growing Maritime Power', *Force*, December 2012, pp. 10-14.
21. 'India Is Building Six Nuclear Attack Subs to Contain China', 25 February 2015, http://ipanewspack.com/india-is-building-6-nuclear-attack-submarines-to-contain-china/, accessed on 18 May 2015.
22. Ruchika Chitravanshi, 'Port Projects in Troubled Waters', *Business Standard*, 19 June 2012, http://www.business-standard.com/article/economy-policy/port-projects-in-troubled-waters-112061902008_1.html, accessed on 18 May 2015.
23. Captain A.T. Mahan, *The Influence of Sea Power upon History: 1660–1783* (Boston: Little Brown, 1905), p. 58.
24. Admiral Arun Prakash (retd), Y.B. Chavan Memorial Lecture, Institute for Defence Studies and Analyses, 26 November 2013.

25. Captain A.T. Mahan, *The Influence of Sea Power upon History: 1660–1783* (Boston: Little Brown, 1905), p. 50.
26. In a book titled *1421: The Year China Discovered the World* (London: Bantam Press, 2002), sponsored and funded by the Chinese government, a retired Royal Navy officer, Gavin Menzies, has put forth a thesis that a massive armada of Chinese junks, led by the eunuch Admiral Cheng Ho, sailed in March 1421 on an epic voyage at the behest of Emperor Zhu Di, and circumnavigated the globe. In the process, they discovered Africa, South and North America, Antarctica, Australia, New Zealand and Greenland. On return to China, the death of the Chinese emperor led to the total destruction of all maps, charts and records of the armada's voyages. According to Menzies's fertile imagination, these Chinese fleets made all the discoveries for which history has subsequently given credit to Diaz, Vasco da Gama, Magellan, Columbus and Captain Cook. He also suggests that European navigators used copies of Cheng Ho's charts, stolen by an Italian while the Chinese mariner was in the Indian port of Cochin!

11. Managing Internal Security Challenges

1. At least 43,758 lives have been lost in this conflict between 1988 and 31 May 2015. See 'J&K: Fatalities in Terrorist Violence 1988–2015', South Asia Terrorism Portal, http://www.satp.org/satporgtp/countries/india/states/jandk/data_sheets/annual_casualties.htm, accessed 2 June 2015.
2. 'India: Chronic Conflict Map 2015', South Asia Terrorism Portal, http://www.satp.org/satporgtp/countries/india/database/conflictmapindia.htm.
3. Total fatalities in all major insurgencies and terrorism across India (including J&K) have dropped from a peak of 5,839 in 2001 to 976 in 2014. In the first half of 2015, 296 people were killed in insurgent and terrorist violence. 'India Fatalities 1994–2015', South Asia Terrorism Portal, http://www.satp.org/satporgtp/countries/india/database/indiafatalities.htm.
4. *Crimes against Scheduled Castes*

1993	1995	1997	2002	2003	2004	2005	2006	2007	2008	2009	2010	2011	2012	2013
32,462	35,304	17,044	33,507	26,252	26,887	26,127	27,070	30,031	33,615	33,594	32,712	33,719	33,655	39,408

Crimes against Scheduled Tribes

1990	1995	2002	2003	2004	2005	2006	2007	2008	2009	2010	2011	2012	2013
3,578	5,608	6,774	5,889	5,889	5,713	5,791	5,532	5,582	5,425	5,885	5,756	5,922	6,793

(Data compiled from annual figures, 'Crime against Persons Belonging to SCs/STs', Crime in India, National Crimes Record Bureau, Ministry of Home Affairs, Government of India, http://ncrb.gov.in/.)

Communal Violence

Year	2003	2004	2005	2006	2007	2008	2009	2010	2011	2012	2013	2014
Incidents	711	677	779	698	761	943	826	701	580	640	823	644
Fatalities	193	134	124	133	99	167	125	116	91	93	133	95

(Data compiled from Annual Reports, Ministry of Home Affairs, Government of India, http://mha.nic.in/AnsnualReports.)

5. 'Tighten the noose', *Daily Excelsior*, 15 October 2013, http://www.dailyexcelsior.com/tighten-the-noose/.
6. Aman Sharma, 'Economic terror no fake threat', *India Today*, 5 August 2009, http://indiatoday.intoday.in/story/Economic+terror+no+fake+threat/1/55177.html.
7. 'Fake Indian Currency Notes', Press Information Bureau, Ministry of Home Affairs, Government of India, 17 December 2014, http://pib.nic.in/newsite/PrintRelease.aspx?relid=113525.
8. Shrideep Biswas, 'FICN: Currency of Terror', *South Asia Intelligence Review*, Vol. 9, No. 49 (13 June 2011), http://www.satp.org/satporgtp/sair/Archives/sair9/9_49.htm.
9. 'Rs 16,000 cr in fakes "printed in Pakistan" and circulated all over', *Indian Express*, 10 June 2012, http://expressindia.indianexpress.com/karnatakapoll08/story_page.php?id=960280.
10. Yatish Yadav, 'Pakistan Takes Mission Route to Fake Currency', *New Indian Express*, 28 September 2014, http://www.newindianexpress.com/thesundaystandard/Pakistan-Takes-Mission-Route-to-Fake-Currency/2014/09/28/article2452720.ece.
11. Sanchita Bhattacharya, 'Bankrolling Terror', *South Asia Intelligence Review*, Vol. 13, No. 4 (28 July 2014), http://www.satp.org/satporgtp/sair/Archives/sair13/13_4.htm#assessment1.
12. Sanjib Kr Baruah, 'Pakistan gangs use Indian banks for fraud', *Hindustan Times*, 21 July 2014, http://www.hindustantimes.com/india-news/pakistan-gangs-use-indian-banks-for-fraud/article1-1242733.aspx.
13. 'Property Stolen and Recovered', Chapter 8, Table 8.10, 'Crime In India (2013)', National Crime Records Bureau, Ministry of Home Affairs, Government of India, http://ncrb.gov.in/index.htm.
14. 'Crores being pumped into India by ISI to finance terror', 1 April 2013, http://www.rediff.com/news/report/crores-being-pumped-into-india-by-isi-to-finance-terror/20130401.htm.
15. Mateen Hafeez, 'IM got hawala money for 13/7 Mumbai blasts: Anti-terrorism squad', *Times of India*, 11 March 2014, http://timesofindia.indiatimes.com/india/IM-got-hawala-money-for-13/7-Mumbai-blasts-Anti-terrorism-squad/articleshow/31804648.cms.
16. 'Naxal–Drug cartel nexus new headache for para-military forces', *Daily*

Bhaskar, 25 March 2012, http://daily.bhaskar.com/news/BIH-naxal-drug-cartel-nexus-new-headache-for-para-military-forces-3014987.html; Amarnath Tewary, 'India naxals turn to poppy for funds', Naxal Terror Watch, 10 June 2007, http://naxalwatch.blogspot.in/2007/06/india-naxals-turn-to-poppy-for-funds.html.

17. 'Narcotics trade gain for rebels', *Telegraph*, 23 May 2010, http://www.telegraphindia.com/1100523/jsp/northeast/story_12478174.jsp.
18. Ajit Kumar Singh and Sachin Bansidhar Diwan, 'Red Money', *South Asia Intelligence Review*, Vol. 8, No. 39 (5 April 2010), http://www.satp.org/satporgtp/sair/Archives/sair8/8_39.htm#assessment1.
19. Unstarred Question No. 3086, Lok Sabha, Ministry of Home Affairs, Government of India, http://mha1.nic.in/par2013/par2013-pdfs/ls-110214/3086.pdf.
20. Sandeep Pai, 'How Maoists got hold of 15 lakh kg of industrial explosives', *DNA*, 23 March 2015, http://www.dnaindia.com/india/report-15-lakh-kg-explosives-stolen-in-three-years-2071099.
21. 'New NBDC data shows India had more blasts than Afghanistan in 2014', 12 February 2015, http://firstpost.com/business/corporate-business/new-nbdc-data-shows-india-blasts-afghanistan-2014-2095863.html.
22. Ajai Sahni, 'Ever Unready', *South Asia Intelligence Review*, Vol. 12, No. 39 (31 March 2014), http://www.satp.org/satporgtp/sair/Archives/sair12/12_39.htm#assessment1.
23. Praveen Swami, 'No funding this year for network to track crime', *Indian Express*, 1 June 2015, http://indianexpress.com/article/india/india-others/no-funding-this-year-for-network-to-track-crime-2/.
24. 'India: Broken System – Dysfunction, Abuse and Impunity in the Indian Police', Human Rights Watch, 2009.
25. Ajai Sahni, 'See no evil, hear no evil, do no good', *South Asia Intelligence Review*, Vol. 10, No. 10 (13 September 2011), http://www.satp.org/satporgtp/sair/Archives/sair10/10_10.htm.
26. 'Police system neglected, needs urgent reform: Chidambaram', 27 October 2009, http://www.sify.com/news/police-system-neglected-needs-urgent-reform-Chidambaram-news-jk1s4bgehfc.html.
27. P. Chidambaram, 'A New Architecture for India's Internal Security', Intelligence Bureau Centenary Endowment Lecture, 23 December 2009, http://mha.nic.in/pdfs/HM-IB-Endowment231209.pdf.
28. Ajai Sahni, 'Weakness Compounding Weakness: The Centre and States in Indian's Internal Security', paper presented at the seminar on the 'Role of the Union Government in Internal Security', Nehru Centre, Mumbai, 8 June 2012.

29. Ibid.
30. Aman Sharma, 'Govt can use any element of its national power against Maoists: Rajnath Singh's new anti-Naxal Policy', *Economic Times*, 17 October 2014, http://articles.economictimes.indiatimes.com/2014-10-17/news/55148242_1_new-policy-interventions-insurgency.

12. Financial Support for National Security

1. C. Christine Fair, *Fighting to the End: The Pakistan Army's Way of War* (New York: Oxford University Press, 2014), p. 65.
2. A full-fledged system of seventeen departmentally related standing committees—the Committee on Defence being one of them—was introduced in April 1993.
3. Budget speech 1947-48, pp. 10-12, http://indiabudget.nic.in/bspeech/bs194748.pdf.
4. Ibid, p. 16.
5. All these figures have been gleaned from the Union budget speeches of the relevant years.
6. Budget speech 1949-50, p. 10, http://indiabudget.nic.in/bspeech/bs194950.pdf.
7. See the budget speeches of the relevant years, http://indiabudget.nic.in/bspeech.htm.
8. Budget speech 1950-51, p. 14, http://indiabudget.nic.in/bspeech/bs195051.pdf.
9. Budget speech (interim) 1957-58, p. 1, http://indiabudget.nic.in/bspeech/bs195758%28I%29.pdf.
10. 'Forward Policy of Nehru govt blamed for 1962 debacle', *Deccan Herald*, 18 March 2015, http://www.deccanherald.com/content/392828/forward-policy-nehru-govt-blamed.html.
11. Budget speech 1959-60, p. 9, http://indiabudget.nic.in/bspeech/bs195960.pdf.
12. These and other sporadically quoted figures have been gleaned from the budget speeches of the relevant years.
13. Budget speech 1962-63 (interim), p. 6, http://indiabudget.nic.in/bspeech/bs196263%28I%29.pdf.
14. Budget speech 1963-64, pp. 5-6, http://indiabudget.nic.in/bspeech/bs196364.pdf.
15. Ibid, p. 4.
16. Ibid, p. 5.
17. Budget speech 1964-65, pp. 8-9, http://indiabudget.nic.in/bspeech/bs196465.pdf.

18. Budget speech 1966-67, pp. 8-9, http://indiabudget.nic.in/bspeech/bs196667.pdf.
19. Ibid, p. 3.
20. 'Defence Budget: A Statistical Digest', Finance Division, Ministry of Defence, Government of India, December 2006, p. 7.
21. Budget speech 1972-73, p. 6, http://indiabudget.nic.in/bspeech/bs197273.pdf.
22. 'Defence Budget: A Statistical Digest', Finance Division, Ministry of Defence, Government of India, December 2006, p. 7.
23. Ibid, pp. 3-4.
24. The MoD did from time to time reveal some information to the Standing Committee on Defence but this was in general, non-quantifiable terms. See, for example, 'Eleventh Report of the Standing Committee on Defence (14th Lok Sabha)', Lok Sabha Secretariat, New Delhi, May 2006, pp. 31-32. In any case, no authentic report on the outcome of these plans is available in the public domain.
25. 'Defence Budget: A Statistical Digest', Finance Division, Ministry of Defence, Government of India, December 2006.
26. Budget speech 2000-01, p. 3, http://indiabudget.nic.in/bspeech/bs200001.pdf.
27. 'Defence Budget: A Statistical Digest', Finance Division, Ministry of Defence, Government of India, December 2006, p. 7.
28. Budget speech 2001-02, http://indiabudget.nic.in/ub2001-02/bs/speech.htm.
29. 'Bharatiya Janata Party Election Manifesto 2014 (Abridged)', p. 35, http://www.bjp.org/images/bjp_manifesto_an_abridged_version_english_26.04.14.pdf.
30. Budget speech, 10 July 2014, pp. 25-26, http://indiabudget.nic.in/ub2014-15/bs/bs.pdf.
31. For a detailed analysis, see the author's 'Metamorphosis of the Defence Budget 2016-17', IDSA Comment, 2 March 2016, Institute for Defence Studies and Analyses, http://idsa.in/idsacomments/metamorphosis-of-the-defence-budget-2016-17_acowshish_020316; and 'Reorganisation of Defence Outlay for 2016-17: A Tepid Affair', *Journal of Defence Studies*, Vol. 10, No. 2 (April 2016), http://idsa.in/jds/jds_10_2_2016_%20reorganisation-of-defence-outlay-for-2016%E2%80%9317.
32. For a detailed analysis, see the author's 'Discontinuance of National Five Year Plans: Time to Revaluate Defence Planning', IDSA Comment, 11 April 2016, Institute for Defence Studies and Analyses, http://idsa.in/idsacomments/national-five-year-plans-defence-planning_acowshish_110416.

33. 'Statistical Handbook on Defence Expenditure', Controller General of Defence Accounts, Ministry of Defence, New Delhi, 2015.
34. Report No. 19 of 2015—Union Government (Defence Services—Army and Ordnance Factories), Comptroller and Auditor General of India, May 2015.
35. Standing Committee on Defence (14th Lok Sabha), Eleventh Report, May 2006, p. 29.
36. Based on the Defence Services Estimates of the relevant years.
37. Standing Committee on Defence (15th Lok Sabha), Sixth Report, April 2010, pp. 21-22.
38. Based on the Defence Services Estimates of the relevant years.
39. Based on the data gleaned from various reports of the Standing Committee on Defence.
40. Palash Ghosh, 'How Many People in India Pay Income Tax? Hardly Any', *International Business Times*, 6 June 2013, http://www.ibtimes.com/how-many-people-india-pay-income-tax-hardly-anyone-1294887.
41. 'Fiscal Responsibility and Budget Management Act 2003', http://finmin.nic.in/law/frbmact2003.pdf.
42. See Gazette Notification dated 2 July 2004, http://www.finmin.nic.in/law/frbm_rules_2004.pdf.
43. 'Key Features of Budget 2015-16,' http://indiabudget.nic.in/ub2015-16/bh/bh1.pdf.
44. Based on the Defence Services Estimates of the relevant years.
45. This is based on the data gleaned from the Defence Services Estimates for the relevant years and the author's understanding of what comprises 'capital acquisition' budget.
46. 'Statistical Handbook on Defence Expenditure', April 2015, pp. 110-11, and Expenditure Budget 2016-17.
47. This has been reorganized and renamed as the Demand for Grant for Ministry of Defence (Miscellaneous) starting from 2016-17.
48. 'Statistical Handbook on Defence Expenditure', April 2015, pp. 115-16.
49. Ibid, pp. 119-20, and Demand for Grant No. 20 for the Ministry of Defence, 2016-17.
50. Ibid., p. 134, and Demand for Grant No. 20 for the Ministry of Defence, 2016-17.
51. Standing Committee on Defence (15th Lok Sabha), Lok Sabha Secretariat, New Delhi, February 2014, Twenty-second Report, http://164.100.47.134/lsscommittee/Defence/15_Defence_22.pdf.
52. Standing Committee on Defence (16th Lok Sabha), Lok Sabha Secretariat, New Delhi, August 2015, Tenth Report, http://164.100.47.134/lsscommittee/Defence/16_Defence_10.pdf.
53. Standing Committee on Defence (16th Lok Sabha), Lok Sabha Secretariat,

New Delhi, December 2014, Second report, p. 7, http://164.100.47.134/lsscommittee/Defence/16_Defence_2.pdf.

54. Rajat Pandit, 'Fund crunch hits Army's new strike corps', *Times of India*, 16 April 2015, http://timesofindia.indiatimes.com/india/Fund-crunch-hits-Armys-new-strike-corps/articleshow/46940064.cms.
55. 'Statistical Handbook on Defence Expenditure', p. 106.
56. Standing Committee on Defence (15th Lok Sabha), Lok Sabha Secretariat, New Delhi, December 2009, p. 10, http://164.100.47.134/lsscommittee/Defence/15_Defence_9.pdf.

16. Economic Warfare to Support National Security

1. Boris Kondoch, 'The Limits of Economic Sanctions under International Law: The Case of Iraq,' Report of Campaign against Sanctions on Iraq, http://www.casi.org.uk/info/kondoch01.pdf.
2. George Shambaugh, 'Economic warfare', Encyclopedia Britannica, http://www.britannica.com/topic/economic-warfare.
3. Robert A. Pape, 'Why Economic Sanctions Do Not Work,' *International Security*, Vol. 22, No. 2 (1997), p. 97.
4. Stephen D. Collins, 'Democracy Sanctions: An Assessment of Economic Sanctions as an Instrument of Democracy Promotion', *Taiwan Journal of Democracy*, Vol. 5, No. 2 (2009), p. 106.
5. James Mayall, 'The Sanctions Problem in International Economic Relations: Reflections in the Light of Recent Experiences', *International Affairs*, Vol. 60, No. 4 (Autumn 1984), pp. 631-42.
6. 'India–Bhutan Relations', Ministry of External Affairs, 20 July 2015, http://www.mea.gov.in/Portal/ForeignRelation/Bhutan_2015_07_20.pdf.
7. 'European Union, Trade in Goods with Bangladesh', Directorate-General for Trade, European Commission, 10 April 2015, http://trade.ec.europa.eu/doclib/docs/2006/september/tradoc_113349.pdf.
8. 'European Union, Trade in Goods with Bangladesh', Directorate-General for Trade, European Commission, 10 April 2015, http://trade.ec.europa.eu/doclib/docs/2006/september/tradoc_113349.pdf.
9. 'European Union, Trade in Goods with Sri Lanka', Directorate-General for Trade, European Commission, 10 April 2015, http://trade.ec.europa.eu/doclib/docs/2006/september/tradoc_113449.pdf.
10. Anurag Kotoky, 'Ambitious India Port Bets on Policy Shift to Steal Colombo Trade', 10 August 2015, http://www.bloomberg.com/news/articles/2015-08-09/ambitious-india-port-bets-on-policy-shift-to-steal-colombo-trade.
11. Katharine Houreld and Maria Golovnina, 'World Bank Approves $12 Billion, Five-year Loan for Pakistan: Finance Minister', 2 May 2014, http://www.reuters.com/article/2014/05/02/us-pakistan-worldbank-loan-idUSBREA4108N20140502.

12. Shahbaz Rana, 'Seventh Review: IMF Approves $506m Loan Tranche for Pakistan', *Express Tribune*, 26 June 2015, http://tribune.com.pk/story/910392/seventh-review-imf-approves-506m-loan-tranche-for-pakistan/.
13. Mehreen Zahra-Malik, 'Saudi Arabia Loans Pakistan $1.5 Billion to Shore up Economy', 13 March 2014, http://www.reuters.com/article/2014/03/13/us-pakistan-saudi-idUSBREA2C13G20140313.
14. Shahbaz Rana, 'Asian Development Bank Approves $6b Loan for Pakistan', *Express Tribune*, 26 August 2015, http://tribune.com.pk/story/944875/development-financing-adb-approves-6b-loan-for-pakistan/.
15. K. Alan Kronstadt, 'Pakistan–US Relations: Issues for the 114th Congress', Congressional Research Service, 14 May 2015, http://www.fas.org/sgp/crs/row/R44034.pdf.
16. Ibid.
17. 'Gross Domestic Product 2014', World Bank, 18 September 2015, http://databank.worldbank.org/data/download/GDP.pdf.

17. Challenges and Strategy for Energy Security

1. 'Executive Summary, Power Sector', Ministry of Power, Central Electricity Authority, Government of India, January 2015, http://www.cea.nic.in/reports/monthly/executive_rep/jan15.pdf.
2. Durgesh Kumar Dubey, 'Issues and challenges in electricity sector in India', *The Business & Management Review*, Vol. 5, No. 4 (January 2015); and CEA, January 2015.
3. 'India to eclipse China as top coal importer in 2015', 20 May 2015, http://in.reuters.com/article/2015/05/20/india-china-coal-idINKBN0O51CD20150520.
4. Promit Mukherjee, 'India's gas output to grow by 50% in the next three years', 13 May 2015, http://www.livemint.com/Politics/b6JtJvYh7o7sSbHU9OzQyO/Indias-gas-output-to-grow-by-50-in-the-next-three-years.html.
5. Anil Sasi, 'Gensets add up to under half of installed power capacity', *Indian Express*, 18 August 2014, http://indianexpress.com/article/india/india-others/gensets-add-up-to-under-half-of-installed-power-capacity/.
6. 'Natural gas production in 2017-18 projected to be 138.33 MMSCMD', *Economic Times*, 13 May 2015, http://energy.economictimes.indiatimes.com/news/oil-and-gas/natural-gas-production-in-2017-18-projected-to-be-138-33-mmscmd/47266877.
7. Siddhartha P. Saikia and Huma Siddiqui, 'Pradhan: Oil diplomacy has seen paradigm shift in new Govt', *Financial Express*, 25 November 2014, http://www.financialexpress.com/article/economy/pradhan-oil-diplomacy-has-seen-paradigm-shift-in-new-govt/12334/.
8. 'Biofuel Promotion in India for Transport: Exploring the Grey Areas', TERI

Policy Brief, February 2015, http://www.teriin.org/policybrief/docs/biofuel.pdf.

9. 'Hydropower in India: Key enablers for a better tomorrow', FICCI, PWC, 2014, https://www.pwc.in/en_IN/in/assets/pdfs/publications/2014/hydropower-in-india-key-enablers-for-better-tomorrow.pdf.
10. 'Small Hydro Power Programme', Ministry of New and Renewable Energy, Government of India, http://www.mnre.gov.in/schemes/grid-connected/small-hydro/.

19. Contours of India's Grand Strategy

1. Craig Whitlock, 'Pentagon weighs future of its inscrutable nonagenarian futurist, Andrew W. Marshall', *Washington Post*, 28 October 2013, http://www.washingtonpost.com/world/national-security/pentagon-weighs-future-of-its-inscrutable-nonagenarian-futurist-andrew-marshall/2013/10/27/f9bda426-3cac-11e3-b6a9-da62c264f40e_print.html, accessed on 11 March 2015.
2. Pavan K. Varma, *Chanakya's New Manifesto to Resolve the Crisis within India* (New Delhi: Aleph Book Company, 2013), p. 9.
3. Hal Brands, 'The Promise and Pitfalls of Grand Strategy', Strategic Studies Institute, US Army War College, http://www.strategicstudiesinstitute.army.mil/, accessed on 14 November 2013.
4. Ibid.
5. Aam Aadmi Party, http://delhi.aamaadmiparty.org/Delhi-Elections-2013/Shaziallmi, accessed on 15 March 2015.
6. Ashley J. Tellis, 'Between the Times: India's Predicaments and Its Grand Strategy', Carnegie Endowment for International Peace, 3 December 2012, http://carnegieendowment.org/2012/12/03/between-times-india-s-predicaments-and-its-grand-strategy-pub-50223.
7. K.S. Bajpai, 'Our Grand Strategy', *Indian Express*, 31 December 2009.
8. Ajay Shah, 'Economic Policy Dimension of India's International Strategy' in V. Krishnappa and Princy Marin George, eds., *Grand Strategy for India: 2020 and Beyond* (New Delhi: Institute for Defence Studies and Analyses, 2012), p. 163.
9. Pradeep Chhibber and Rahul Verma, 'A bureaucracy that governs, not reigns', *Indian Express*, 16 October 2013, http://archive.indianexpress.com/news/a-bureaucracy-that-governs-not-reigns/1183104/.
10. Statement attributed to Prashant Bhushan, noted Supreme Court lawyer, activist and public intellectual. See http://www.voiceofbharat.org/judiciary/voices_prashantbhushan.asp, accessed on 16 April 2015.
11. For an illuminating discussion on the structural impediments that line India's path, see Dipankar Gupta, *The Caged Phoenix: Can India Fly?* (London: Viking, 2009).

12. 'Tunnel Vision: UPA's hostility to business weakens financial foundations of the welfare state', *Times of India*, 21 October 2013.
13. Deepak Nayyar, 'Catch-up in industrialisation', *Hindu*, 26 October 2013, http://www.thehindu.com/opinion/lead/catchup-in-industrialisation/article5272993.ece.
14. 'Economy Rankings', http://www.doingbusiness.org/rankings, accessed on 17 February 2015.
15. Nandan Nilekani, Keynote Address, Eisenhower Foundation Lecture on 'India's Journey to 2018'. See 'It has to be integration of bazaar, samaj and sarkar to take India to the next level', *Indian Express*, 22 October 2013, http://archive.indianexpress.com/news/it-has-to-be-integration-of-bazaar-samaj-and-sarkar-to-take-india-to-the-next-level/1185641/.
16. 'The Needler', *Mail Today*, 9 November 2013, p. 14.
17. A point made by Shyam Saran in an interesting article, 'Revisiting India's Growth Strategy', *Business Standard*, 12 May 2015, http://www.business-standard.com/article/opinion/shyam-saran-revisiting-india-s-growth-strategy-115051201522_1.html.
18. Nitin Desai, 'Towards 2050: Social Protection', *Business Standard*, 17 October 2013, http://www.business-standard.com/article/opinion/nitin-desai-towards-2050-social-protection-113101600920_1.html.
19. Shyam Saran, 'Revisiting India's Growth Strategy', *Business Standard*, 12 May 2015, http://www.business-standard.com/article/opinion/shyam-saran-revisiting-india-s-growth-strategy-115051201522_1.html.
20. Wolfers Arnold, 'National Security as an Ambiguous Symbol', *Political Science Quarterly*, Vol. 67, No. 4 (December 1952), p. 488.
21. Leading national security professionals like the former NSA, Shivshankar Menon, may themselves be guilty of stoking such a refrain by often making the point that national security is much more than the military and that the usability of hard power is waning, which is of course true but only superficially. The deeper connotations need to be explored. See the keynote address by the NSA at the anniversary dinner of the Council on Energy, Environment and Water (CEEW), New Delhi, on 23 August 2012, http://www.youtube.com/watch?v=bpV9WZF5nlc, accessed on 6 May 2015.
22. For an insightful account of the many benefits of defence diplomacy, see Bhubhindar Singh and See Seng Tan, *From Boots to Brogues: The Rise of Defence Diplomacy in Southeast Asia*, (Singapore: S. Rajaratnam School of International Studies, 2011), Monograph No. 21.
23. Statement attributed to Admiral Arun Prakash (retd), former Chief of Naval Staff.
24. For a detailed account, see Raj Shukla, 'Civil–Military Relations in India', Manekshaw Paper No. 36, 2012, Centre For Land Warfare Studies, New Delhi.

25. A useful model for reform could be the one spearheaded by Bernard Gray in the UK, commonly known as the Bernard Gray Review of Acquisition, a study commissioned by the UK MoD. For details visit www.mod.uk.
26. For an informed account of how we are neglecting this vital issue and the rapid strides being made by the PLA in comparison, see Roy Kamphausen, Andrew Scobell and Travis Tanner, 'The People in the PLA: Recruitment, Training and Education in China's Military', September 2008, http://www.strategicstudiesinstitute.army.mil/, accessed on 24 January 2015.
27. For a useful account of the problem, see Manoj Joshi, 'India needs more wings for its bucks', *Mail Today*, 9 October 2013, http://www.dailymail.co.uk/indiahome/indianews/article-2449912/THE-BIGGER-PICTURE-India-needs-wings-bucks.html.

20. The New Arthashastra: A Security Strategy for India

1. Charles Krauthammer, 'The Unipolar Moment', *Foreign Affairs*, Vol. 70, No. 1 (1990-91), Council on Foreign Relations, pp. 23-33.
2. Some Indian commentators have averred that the new century will be an Indian century.
3. Lauren McCauley, 'Beyond Blackwater Massacre, Renewed Concern over Rise of Mercenary Armies', 15 April 2015, http://www.globalresearch.ca/beyond-blackwater-massacre-renewed-concern-over-rise-of-mercenary-armies/5443161.
4. Andrew Small, *The China–Pakistan Axis: Asia's New Geopolitics* (New Delhi: Random House India, 2015), p. 3.
5. According to Andrew Marshall, former director of the Office of Net Assessments in the Office of the Secretary of Defense: 'A Revolution in Military Affairs (RMA) is a major change in the nature of warfare brought about by the innovative application of new technologies which, combined with dramatic changes in military doctrine and operational and organizational concepts, fundamentally alters the character and conduct of military operations.' Lothar Ibrugger, 'The Revolution in Military Affairs', http://iwar.org.uk/rma/resources/nato/ar299stc-e.html#top, accessed 24 July 2016.
6. 'National Security Environment', Ministry of Defence, Government of India, Annual Report 1995-96, pp. 2-6.
7. 'History has worked in reverse: Thanks to nuclear weapons, the days of large-scale interstate war, if not over, are in their death throes; in their place, we will witness the rise of "crummy little wars"—fought by terrorists, bandits, guerrillas, drug cartels, and criminal networks.' Martin van Creveld, cited by P.H. Liotta, 'Strategy under Uncertainty', presentation at the United Service Institution, New Delhi, 9 January 2004.

8. 'Wars of Intervention: Why and When to Go In', *Economist*, 6 January 2001.
9. John M. Collins, *Grand Strategy: Principles and Practices* (Annapolis, Maryland: Naval Institute Press, 1973), p. 14.
10. Basil H. Liddell Hart, *Strategy* (London: Faber & Faber, 1967), p. 322.
11. 'A National Security Strategy for a New Century', White House, Washington, DC, December 1999.
12. Most of the invaders came in from the Khyber Pass in the Hindu Kush Mountains, where 400 men could have stopped an army. But Indian kings never fought them there when the threat was still nascent. The 'Panipat Syndrome' implies that when we do fight, we fight when the invaders have reached Panipat and are preparing to knock on the gates of Delhi.
13. In Indian mythology, the Lakshmana Rekha was a protective line drawn by Lord Rama's younger brother Lakshmana around the hut he shared with his brother and Rama's wife Sita at Panchavati near Nashik in Maharashtra during the period that Rama had been banished from Ayodhya. The line was meant to protect Sita, but a wily Ravana succeeded in abducting her anyway.
14. India's application for membership of the NSG came up at the plenary meeting at Seoul on 23 and 24 June 2016 but was opposed by China and a few other countries on procedural grounds despite strong support from France, the UK and the US, among many others. It appears that India will have to wait for another year or two before the procedural issues are resolved.
15. Several analysts have averred that during the Kargil conflict in 1999, Operation Parakram in 2001-02 and in the wake of the Mumbai terror strikes on 26 November 2008, the Indian political leadership was apprehensive of Pakistan's nuclear retaliation if certain military options were exercised. See, for example, Vipin Narang, *Nuclear Strategy in the Modern Era: Regional Powers and International Conflict* (Princeton: Princeton University Press, 2014), pp. 257-82.
16. The programme of 'four modernizations' was initiated by President Deng Xiaoping in 1975 and included the modernization of agriculture, industry, science and technology and the military.
17. Deng Xiaoping's twenty-four-character strategy for China was: 'Observe calmly; secure our position; cope with affairs calmly; hide our capacities and bide our time; be good at maintaining a low profile; and never claim leadership.' Deng Xiaoping's 24-Character Strategy, http://www.globalsecurity.org/military/world/china/24-character.htm.
18. Throughout history, the traditional name that China used to refer to itself was Zhonggou, which means Middle Kingdom. It was based on the belief that China was the 'centre' of the world. Some people still refer to their country as the Middle Kingdom with a sense of pride and with the belief that they play a significant role in the world.

19. Ananth Krishnan, 'One step forward, two steps back', *India Today*, 11 June 2015, http://indiatoday.intoday.in/story/china-india-lac-modi-visit-xi-jinping-border-dispute/1/443886.html, accessed on 24 July 2016.
20. Blue water capability implies the ability to conduct and sustain naval operations on the high seas, that is, well away from territorial waters. A blue water navy is one that can project power and would normally have one or more fleets based on an aircraft carrier with battleships and submarines and be self-contained for logistics support for a specified duration.
21. According to China's Academy of Social Sciences (CASS), the top ten countries in the world in terms of their CNP are: the US (90.62 per cent), the UK (65.04), Russia (63.03), France (62), Germany (61.93), China (59.10), Japan (57.84), Canada (57.09), South Korea (53.20) and India (50.43). Excerpted from 'China's Resurgence: An Insight', a talk delivered by Major General G.G. Dwivedi at the United Service Institution, New Delhi, on 12 November 2008, *Journal of the United Service Institution of India*, Vol. CXXXIX, No. 575 (January-March 2009), http://usiofindia.org/Article/?pub=Journal&pubno=575&ano=305.
22. A good example of 'jobless growth' is the multi-billion-dollar oil and gas refinery on India's west coast, with a capacity of 1.24 million barrels per day, incidentally the world's largest single refining complex. It employs a total of 2,500 people working in three shifts—and many of them are gardeners.
23. The 'just war' doctrine pertains to military ethics to be observed during the conduct of war. According to this doctrine, care should be exercised and a distinction made between combatants and civilians; the latter must never be targeted. The principle of necessity seeks to ensure that a state wages war only if it is absolutely necessary. It must be ensured that the quantum of force applied is proportional to the aim to be achieved and that it is not excessive. Both necessity and proportionality also imply that minimum harm must be caused to non-combatants. For details, see 'War' in the *Stanford Encyclopedia of Philosophy*, http://plato.stanford.edu/entries/war/, accessed on 3 May 2016.
24. The universally acknowledged Responsibility to Protect (R2P) places the onus of protecting citizens first on the state and, if it fails to do so, on the international community, even to the extent that a military intervention may be necessary. In such a case, the dilution of sovereignty is considered justified. For details, see 'The Responsibility to Protect' in 'Prevention of Genocide', http://www.un.org/en/preventgenocide/adviser/responsibility.shtml.

Index

About the Editor

BRIGADIER GURMEET KANWAL (RETD) is Distinguished Fellow, Institute for Defence Studies and Analyses, New Delhi; and Adjunct Fellow, Centre for Strategic and International Studies (CSIS), Wadhwani Chair, Washington, DC. He was Director, Centre for Land Warfare Studies (CLAWS), New Delhi (January 2008–March 2012), the Indian Army's think tank. He has co-founded two Delhi-based think tanks: Forum for Strategic Initiatives (FSI) and the South Asian Institute for Strategic Affairs (SAISA).

Brigadier Kanwal commanded an infantry brigade in the high-altitude Gurez Sector on the LoC with Pakistan (Operation Parakram, 2001–03) in northern Kashmir and an artillery regiment in counter-insurgency operations in the Kashmir Valley (Operation Rakshak, 1993-94). He has served as Deputy Assistant Chief of Integrated Defence Staff (Doctrine, Organization and Training) at HQ IDS, New Delhi; Director MO-5 in the Directorate General of Military Operations at Army Headquarters (dealing with threat, strategy and force structure); United Nations Military Observer in UNTAG, Namibia; Brigade Major of an infantry brigade and Instructor-in-Gunnery at the School of Artillery, Devlali.

He opted for voluntary retirement in 2003 and joined the Observer Research Foundation (ORF), New Delhi, as Director, Security Studies, and Senior Fellow. He has also served as Senior Fellow, Institute for Defence Studies and Analyses (IDSA), New Delhi; and Senior Fellow, Centre for Air Power Studies, New Delhi. He has been a Visiting Research Scholar at the Cooperative Monitoring Centre (CMC), Sandia National Laboratories, Albuquerque, United States, and in other think tanks in London and Singapore.

Brigadier Kanwal has authored several books: *Nuclear Defence: Shaping the Arsenal*; *Indian Army: Vision 2020*; *Pakistan's Proxy War*; *Heroes of Kargil*; *Kargil '99: Blood, Guts and Firepower* and *Artillery: Honour and Glory*. He has edited and co-edited many books on defence.

He has contributed extensively to various journals and leading newspapers, including a column in the *Statesman* for over two years. He is a regular speaker at well-known international think tanks and military institutions.